# Sacred Fire

# Sacred Fire

## Torah from the Years of Fury 1939-1942

### Rabbi Kalonymos Kalmish Shapira

translated by
J. Hershy Worch

edited by
Deborah Miller

JASON ARONSON INC.
*Northvale, New Jersey*
Jerusalem

This book was set in 11½ pt. Perpetua by Alpha Graphics of Pittsfield, NH and printed and bound by Book-Mart Press, Inc. of North Bergen, NJ.

Copyright © 2000 by Deborah Miller & J. Hershy Worch

10  9  8  7  6  5  4  3  2  1

All rights reserved. No part of this book may be used or reproduced in any manner whatsoever without written permission from Jason Aronson Inc. except in the case of brief quotations in reviews for inclusion in a magazine, newspaper, or broadcast.

**Library of Congress Cataloging-in-Publication Data**

Kalonimus Kalmish ben Elimelekh, 1889–1943.
   [Esh kodesh. English]
   Esh kodesh = Holy fire / translated by J. Hershy Worch ; edited by Deborah Miller.
   p. cm.
   ISBN 0-7657-6127-0
   1. Bible. O. T. Pentateuch—Meditations.  2. Holocaust, Jewish (1939–1945)—Poland—Warsaw.  3. Suffering—Religious aspects—Judaism—Meditations.  I. Title: Holy fire.  II. Worch, J. Hershy.  III. Title.

BS1225.4 .K275 2000
296.4'7—dc21                                                       99-048146

Printed in the United States of America on acid-free paper. For information and catalog write to Jason Aronson Inc., 230 Livingston Street, Northvale, NJ 07647-1726, or visit our website: www.aronson.com

## *Acknowledgments*

I owe gratitude to the Living God who has carried me this far, and has not, in His mercy and Loving-Kindness, abandoned His servant. Thank You.

I owe thanks to my children and family; to friends, acquaintances, and all the people who have helped me on my journey this far; and most of all to my students. Thank you.

I owe debts of every kind to my children and family, and to friends, acquaintances, and people all over the world who wait patiently to be paid.

I owe amends to all of you who know me. Please accept this work as your due.

—J. H. W.

Dedicated to
\*\*\*
Yaakov Yitzchok
Kalonymos Yehuda
Sheind'l
Shmuel Chaim
Sima Gitt'l Baylah
Meshulem Shragge Feivish
Mordechai Yosef
Wolf
and
Liba Roisa

The children: may they enjoy all the blessings promised in this book.

Finally, I want to acknowledge the living memory of all the Holy Jewish Martyrs to whom this work is a testimony, among them my grandparents and their extended families. I have missed them all my life.
—J. Hershy Worch

The Book of
SACRED FIRE Holy Sayings from the Years of Destruction 1939–1942
said on Sabbaths and festival days in the tormented ghetto of Warsaw

by

His Honor, His Holiness, Jewish Saint and Exilarch,
Lamp of Holy Light, Pious and Abstemious, Scion of a Holy Dynasty, etc.,
The Holy, our Teacher, our rabbi, Rabbi Kalonymos Kalmish,
of Saintly Blessed Memory. God will avenge his blood.
Head of the Rabbinical Court of the Community of Piacezna.
Author of the book *Duties of the Student*.

Son of His Honor, His Holiness, our Master, teacher and rabbi, The Saint,
Holy Man of God, Scion of the Holy Dynastic Chain of Distinguished Lineage,
our Teacher, our rabbi, Rabbi Elimelech, of Saintly Blessed Memory.
Head of the Rabbinical Court of the Community of Grodzysk.
Author of the books *Words of Elimelech* and *Speech of Elimelech*.

Son-in-Law of His Honor, His Holiness, our Master, teacher and rabbi,
The Saint, Holy Man of God, Scion of the Holy Dynastic Chain of
Distinguished Lineage, our Teacher, our rabbi, Rabbi Yerachmiel Moshe,
of Saintly Blessed Memory. Elegant preacher and head of the
Rabbinical Court of the Community of Koznitz.

May their merit shield us and all of Israel;
Amen.
The Holy City Jerusalem, May it be rebuilt swiftly.
This year 5720 (1950).

Published by the Committee of Piacezna Hasidim, with permission of the author's
nephew, our Teacher, our rabbi, etc., Rabbi Elimelech. May he be blessed with long life,
Son of the Rabbi R. Yeshaya Shapira of Saintly Blessed Memory.
80 Sokolov Street, Corner Amos 2, Tel Aviv

# Translator's Note

**ESH KODESH**

This project began as a series of classes on the Sacred Fire text. The recordings were transcribed, and out of them grew the idea of a complete, unabridged translation of the Sacred Fire in to English. The production of the entire manuscript for publication, from conception to completion, was a collaborative effort between the translator and Deborah Miller, who transcribed all the tapes, transposed them into written text, and subsequently edited the emendations and corrections made to them.

Please note: The author's original Hebrew text of Sacred Fire is spare, elegant, and lucid. If the translation is overwrought, clumsy, or dense in places, it is solely the fault of the translator.

# Contents

| | |
|---|---|
| Introduction | xv |
| Notice | xxxi |
| Memorial | xxxiii |

**Jewish Year 5700: September 14, 1939–October 2, 1940**     1

| | |
|---|---|
| Rosh Hashanah (New Year)—September 14–15, 1939 | 3 |
| Shabbat Tishuvah (Sabbath of Repentance)—September 16, 1939 | 10 |
| Chayay Sarah—November 4, 1939 | 13 |
| Toledoth—November 13, 1939 | 15 |
| VaYetzeh—November 18, 1939 | 17 |
| VaYishlach—November 25, 1939 | 19 |
| VaYeshev—December 2, 1939 | 21 |
| Miketz—December 9, 1939 | 24 |

| | |
|---|---|
| *VaYigash*—December 16, 1939 | 26 |
| *VaYechi*—December 23, 1939 | 28 |
| *VaEra*—January 6, 1939 | 30 |
| *Bo*—January 13, 1940 | 33 |
| *BeShalach*—January 20, 1940 | 35 |
| *Yithro*—January 27, 1940 | 38 |
| *Mishpatim*—February 3, 1940 | 40 |
| *Ki Thisa*—February 24, 1940 | 43 |
| *VaYakhel*—March 2, 1940 | 45 |
| *Pekudey (Parshat Shekalim)*—March 9, 1940 | 48 |
| *VaYikra*—March 16, 1940 | 52 |
| *Parshat Zachor*—March 23, 1940 | 55 |
| *Purim*—March 24, 1940 | 58 |
| *Parshat HaChodesh*—April 6, 1940 | 59 |
| *Shabbat HaGadol* (The Great Sabbath)—April 20, 1940 | 63 |
| *Pesach* (Festival of Passover)—April 23–30, 1940 | 67 |
| *Shabbat Chol HaMoed* (Sabbath During the Week of Passover)—April 27, 1940 | 72 |
| *Shevi'i Shel Pesach* (Seventh Day of Passover)—April 29, 1940 | 76 |
| *Acharon Shel Pesach* (Last Day of Passover)—April 30, 1940 | 79 |
| *Metzorah*—April 13, 1940 | 82 |
| *Kedoshim*—May 4, 1940 | 84 |
| *Emor*—May 11, 1940 | 87 |
| *B'Har*—May 18, 1940 | 92 |
| *B'Chukothai*—May 25, 1940 | 95 |
| *Naso*—June 8, 1940 | 98 |

| | |
|---|---|
| *Naso*—June 8, 1940 | 98 |
| *Shavuoth* (Festival of Weeks)—June 12, 1940 | 102 |
| *B'Ha'aloth'cha*—June 15, 1940 | 107 |
| *Sh'lach*—June 22, 1940 | 110 |
| *Balak*—July 13, 1940 | 111 |
| *Pinchos*—July 20, 1940 | 114 |
| *Ki Thetze*—September 14, 1940 | 118 |
| *Ki Thavo*—September 21, 1940 | 121 |
| *Nitzavim*—September 28, 1940 | 124 |

### Jewish Year 5701: October 3, 1940–September 21, 1941 — 127

| | |
|---|---|
| *Rosh Hashanah* (New Year)—October 3–4, 1940 | 129 |
| *Shabbat T'shuvah* (The Sabbath of Repentance)—October 5, 1940 | 135 |
| *Yahrzeit* (16 *Tishrei*)—October 18, 1940 | 138 |
| *Shimini Atzeret* (The Eighth Day Festival)—October 24, 1940 | 143 |
| *Be'reshith*—October 26, 1940 | 147 |
| *Noah*—November 2, 1940 | 150 |
| *Toldoth*—November 30, 1940 | 154 |
| *VaYishlach*—December 14, 1940 | 157 |
| *VaYeshev*—December 21, 1940 | 159 |
| *Parshat HaChodesh*—March 29, 1941 | 162 |
| *Shabbat HaGadol* (The Great Sabbath)—April 5, 1941 | 167 |
| *Pesach* (Festival of Passover)—April 12–19, 1941 | 172 |
| *Shevi'i Shel Pesach* (Seventh Day of Passover)—April 18, 1941 | 182 |
| *BeHa'aloth'cha*—June 14, 1941 | 188 |

| | |
|---|---|
| *Chukath*—July 5, 1941 | 190 |
| *Massay*—July 26, 1941 | 196 |
| *Shabbat Nachamu* (Sabbath of Consolation)—August 9, 1941 | 200 |
| *Ekev*—August 16, 1941 | 204 |
| *Re'Eh*—*Rosh Chodesh Elul*—August 23, 1941 | 210 |
| *Shoftim*—August 30, 1941 | 212 |
| *Ki Thavo*—September 13, 1941 | 214 |

### *Jewish Year 5702: September 22, 1941–September 11, 1942* — 217

| | |
|---|---|
| *Rosh Hashanah*—September 22–23, 1941 | 219 |
| *Shabbat Shuva* (Sabbath of Repentance)—September 27, 1941 | 226 |
| *Sukkoth* (Festival of Tabernacles)—October 6–12, 1941 | 231 |
| *Hoshanna Rabbah* (Seventh Day of *Sukkoth*)—October 12, 1941 | 236 |
| *Sh'mini Atzeret* (Eighth Day of *Sukkoth*)—October 13, 1941 | 237 |
| *Be'reshith*—October 18, 1941 | 239 |
| *Toldoth*—November 22, 1941 | 241 |
| *VaYishlach*—December 6, 1941 | 245 |
| *Chanukah*—December 15–22, 1941 | 249 |
| *VaYigash*—December 27, 1941 | 254 |
| *Sh'moth*—January 10, 1942 | 257 |
| *VaEra*—January 17, 1942 | 262 |
| *Bo*—January 24, 1942 | 268 |
| *B'Shalach*—January 31, 1942 | 275 |
| *Yithro*—February 7, 1942 | 279 |
| *Mishpatim* (*Parshat Shekalim*)—February 14, 1942 | 286 |
| *Parshat Zachor*—February 28, 1942 | 293 |

| | |
|---|---|
| *Purim*—March 3, 1942 | 302 |
| *Parshat Parah*—March 7, 1941 | 305 |
| *Parshat HaChodesh*—March 14, 1942 | 309 |
| *Rosh Chodesh Nissan*—March 19, 1942 | 318 |
| *Chukath*—June 27, 1942 | 322 |
| *Mattoth*—July 11, 1942 | 330 |
| *Shabbat Chazon*—July 18, 1942 | 337 |

# *Introduction*

*Sacred Fire* is unique among the voluminous Jewish literature of the last thousand years. Students or readers of the first chapters can have no inkling of the places they will visit, should they persevere with this book.

*Sacred Fire* is not a diary or record of three years in the life of a Rabbi caught up in the maelstrom of the Warsaw Ghetto. It is not a book of reflections upon pain, terror, and horror, or a book about agony, futility, and loss.

*Sacred Fire* is a collection of Torah on the *Sidra*, or Portion of the Week, a format at once so classic and cliché as to invite immediate and critical comparisons. It includes a number of lengthy sermons around major Jewish Festivals and a few elegiac discourses alluding to people loved and lost. Because writing is not permitted on the Sabbath, the Torah was transcribed from memory, after the Sabbath or Festival had ended.

Like hundreds of rabbinical efforts preceding it, the Torah in this volume has a formulaic structure designed and developed in the *beis haMedrash* (study hall) of Eastern Europe: Quote a verse or a passage from Scripture, pose a question, give a simplistic solution and then follow it with an alternative, a sophisticated *pilpul*— casuistry at its best or worst, depending upon the reader's taste. But *Sacred Fire* defies any scholarly deconstruction or side-by-side comparisons and analyses. There are too many forces at work in its composition.

In addition to the classical norms constraining the format of this work as a Torah of the Week compendium, it is also informed by the less massive but no less influential genre of *Chasidishe*, Hasidic Torah.

The Rebbe of Piacezna, R. Kalonymos Kalmish Shapira, was a Hasid, and who but a Hasid could have written this book? Having said that, it would be a mistake to attempt comparisons with any other Hasidic Torah—with, for instance, the books *Noam Elimelech*, *Kedushath Levi*, or the *Tanya*; or any one of the basic Hasidic texts often quoted in *Sacred Fire*. There is too much growth; too much gritty, real life; or else, too much pathos.

In an introduction of this sort, certain matters have to be addressed and discussed. For which readers or students was this book intended—to whom did the author address his thoughts? What was the purpose of the book—was it intended to convey a particular meaning? Was the manuscript thoroughly edited by the author—did he remove certain telling passages or sections?

The following is a quote from *Sacred Fire*, written December 6, 1941.

> This explains the significance of the Torah we say in times of suffering. For when we say Torah, some of the pain, prayers, and salvation enter into the words of Torah, in the same way that they enter into our words during prayers, thus drawing down and revealing the *chesed* (loving-kindness) [hitherto hidden in the Mind of God] into the Universe of Speech. . . .

Almost all questions concerning the intentions and purpose of the book are answered on contemplating the single most significant thread running through its fabric: the martyrdom of R. Akiba and his affirmation of the unity of God. Another quote from the same passage written December 1941:

> We learn in the Talmud (*Berachoth* 61b), When they took R. Akiba out to kill him, it was time for recitation of the morning *Sh'ma*. They tore his flesh with iron combs, while he took upon himself the yoke of heaven. His students said to him, 'Our rabbi, this far?' He replied, 'All my days have I been at pain over the verse in Scripture (Deut. 6:4–5) Love God your Lord with all your heart, all your soul, and all your might. 'When will I ever have the opportunity to fulfill it?' I asked myself. And now that I have the opportunity, should I not fulfill it?" He was drawing out the word "One" and meditating upon it when his soul departed.' With total self-abandonment, and through the elevation of his thoughts, he unified the name of God as he meditated upon the word "One".

*Sacred Fire* is a meditation upon the word "One" in the verse from *Sh'ma*, "Hear O Israel, God our Lord, God is One."

In a nutshell, the whole thesis of the book revolves around a single thought. All is from God, and it is all happening to God. God is at the center, and He surrounds every event. There is nothing else, no duality. There is no evil power, no satanic insurrection, no forces fighting for supremacy. There is only God and *hesed*, loving-kindness. Sometimes it is unbearable, insufferable, unspeakable, uncontainable *hesed*—but it is ever only One God's singular loving-kindness.

I doubt very much whether the author in his wildest dreams imagined that the manuscript would be translated for the English-speaking world at the end of the twentieth or any other century. In the directions accompanying the original manuscript written January 3, 1943, the Rebbe wrote:

> I take the honor to allow myself a request of the esteemed personage or the esteemed institute who will find these the following, my manuscripts. "The Preparation of Young Men," "Entrance to the Gates (of the Duties of the Young Scholar)," "Command and Exhort," "Torah Novellae" on the weekly portions from the years 1939–42. Please be so kind and take the pains to convey them to the Holy Land to the following address: "Rabbi Yeshaya Shapira, Tel Aviv, Falestina (Palestine)," including with them the attached letter. If God will be merciful and I am among the remaining Jews who survive the war, I ask that you please forgive me and return it all to me, or to the Warsaw Rabbinate for Kalonymos.

Later in that same missive he made the following request:

> I beg of you my dearest beloved, that when God helps and these booklets reach your hands . . . that you endeavor to print them, be it individually or together, as you see fittingly appropriate. Also that you deign and endeavor to "distribute them among Jacob and disperse them among Israel." Please print in all my booklets that I beg and plead with every individual Jew to study my books, and I am certain that the merit of my holy ancestors of blessed memory will stand by him and his entire household, in the present and in the future. May God have mercy upon us.

Knowing that the author conceived, or at the very least prayed, that his manuscript would become a book studied by Jews everywhere, I have taken his words as permission to translate it into English.

The tone of the book is pedagogical throughout, never allowing the reader to forget for an instant that lessons are there to be learned, life's challenges to be met, and character flaws to be rectified—all rather predictable, and in any other circumstances unremarkable. What elevates *Sacred Fire* quite beyond the ordinary are two features that beggar description.

The first is a foray into uncharted territory vis-à-vis the Torah itself. *Sacred Fire* is filled with exquisite, blinding, and breathtaking profundities. In the following example the author proffers simple sentences sketching the murkiest theological cartography in terse, daring periods. A passage from a chapter written August 9, 1941:

> At the end of Lamentations (5:21) we pray, "Return us to You, O God, and we will return." How dare we ask of God that He return us? We sinned, we strayed, and He should bring us about? But note how the text says ". . . and we will return." Let us, as it were, both return. We both need to repent, because if we humans have sinned, then the part of us that is God has also sinned. . . .

The second is the portrait of a man, the subtext from which the author emerges, as insubstantial and persistent as the afterimage of a searing, bright flash of light. Imagine if you can, how devout is the person sharing the following insight, from a passage dated January 10, 1942:

> And now, while every head sickens and every heart grieves, and some say that this is not the time to talk of piety, repentance, or fear—whether of this sort or that—that it is enough just to observe the simple, practical commandments. I say they are mistaken, for two reasons. First, because even now we must worship with all the means at our disposal, with every type of worship. The second reason—which argues quite to the contrary—is this: Any person practicing spiritual reflection, suffering the fears we have described, worrying about himself and whether he may be sinning this way or that, and always looking inside himself for any kind of blemish, eventually experiences the most profound joy. After periods of introspection such as these, he begins to feel elevated and, because his fear is pure, tastes the sweetest, most rapturous essence of fear, described in the Sabbath hymn "God I desire" (by R. Aaron the Great of Karlin). It is a supernal fear, which elevates the man.

Students or readers looking for answers to age-old questions, for why bad things happen to good people, or any people, will find scant to satisfy them in this volume. Holocaust survivors looking for an indictment of God will find slim pickings. Consider this quote, from December 15, 1941:

> In all honesty, what room is there, God forbid, for doubts or questions? Admittedly, Jews only endure suffering of the sort with which we are currently afflicted every few hundred years. But still, how can we expect or hope to under-

The Jewish people, on the other hand, say repeatedly in the liturgy of the High Holy Days, "You, God, are true." God, blessed be He, is true, and nothing else is true. Any truth that exists in the world is only true because God commanded it so, and wanted it so. Because God, blessed be He, is true, therefore it, also, is true. We are forbidden to steal because God, Who is the Truth, so commanded. And because of God's commandment, it became the truth. And when God commands the opposite, and the Jewish court declares property ownerless, making it legally ownerless and removing a person's title to his own property, then this also becomes true. When He commanded our father Abraham to sacrifice his son Isaac, then the binding of Isaac became the truth, and if He had not later commanded Abraham not to harm him, then the truth would have been to slaughter him.

For its treatment of the immanent themes of pain and faith, *Sacred Fire* will have earned itself an unenvied place in the canon. But to describe it solely in those terms is to ignore all of its glittering and many-faceted gems.

Nowhere in modern Jewish literature are there such paeans in praise of womanhood as can be found in the oblique and kabbalistic references to his late wife, Miriam. In discussing the biblical narrative surrounding the death of Miriam the prophet, whose yearly cycle of readings coincide with his wife's *yahrzeit*, the Rebbe makes some of his most innovative remarks. Beginning with a somewhat esoteric discussion of the effects of human emotions on the spiritual forces passing through the body, the Rebbe notes how man's noblest spiritual ambitions may be thwarted by common frailties such as fear and self-obsession, and how man's frail corpus can make spiritual concepts a physical reality. From July 5, 1941:

As is well known from the sacred literature, there are occasions when salvation has already been decreed from heaven on Israel's behalf, but it tarries because it is abstract and cannot come down to this world and clothe itself in physical, practical reality. So, when a Jew knows, not just intellectually but also by feeling with the very core of his body, that he must support and help his fellows, then mercy becomes a part of his body. When next he prays on behalf of his fellow Jews, he prays with a body full of compassion. Then, the salvation that was stopped for want of a channel through which to flow finds in this person a perfect conduit and spreads to meet physical needs as well.

This is exactly what is meant in the Talmud (*Megillah* 14b): When King Josiah was in trouble, he sent for Hulda the prophetess (II Chronicles 34:22) even though the leading prophet of that era was Jeremiah. "But how could Josiah himself pass over Jeremiah and send to her?" the Talmud asks. Members of the school of R. Shila replied, "Because women are more compassionate."

A woman has more compassion than a man has because her physical body is more compassionate, and therefore women can bring salvation down into this world faster than can men. . . . The Torah tells us (Numbers 20:1), "The Children of Israel, the entire congregation, came to the Tzin Desert in the First Month. The people settled in Kadesh, Miriam died there and was buried there." Rashi (ibid.), interpreting the repetition of the word 'there,' comments, "It is as though in the Torah were written that Miriam died "at the Mouth of God [as did her brothers Moses and Aaron]." . . . And Miriam was like a mother even to Jews who were not her children. She is an archetypal mother, and this role did not end with her death. In heaven she is still our mother, continually arousing mercy on behalf of all Israel, even for those who are not directly her descendants.

The following year, in a discourse on the death of Miriam, there are some even more remarkable passages. Referring to the Mystical Kiss of God, whereby the pious give up their souls to their Maker and pass blissfully from life to death, the author breaks new ground. While Rashi, the medieval commentator, remarks that Miriam also died with the Kiss, but the Torah omits this information because it is not "the respectful way from on high" to credit God with kissing Miriam, *Sacred Fire* takes a unique and unassailably transcendental view of the whole matter. What it amounts to is this: The Torah does not say Miriam died at the Mouth of God because then one might be led to believe that she was only as great as Moses or Aaron. She was much greater than they were! Her inspiration was innate, while her brothers Moses and Aaron had to be inspired by God. They may have died when God kissed them, but Miriam died when she kissed God. June 27, 1942:

Every Jew needs to know that even when he believes he is having a spiritual awakening as a result of his own actions, it is still always God, infusing him with belief and desire from above, Who engenders his awakening from below. . . . It follows from this that if a woman becomes a saint, studying Torah and fulfilling the commandments, these must be counted as her own accomplishments, because women are not commanded to do such things. If she was not ordered to fulfill the commandment then she cannot have been inspired with an awakening from on high.

And so, if Miriam also died with the Mystical Kiss, why then does the verse not say that Miriam died at the Mouth of God? And how does the statement

> made by Rashi (ibid.), "Because it was not the respectful way from on high," answer the question? The answer is as follows: We have established that Miriam attained her exalted level not as a result of an 'arousal from on high,' but entirely through an 'awakening from below.' In light of this it is simply not accurate to say of Miriam, "at the Mouth of God." And because the source of Miriam's worship originated within herself, flowing out of her, it was truly Miriam's merit that provided the wellspring, the source from which flowed the living, holy water that sustained all the Jewish people. . . . While Miriam was alive, as we said above, she performed even those deeds that she was not obliged to perform. It was obvious that the force driving her to such exalted heights of piety was her own exceptional yearning, springing from within her. With it she was able to inspire the whole Jewish people with the longing to yearn for God, and with which they would be able to prepare themselves properly to receive the supernal Light that our teacher Moses was to bring down for them. As we have already quoted from sacred literature, 'our teacher Moses was equerry to the King.' His function was to bring down to the people the Light from Above. But once Miriam died, the Jewish people were no longer able to access this great yearning, and so they were no longer properly prepared to receive the Light that Moses brought down from Above. . . .

In talking of the death of his only son, Rabbi Elimelech Benzion, who died on September 29, 1939 after having been grievously wounded by gunfire, the Rebbe asserts that all Jewish martyrdom is part of an unfolding cosmic drama. On October 28, 1940, the first *yahrzeit* (anniversary) of his son's death, he wrote:

> The *Akeidah* (Binding of Isaac) was a test of the desire and intention of Abraham and Isaac. It was never actually accomplished or completed because the angel said to Abraham (Genesis 22:12) "Do not harm the lad." For this reason, the murder of a Jew by idolaters, which as an action devoid of worshipful intention is in absolute antithesis to the *Akeidah*, actually consummates the *Akeidah*. The *Akeidah* was just the beginning, the expression of intent and desire, while the murder of a Jew is the conclusion of the act. Thus, the *Akeidah* and all the murders of Jews since are components of one event.

In the following year on October 7, 1941, upon his son's second *yahrzeit*, he added another dimension to the tragedy. By connecting it with the talmudic Midrash of the martyrdom of the ten Tannaitic Rabbis in Roman times, the death of his son becomes one of the mysteries of Judaism that even Moses on Sinai was not given to understand. He wrote:

Besides the simple wish to be the first to die and not have to watch his friend's death, perhaps R. Shimon b. Gamliel meant something more when he said, "Please, kill me *t'chilah*—first." It could be that he wanted to initiate the new pathway in worship that was being worked out. The new pathway requires someone to have such profound love for Jews that he would rather die first than watch his friend die, even though the friend gains no reprieve from his death. . . .
It is not just those who explicitly express this sentiment, the desire to die rather than watch a Jew be killed, who are included in the category of those walking the path of R. Shimon b. Gamliel by worshipping God in his footsteps. Many among those who have died or been killed in these last years, and also among those who died in the pogroms that occurred earlier—may God have mercy, and say, "Enough"—were saints who walked this very path. They were people whose love for Jews was so great they were always in the most profound readiness to give up their life rather than watch a Jew in pain. And so, it was arranged in heaven that they should die first. This kind of love for Jews comes of loving God with a powerful, self-sacrificial, self-abandoning love.

There are number of complex leitmotifs forming a background, almost a framework, for the whole tapestry of the *Sacred Fire*. The first, *Yir'at Shomayim*—Fear of God or, more correctly, Fear of Heaven—appears in the opening paragraphs and pervades the book. So that the reader not confuse the concept with fear of pain, fear of punishment, or fear of loss, let it be said at the outset that for the Rebbe of Piaczena, Fear of God and Rapturous Bliss seem to be synonymous emotions or states of consciousness. The highest goal, the prized and cherished reward for endeavoring to approach God, is the promise of heightened Fear of God.

The second motif, appearing in the second chapter, is Cosmic Reciprocity: "as above so below, as below so above." From September 16, 1939:

> It is a well-known teaching of the Rabbis (Jerusalem Talmud, *Rosh Hashanah* 7b; Exodus Rabbah, *Mishpatim* 30:9) that God observes all of the commandments of the Torah. How then does He observe the commandment to repent, to do *t'shuvah*?
>
> God fulfills this commandment when He repents of the evil that He has rendered, God forbid, to His people Israel, or that He has decreed to befall them. This is God's repentance, His *t'shuvah* as it were. . . . But when God's repentance is only for that which He has already done, or for what He has decreed, then the Jewish people remain, God forbid, in the same desperate straits as always. . . . They remain in the same very poor condition they were in before the troubles began.

We read in Psalm 90: "Return O God, how long? . . . Satisfy us in the morning with Your kindness. . . ." What we really mean when we say "Return O God" is "God, please repent." . . . And we end by adding the phrase "Satisfy us in the morning with Your kindness, that we may rejoice and be glad all our days," We mean "This is the repentance that we want of You, so to speak. Satisfy us in the morning with Your kindness. . . ."

But this is exactly the kind of repentance required of us, likewise. For when a person repents only of a sin committed . . . he still finds himself back in the state he occupied before he committed the sin. . . . The chief principle of repentance, however, is "Return, O Israel, to God your Lord." Lest you think that contrition for your sins is all you need, the prophet cautions that the repentance must continue all the way, until you reach God. . . .

The next oft-appearing idea is the Martyrdom of R. Akiba, also introduced in the second chapter. Its chief sources are two talmudic midrashim. The first, already mentioned, is the Talmud *Berachoth* 61b, beginning with a discussion of the meaning of the Scriptural verse "Love God your Lord with all your heart, all your soul, and all your might." (Deut. 6:4–5) R. Akiba said, "'With all your soul' even if God takes your soul." The Talmud uses the discussion as a springboard to launch into a description of how R. Akiba was arrested for teaching Torah in public and subsequently executed in the most horrible way imaginable. The second midrashic source is also talmudic, *Menachoth* 29b. Moses was shown R. Akiba and his Torah.

Moses said to God, "You have someone like this, yet You give the Torah through me?" God responded, "Silence! It arose thus in the thought before Me." Moses asked of God, "You have shown me his Torah; now please show me his reward." "Turn around," commanded God. Moses turned around and saw them weighing R. Akiba's flesh in the slaughterhouse. "Is this the Torah and its reward?" he asked. "Silence!" spoke God. "It arose thus in the thought before Me."

The martyrdom of R. Akiba and his nine colleagues is the subject of much discussion in rabbinic literature, particularly in the Lurianic Kabbalah, where it is connected with the Genesis story of the sale of Joseph into Egypt by his brothers. Each of the ten martyred rabbis had to expiate the guilt of one of the nine brothers involved in Joseph's kidnap and sale. R. Akiba, the tenth, stood in place of God, Who was the tenth conspirator in the sale of Joseph.

Another recurrent theme of *Sacred Fire*, is Loss of Self as a result of trauma. This is first remarked upon in a Torah written November 13, 1939, in a discussion of the difference between someone who has been cast out and someone who is lost.

When troubles are as great as they are at present and, as we see plainly, Jewish men have had their beards shorn off, they become unrecognizable as Jews from the outside. Then, as the terrible persecutions and unbearable tortures beyond description persist, we watch people becoming unrecognizable even from the inside. In these terrible circumstances, a person may lose himself completely and be unable to recognize himself at all (in Yiddish, *ehr fahrliert sich*). He can no longer recall how he felt on the Sabbath even one year ago, or how he felt during the week, before praying or after praying, etc. He has been stepped upon and crushed until he no longer feels that he is a Jew or knows whether he is a human being at all, or an animal without any faculties with which to feel. This is the level of being truly lost and absent. . . .

Whenever describing the effects of trauma or post-traumatic stress on those around him, the author's language, while calm, may convey some desperation, as he gropes in vain to find the words for concepts essentially outside the scope of the classical Hebrew language. Bear in mind that Psyche is a Greek mythological personification, while the modern use of the term "psyche" follows an essentially non-Jewish attempt to distinguish among the "lower soul" or animal principle and the "higher soul" or spirit. The closest Hebrew approximations are "soul," "spirit," or "mind," all of which are woefully inadequate in descriptions of the effects the Warsaw Ghetto was having on mid-twentieth century humanity. The phrase "cognitive dissonance," while obviously applicable, may require more than a few sentences in Hebrew. From August 30, 1941:

A person in distress, who still has some spirit left in him, may respond to good news with joy and credulity. But if he has been so beaten and tortured that he is utterly broken and effaced by pain and poverty, then even if he is cognizant and believes that everything will turn out well, there is no longer a person capable of rejoicing. There is no one left to be convinced or encouraged. I have actually seen something like this happen. Therefore, the Torah informs us, "They did not listen to Moses," even though they believed in him. "Because they were dispirited and because of their hard work," there was no one left to be encouraged or to pay attention to the good tidings. . . .

The fifth idea treats a complex theological idea proposed in the Midrash and Zohar, quoted by Rashi, Genesis 1:1. Rashi says: "God originally intended to create the world to be governed with the rule of law. Upon seeing, however, that the world would not be able to withstand the pressures of *Midath HaDin*, Rule of Law, God preceded it with *Midath HaRachamim*, Quality of Mercy—making them both, *Din* and *Rachamim,* Judgment and Mercy, partners in governance of the world." Discussion of this concept appears first on December 9, 1939, in a peculiarly prescient paragraph. "Why was it not enough for God to associate Mercy and Judgment, as He ultimately does when it is needed? Why do we need to be told that God preceded Judgment (*Hikdim*) with the attribute of Mercy? Perhaps this was necessary because there are situations when 'on time' is too late, times when the universe simply cannot stand another moment without Mercy, and so it has to come before its time." Again and again he examines the midrashic quote from Rashi, as though it contains some essential cipher to explain events unfolding around him.

The final motif, God's Pain, does not overtly appear until March 16, 1940, but once visible it can be found beneath all subsequent Torahs and can retrospectively be discerned, albeit vaguely, in earlier chapters as well.

> God is connected to man, as it is written (Psalm 91:15), "I am with him, in pain." In the Midrash (Exodus Rabbah 2:12) we learn, about the verse "God called to him from amidst the [burning] bush" (Exodus 3:4), that God called "Moses Moses!" without a comma punctuating the repeated name—while at the *Akeidah*, the Binding of Isaac, when God called to Abraham to still his hand from hurting Isaac, God used the comma and called, "Abraham, Abraham!" (Genesis 22:11) The Midrash explains this with the parable of a man foundering beneath an unbearable weight. He calls urgently to whomever is nearest, "Hey you you come quick. Help me shed this load!" So it was that God called upon Moses to relieve Him, as it were, of His burden; and Moses helped to relieve God of the unbearable burden of Jewish suffering.

The theme of God in Pain is given more and more attention as *Sacred Fire* develops, until it takes over from most other threads, absorbing them into its own fabric. December 14, 1940: "At another level, however, when the pain of Jews is so great that they have no strength to bear it, then the strength to endure, to remain alive in the midst of such terrible hardships and brutality, is provided solely by the Holy Blessed One. Then, the brunt of the burden is, as it were, upon God. It is not human, Jewish strength, that endures such agony and remains resolute; it is God's strength, the strength that He has given to the Jewish people. God carries by far the greater burden of the pain, and so God calls out to the Jewish people, as He called out to Moses, 'Come quick; help Me shed this load!'"

There is only one sin considered unforgivable by the author of *Sacred Fire*, and whatever harsh words he can summon are reserved for only one sort of person: someone who loses faith. Alluding to the traditional Jewish belief that even the wickedest sinners are not condemned to more than twelve months in Hell, on December 15, 1941, he wrote:

> Faith is the foundation of everything. If the faith of a person is, God forbid, damaged, then the person is torn asunder and distanced from God. Souls condemned to Gehenna emerge purified and cleansed after having repented. We hope to God that all those suffering these tortures now will rise, cleansed, purified, and closer to Him. But the soul of someone whose faith is damaged is like a soul enduring Gehenna while continuing to add offenses to its sins. After a time, upon examining itself, the soul sees the situation and asks itself, "What have I achieved with all this suffering, if I am just as sullied now as I was before?"

One of the most astonishing facets of personality to emerge from *Sacred Fire* is the Rebbe's ability to maintain perspective. He consistently distinguishes "personal" from "important," and lives his life with this salient factor in the forefront of his mind. Throughout *Sacred Fire* he expresses the unbending principle of *Tziduk HaDin*, Justifying God's Right, which obliges every individual to accept whatever is happening as Divine justice. From August 23, 1941: "A Jew must believe and perceive that everything happens at the hand of God, and that the Holy Blessed One does not execute judgment without justice, God forbid. This is fundamental. It is one of the Thirteen Principles of the Jewish Faith. . . . Besides this, it is also a source of strength and joy in times of suffering. . . ." However, the opposite applies when thinking about Jews as a nation. On December 15, 1941, the author emphasized what he thought made it all worthwhile, writing: "If only people would bear in mind that it is not because we robbed or did anything wrong to anyone that we are being persecuted, but because we are Jews—Children of Israel, bound to God and to His holy Torah."—as though, somehow, with this thought in mind, the Jewish people could endure and survive anything the cosmos might throw at them. This theme takes on greater and greater weight as the escalating tragedy in the Warsaw Ghetto approaches its apogee.

Amid all this Torah of pain is a Torah of laughter. It comes at the beginning of the book, January 13, 1940, and deserves comment. It begins, as do many of the *Sacred Fire* chapters, with a quote from Rashi: "Rashi explains that the words 'how I made a mockery of Egypt' mean 'how I played and toyed with the Egyptians.'"

The author brings midrashic proof that God never rejoices in destruction, even of the wicked. "So how can it be that in our text, God is saying, 'You will tell your children and grandchildren how I made a mockery of Egypt, and laughed at their downfall?'" By distinguishing among punishment and educational correction, the author of *Sacred Fire* reconciles the difficulties. The first, he points out, is merely painful; the second is salutary.

> Perhaps God doesn't refrain from rejoicing in the downfall of the wicked, if the downfall also conveys an important lesson to Israel. Throughout history, Jewish people have suffered so much anguish, on so many occasions, simply so that they would be purified in the process, and aroused to the fear of God. But during the Exodus from Egypt, as the Jewish people approached redemption, God said, "This time, it is My great pleasure and joy to bring awareness and knowledge of Myself to the Jewish people, through tormenting and afflicting plagues upon the Egyptians, and not the Jews." . . .
>
> With this we can answer the question posed by our early sages, of blessed memory: Why was Pharaoh punished for being stubborn, when the text tells us plainly that he had no free will? God often says of Pharaoh, "I have hardened his heart, so that he will not obey." But now we can understand it without too much difficulty. If the Jewish people can be punished, tormented, and abused so often without any fault to be found in them, but simply in order to make them aware of God and to awaken in them the fear of Him, then Pharaoh also can suffer a little, so that Israel may know that "I am God."

In fact, the holy Piacezna Rebbe is indulging in a little Cosmic Reciprocity, laughing because God was laughing, mocking because God mocked. Throughout this Torah, there is the rumbling belly laughter of someone getting an insider's joke. It is all the more tragic that of all the Torahs in *Sacred Fire*, this one ends with the words, "I am unable to recall any more of my words on this matter."

J. Hershy Worch<br>
Chicago, Illinois

# *Notice*

By the grace of God. I take the honor to allow myself a request of the esteemed personage or the esteemed institute who will find these the following, my manuscripts: *The Preparation of Young Men*, *Entrance to the Gates (of the Duties of the Young Scholar)*, *Command and Exhort* and *Torah Novellae* on the weekly portions from the years 1939–42. Please be so kind and take the pains to convey them to the Holy Land to the following address: "Rabbi Yeshaya Shapira, Tel Aviv, Falestina (Palestine)," including with them the attached letter. If God will be merciful and I am among the remaining Jews who survive the war, I ask that you please forgive me and return it all to me, or to the Warsaw Rabbinate for Kalonymos. May God have mercy upon us, the remnants of Israel who are anywhere at all: Save us, restore us, and deliver us in the blink of an eyelid.

With profound and heartfelt thanks,
Kalonymos

On the eve of Monday, in the week of Vaera, Teveth 27, 5743 [January 3 1943].

By the grace of God. To his honor, the honored Rabbi, Rabbi Yeshaya Shapira, may he live a long, good life; Amen.

To his honor, my illustrious friend R. Avner Bienenthal, may his light shine brightly. To his honor, my trusted friend R. Elimelech Ben Porath, may his light shine brightly. To the honorable, beloved brothers and friends, who have been joined to my heart forever, may they be well.

Printing of the booklet *The Preparation of Young Men*, had already begun before the war, and was interrupted by the outbreak of war. Now that we are in constant peril of our lives, God forbid, I beg of you my dearest beloved, that when God helps and these booklets reach your hands *The Preparation of Young Men, Entrance to the Gates (of the Duties of the Young Scholar), Command and Exhort*, and *Torah Novellae* from the Years of Fury, 1939–42—that you endeavor to print them. This may be individually or together, as you see fittingly appropriate. Also that you deign and endeavor to "distribute them among Jacob and disperse them among Israel." Please print in all my booklets that I beg and plead with every individual Jew to study my books, and I am certain that the merit of my holy ancestors of blessed memory will stand by him and his entire household, in the present and in the future. May God have mercy upon us.

Now, in the booklet *The Preparation of Young Men* that was already being printed, I displayed an inscription dedicated solely to the blessed memory of my pious, saintly wife—for at that time, things were still well with me. My mother, my guide, the saintly Rebbetzin of blessed memory was still alive; my holy son, the Rabbi of blessed memory; and his wife, my holy daughter-in-law, the Rebbetzin of blessed memory, were alive. But now, to my grief and my great woe I have lost, for my many sins, all this treasure. The light of my eyes is dimmed, may you be spared. Therefore, I request that you print the memorial inscriptions that I will record here.

God will have mercy and say "Enough!" to the suffering of the Jewish people and to my own suffering. He will give me back my dearest, most precious, modest daughter, Ms. Rechil Yehudis, may she live a long and good life; Amen. She was snatched from me on the second day of Rosh Chodesh Elul, Friday in the week of Shoftim, 5702 [August 1942].

Also endeavor to print on the frontispiece of all the books mentioned above my name with the names of my father, the holy Rabbi of blessed memory, and of my father-in-law, the holy Rabbi of blessed memory.

More, I am unable to write. May God have mercy and preserve me with the remnants of Israel, that I also merit to join in the work of printing them.

The words of your loving friend and brother, who yearns for you, who is broken and shattered with his own torments and with the torments of all the Jewish people, which are as deep as the manifold abyss and high as heaven's heavens, who anticipates God's salvation in the blink of an eye.

Kalonymos

## *Memorial*

The memory of saintly men and women is eternal. Behold Her Honor and Holiness my mother, my guide, the Rebbetzin and saint, noblest woman, scion of the holy dynastic chain of distinguished lineage, Mrs. Hannah Bracha, of blessed memory. Daughter of the sainted, holy Rabbi, R. Chaim Shmuel the Levi, may the memory of the saintly be a blessing, from Chentshin. She served God with all her abilities, in heart and in soul. With the utmost exertion, she raised her children to the Torah. Her holy soul rose heavenward in purity, on the eve of Friday, the eve of Sabbath, 7th of Cheshvan 5700.

Her honor my wife, the saintly, modest, pious Rebbetzin, scion of the holy dynastic chain of distinguished lineage, Mrs. Rachel Chaya Miriam, of blessed memory. Daughter of the sainted, holy Rabbi, R. Yerachmiel Moshe, may the memory of the saintly be a blessing; head of the rabbinical court, Koznitz. Her virtues were bounteous; she also studied Torah every day. She was a compassionate mother toward embittered souls in general and of Torah scholars and Hasidim in particular. In the fullness of her life, her holy soul rose in purity, heavenward. On the Sabbath, in the week of the reading "And Miriam died there" [Chukath], Tamuz 10, 5697.

His Honor my only son, treasure of my heart and soul, the holy, the Rabbi, the pious, scion of the holy dynastic chain of distinguished lineage, our Rabbi, the Rabbi R. Elimelech Benzion, of blessed memory. A man of truth, master of the purest, good character, plumbing the depths of the Torah, he was a sage and lover of Jews. He left behind Torah novellae on the Tractate *Shabbat* and one volume on the *Yoreh Deah*.

He was mortally wounded at a time of great distress for Jacob, on Monday 12, Tishrei 5700. In great pain and bitter anguish, his holy soul fled heavenward on the 16th of Tishrei, the second day of Sukkot.

Her honor his wife, my holy daughter-in-law, transparent, modest, scion of the holy dynastic chain of distinguished lineage, Mrs. Gittel, of blessed memory. Daughter of the sainted Rabbi, the Rabbi, our Rabbi R. Shlomo Chaim, may he live a long and good life, [of blessed memory], from Balachov. As she stood, utterly selfless, at the hospital where her husband, my holy son of blessed memory, lay wounded, she was killed Tuesday 13, Tishrei, 5700.

The Master of Compassion will hide them within the secrets of His wings forever, wrapping their souls in the assemblage of eternal life. God is their lot, and may they rest in peaceful repose; Amen.

*The Jewish Year 5700:
September 14, 1939–
October 2, 1940*

# *Rosh Hashanah* (New Year)—
# September 14–15, 1939

The two following verses are found in the liturgy recited before blowing the *shofar*:

> *"Out of my straits I called upon God; He answered me with divine alleviation."* (Psalms 118:5)

> *"You hear my voice; please be not deaf to my plea for well-being."* (Lament. 3:56)

In the Midrash (Eccles. Rabbah 9:3 on the verse Eccles. 9:7) "Go, eat with joy your bread, and with a glad heart drink your wine, for God has already favored your works," we learn the following:

They said in the name of R. Levy: This verse is an allusion to Rosh Hashanah and Yom Kippur.

A parable: A city owed tax arrears to the crown. The king with his treasury agents went to collect the debt. Ten miles from the city, the nobility came out and greeted the king with praises; He forgave them one third of their debt. Five miles from the city, people of the middle classes greeted the king with praises; He forgave them another third of their debt. As he approached the city, men, women, and children came out to greet him, singing his praises; He forgave them their whole debt, saying to them, "What has passed has passed, let us now begin a fresh reckoning." So it is on the eve of Rosh Hashanah when the leaders of the generation fast God forgives a third of their sins, as it is written (Psalm 130:4), "Forgiveness is with You, so that You be feared." Certain individuals fast on those days between Rosh

Hashanah and Yom Kippur, and God forgives them another third of their sins. On the day of Yom Kippur, everyone fasts, men, women, and children alike, and God forgives them all their sins, saying, "Whatever has passed has passed; let us now begin a fresh reckoning." Then a voice goes out from heaven saying, "Go, eat with joy your bread and with a glad heart drink your wine, for God has already favored your works."

R. Acha said, "Forgiveness is all readied and prepared at Rosh Hashanah, as it is written, 'Forgiveness is with You, so that You be feared.' So that fear be upon all Your creatures, God."

The Midrash makes clear two noteworthy ideas: that forgiveness is readied and prepared at Rosh Hashanah, and that the reason for this is so we should fear God. In fact, we have previously learned that the reason the Holy Blessed One created the entire universe was in order that we fear Him, as it is written (Eccles. 3:14), "And God made it, in order that they fear Him."

But what this Midrash adds is the idea that even the concept of forgiveness was conceived only to enable us to fear God.

When all of his blunders and previous errors torment a person, it is impossible for him to fear God honestly, with dread and reverence of God's blessed greatness and His awesome power. Real fear of God is the awe of His very greatness that is experienced by every Jewish soul, each according to his own level of sensitivity. There is, for instance, the person for whom the fear of the tremendous holiness of God is felt viscerally, who trembles at the very idea of erring, God forbid, or of acting against the wishes of God. And then there is the person whose fear is experienced merely as a fear of punishment. This fear also stems from his soul, which fears God's greatness, but because of the person's self-centeredness and insensitivity to his soul, it is experienced as fear of being punished or fear that his personal needs will not be sufficiently met.

All this is true only at those times when the essential Jewish soul predominates, for only then can it feel its genuine closeness to God and tremble at the fear of God. This cannot happen when a person is miserable because of his blunders and is tormented by them. Then, crushed and declining, he may be totally numbed in body and soul, unable to feel anything at all, let alone the fear of God or a trembling at His awesome power. This is the meaning of the verse (Psalm 130:4) "Forgiveness is with You, so that You be feared." As we read in the Midrash above, from Rosh Hashanah the forgiveness—including not only exoneration but also remission and salvation—is all prepared and readied "so that fear be upon all Your creatures, God."

Rosh Hashanah, the Ten Days of Repentance, and Yom Kippur are particularly favorable times in which to find the Holy One, blessed be He. Our sages of blessed memory explained the verse "Seek God while He may be found" (Isaiah 55:6) by asking, "When may a person find God?" and answering, "He may be found during the ten days between Rosh Hashanah and Yom Kippur." (Talmud, *Rosh Hashanah* 18a) The sages were saying that during this period the revelation of God is manifest in the soul of every person, and so the fear of God is awakened in each person with greater clarity and greater strength.

Why are the perceived closeness and the manifest revelation of God most noticeable at this time of the year? In order to reveal God's sovereignty. We say in the Rosh Hashanah liturgy, immediately upon blowing the Shofar, "Today is the birthday of the world." As was said earlier, the purpose of Creation is to reveal God's sovereignty over the Jewish people, and so it follows that in this period, at the birthday of the world, God's sovereignty is felt most acutely.

And so the meaning of the Midrash quoted above, with the parable about the people of the city who came out to sing the praises of the king, becomes clear. The people came out to sing praises of the King because this was their way of acknowledging His sovereignty. The parable compares our fasting during the period of the Ten Days of Repentance to their singing of the praises of the king. It might then be asked: What kind of praise is fasting? With what we have already said, we can readily explain what the Midrash means. It is not only the songs and praises that we sing on these days; or the prayers, crying, and beseeching we do; that sing the praises of God, but even our fasting and acts of self denial are acknowledgments of God. They stress our feeling that the soul within us, our viscera, feels the revelation and imminence of God. That we tremble before Him, and shudder at the mere thought of sinning.

There is great need for us to arouse and excite our own fear of heaven during this period, because the fear itself is an acceptance of the yoke of God's sovereignty upon us. All the cries of the Jewish people heard in this period are a revelation of God's sovereignty and an acceptance of God's sovereignty upon us. Even those pleas and prayers in which we beseech God to take care of our physical needs are also a kind of revelation of His sovereignty and a praising of Him. God has revealed His majesty to us and we have accepted His sovereignty over us. We have returned to Him, and so we also ask of Him that He meet our needs. Who else can fill the needs of His people and His servants if not God, King of kings, the Holy Blessed One? This is the praise we sing to God: the fact that we acknowledge and accept upon ourselves God's sovereignty.

A person may take it as a sign that his fears flow from his soul's awareness of the proximity and revelation of God if he finds himself anxious and fearful during this period. If he finds himself doing a personal inventory, examining himself without any thought of self-justification, but, on the contrary, reviewing his own behavior and scrutinizing the very smallest of his sins; if there arise in him feelings of remorse and even anger at himself, such that he says, "Woe, that I sinned against God. How am I acknowledging Him as Sovereign over me?"; if during this period he feels himself donning the yoke of the fear of heaven, accepting the weight of God's sovereignty upon himself, for the year to come, then his pleas—even those related solely to his own needs—are all forms of worship and a singing of God's praises. In fact, it is especially appropriate that we cry out to God to meet our needs during these days more so than all the rest of the year.

There is a parable of a prince who was captured and held captive by the most contemptible people, who afflicted him. Suddenly, the prince, sensing the proximity of the king, started shouting and crying bitterly, "Help me, father! Help me, my liege!"

The prince felt the king's manifest nearness, and so his increased weeping was an indication that he was experiencing a revelation of the king's closeness. Similarly, the increase in the intensity of crying heard from all Jews at this time, over their own suffering—the suffering of loved ones and the suffering of all Israel—is a sign that they are experiencing the manifest revelation of God's sovereignty. Of course, this is only true when and if a person genuinely feels his fear of God growing stronger and his yearning to crown God as King growing more powerful.

Now, it is also true that people repent each in his own way, all year round, and that every day we pray for our life, health, and sustenance. Why then should Rosh Hashanah be considered so unique? What makes the day so easily distinguishable is the sounds associated with it—not only those of the shofar, but also more generally the piercing sounds made by our voices of repentance and the poignancy of our pleas for sustenance. Rosh Hashanah is unique because at this time our souls feel the revelation of our Father, our King. As we said above, we are like the prince who at the time when he feels his father, his king, close to him cries out with all his heart and all his strength, quite unlike the way he calls out during the rest of the year. This is how our praying ought to be on Rosh Hashanah. In addition to the sound of the blowing of the shofar, the whole day ought to resound with the sounds of our prayers and the strength of our cries. They are signs that we are in touch with our awareness of the revelation of God's sovereignty and our acceptance of the yoke of heaven. A person's prayers at this time of the year should not resemble those of the whole year round, for if his prayers display no emotion and do not cry out loud, though he recite all the poems in the liturgy, it is a sign that he has not noticed his Father is close and unveiled. When a person prays with great passion and clamor, however, it is a sign that he knows his Father is revealed, and that he accepts upon himself the yoke of heaven.

We are able to understand this with the help of a well-known parable expounded by his honor, my holy father and teacher, my rabbi, of holy blessed memory, in his holy book, *Imrei Elimelech.* (p. 330) A prince began to stray from the proper path, giving his life to vain, empty things and to the company of base and reckless people. Courtiers began complaining to the king about the prince and his behavior. They claimed that he disobeyed the king's decree and did nothing to glorify his father, the king, or to acknowledge his father's sovereignty at all. Furthermore, it was charged that in addition to all the things of which the prince already stood accused, he had become so insensible with fickleness that he did not even acknowledge his father as sovereign, and could not distinguish between his father and a commoner.

The prince was exiled from the king's presence and sent to live among vulgar people who maltreated him, making him suffer, until in his great anguish he began to ask himself, "Why am I in this predicament, in so much pain?" He started to heed the decrees of his father, and to plead, "Please, father, have mercy on me; save me. Take me back to you and I will do your bidding. Heal me from all my hurt, for how can I do all that needs to be done when my hands are broken, my heart is broken, and my head is full of wounds?"

But the prince had many enemies in court at that time. There was no shortage of accusers to maintain the deceit that the prince still lacked respect for his father and his father's sovereignty, and that all his cries were simply a response to being exiled from his father's house. They pretended that the prince's cries were due only to the pain of being hurt and beaten; that his cries of "Father, father!" were simply a conditioned reflex, nothing more than childhood memories of his father chastising him; that seeing the faces of people he recognized had jolted his memory somewhat, because the king, his father, had been in the habit of sending trusted advisors to help rehabilitate his son. His accusers offered the king other proofs of their words, saying, "Even now he has no intention of accepting upon himself the king's decree; otherwise, why listen to those vulgar people, and take their advice as well? Obviously he doesn't truly recognize your majesty's sovereignty." The accusers' indictment succeeded so well that despite his pleas and supplications, the prince remained in exile and misery, God forbid.

Once, the king passed before the windows of his son's room at a time when his thoughts were composed, and the prince started to yell out all the cries that he was accustomed to shouting: "Woe, I am in pain! I have no food, Father! Take me back, bring me close to you. . . ." The prince shouted with a voice so piercing and bitter, it caused the doorposts to tremble. His father ran to him, embracing him and taking him close unto himself. When the accusers began muttering their customary charges, that the prince had only been crying because he was accustomed to doing so, that even now he did not really recognize his father or his sovereignty, the king thundered at them: "Now I see that all this time it was only because you hated my son that you denounced him. For who can not instantly hear when cries are genuine? It was obvious he recognized me. He cried when he saw me because he recognized me; he knows that I am the king and that his destiny is in my hands. His repentance came from his acceptance of my sovereignty upon himself. Even his pleas for his physical needs came from his recognition and acceptance of my sovereignty."

The analogy is obvious. The Jewish people are "My son, My firstborn, Israel." (Exodus 4:22) For their sakes God created all the worlds, that they might direct all the worlds. At first they were on the level of "Israel, it is in you am I glorified," (Isaiah 49:3) but later they strayed from the path, and in heaven there began the accusations against them. The charges stated that because of the great capriciousness of the Jewish people, because they were so steeped in their ignorance, they did not even acknowledge God's sovereignty. "And they say to the tree, 'you are my father.'" (Jeremiah 2:27) Consequently, they were banished from the palace of the King, to dwell among people who torture them and cause them suffering. We have long felt our suffering, like the prince who was forced to ask himself, "Why am I in this predicament, in so much pain?" We began to plead, "Please, father, have mercy on us; save us. Take us back to you, and we will do your bidding. You, our King, draw us near to You." But the accusers are not idle. They continue to malign us, saying that even now, God forbid, we do not recognize God's sovereignty; that we have no humility and do not negate our ego before the sovereignty of heaven; that even now, our crying is only because we are in trouble. They say it is only because of the prophets sent by God, who were so plainly manifest in ancient times, and because of the messengers that God secretly sends to us these days, that we are accustomed to repenting and returning; that all our remorse is just force of habit; that we are grown used to the fact that we have to beg and entreat—that we have become habituated to the need to speak words of contrition, but all of this is done without any real recognition of God's sovereignty. The accusers even try to prove the veracity of their words, showing that even as we repent and return, hearkening to God, we also listen to others. They say we listen not just to our own evil inclination, which tries to lure us with manifold seductions, but to every kind of depraved and malign influence.

One can hardly deny that in these modern times there are young people who have abandoned spirituality, straying from the proper road, God forbid. Those influenced by their friends and peers are greater in number than those who are seduced by their own evil inclination. They observe, and then copy others, saying, "If they do this then so must I, or else I will be considered dull, or seen as old fashioned and reactionary," etc. And so the accusers use this to prove that the good that people try to do, their contrition and repentance, is done merely out of habit, from imitating others; that people do not actually recognize the One and only Master of all, or acknowledge the sovereignty of heaven, God forbid, but simply do the bidding of anyone who happens to come along.

This is why even though we repent and return and pray, we are nevertheless still in exile and our troubles intensify. The situation has deteriorated so much, to the point that it is not just our ancestors that lived many hundreds of years ago who would be unable to comprehend our predicament. We ourselves, had we been told just thirty years ago that we would find ourselves in such a serious plight, would have been unable to imagine how it could happen and how we could survive it.

If, however, during this period, our souls really do feel the imminence of God; if in our excitement we shout out all our prayers truly from the depths of our hearts, then our words of contrition and the sounds of the shofar will stop the mouths of all our accusers. This then becomes the proof that we have recognized God's sovereignty, that we accept upon ourselves the yoke of His sovereignty, and that we have truly returned and repented. When this is so, even the requests for our own basic physical needs are also a sign that we recognize the majesty of God that is being revealed to us at this time.

This is why Rosh Hashanah is so noted for the piquancy of its liturgy, the sounds of the shofar and the sounds of the prayers: because at this time we are aware of the revelation of the sovereignty of God.

In the holy Zohar (Vol. II 20a) it is written, R. Yehuda said: "Yelling and crying are the highest forms of prayer. The Hebrew words *tsa'akah* and *za'akah*, meaning 'yelling' and 'crying,' are one and the same thing. They are much closer to the Holy Blessed One than moaned or whispered prayers, as it is written: 'If he shouts to Me, I will listen to his cry.' (Exodus 22:22) It is precisely because we feel God's closeness and recognize only His sovereignty that before blowing the shofar we pray, 'Out of my straits I called upon God.' We also call out to Him, saying 'You hear my voice. . . .' Listen to the cries and shouts of our voices, for it is only You that we recognize. We accept Your sovereignty; therefore, 'Please be not deaf to my plea for well being.'"

# *Shabbat T'shuvah* (Sabbath of Repentance)—September 16, 1939

"Return, O Israel, to God your Lord; for in your sin have you stumbled."
(Hosea 14:2)

It is a well-known teaching of the Rabbis (Jerusalem Talmud, *Rosh Hashanah* 7b; Exodus Rabbah, *Mishpatim* 30:9) that God observes all of the commandments of the Torah. How then does He observe the commandment to repent, to do *t'shuvah*?

God fulfills this commandment when He repents of the evil that He has rendered, God forbid, to His people Israel, or that He has decreed will befall them. This is God's repentance, His *t'shuvah* as it were, as it is written, "And God repented of the evil that He spoke of doing to His people." (Exodus 32:14) What is meant by the word "repented" in the context of this verse? It means that God had, as it were, "regret," which is always the precursor of repentance.

But when God's repentance is only for that which He has already done, or for what He has decreed, then the Jewish people remain, God forbid, in the same desperate straits as always. If God regrets and repents only of the evil that He was going to add, God forbid, to their already precarious predicament, they remain in the same very poor condition they were in before the troubles began.

We read in Psalm 90:13, "Return O God, how long? Have regret concerning Your servants. Satisfy us in the morning with Your kindness . . . ."

What we really mean when we say "Return O God" is "God, please repent." Then we add the phrase ". . . how long? Have regret concerning Your servants."

What we mean is "For how long will Your regret extend only as far as the decrees You have brought upon us or are thinking of bringing upon us?" For even without new decrees, we still remain in the same poor condition.

And so we end by adding the phrase "Satisfy us in the morning with Your kindness, that we may rejoice and be glad all our days." We mean "This is the repentance that we want of You, so to speak. Satisfy us in the morning with Your kindness. . . ."

But this is exactly the kind of repentance required of us, likewise. For when a person repents only of a sin, whether it was committed, God forbid, in thought, in word, or in deed, he still finds himself back in the state he occupied before he committed the sin, when he was not engaged upon any great spiritual journey. So what if he is merely relieved of this particular sin? The chief principle of repentance, however, is "Return, O Israel, to God your Lord." Lest you think that contrition for your sins is all you need, the prophet cautions that the repentance must continue all the way, until you reach God, ". . . for in your sin have you stumbled." Only then will you be completely elevated, in holiness, purity, and worship of God.

In the last Mishnah of Tractate *Yoma* (8.9) we learn; R. Akiba said: "Lucky are you, Israel! Before whom are you being purified? And who is it that purifies you? Your Father in heaven."

In the holy book *Arvei Nachal*, in a commentary on the final chapter of the book of Numbers (*Massei*) in a discourse on the martyrdom of R. Akiba, a responsa of the Maharam, of blessed memory, is quoted: "We have a tradition, bequeathed to us mouth to mouth, that anyone martyred for the sanctification of God's name feels no pain at all."

The author of the *Arvei Nachal* explains that when a person is consumed with passion and the desire to die for the sanctification of God's name, all his senses are elevated beyond the physical plane of existence into the highest realms, the world of thought. Everything becomes clothed in thought. The person's feelings and sensations are muted, his physical body is silenced and divested of all sensations, and all that he experiences is pleasure.

The same applies to all the sufferings of a Jew, though it remains true that pain is difficult to bear—and may God have mercy and ease our pain. Nevertheless, a person who is suffering needs to remember that the pain is washing away his sins and purifying him so that he can draw closer to God. The more deeply he enters into this thought and the more tightly he binds himself to it the lighter grow his pains, and his suffering becomes easier to bear.

What is more, when something occurs below it activates a sympathetic action above. When we enter so deeply into the thought that the pain ultimately brings us closer to God, to the point where we can no longer feel pain any more, then God does the same. He binds Himself to us, to the point where His feelings of wrath and retribution also disappear and His ire toward us is fixed. When this happens, all suffering turns into true salvation and redemption in every aspect.

Now we can understand the quote from R. Akiba in the Mishnah above. R. Akiba said: "Lucky are you, Israel! Before whom are you being purified? And who is it that purifies you? Your Father in heaven."

R. Akiba himself was martyred for the sanctification of God's name, and all his life he cherished thoughts of willingly dying in order to sanctify God's name. At the time of his death, he said (*Berachoth* 61b), "All my days I have been at pains over this verse in the *Sh'ma* (Deut. 6:5) 'Love God your Lord with all your heart, with all your soul, and with all your might.' I asked myself, 'When will I ever have the opportunity?'"

Therefore, in the Mishnah quoted above, R. Akiba is saying or means to say "Even in your suffering you can rejoice, O Israel! When you remember before whom are you being purified, then your physical sensations will be nullified, and you will not feel the pain. And even more than this: when you rejoice this way, He becomes your "Father" in heaven, and like a father who nullifies his anger for the good of his child, so God will do everything for your sake. And consequently all the judgments will be nullified, as we explained above, and you will be truly saved and you will rejoice, O Israel."

# *Chayay Sarah*—November 4, 1939

*"Sarah lived to be one hundred years and twenty years and seven years old. These were the years of the life of Sarah."* (Genesis 23:1)

Rashi (ibid.) explains: "The numbers of years are written separately—one hundred years and twenty years and seven years—for a reason. They are set out in this way to tell us that just as a person younger than twenty years of age is legally considered a minor, and hence without sin, so Sarah, when she was one hundred years old, was also without sin. The verse ends with the words 'These were the years of the life of Sarah' because Sarah's years at all these ages were equally virtuous."

What is this chapter teaching us? Of all the great saints and righteous women mentioned in the Torah, none are spoken of as highly as is Sarah. The puzzle becomes even greater when considered in light of what is written of Abraham upon his death. When Abraham our father dies, the Torah also says, "He lived a total of one hundred years and seventy years and five years," (Genesis 25:7) and Rashi there explains that this also was because Abraham lived without sin. And yet, at the end of this verse we do not find the words "These were the years of the life of Abraham," which might tell us, as with Sarah, that all the sets of years were considered equal in virtue.

In the holy book *Ma'or V'Shemesh*, we find a quote from R. Menachem Mendel of Rymanov, taken from his commentary on the beginning of chapter 6 in Exodus. It concerns a teaching found in the Talmud (*Berachoth* 5a). R. Simeon b. Lakish said, "The Torah uses the word 'covenant' in its description of salt (Leviticus

2:13). It also uses the word 'covenant' in its description of suffering (Deut. 28:69). This teaches us that just as salt purges meat, so does suffering purify a person."

R. Menachem Mendel of Rymanov adds the following: "And similarly, just as meat is ruined when overly salted, so can a person be damaged by unbearable suffering. For a person to be properly seasoned by suffering, the suffering must be administered with mercy and properly offset against the person's ability to cope."

Rashi asks, "Why does the Torah recount the death of Sarah directly after the account of the binding of Isaac?" Is the text suggesting some connection between these two events? Rashi answers, "When Sarah was told of the binding of Isaac—of how he was prepared for slaughter, of how the knife was laid at his throat—her soul fled, and she died."

So Moses our teacher, the trusted shepherd, deliberately edited the Torah. He placed these two events—the death of Sarah and the binding of Isaac—side by side in the text in order to advocate on our behalf. By doing this, Moses is suggesting that if the anguish is, God forbid, unbearable, then death can result. He is showing us something important: that if this could happen even to Sarah—who was of such stature that the Torah goes to great lengths to tell us how when she was a hundred years old she was as virtuous as a girl of twenty, and when she was twenty years she was as innocent as a child of seven; that in fact all her life she was equally virtuous—if she, Sarah, was unable to bear such pain, how much less so can we.

The Torah may also be telling us that our mother Sarah, who took the binding of Isaac so much to heart that her soul flew out of her, died for the good of the Jewish people. She died in order to show God that a Jew should not be expected to suffer unlimited levels of anguish. Even though a person, with the mercy of God, survives and escapes death, nevertheless elements of his capability, his mind, and his spirit are forever broken and, as a result of his ordeal, lost to him. In the final analysis, what difference does it make, whether all of me or part of me is killed?

Perhaps the text itself is answering the question by saying, "These were the years of the life of Sarah." One might tend to judge Sarah as having sinned against the remainder of her years, because if she had not taken the binding of Isaac so much to heart, she would have lived longer. However, since this taking to heart was done for the good of the Jewish people, the verse hints that the years Sarah might have lived beyond her 127 years were not wasted, and so she did not really sin against those years. Therefore let God quickly send us spiritual and physical salvation, with revealed kindness.

# *Toledoth*—November 13, 1939

*"And God will give you . . ."* (Genesis 27:28)

Rashi (ibid.) explains the word "And" in this context: "He will give you, and then He will return and give you again."

The question is obvious and well known: When the Torah says "And God will give you," it already implies constant giving, so why then do we need Rashi's comment "and then He will return and give you again"? When a person blesses his friend with abundance, he does not need to say, "May God give you abundance, and then may He give you abundance again," because it is obvious that consistency is part of the blessing.

This is the explanation: When a person gives his friend money for the first time, then he is indeed the giver. If, however, the recipient had previously given the money to the person who is giving it now, then the giver is only returning what he has previously received.

Although it is true that we must worship God without thought of obtaining any reward, nevertheless when a Jew worships God, and deserves a reward, then the reward that God gives him is actually in return for his worship. If, however, God bestows good upon a person who does not deserve a reward, then God really is the giver.

This then is the blessing that Isaac gave to Jacob, "And God will give you . . ." In Rashi's explanation this means that first God will give, even if the Jew has done nothing to deserve the favor. Then "He will return and give you again," because by the second giving God will be giving in return for what the person has already given Him in worship. This is only proper; after all, how can anyone worship God properly while enduring great suffering, God forbid, unless God gives first? It is only when God gives, even to the undeserving person, that afterwards the giving can be at the level of "a return," as we have just explained.

Another explanation may be found in the verse "They will come, those who are lost in the land of Assyria, and those who are outcast in the land of Egypt. . . ." (Isaiah 28:13) There are people who are really "lost," and then there are those who are simply "outcast." The outcast person has merely been exiled from his location to another place, but he can still be seen and recognized. A person who is lost, however, is neither visible nor recognizable.

When troubles are as great as they are at present and, as we see plainly, Jewish men have had their beards shorn off, they become unrecognizable as Jews from the outside. Then, as the terrible persecutions and unbearable tortures beyond description persist, we watch people becoming unrecognizable even from the inside. In these terrible circumstances, a person may lose himself completely and be unable to recognize himself at all (Yiddish, *ehr fahrliert sich*). He can no longer recall how he felt on the Sabbath even one year ago, or how he felt during the week, before praying or after praying, etc. He has been stepped upon and crushed until he no longer feels that he is a Jew or knows whether he is a human being at all, or an animal without any faculties with which to feel. This is the level of being truly lost and absent, described in the verse "And they will come, those who are lost . . ."

The Talmud (*Kiddushin* 2b) says: "The loser must return in search of his lost article." This is because a truly lost object cannot be seen or recognized, and so its owner must go around looking for it in order to find it, raise it, and bring it back to him.

God is our owner, and we are his lost articles. So Isaac blessed Jacob our father, saying "And God will give . . ." The blessing is that God will give not only when the Jew is visible and recognizable but also when he is lost, when he is neither visible nor recognizable as a Jew. At such times God will "return" and give again. The owner of the lost object will return to search for us and find us, give us everything good, and return us to Him and redeem us with the salvation of our bodies and our souls, with great mercy and good deliverance.

# *Va Yetzeh*—November 18, 1939

*"And behold, he saw God standing over him."* (Genesis 28:13)

Rashi (ibid.) explains: "God was standing over Jacob in order to protect him."
We need to understand: Why wasn't it sufficient for one of the angels who were going up and down the ladder (in Jacob's dream) to guard him? Further on in the text of the dream we find again: "Behold, I am with you and I will protect you." (Genesis 28:15) Why did Jacob need to be guarded in this place, while he was asleep?

It might be argued that first God promised to guard Jacob on his journey, and then afterwards He promised to guard him while asleep that night. Nevertheless, we still need to understand why guarding is mentioned twice, and not just once, to cover the entire period until Jacob's return.

There is one well-known opinion (Genesis Rabbah 68:14) stating that the angels who were going up and down on the ladder in Jacob's dream were lords representing the nations of the world, who rise and fall. When there is war between these lords, one rising and trying to push the other down and vice versa, then the Jew stands in the greatest need of the mercy of heaven. So we are told, "God stands over him to protect him."

Angels have little patience, as it is written (Exodus 23:20–21), "Behold I send an angel before you to guard you on the road and to bring you to the place I have prepared. Be heedful of his face, and hearken to his voice, for he will not bear your sins . . ." whereas God, blessed be He, is boundlessly merciful. So when God says to Jacob in the dream, "I am the God of Abraham your father . . ." (Genesis 28:13) He means "I am still the God of Abraham your father even if, God forbid, you have no merits of your own. If I am unable to say to you 'I am God your God,' I will still be able to say, 'I am the God of your father.'" And so in the merit of his father, "God stands over him to protect him."

In these verses in which God speaks to Jacob in the dream, God first says, "I am God," (Genesis 28:13) using the Hebrew word *Ani* for "I." Then afterwards God says, "I am with you," using the Hebrew word *Anochi* for "I," Why does God use two different words, both meaning "I"? The difference between these two is the Hebrew letter *kaf*, which appears in *Anochi* but not in *Ani*. We learn in the Talmud (*Shabbath* 105a) that the Hebrew word *Anochi* is a notarigon, an aramaic acrostic meaning, "I Myself have written, have given." The word *Ani* is lacking only the letter *kaf*, which in the acrostic refers to the word "written." So the difference between *Anochi* and *Ani* is the difference between script and speech. In the word *Anochi*, God refers to having written and then given Himself, while *Ani* means only that God has spoken and given Himself. The obvious difference is that when something is written, it exists even after the action of writing is completed, while the spoken word exists only while it is being spoken.

This may well be the meaning of the dictum in the Talmud (*Pesachim* 50a) referring to the name of God, about which it says, "Not as I am written am I spoken." Also in the Talmud (*Sotah* 38a), we learn that it was only in the Temple that the High Priests spoke God's name as it was written, because they had achieved with their speech an active internal holiness that remained with them as though it had been written inside them. The High Priests spoke the name of God as it is written because their speech was comparable to the act of writing. However, this is not the case with us now. Our speech is not comparable to writing, for the impression of holiness has grown feeble, and so we must not pronounce the name of God as it is written.

In times of distress, when we are in pain because the lords of nations of the world rise and fall, and generally in times of suffering, while our hearts yield before God and we fear Him, we need to etch these things into our hearts. Only then will we be able to maintain our fear of God and subjugation to Him after He has saved us from all our troubles. So, when God helps us soon, and saves us from all our troubles, we will remain bonded to Him and truly worshipful of Him with love and fear. This is why at the beginning of the chapter on Jacob's dream it is written, "I (*Ani*) am the God of your father," and only afterwards it is written, "I (*Anochi*) am with you." We must strive to attain the level of *Anochi*, which is "I am written into you." God is saying, "Work to etch Me (*Ani*) indelibly within you, and then I (*Anochi*) will be with you always."

# *Va Yishlach*—November 25, 1939

*"And he said to him, 'I will not let you leave unless you bless me.'"* (Genesis 32:27)

Let us try to understand why our father Jacob needed the blessing of the angel with whom he had struggled, after God had already blessed him, and also why the angel answered Jacob with the question "What is your name?" Could it be that he did not know Jacob's name?

The stories of the lives of the patriarchs always convey a lesson for us. Jacob encountered the angel, struggled with him, and sustained damage when the angel touched upon his sciatic nerve. Then the angel made his preparations to leave, and Jacob said, "Is that it? Is this to be the fate of my children? After they have suffered all the pain and sustained all the damage inflicted on them, is this to be their whole victory—that they survived, that their enemies failed to finish them off? And will they then simply revert to the same state they were in before all their suffering? It must not be!" This is why Jacob said, "I will not let you leave unless you bless me." He was trying to ensure that after the suffering, not only would their enemies leave them alone, but that there would also be salvation from God.

It is well known that the angel of Esau, with whom Jacob struggled, is called *Sammael* in Hebrew, and that in the future the Hebrew letter *mem* will be removed from his name, because the *mem* belongs to the Hebrew word *mavet*, or "death." The *mem* will be removed because, in the future, "Death will be swallowed up for ever." (Isaiah 25:8)

In the world to come, the angel's name will be *Sael*, which in gematria (attributing numerical value to each of the Hebrew letters) adds up to the number 91, which is equivalent to the sum of the four letter name of God, *YHVH*, (26) and the name *Adonai* (65). And so when this angel is called *Sael*, it will become holy and take its place among all the other holy angels.

Our father Jacob struggled with the angel of Esau, in order to fix his part in that angel, so that the angel would be ready for the future redemption and the changing of his name to *Sael*. Therefore, after this struggle the angel had already become a holy angel, and wanted only to act for the good of Israel. When the angel asked Jacob, "What is your name?" and Jacob answered "Jacob," the angel was making a profound statement.

The name "Jacob" was given to him because of the circumstances surrounding his birth. Jacob and Esau were twins. When Esau, the elder sibling was born, Jacob was grasping Esau's heel. The word "Jacob" means "he that holds onto the heel of." So it had been throughout the ages, whatever victories had come unto Jacob's hands had come to him only after Esau had trodden on them with his heel. But now, after the struggle, Jacob is free of the heels that have been treading upon him, for now the angel of Esau has been fixed and desires only the good of the Jewish people. "Now," says the angel to Jacob, "you don't need to demand my blessing after your victory, or pray that in the future your children will come away with more than the mere victory of survival. There is no need for that, because from now on your name will be Israel, meaning 'victory.' The victories will be yours from the outset, and you will overpower the angel."

The angel also hinted to Jacob another aspect of his new name. The name "Israel," as the angel explained to Jacob, means "You struggled with angels and with men and you won." The Hebrew word for "struggle" is *sar*, and stems from the Hebrew word for "lord." The angel was saying, "First you were a lord, and then you were victorious. Even before the battle was decided you had already won, because even when you were in dire straits, you still ruled your spirit and never allowed it to fall. Even in those difficult times you were still, inside yourself, always a lord."

# *Va Yeshev*—December 2, 1939

*"Jacob settled in the area where his father had lived in the land of Canaan."*
(Genesis 37:1)

Rashi (ibid.) explains: "Jacob wanted to live in serenity, but the anguish of Joseph leapt upon him. Righteous people want to live in serenity in this world, but the Holy One, blessed be He, says to them, 'Is it not enough that you will enjoy serenity in the world to come, that you should want it in this world as well?'"

My father and teacher, his holiness R. Elimelech, of blessed memory, comments on this in his writing, (Divrei Elimelech, p. 89) asking if God's answer to righteous people, as explained by Rashi, does not hold more than just the simple, obvious meaning. Would God begrudge the saint a serene life?

It may perhaps be understood as I heard explained by my father-in-law, his holiness, our master, teacher and rabbi, R. Yerachmiel Moshe, of blessed memory, who said the following in the name of the holiest of the holy, leader of the Diaspora, the Rebbe, R. Baruch'l of Medzbusz: "In the song *Kol Mekadesh* that we sing on Friday night, in the verse 'Help those who sanctify the Seventh Day by desisting from plow and harvest . . .' the Hebrew word *charish*, 'plow,' may also be translated as 'silence' (the two words, meaning 'plow' and 'silence,' are identical in Hebrew). The verse then reads, 'Help those who sanctify the Seventh Day with silence.' They sanctify the day, because they do not speak."

The very simplest interpretation of this teaching may refer to the talmudic teaching (*Shabbath* 113a) on the verse "If for the Sabbath's sake you rest your feet, nor do your fancy on My holy day. If you call it a pleasure to honor God's holy day, refraining from your business, looking out for your interests, nor talking your words, then will you delight yourself in the Lord. . . ." (Isaiah 58:13–14) The Talmud explains that one's conversation on the Sabbath should not be like weekday speech.

The verse from the song *Kol Mekadesh* may also be interpreted another way. It could be referring to those righteous people who attain such rapture on the Sabbath that they are unwilling to articulate with mere words what they are experiencing or feeling. If this is the meaning of Reb Baruch'l's teaching, then the verse "Help those who keep the Seventh Day with silence," is talking about the silence that is, somehow, demanded by the experience itself.

What then is the difference between the Hebrew words *charish* (silence) and *almut* (muteness)? When the Torah uses the word *charish*, there is generally plenty to be said but the subject refrains from speaking. For example, when Mordechai tells Esther, "If you remain silent at this time (*Im hacharaish tacharishi*) then relief and deliverance will appear for the Jews from elsewhere; but you and your father's house will perish," (Esther 4:14) or as Moses says to the Jews on the banks of the Red Sea, "God will fight for you, and you be silent (*tacharishun*)." (Exodus 14:14) and so forth. In all of these examples, there is plenty that might have been said, but people were silent. Very different is the Jewish person who is, God forbid, so broken and crushed that he has nothing to say; who does not appreciate or understand what is happening to him; who does not possess the faculties with which to assess or assimilate his experiences; who no longer has the mind or the heart with which to incorporate the experience. For him, silence is not a choice; his is the muteness of one incapable of speech.

There are times, it is understood by the Jew, when survival means being reduced, God forbid, to petty, small-minded, and spiritually diminished behavior. Then the Jew cheers himself, adapts and adjusts to the times and the difficulties, until the wrath passes. He says to himself, "It is true that now I am mute, but even a mute can communicate a little with grunts and gestures. I too will speak a little in this way, communicating even in my muteness."

When, however, the suffering of the Jewish people continues growing, and everyone is even more broken and crushed, then we reach the level we read of in this week's portion. Joseph describes his first dream to his brothers: "Behold," he tells them. "We were binding sheaves in the field. Then my sheaf stood up erect, and your sheaves surrounded it and bowed down to my sheaf." (Genesis 37:7) The Hebrew for the binding of sheaves is *meAlmim alumim*, which is identical to the Hebrew for being made mute—as though Joseph had said, "We were struck dumb in the field. . . ."

The word "field" in Joseph's dream is a reference to the kabbalistic concept of the "holy field" in which all Jews toil. "Look," said Isaac of Jacob, "The scent of my son is the scent of a field blessed by God." (Genesis 27:27)

Rashi (ibid.) connects it with an ancient kabbalistic concept, that of the "field of holy apples." All Jewish worship is "harvesting the field."

Joseph explains the prophetic meaning of his dream: "We were harvesting the field, and when the exile reached the state of *meAlmim alumim*, 'dumbstruck muteness,' we were bereft of the ability to communicate even in our Torah and our worship of God. Then, behold *alumati*, my 'muteness' suddenly stood up erect. At first I tried bending my shoulders to the yoke, thinking to adjust myself to the difficulties and to live a life of muteness, but when I saw that even the muteness was dumbstruck, I could not bear it. I took the courage to cry out to God even louder, when *alumoteichem*, your 'muteness' surrounded mine and you took strength from me."

This is the meaning of the original quote from Rashi with which we began this chapter. "Righteous people want to live in serenity in this world." They want to adjust and adapt themselves to the exile and the troubles. But the Holy Blessed One says, "It is not enough for the righteous to be satisfied that the future will be good, that they will survive. Even now, they must toil to arouse heavenly mercy, so that God will save Israel immediately."

# *Miketz*—December 9, 1939

*"May God Almighty grant you mercy before the man . . ."* (Genesis 43:14)

    Are we to understand that it is possible that our father Jacob actually blessed his children with a blessing that the man whom he thought to be a wicked Egyptian should have mercy upon them? Why did he not bless them that the man should not be able to hurt them at all, and that God would have mercy on them and save them?

    We know from the Midrash (Genesis Rabbah 5:8) that the name "God Almighty" (in Hebrew, *El Shaddai*) is interpreted by our sages to mean "God who said 'Enough' to the universe." The implication is that if God had not said "Enough" to the world, it would have continued to expand and evolve infinitely.

    What really happened at the creation of the world is beyond our grasp, but this could perhaps teach us something about the present and our current circumstances. God created the world so that His sovereignty should be revealed through it. But since He created the world to run according to the laws and designs of nature, through cause and effect, there are times when a lengthy delay occurs while a situation evolves and develops before salvation comes and God's sovereignty is revealed. An example of this is when God's salvation and sovereignty are revealed through His healing of the sick. Since salvation and healing are camouflaged and dressed in causality, they may take the form of a particular medication or a particular doctor. The doctor must pay his visit and the medication must be purchased, etc., and so the whole process develops and evolves. But when, God forbid, the sick person is in so much danger that he will not survive while the process takes its time to evolve, then the Holy One, blessed be He, says, "Enough" to development and evolution. Then the salvation and the sovereignty of heaven are revealed immediately and straight away.

This is also the case with other forms of deliverance. When the Jewish people are unable to withstand their troubles another moment, and to continue while this nation is defeated or that nation is victorious, then God says "Enough" to the developing situation and saves them immediately.

Rashi (Genesis 1:1), commenting on the verse "On the day that *YHVH-Elohim* created heaven and earth" (Genesis 2:4) explains: "Originally, it arose in the Thought to create the world with the attribute of Judgment (*Elohim*). Seeing, however, that under these conditions alone the world could not long exist, God preceded it with the attribute of Mercy (*YHVH*) and associated Mercy with Judgment."

Why was it not enough for God to merely associate Mercy and Judgment, as He ultimately does when it is needed? Why do we need to be told that God preceded Judgment (*Hikdim*) with the attribute of Mercy? Perhaps this was necessary because there are situations when "on time" is too late, when the universe simply cannot stand another moment without Mercy, and so it has to come before its time.

Our father Jacob could see prophetically that salvation would come eventually through this Egyptian man, but because Jacob's suffering had reached the point of being unbearable, he said, "May God Almighty grant you mercy before the man." That is, even before the man grants you mercy, God should have mercy and rescue you. The name of God, "*El Shaddai*," is used because it is the name with which God said to His world, "Enough," that it should no longer continue to develop and evolve naturally because salvation must come now, at this very moment.

# *Va Yigash*—December 16, 1939

*"Joseph fell weeping upon the neck of his brother Benjamin, while Benjamin wept on Joseph's neck."* (Genesis 45:14)

Rashi (ibid.) explains that the two brothers were crying over the future destruction of the Holy Temple, which was to be situated on their territory in the Land of Israel.

Let us understand: The text of the following verse (Genesis 45:15) says, "Joseph kissed his other brothers and cried over them." Yet why is it that Rashi does not explain the crying in this instance to be over the future destruction of the Temple?

Perhaps the answer is related to what we have learned in the Talmud (*Rosh Hashanah* 28a) that "Commandments were not given to provide enjoyment." Rashi explains that commandments were given in order to be a yoke on the neck of the people.

This explains why the brothers cried "on each other's neck." They were lamenting the yoke of the commandments that would be shrugged off at the time of the destruction of the Temple.

Every Jewish person has a yoke around his neck. He must do this and that, learning Torah and observing commandments, every day. His thoughts and his speech must also be holy, and even when he is prevented from physically observing commandments he must brace himself for even greater effort, because of the yoke that remains on his neck.

In catastrophic times, however, when suffering is overwhelming and everything holy and Jewish is destroyed, God forbid, people not only give up on specific things because of the difficulties in observing commandments, but the yoke itself is shrugged off, God forbid, because of all the pain and degradation that must be endured. This is why Joseph and Benjamin cried, each upon the neck of the other, and why, when explaining this verse, Rashi makes his comment about the destruction of the Temple. Rashi does not suggest that Joseph was crying over the destruction of the Temple when he refers to Joseph crying over his other brothers because there is no mention of their falling on their necks.

With this we can also answer a question arising from a subsequent text, namely, why Joseph later falls upon the neck of his father Jacob and weeps, whereas Jacob does not fall on the neck of Joseph (Genesis 46:30). Rashi explains that instead of falling upon the neck of Joseph, Jacob recited the *Sh'ma*. My father, his holiness, my teacher, R. Elimelech, of blessed memory, asks the well-known question, "Why did Jacob recite the *Sh'ma* at that particular time, and why did Joseph not also recite the *Sh'ma*?"

With what has been said above, we can now understand the text. Upon meeting his father, Joseph began once again to weep over the future destruction destined to meet the Jewish people, and the shedding of the yoke associated with that catastrophe. This is the reason for the reference to the neck of his father. The Jewish people were entering into their exile in Egypt, and so Joseph wondered how, under these circumstances, they would manage to keep the yoke of the commandments around their necks. Jacob the patriarch answered simply, "With self-sacrifice." He gave this answer by reciting the *Sh'ma*. When we recite the *Sh'ma*, we give our soul back to God, utterly and without reservation. And, as we learn in the holy book *Ma'or V'Shamesh*, whoever recites the *Sh'ma* properly in the morning will find that his worship is successful all day long.

# *Va Yechi*—December 23, 1939

*"Jacob lived in Egypt seventeen years."* (Genesis 47:28)

Rashi, quoting the Talmud, asks, "Why is this chapter 'closed'?" That is, why in its written format does the Torah text continue directly from the previous narrative, without the space that usually precedes a new paragraph or chapter? Rashi explains: "Because as soon as our father Jacob died, the eyes of the Jewish people were closed and their hearts were blocked. Another explanation is that Jacob wanted to reveal the end of the exile to his children, but it was blocked from him."

We need to understand the quote "Jacob wanted to reveal the end of the exile to his children, but this was blocked from him." Does it mean that the desire of our patriarch Jacob in this matter was thwarted?

The holy Zohar (vol. I, 227b) on the verse "Jacob blessed Joseph, and said . . ." (Genesis 48:15) asks the following: What blessing did Joseph receive, when Jacob blessed only Joseph's sons? Why then does the verse say, "Jacob blessed Joseph?" The holy Zohar answers as follows: Joseph was blessed because the child's blessings are the blessings of his parents. Consequently, the blessing of Joseph's children was Joseph's blessing.

With this, we can understand this quote from the Talmud (*Berachoth* 7a): "God said, 'Ishmael, My son, bless Me.' R. Ishmael b. Elisha blessed God, saying, 'May it be Your will that Your mercy suppress Your anger, that Your mercy prevail over Your other attributes, and that You deal with Your children with Your attribute of mercy. And may You never be judgmental of them.' God nodded his head."

When the Holy One said to R. Ishmael, "Bless me!" R. Ishmael blessed the Jewish people that God should treat them mercifully. From what we have discussed above, we can easily understand this talmudic story, because "The child's blessings are the blessings of his parents."—and so, the blessings of the Jewish people are the blessings of God. Conversely, when our father Jacob died the Jewish people descended into the depths of suffering, to the point where even the Torah was damaged and wounded—This, then, is our greatest and ultimate hope: that if our suffering has such an effect and causes damage at such supernal levels, then surely God will save us.

"Our father Jacob wanted to reveal the end of the exile to his children, but it was blocked from him." This circumstance in itself heralds the end of the exile. If this chapter of the Torah text is "blocked off" because our father Jacob was blocked and prevented from revealing the end, which suggests that knowledge of the end was denied him, then the damage was indeed cosmic. Similarly, whenever we see that the troubles have grown so great that the Torah itself and the study halls of the synagogues and the yeshivahs are all closed and locked, we can take heart—for it is clear from these circumstances that the damage is cosmic and reaches the small and the great, and so we can surely trust to God that the end is close.

# *VaEra*—January 6, 1940

"God (Elohim) spoke to Moses, saying to him, 'I am YHVH. I revealed Myself to Abraham, Isaac, and Jacob as God Almighty (El Shaddai), and did not allow them to know Me by My name YHVH. I also made My covenant with them, promising to give them the land of Canaan, the land of their sojourn, where they lived as foreigners. . . .'"

"Moses related this to the Israelites, but because of their shortness of breath and their hard work, they could not hear him."

"God (YHVH) spoke to Moses, saying, 'Go, speak to Pharaoh, king of Egypt, and he will let the Israelites leave his land.' Moses spoke, interrupting the revelation. 'Even the Israelites will not listen to me,' he said. 'How can I expect Pharaoh to listen to me? I have no self-confidence to speak.'"

"God (YHVH) then spoke to Moses and Aaron. He commanded them regarding the Israelites and Pharaoh, king of Egypt, so they would be able to get the Israelites out of Egypt." (Exodus 6:2–13)

Rashi (ibid.) explains: "God commanded Moses and Aaron to lead the Jewish people gently, to sustain them."

We need to understand how the events described in the text follow one another. If the Jewish people did not listen to Moses because of the suffering they endured under Pharaoh, why then should Moses and Aaron have to be commanded to lead them gently? Furthermore, what was to be gained from leading them gently, if Pharaoh was still torturing them, God forbid?

In the morning service, in the blessings over the Torah, we pray, "Grant us today and every day grace, loving-kindness, and mercy in Your eyes and in the eyes of all who look at us, and bestow beneficent kindness upon us. Blessed are You, God, Who bestows beneficent kindness upon His people Israel."

We seek grace first because grace is given without regard to merit, even to someone who, God forbid, does not deserve to be saved, as it is written (*Sanhedrin* 108a; Genesis Rabbah 29:1), "And Noah found grace in the eyes of the Lord." (Genesis 6:8) Noah was not worthy of salvation, but nonetheless he found grace in the eyes of God.

After grace we ask for loving-kindness, for as we know, loving-kindness is boundless, extending equally to the undeserving as to those who are deserving of it. Mercy, however, contains an element of judgment. Mercy is not made up entirely of judgment, nor is it all boundless forgiveness that embraces the undeserving. Mercy is extended only to someone who is at least partially deserving of it.

We need to pray in this particular order because it is obvious that we ourselves are quite undeserving. Not only are we unable, because of the trouble we are in, to bear examination by a judgmental eye and expect any deserved reward, but even under examination in a merciful light our lives are so undeserving that we must resort to begging grace and freely given kindness. All of this is because of the terrible suffering we endure. So we pray first for grace and loving-kindness, which will save us from the agony that makes it impossible for us to reach any level of entitlement. Only then will we have the resources to become deserving of at least a little mercy. Not only does the profound suffering of our current circumstances make it impossible for us to busy ourselves with Torah and do everything that we are supposed to do, but even the duties we do perform are devoid of living spirit. They are done cheerlessly, grudgingly, and without joy, God forbid.

When our teacher Moses said to God, "O Lord, why do You mistreat Your people? Why did You send me? As soon as I came to Pharaoh to speak in Your name, he made things worse for the people. You have done nothing to save Your people," (Exodus 6:1) God (*Elohim*, the attribute of Judgment) answered, saying "I am God (*YHVH*, Mercy)."

In this verse God of Judgments speaks to Moses, saying that as the God of Mercy He is foretelling that the Jews will be treated mercifully, that the severity of their suffering has earned them a reprieve, and that their exile will end earlier than originally ordained, as is well known. The verse is telling us that even God of Judgments had to admit that the Jews had earned some remission, in the form of Mercy mixed with Judgment.

When Moses conveyed God's message to the Jews, however, the Jews would not listen to Moses "because of their shortness of spirit and their hard work."

Their response was cheerless and joyless. This explains why they needed to be led with a more gentle hand. Whenever the Jews earned God's mercy only through suffering, their response was always "short of spirit," and devoid of life. This is why they could not hear Moses: because of the lack of spirit that affected everything they did. Therefore, "God (*YHVH*, Mercy) spoke to Moses and Aaron. He commanded them regarding the Israelites."

Earlier in the chapter it was God (*Elohim*, Judgment) Who first spoke, saying, "I am God (*YHVH*, Mercy)." In the second part of the text, however, it is God—Merciful—Who speaks right from the outset, saying, "He commanded them regarding the Israelites." And so, Rashi explains, "God commanded Moses and Aaron to lead the Jews gently." It was imperative to change the order of things. At this time the order could not be Judgment followed by Mercy, because the Jewish people had to be led gently right from the beginning.

# *Bo*—January 13, 1940

*"God said to Moses, 'Come to Pharaoh. I have made him and his advisors stubborn, so that I will be able to demonstrate these miraculous signs among them. You will then be able to relate to your children and grandchildren how I made a mockery of Egypt, and how I performed miraculous signs among them. Then you will know that I am God.'"* (Exodus 10:1)

Rashi explains that the words "how I made a mockery of Egypt" mean "how I played and toyed with the Egyptians."

In a well-known Midrash (*Megillah* 10b) we learn the following: That night, while the Egyptians were drowning in the Red Sea and the ministering angels in heaven wanted to sing their established song, the Holy Blessed One said, "The works of my hands drown in the sea, and you want to sing?" And so, on that day, the angels were forbidden to sing, because God does not rejoice in destruction, even when it involves the downfall of the wicked. So how can it be that in our text God is saying, "You will tell your children and grandchildren how I made a mockery of Egypt, and laughed at their downfall?"

The answer might be found in God's words to Moses by the sea: "Speak to the Israelites and tell them to turn back and make camp. . . . I will triumph over Pharaoh and his entire army, and Egypt will know that I am God." (Exodus 14: 1–4)

At the Red Sea, we read, "Egypt will know that I am God," whereas in the verse previously quoted (Exodus 10:1) it is written, "You will know that I am God," meaning "Israel will know that I am God."

Perhaps God does not refrain from rejoicing in the downfall of the wicked if the downfall also conveys an important lesson to Israel.

Throughout history, Jewish people have suffered so much anguish, on so many occasions, simply so that they would be purified in the process, and aroused to the fear of God. But during the Exodus from Egypt, as the Jewish people approached redemption, God said, "This time, it is My great pleasure and joy to bring awareness and knowledge of Myself to the Jewish people, through tormenting and afflicting plagues upon the Egyptians, and not the Jews."

The situation at the sea, however, was different. There the Jews were told, "Turn back and make camp. . . . I will triumph over Pharaoh and his entire army, and Egypt will know that I am God." In this case God did not rejoice, because His desire for the Egyptians to know Him is nothing like His yearning to be known by the Jewish people. In our tradition it is well known that the world was created because of God's yearning to be known by the Jewish people—"Because I want them to know Me." As well, God did not rejoice in the drowning of the Egyptians in the sea, because by the time the Jews had reached this point, they were no longer being tortured.

With this we can answer the question posed by our early sages, of blessed memory: Why was Pharaoh punished for being stubborn, when the text tells us plainly that he had no free will? God often says of Pharaoh, "I have hardened his heart, so that he will not obey." But now we can understand it without too much difficulty. If the Jewish people can be punished, tormented, and abused so often without any fault to be found in them, but simply in order to make them aware of God and to awaken in them the fear of Him, then Pharaoh also can suffer a little, so that Israel may know that "I am God."

"Come to Pharaoh . . ." says God, "And if you are wondering how I can punish Pharaoh when he really has no free will, as it is written, 'I have made him and his advisors stubborn,' then let me tell you. I will demonstrate these miraculous signs among them, and then you will be able to tell your children and grandchildren that I am God. And I do it with such glee and take such joy in Egyptian suffering, because through it I am teaching you and your children something new, for you will know that I am God." From this it follows that Pharaoh can be punished regardless of his lack of free will.

I am unable to recall any more of my words on this matter.

# *BeShalach*—January 20, 1940

*"And God goes before them—by day, with a pillar of cloud, to guide them along the way, and by night, with a pillar of fire providing them with light—to travel day and night. Neither the pillar of cloud by day nor the pillar of fire at night leave their station in front of the people."* (Exodus 13:21)

Until this verse, all the preceding text is stated in the past tense, as in: "When Pharaoh let the people leave . . ." (Exodus 13:17); "Moses took Joseph's remains with him . . ." (ibid. 19); "They traveled on from Sukkoth . . ." (ibid. 20). But this verse, "And God goes before them . . .", is the first place in which the text speaks in the present tense.

We learn in the Midrash (Genesis Rabbah 51:2) that the phrase "And God" always connotes "God and His court of law." And so we ask: What aspect of judgment was hinted at in the verse "And God goes before them . . ."? The fire (judgment) was for the Jewish people's own good, since it lit up the darkness for them. What then is so judgmental about the text, connoting God and His court of law?

Rashi explains that the verse "And these are the laws that you must set before them," (Exodus 21:1) means that the laws should be set out like a table laid before them, so that each individual should find the Torah arranged plainly and clearly for him according to the level of his intelligence. This is also what is meant by the words of our text above, "And God goes before them." God and His court of law are "before them," adjusting and setting the judgments according to the level of need of each individual Jew. This is why the fire—i.e., the judgment—is plainly and clearly beneficial, lighting the darkness for each person.

We must always use the judgments and suffering we endure properly, utilizing them to worship God, to keep going day and night. We learn this from that part of the text that speaks in the present tense and refers to the necessity for the Jewish people to keep going, day and night. Furthermore, from what we have already said the deeper implication becomes plain and clear: Not only when the going is soft and easy must we go in God's ways, climbing higher and higher spiritual heights, but also when, God forbid, we are in pain and darkness. For when a person enjoys generous good fortune, it is easy for him to worship God joyously, passionately, and with love. Nevertheless, when he is suffering, God forbid, he must take advantage of that situation also, to worship God with his broken heart and with an outpouring of the soul.

We learn in the Talmud (*Berachoth* 3a): "When R. Jose entered one of the ruined houses of Jerusalem in order to pray, he heard a heavenly echo." In the same Talmudic passage we learn that R. Jose was told by the Prophet Elijah that the heavenly voice speaks not only in the ruins, but whenever Jewish people go into synagogues anywhere, in order to pray. Why then did R. Jose not hear this echo when praying in his own synagogue?

We do not presume to understand the essence of R. Jose's experience, but the lesson in it for us is this: It was precisely because R. Jose was praying amidst the ruins of Jerusalem, because his heart was broken in response to the destruction around him, that he was able to hear the heavenly echo. And so it must be with us, when commerce is brought to a standstill and businesses are closed, God forbid. It may indeed be a very sad and bitter reality—for, after all, the Jewish people need and deserve a livelihood. Nevertheless, regardless of the reason for our having so much free time, let us not waste the time or the opportunity. If there is nothing for us to do, then let us recite the Psalms, and so forth. Let us keep going, day and night. And God Who is merciful will have mercy, and will turn the judgments around so that they become entirely beneficial, "going before them," to meet each individual need.

With this, we may possibly answer another question. It is taught in the Talmud that the manna that fell from heaven was used to judge arguments and disputes that occurred among the Jewish people. For instance, we learn in the Talmud (*Yoma* 75a): "If two men both claimed to own the same slave, the issue was decided by watching to see into which litigant's house the slave's portion of manna fell."

Why was it, then, that we did not determine the halachic (legal) time of changeover from day to night simply by looking to see whether we were following a pillar of cloud or a pillar of fire? It should have been obvious which pillar we were following. From this observation we should have been able to calculate the period between sunset and nightfall to the exact satisfaction of all the legal requirements. Why is it, then, that the precise moment of nightfall is still legally undetermined?

As we have learned, the phrase above, "God goes before them by day . . ." means not only that when it is really daytime the pillar of cloud is there and the pillar of fire is not, "before them" means "according to their needs." And so it is possible that there were times when the Jewish people for one reason or another could not see so well, although it was still daytime, and so the pillar of fire came to light the way for them.

# *Yithro*—January 27, 1940

*Author's note: By the Grace of God. Yithro. This Sabbath I was in hiding.*

*"Moses' father-in-law, Jethro, sheik of Midian, heard about all that God had done for Moses and His people Israel, when He brought Israel out of Egypt." (Exodus 18:1)*

Rashi (ibid.) asks: "What was it that Jethro heard, that made him come to Moses? Jethro heard about the splitting of the Red Sea and the battle with Amalek."

A well-known question, found in works of my father, of blessed memory, and in other sacred texts, asks what Rashi could have meant by asking, "What was it that Jethro heard?" The text itself states explicitly that he heard "about all that God had done for Moses and His people Israel when He brought Israel out of Egypt." Why does Rashi answer that Jethro heard about the splitting of the sea and the battle with Amalek, instead of quoting what is written in the text?

We learn in the holy book *Beit-Aharon* that the fact that God gave the Torah to the Jewish people in the wilderness was of great significance. The *Beit-Aharon*'s teaching is in reference to Rashi's explanation of the verse (Deut. 6:5) "You must Love God your Lord with all your heart." Rashi (ibid.) explains: "Your heart should not be divided against God." The Hebrew name for God used in this Rashi is *HaMakom*, which in this context is translated as "Omnipresent," but normally translates as "Place." The *Beit Aharon* explains Rashi as saying, "Your heart should not be divided against the place."—that we must never say, "In this place I can worship

God, but in another place it would not be possible." Wherever we are, we must worship God.

If the Jewish people had received the Torah in their own land, the Land of Israel, they might have assumed that they could fulfill the commandments only in their own homes, and not when they were exiled and preoccupied with survival. This is why God gave them the Torah in the wilderness, while they were traveling and busy—so that they would know to keep the Torah everywhere, as we said above, "that your heart should not be divided against the place."

It is therefore possible that Rashi, in questioning Jethro's response, is asking: What specific thing did Jethro hear that made him leave his place "and come" to the wilderness? Why did he need to come at all? He might just as well have sat in his own home and sent a message to Moses, asking for a teacher to be sent to him, to proselytize and teach him Torah, just as later we see that Jethro himself returned to his home to convert his family to Judaism.

Now we can better understand Rashi's answer, "Jethro heard about the splitting of the Red Sea and the battle with Amalek." Amalek wanted, above all else, to cool the ardor of the Jews for their God. But how could he possibly have imagined being able to chill the enthusiasm of a people who had just witnessed the splitting of the Red Sea? The splitting of the Red Sea, the Talmud tells us, was a moment when even the lowliest, heathen maidservant saw visions of God not revealed to Ezekiel the prophet. But because the Jewish people were traveling, busy, and weary, Amalek thought that he might be victorious over them, God forbid, even though they had just enjoyed an apotheosis of spiritual revelation. This is why it is written (Deut. 25:17): "Remember what Amalek did to you on the road out from Egypt. Who chilled you on the road . . ."

Jethro said to himself, "If this is any indication of how things are, it will not be enough for me to receive the Torah in my own house. I must go out on the road, and receive the Torah there also, and only then will I be able to be a Jew in my home."

This, then, is the meaning of Rashi's remark, "He heard about the splitting of the Red Sea and the battle with Amalek." When Jethro heard that even after the splitting of the sea there was still a battle to be fought with Amalek and that Amalek actually thought he could prevail against the Jews, Jethro realized that to become a Jew, one must leave home and be on the road, in the wilderness.

# *Mishpatim*—February 3, 1940

"*(Moses) took the Book of the Covenant and read it aloud to the people. They replied, 'All that God has declared, we will do and we will listen.'*" (Exodus 24:7)

It is the opinion of the Talmud, and Rashi (ibid.) concurs, that the events described in the text above occurred before the Giving of the Torah. This means that the Jewish people's saying "We will do and we will listen" happened before the events at Sinai. What we need to understand, then, is why the Torah narrative places this event after the Giving of the Torah. Even though, as is well understood, there is no chronological "before" or "after" in the Torah, nevertheless the juxtaposition of these events in the text must surely be teaching us something.

Rashi explains that the Book of the Covenant that Moses read aloud to the people at that time was the story from Creation to the Giving of the Torah. Why then did the Jews, upon hearing only this much of the narrative, when Moses had read only Genesis and the first chapters of Exodus, feel moved to reply, "All that God has declared, we will do and we will listen," as though they were receiving the whole Torah? Furthermore, the declaration "We will do and we will listen" is everywhere assumed to be our acceptance of the entire Torah text. So, we need to understand why it was that after such a partial reading of the Torah, we declared "We will do and we will listen" to all the subsequent Torah?

We learn the following in the Talmud (*Shabbath* 88a) about the verse "And they stood under the mountain" (Exodus 19:17): "This teaches us that the

Holy Blessed One tore out the mountain at its roots and held it over them like a barrel, and said to them, 'If you accept the Torah, well and good; if not, there shall be your burial site.' R. Acha b. Yaakov observed, 'This furnishes a strong protest against the Torah.' Rabba responded, 'Yet even so, they reaffirmed their acceptance, voluntarily, in the days of Ahasuerus, as it is written, "(The Jews) accepted, and observed . . ." (Esther 9:27) which means they reaffirmed what they had previously accepted.'"

In their commentary on this talmudic passage, the Tosaphists conclude that there is a distinction between our acceptance of the Torah per se, and our commitment to observe and fulfill all its demands. Because we did accept the Torah voluntarily in the covenanted ceremony described in the text above, it is untrue for us to claim that the Torah was forced upon us. Nevertheless, we still had the right to protest that we had been coerced to commit to the observance of all the Torah's commandments. This latter claim held true until we voluntarily reaffirmed our commitment to the Torah in the time of Ahasuerus.

Perhaps, therefore, the phrasing of our speech, putting "we will do" before "we will listen," was a way of saying that even if we were presented with an opportunity to protest that we had been forced to commit to the observance of the Torah, we still promised to fulfill its dictates nonetheless.

The question then is this: How did they know, during the ceremony described in the text above, which happened before the Giving of the Torah, that they would be forced into committing to observe the Torah? The answer is this: From Moses' reading of the book of Genesis—the story of the patriarchs, and the covenants that God made with them—the Jewish people realized that they were going to be forced into this commitment, even under duress. They heard how God had committed to the patriarchs, as it is written (Deut. 4:27): "And because He loved your fathers, and chose their descendants after them . . ."

If this was the case, then placing the narrative of the declaration "All that God has declared, we will do and we will listen" in the text after the Giving of the Torah has a definite purpose. It is a way of telling us that the Jewish people intended to commit voluntarily to the entire Torah they would receive at Sinai, even if they were also forced to commit to it under duress.

Perhaps this is why Moses sprinkled half the blood of the people's sacrifice on the altar before they answered "We will do and we will listen," and the other half after they made their declaration (Exodus 24:6–8). The sprinkling of the blood on the people was the sealing of a covenant, as Moses said, "This is the blood of the covenant that God is making with you regarding all these words." (ibid.) God was binding Himself in an irrevocable covenant to rescue the Jewish people whether they were deserving of His salvation or whether, God forbid, they were not—and we were committing to observe the Torah even when we had the right to protest that we were being coerced.

The covenant is always reciprocal. Because we said "We will do and we will listen" regarding observance of the Torah, even when we had the right to protest that we were being coerced, God was forced into the same kind of covenant. He must save us, even when protesting that He is being forced into so doing. And we, whether we are bound to do so or have the right to protest, will always worship God.

# Ki Thisa—February 24, 1940

*"Moses went back up to God and said, 'The people have committed a terrible sin by making a golden idol. Now, if You would, please forgive their sin. If not, You can blot me out from the book that You have written.'"* (Exodus 33:31)

The question arising from this is well known. If Moses was coming to plead for God's forgiveness on behalf of the Jewish people, why did he exaggerate their sin?

My father, my teacher, R. Elimelech, of blessed memory, asks another question. (Divrei Elimelech, p. 175) Why is it that before the sin of the golden calf Moses does not demur when God says that He will send an angel to lead the people (Exodus 23:20), whereas after the sin Moses says, "If Your presence does not accompany us, do not make us leave this place" (Exodus 33:15)?

Perhaps with a teaching from the work of my holy father, of blessed memory, we can understand the text quoted above. My father teaches that a person who gives his life to save a fellow Jew is greater than a person who gives his life for the sake of God alone. The former person is like someone who gives his life to save the son of the king. His love for the king is so great that he is willing to give his life not only for the sake of the king, but also for the king's son.

With this teaching, it is possible to understand the actions of our teacher Moses. When he saw that the Jewish people were in need of great mercy—needing forgiveness even for this terrible sin—there awoke within him such love for the

Jews that he was prepared to give his life for them—and not just for the righteous among them, but also for the sinners who committed this grievous wrong. The Jewish people are the children of God, and Moses loved the Holy Blessed One so much, his love aroused in him the desire to give his life not only for God but also for His children. This arousal in turn awakened God's great love—not just for Moses, but for the entire Jewish people.

Moses exaggerated the sin of the Jewish people, calling it "a terrible sin," because he wanted to conclude by saying to God, on their behalf, "Despite all this, if You do not forgive them, then You can blot me out from Your book."

Why was Moses able to refuse to accept the angel God wanted to send to accompany them? To understand the answer to this question, we must first answer the following: What did God mean when He said of the angel, "He will not bear your sins" (Exodus 23:21)? How can forgiveness depend upon an angel? Surely everything must depend solely upon the Holy Blessed One.

We learn in the sacred literature, in the verse "God bears iniquity," (Exodus 34:7) that the Holy Blessed One carries, as it were, the sin upon Himself, as though to say, "I am responsible for this." Similarly, we learn in the Talmud (*Berachoth* 31b); R. Elazar said, "Elijah the prophet traduced calumny against the Almighty when he said 'God, You have perverted their hearts and turned them against You.'" (I Kings 18:37) R. Shmuel b. Yitzchak said: "How do you know that God turned around and admitted as much to Elijah? It is written, 'I will gather the lame and the halt and the outcast and those whom I have misled.'" (Micha 4:6)

When God says of the angel, "He will not bear your sins upon himself," He means "He will not consider himself responsible when you sin." On the contrary, angels act as accusers, even complaining when God shows special favor toward the Jewish people, as we learn in the Talmud (*Berachoth* 20a).

Therefore, after Moses has offered to die for the Jewish people, he is in a position to argue, saying, "I do not agree to being led by anyone who is unwilling to bear upon himself the sins of the Jewish people, even if he is an angel." And so God answers, "My presence will go, and I will lead you."

# *VaYakhel*—March 2, 1940

*"Moses assembled the entire community of Israel and said to them, 'These are the words that God has commanded for you to do. You may do work during the six weekdays, but the seventh day must be kept holy as a Sabbath of Sabbaths to God. Whoever does any work on that day shall be put to death. Do not ignite any fire on the Sabbath, no matter where you may live.'"* (Exodus 35:1)

A well-known question from the sacred literature asks: Why does the Torah need to command the people to work during the six weekdays, when surely they would work anyway on those days? Why then were we not simply given the commandment regarding the Sabbath?

An explanation may be found in the following text from the Talmud (*Shabbath* 70a). The phrase that Moses used above, *Eleh haDevarim* ("These are the words") hints at the thirty-nine forbidden Sabbath labors taught to Moses at Sinai. Moses' use of the plural, "words" instead of "This is the word of God," implies at least two. By saying "the" words, instead of simply "This is God's word," he implies three. Using the Hebrew letter *heh* attached to the word *devarim*, making it *haDevarim*, is an extension implying a greater number than two—i.e., three. Finally, the Hebrew word for "these," *Eleh*, has the gematria, or numerical value, of thirty-six, thus totaling thirty-nine in all.

We expound gematria in the Torah because the script of the Torah is unlike all other scripts. The main purpose of other scripts is to convey the intention and thought of the writer. Since it is impossible to convey a thought in writing without resorting to depiction and symbol, we have agreed upon certain symbols—the letters of the alphabet with which we build words—to convey our intention and thought. The letters themselves are just symbols, as we have said, and the symbolism arbitrarily agreed upon for a certain letter might just as effectively have been attributed to a different letter. This is not the case, however, with the letters of the holy Torah. Here, each letter is exactly what it is, and could not possibly have any other form. *Alef* cannot be *beth* and *beth* cannot be *alef*, and so forth. This is because it is not only the thoughts and the ideas contained in the words of the Torah that are holy: The vessels and physical shapes that carry these thoughts—the letters—are also holy. The holiness permeates the vessels, until it saturates every facet of their being. Not only are the letters holy, but their filling, *miluy*, is likewise holy.

[Translator's note: *Miluy* is best described as follows. When referring to the tenth Hebrew letter, *yud*, in writing, the Hebrew letters *vav-daleth* are added to the *Y* thus, *y-ud*, to create a word. When the first Hebrew letter *alef* is referred to, *lef*—comprising *lamed feh*—is added to *A* to create the word *alef*. It is understood that all three letters comprising the filling (*miluy*) of the word *yud* share the character of the letter *yud*, etc.]

Not only the letters but also the gematria, the numerical values, of the letters are holy. And because there is something to be learned just from counting the number of letters, then that sum is also holy.

We learn in the holy Zohar (vol. III, 94a); What is the difference between the Sabbath day and a Festival day? The festivals are "called holy" (Exodus 12:16) because we call the holiness upon them by preparing for them and thus sanctifying the day. The Sabbath, however, is intrinsically holy, as it is written, "It is holy for you." (Exodus 31:14) This is why there is no special commandment to fulfill on the Sabbath itself. On Rosh Hashanah we are commanded to blow the shofar, on Yom Kippur we must take upon ourselves the five hardships of Yom Kippur, and on Sukkoth we are commanded to take the four species and dwell in a *sukkah*; but on the Sabbath all that is required is that we refrain from working. Moreover, it is well known that because the Sabbath is capable of sanctifying the other six days of the week, the holiness of the Sabbath suffuses the six days. Until Wednesday we receive the holiness from the previous Sabbath, and from Wednesday onwards we receive holiness from the Sabbath that is coming. In the same way that physical bodies become holy on the Sabbath, so also are the days of the week sanctified, and this is why the Sabbath requires no special commandment, making us responsible to prepare it for sanctification.

The Talmud (*Shabbath* 118b) says: "If only the Jewish people would keep two Sabbaths, they would be redeemed immediately." Considering what we have said above, this may be understood to mean that the first Sabbath is the seventh day, while the second Sabbath is that which occurs during the six weekdays. The commandment is to draw the holiness of the Sabbath into the weekdays. So the text with which we began this chapter now reads "Work during the six weekdays, *and* keep Saturday holy as a Sabbath of Sabbaths to God." Make Sabbath pervade your weekdays, while observing the seventh day as the Sabbath of Sabbaths. This is the meaning of the "two Sabbaths" mentioned in the quote from the Talmud.

In this injunction, the Torah uses gematria to teach the thirty-nine forbidden labors precisely in order to show us the nature of the sanctity of Sabbath. We see how the Sabbath spreads its holiness, pervading even the gematria, and so we realize that there is Torah to be learned even from this.

# *Pekudey* (Parshat *Shekalim*)— March 9, 1940

*"Moses saw that all the work had been so done; as God commanded, it had been so done. Then Moses blessed them."* (Exodus 39:43)

According to Rashi (ibid.), Moses' blessing was: "May it be the Divine Will that God's presence comes to dwell in the work of your hands."

We need to understand why the words "so done" appear twice in the text.

In Rashi's commentary to the beginning of this chapter, he refers to the talmudic account (*Berachoth* 55a) of these events. At the time when the Holy Blessed One said to Moses, "Go and tell Bezalel to make me a Tabernacle, an Ark and Vessels." Moses went and reversed the order, saying to Bezalel, "Make an Ark and Vessels and a Tabernacle." Bezalel said to him, "Our teacher Moses, as a rule a man first builds a house and then brings vessels into it; but you say, 'Make me an Ark and Vessels and a Tabernacle.' Where shall I put the vessels that I am to make? Could it be that the Holy Blessed One told you to make a Tabernacle, an Ark and then Vessels?" Moses replied, "You must have been in the shadow of God, as he was speaking to me!" The Hebrew *bezal-el* means "in the shadow of God."

However close Bezalel stood "in the shadow of God," he was still nowhere near as close to God as was our teacher Moses. So, should not Moses have known more than Bezalel?

A possible explanation can be found in the Talmud (*Yebamoth* 49b): Manasseh, King of Israel said to Isaiah the prophet, "Your teacher Moses said, 'For man cannot see Me and live,' (Exodus 33:20) and yet you say, 'I saw the Lord sitting on a throne, high and exalted.'" (Isaiah 6:1) The Talmud answers that while Isaiah looked "through a glass darkly," Moses looked through a sparkling, clear glass.

Although there are millions of degrees of incomparability, nevertheless we may perhaps draw an analogy between looking at God and looking at the sun. It is impossible to look at the sun through clear glass; only through smoked glass can one look at the sun. And so, when looking through clear glass it is true that "Man cannot see Me and live." When Isaiah said, "I saw the Lord," it was because he was looking through a glass darkly.

The rule that God can be seen when looking through a glass darkly but cannot be even looked at with unclouded vision applies not just to prophetic revelation but also to the revelation of God that comes through worship and fulfillment of the commandments. There are *kavanot*, sacred meditations and acts of divine unification, that are specific to each commandment, but they are utterly without value unless the commandment is observed and practiced. If a person has all the correct intentions and meditations for putting on phylacteries (*t'fillin*) but, God forbid, does not physically don the *t'fillin*, then all his meditations and intentions of divine unification are worthless and void.

Only here in this world, where the presence of God is so concealed, can the commandments be physically observed, and can there be a revelation of God through the meditations and unification. This cannot happen above, in heaven, where all is void in the presence of God—the angels are nullified, they have no free will, and even the higher realms and their characteristics are nothingness in the presence of God. If everything is null and void, then there is nothing to cloud one's view of God and so, above, God cannot be looked at. On the other hand, in this world, the World of action, where God is most hidden, He can be perceived, because this is the world in which we can look at God through a glass darkly (but not in any other way).

It was Bezalel who in practice actually made the Tabernacle, while our teacher Moses only commanded its making. Jews made donations to the building fund because they wanted Bezalel and his people to build the Tabernacle, and it was his actual labor that built it. Therefore, more details about the Tabernacle were revealed to Bezalel than to Moses. This is why Moses said to Bezalel, "You were in the shadow of God."

The reference to Bezalel's being "in the shadow" points to what we said above. Being in the shadow, the world of clouded vision, the practical world, the World of action, where God is hidden, is an opportunity to look at God in ways that Moses with his unclouded vision could not. Isaiah said, "I saw the Lord . . ." because he was looking through a glass darkly, as we explained above.

It is possible that this is also what is hinted at in the Midrash (*Tanchuma* Exodus, *Ki Thisa* 3). Moses said to God, "But once I am dead, I will not be remembered." God replied, "I promise you, just as you are standing here now and giving them the reading of the *shekels*, so every year as they read the chapter of *shekels* before Me, it will be as though you were standing here at that time and raising their heads." The Midrash explains that this is why the verse in the Torah does not say "Count their heads," but rather "You will count their heads." (Exodus 30:12)

It might simply be asked: What did Moses mean when he said, "Once I am dead, I will not be remembered?" After all, Moses is mentioned throughout the Torah, as in "and Moses spoke," "and God said to Moses," and so forth.

It may perhaps mean the following. We learn in the holy *Tikunei Zohar* (*Tikun* 6:22b): "Lucky is the person who makes God a dwelling place in his heart." It is also written (Exodus 25:8), ". . . and I will dwell inside them." Our sages of blessed memory explain (*Ohr Hachaim*, ibid.): "It says 'inside them' instead of 'inside him,' because the Holy One, blessed be He, dwells inside all Jewish people. This is not only to satisfy the need of every Jew; it is also God's need, the need of the *Shechinah*, because besides the fact that God loves the Jewish people very much and so wishes to dwell among them, it is also His desire to be revealed and known in this world." Now, as we explained above, the only real revelation of God is in this very world, the world of action, because in higher realms everything is canceled out to the utmost nullification. And as we learned in the Talmud (*Berachoth* 3a), "When R. Jose went into one of the ruined houses of Jerusalem to pray, and heard there a divine voice saying, 'Woe to me, that I destroyed My house!' the Prophet Elijah told him, 'It is not only now that the divine voice can be heard, but thrice each day. And more than that, whenever the Jewish people go into their synagogues and schoolhouses and respond: "May His great name be blessed!" the Holy One, blessed be He, shakes His head and says, "Happy is the king who is thus praised in this house!"'"

From this talmudic passage it is clear that not only are we humans fortunate to have God revealed to us, but also God, the Almighty King, is lucky to be revealed thus to us and among us. And so the Divine voice that R. Jose heard in the ruined house said, "Woe, that I destroyed My house!" If God has regrets about destroying temple we can infer He now lacks something and suffers. God also regrets not being revealed in the world.

This also explains why it is that after they depart this world, souls ascend to a much higher level in the Garden of Eden than the level they occupied before they came into this world. All the realities and practical details of holiness are found only in this world, the world of Action, and in the physical observance of the commandments, which can only happen in this world. Therefore, besides from the saying of *Kaddish* and the learning of Mishnah after someone has died, the soul of a departed person also benefits when his name is mentioned by someone who is about to observe a commandment or learn Torah. The benefit comes not merely from mentioning the dead person's name but from binding oneself to him, so that he is actually observing the commandment and learning Torah together with the living person. When this happens the departed soul becomes clothed once again in the physical world of Action, and from the learning and the observance there comes a further revelation of holiness and an ascension to yet higher levels of the Garden of Eden.

If God, as it were, wants so much to dwell inside every Jewish person, how much stronger is the desire of the souls who have departed this world? They desire that some part of them dwell inside the Jewish people, to learn Torah and observe commandments together with them.

This is what Moses our teacher meant when he said, "Once I am dead, I will not be remembered," for in the Torah when it says, "God spoke to Moses . . ." and "Moses spoke to the Jewish people . . ." Moses will only be remembered as having lived at some time in the past. Thus, he was asking, "After I am dead, will I also be remembered in the present?" referring to the kind of remembrance mentioned above, whereby Moses could actually be found inside a Jewish person, and whereby Moses may actually be observing the commandments together with the living person. And so, God replied, "I promise you, just as you are standing now and giving the people the reading of the *shekels*, so every year as they read the chapter of the *shekels* before Me, it will be as though you were standing there and raising their heads." The verse in the Torah does not say "count their heads," but rather "you will count their heads," because Moses our teacher is reading the chapter of the *shekels* now, with us, and it is so done. Every year Moses performs this deed, and by so doing he lifts up our heads. Since Moses our teacher is inside us, then all year round whenever we learn Torah and observe commandments we are learning and observing with Moses, who continues to expand and permeate through us, and it is so done.

# *VaYikra*—March 16, 1940

*"God called to Moses and said to him . . ."* (Leviticus 1:1)

Rashi (ibid.) explains: "Whenever God commanded, instructed, or spoke to Moses, He always called to Moses first. *Kriah*, 'calling,' is an expression of tenderness and affection. It is an expression used by the ministering angels, as it is written, 'One angel calls another, saying: "Holy, holy, holy is God, Lord of Hosts, the whole world is filled with His glory."'" (Isaiah 6:3)

Why does Rashi make this comment about the expression of affection—*Kriah*—when it appears at this point in the Torah text, rather than at an earlier opportunity? For instance, at the burning bush, where it is written, "God called to him from amidst the bush, and said . . ." (Exodus 3:4) or at the revelation on Sinai, where it is written, "God called to him from the mountain, saying . . ." (Exodus 19:3)

When God tested Abraham at the *Akeidah*, the Binding of Isaac, it is written, "He went, took the ram, and sacrificed it as a burnt offering in his son's place." (Genesis 22:14) This is true of every animal sacrifice: It is always in place of a person. The verse quoted above (Leviticus 1:1) continues, "When a man of you brings a sacrifice to God . . ." The verse emphasizes the words "of you" because the animal is really in place of the person himself. On fast days, we pray: "May the fat and blood that I lose as a result of this fast be accepted as a sacrifice upon the altar before You." In fact, suffering per se scours away the sins of a person because it diminishes a person's strength as well as his fat and blood. All the sufferings of the Jewish people are a kind of sacrifice. That is why Rashi chooses this text, which begins the chapter on animal sacrifices, to make his point. He is telling us that any sacrifice we make, whether like those in the text that follows—with an animal in place of a person—or our own suffering, is God "calling" to us. They are expressions of tenderness toward us from the Holy Blessed One.

There may be another, deeper explanation as well. The verse from Isaiah mentioned above (Isaiah 6:3) is quoted in the liturgy of the morning service, *Uva L'Tzion*: "One angel calls another, saying, 'Holy, holy, holy is God. . . .'" An ancient Aramaic translation of this reads: "They receive from one another and say 'Holy, holy, holy. . . .'" In this translation from the *Targum* of Yonathan b. Uziel, "calling" is translated as "Receiving." It is taught in the holy book *Tikunei Zohar* (cap. 19) that the Jewish people empower angels to receive from one another. When one Jew learns Torah from another, or receives money or a favor from another Jew, then the angels are empowered to receive from one another.

Angels receive from one another not only when Jewish people give charity and perform acts of kindness for one another: even when one Jew simply listens to the troubles of his fellow Jews, angels are empowered. If a Jew hears of the suffering of others and does what he can to help, and if his heart breaks and the blood congeals in his veins at the story of his friend's troubles, then angels are empowered. If from this broken heart the Jewish person has thoughts of penitence and returns to God, praying to the Holy Blessed One on behalf of the Jewish people, then this also is an instance of Jews receiving from one another. One receives from his fellow a broken heart and thoughts of repentance, while the other receives mercy and favors that may be done for him, as well as the prayers that are offered up in return. With this action below there is a reciprocal action above, and so the angels also receive from one another.

We learn in the Midrash (Deut. Rabbah 2:36): "When Moses was in heaven receiving the Torah, he heard the ministering angels praising God, saying, 'Blessed is the Name of His glorious kingdom for all eternity.'" When Moses came down, he taught this to the Jewish people, who say it quietly in their daily liturgy, *Sh'ma*. Thus we received an important piece of our liturgy from the angels, while in return they received from us the "Calling" that one receives from another. The prayer that we have from the angels ("Blessed is the Name of His glorious kingdom for all eternity") we recite quietly, while the "Calling" that the angels received from the Jewish people is very loud. It is so loud that when it is said, everything moves, as it is written: "One angel calls another, saying, 'Holy, holy, holy is God, Master of Legions, the whole world is filled with His glory.' The doorposts shake at the voice of him that cries, and the house is filled with smoke." (Isaiah 6:3–5) The reason for the difference in volume is this: The angels' calling/receiving from one another, which is empowered by the Jewish people receiving from one another, has in it much of the pain of the Jewish people. This is the pain of one Jew broken by the woes afflicting his fellow and another buttressing his fellow through his pain, as we said above. The calling/receiving that comes from sharing suffering and pain is very loud, and so the angels call out to one another in voices loud with compassion for the suffering of the Jewish people.

The prayer we have from the angels ("Blessed is the Name of His glorious kingdom for all eternity.") does not contain the pain of angels—for was there ever an angel who tasted the pain of a Jew enduring a beating, or his shame at being persecuted and humiliated, or his terror, or his anguish at being without sustenance, God forbid?

The prophet Isaiah said, "Woe is me, for I am ruined! I am a man of unclean lips, dwelling in the midst of a people of unclean lips; for my eyes have seen the King, the Lord of Hosts. Then one of the angels flew to me holding a live coal, which he had taken with tongs from off the altar. He laid it upon my mouth, and said 'Lo, this has touched your lips; and your iniquity is taken away, and your sin is purged.'" (Isaiah 6:5–7) Our sages of blessed memory (*Tanchuma-Genesis, VaYishlachz*) explained this passage to mean the following: "The Holy One, blessed be He, instructed the angel, 'Burn the mouth that defames my children.'"

In light of what we have said above, God was hinting to Isaiah, "You heard the sound of the angels 'calling to/receiving from' one another. All the power they demonstrated was only that given them by the Jewish people, and the great noise you heard, the noise that shook the doorposts, was from the pain of the Jews. How dare you then traduce the Jewish people?"

The first verse from Leviticus that we quoted at the outset, "God called to Moses and said to him . . ." teaches us that it is not just angels who "call/receive" one another, mirroring the "call/receive" that Jews give to one another, as taught in the *Tikunei Zohar* quoted above. Even God, Himself, "called to Moses," as one angel would "Call" to another. And so, God, blessed be He, by calling Moses, received from Moses in the way that one angel calling upon another both receives and gives. This happens because God is connected to man, as it is written (Psalm 91:15), "I am with him, in pain."

In the Midrash (Exodus Rabbah 2:12) we learn, about the verse "God called to him from amidst the (burning) bush," (Exodus 3:4) that God called "Moses Moses!" without a comma punctuating between the repeated name, while at the *Akeidah*, the Binding of Isaac, when God called to Abraham to still his hand from hurting Isaac, God used the comma and called "Abraham, Abraham!" (Genesis 22:11) The Midrash explains this with the parable of a man foundering beneath an unbearable weight. He calls urgently to whomever is nearest, "Hey you you come quick. Help me shed this load!" So it was that God called upon Moses to relieve Him, as it were, of His burden, and Moses helped to relieve God of His unbearable burden of Jewish suffering.

# *Parshat Zachor—March 23, 1940*

"*Remember what Amalek did to you on your way out of Egypt (Amalek) who encountered you on the road when you were tired and exhausted, they cut off those straggling to your rear, and did not fear God. Therefore, when God gives you peace from all the enemies around you in the land that God your Lord is giving you to occupy as a heritage, you must obliterate the memory of Amalek from beneath the heavens. You must not forget.*" (Deuteronomy 25:17)

Let us attempt to understand why the memory of Amalek must be blotted out "from beneath the heavens." Why does the text not say "from upon the earth," which is more accurately the abode of Amalek?

The reason could be as follows: It is written, "The heaven is my throne, and the earth My footstool." (Isaiah 66:1) As we know from Rashi's commentary to the verse in Exodus 17:15, which speaks of Joshua's battle with Amalek, God's throne will never be whole until the memory of Amalek has been obliterated. Therefore the text stresses "from beneath the heavens,"—that is, until God's throne is once again whole.

Another explanation might be this. We learn in the Midrash (*Tanchuma*, Deut., *Ki Taytzay* 9): "The Rabbis said that the Hebrew words *asher karcha* in the text above, which are usually translated to mean 'who encountered you,' can also be translated as 'who chilled you.' A parable: There was a pool of water so hot, not a single person dared set foot in it. Along came one reckless lout and jumped in.

Now even though the man was burned, those watching him jump in no longer believed the water so hot. When the Jewish people came out of Egypt and God split the Red Sea for them, all the nations of the world were afraid to attack them. But after Amalek had jumped in and made war on them, even though Amalek was roundly defeated, others no longer considered the Jews inviolable."

In the sacred literature, however, we learn that "chilled you," means not that Amalek made the Jewish people seem vulnerable in the eyes of others, but that he actually did succeed in cooling them off. Let us understand, if we can, how it could have been possible for Amalek, the avowed enemy of the Jewish people, whose sole purpose in attacking them was to kill them all, God forbid, could yet succeed in cooling them down? How were the Jewish people made to obey the enemy, who sought only evil? Was this act achieved through unclean powers, God forbid?

This is not the meaning of the sacred literature. It is teaching us something else. There is a teaching in the holy work of my father, of blessed memory, (Imrei Elimelech, p. 148) that the phrase "on the road" in the text above is a euphemism for "thought." With this understanding, the verse reads, "(Amalek) who chilled your thinking."

The gematria, or numerical value, of the word "road" (*derech—daleth resh kaf*) is 224, which is made up of two numerical equivalents or *gematriyot*: 63 plus 161, which equal 224. The four-letter name of God that is associated with the World of Thought has the numerical value of 63. This is the name *YHVH* with its letters *heh* in the *miluy* of *yudin*, written *yud-vav-daleth*; *heh-yud*; *vav-alef-vav*; *heh-yud*. And then there is the name of God *Ehyeh*, meaning "I Will Be Whom I Will Be," and which in its *miluy* is written *alef-lamed-daleth*; *heh-yud*; *yud-vav-daleth*; *heh-yud* and has the numerical value of 161. (Translator's note: For further explanation of *miluy*, see *Vayakhel*—March 2, 1940.)

Given this key, we can understand the verse with which we began the chapter, "Remember what Amalek did to you on your way out of Egypt (Amalek) who chilled your thinking." Before Amalek came to fight with you, there were among you servile people who esteemed the very thinking championed by Amalek. You were impressed with the superficial culture in which Amalek takes such pride. As a result, your response to Jewish culture and the wisdom of Torah was chilly. You were sure that Amalek was very cultured, that his philosophy was quite as good as anything. To be sure, it also had its ethics, and there is profit to be had from it in this world. What did God do? He brought you face to face with Amalek and with all the culture and philosophy he affects. God allowed him to expose to you his evil, the corruption in his wicked heart, the psychosis of his character, and all the putrefaction of his intelligence. Now you see for yourselves the real nature of secular, worldly knowledge.

God did the same for us in Spain, where there were Jews who were attracted to Spanish culture and embraced their philosophy. The Spanish resurgence brought them unremitting torment and bitter exile, etc.

So, when the Torah says, "Remember what Amalek did to you," it is emphasizing what happened to you—you yourself. He "chilled your thinking" to such an extent that he compelled you to agree that his culture is beautiful too, God forbid. Now you have the opportunity to see and feel the full "beauty" of his culture for yourselves. "Therefore, when God gives you peace from all the enemies around you in the land that God your Lord is giving you to occupy as a heritage, you must obliterate the memory of Amalek from beneath the heavens."

Surely, at the very least from now on, when with God's help you will be rescued and Amalek obliterated, you will have admitted that there is not, in all his worldly wisdom, culture, and science, one soupcon of decency. Oh, they can lecture prettily enough, but inside them they are filled with filth and decay. When they feel compelled, or even simply feel an urge, they can use the very same scientific method and intellectual rationale they invented to teach the world ethics and correct behavior, to prove the merit of theft, robbery, murder, and other forms of corruption.

How different, our holy Torah and its holy wisdom! It is not a human invention that can be twisted according to the will, desire, or intelligence of a person. Torah has nothing to do with empty intellectualization. Its substance is the very soul of light, from the breath of the light of the Almighty. All its commandments are statutes commanded by God. Whether or not a person is able to understand them intellectually, commandments are still commandments, and no one has the right to query them—and certainly not, God forbid, to twist any part of the Torah even as much as a hair's breadth. A person who learns Torah and fulfills its obligations cleaves to it with all his body and soul, his spirit and his breath. He is elevated to where he can see some small part of its greatness and goodness, and he becomes incapable of the desire to do anything bad, God forbid, as we learn in the sacred literature.

"Obliterate the memory of Amalek from beneath the heavens. . . ." This is necessary because there are those who straggle behind you, those ejected by the clouds of glory surrounding the Jewish people, who esteem Amalek's cleverness "beneath the heavens," God forbid. An alternative reading of the Hebrew word *tachat* alters "from beneath the heavens" to "instead of the heavens." The stragglers substitute mundane wisdom for the Torah, with which it cannot even be compared. Therefore, the text is saying: "Now that you have seen and experienced all this, go and 'obliterate the memory of Amalek from beneath the heavens.'"

# *Purim*—March 24, 1940

We learn in the *Tikunei Zohar* that Purim is like Yom Kippur. This could be hinting to us that just as on Yom Kippur a person must fast and repent whether he wants to or not, because he is fulfilling a commandment of God, so also the joy of Purim is not dependent on whether or not a person feels happy in himself or whether he is in a situation that facilitates happiness. Even if he is at the lowest level of brokenheartedness and his whole mind and spirit are ground down, it is nevertheless a statute that on Purim he must bring into his heart at least some spark of joy.

The comparisons between Yom Kippur and Purim apply equally to Heaven. The flow from above to below is bound to happen on Purim, just as on Yom Kippur the essence of the day itself atones for a person even if the person has not fulfilled all the requirements of repentance. We learn in the Talmud (*Yoma* 85b); Rebbe said: "Whether one has repented fully or not, the Day of Atonement procures atonement for all transgressions." So also, on Purim: Even if the Jewish person has not really felt joy, as he is commanded to do, and for this reason his worship on Purim was not whole, nevertheless, the salvation and joy that Purim itself achieves for the Jewish people will also work now.

# *Parshat HaChodesh*—April 6, 1940

"*This month shall be the head month to you. It shall be the first month of the year. Speak to the entire community of Israel, saying, 'On the tenth of this month, every man must take a lamb for each extended family, a lamb for each household.*'" (Exodus 12:1)

The juxtaposition of the two Torah commandments, that of counting the month with that of taking a lamb for each household, can be explained as follows. We learn in Rashi (Genesis 1:1); R. Isaac said: "The Torah should surely have commenced with the verse 'This month shall be the head month to you,' which is the first commandment given to the Jewish people. Why, then, does it commence with the account of the Creation?" He answers: "Because of the thought expressed in the verse (Psalms 111:6) 'He declared to His people the power of His works, that He might give them the heritage of nations.' For the nations of the world will one day say to Israel, 'You are robbers: you took by force the Land of Canaan, the land belonging to the seven nations.' Israel can reply to them, 'The land belongs to the Holy Blessed One. He created it and gave it to whomever He pleased. At his will He gave it to them, and when He wanted to, He took it from them and gave it to us.'"

A well-known question asks the following about this Rashi. Surely R. Isaac was not suggesting that the whole Book of Genesis, the stories of the Patriarchs, and the exodus from Egypt be omitted from the Torah? God's creation of the world is one of the foundations of the Jewish faith. R. Isaac must merely have been suggesting that the Torah begin with the first commandment. But if this were so, why then does he answer that the Jewish people needed to have the story of the creation in writing in order to present it as proof to the nations of the world? And if this is not the answer, then what is? If the story of the creation were written after the first commandment, the nations of the world would still be able to see that God created the world. Another puzzling question related to R. Isaac's statement is this: Why was R. Isaac so troubled by the order of events in the Torah in the first place? Why did it matter to him that in the Torah the first commandment comes after the story of the creation, and that the order is as it is? What objection could there be to the Torah beginning with the story of the creation; then describing the exile in Egypt; and then, before the exodus, God saying, "This month shall be the head month to you?"

Perhaps the reason is as follows. We learn in the Talmud (*Baba Kamma* 87a); R. Joseph stated: "Formerly I used to say, 'If someone would only assure me that the ruling (*Halachah*) is in accordance with R. Judah, who declared that a blind person is exempt from the commandments, I would make a feast for our Rabbis, because although I am blind and therefore exempt, I still fulfill the commandments.' But now that I have heard the statement of R. Hanina, who declared, 'Greater is the reward of those who, being ordered to, fulfill their obligation, than of those who, though exempt, do so anyway,' I feel the opposite. If someone were to assure me that the *halachah* is not in accordance with R. Judah, I would make a feast for our Rabbis, because if I were obliged to fulfill the commandments, my reward would be greater." End quote.

Why should the person who fulfills his obligation because he is commanded to do so receive a greater reward than a person who, though not enjoined, fulfills the commandments of his own free will and choice? Surely, the person who performs commandments without being enjoined to do so should be the greater? It is not so, however, because as is well known, when a person is enjoined to perform a commandment he must struggle with his evil inclination, which constantly advises him to disobey (*Tosaphot*, Talmud, *Avodah Zarah* 3a).

Perhaps, also, when a person who is not enjoined to observe a commandment does so anyway, he brings upon himself only that amount of holiness that he, a mere human, is capable of drawing down through his observance of the commandment. A person who is enjoined, however, draws down holiness much greater than that which he could bring upon himself through his own actions. This is because God, blessed be He, Who is above all the worlds, is the source of the commandment, and a person who observes His commandment connects himself to God, Who bestows holiness and light that surpasses everything. In addition, when a person observes a commandment that he is enjoined to observe, not only does he draw down the Divine Light that surpasses everything, but also that spark of originality and individuality that he of himself brings to the observance draws down still more and greater light.

Fundamentally, the person is doing what God commanded, and this is why every commandment (*mitzvah*) has in it the four-letter name of God, *YHVH* (*Yud Heh Vav Heh*). One half of the Holy name, *Yud Heh*, is hidden, and the other half, *Vav Heh*, is revealed, as is well known. The first two letters of the Hebrew word for commandment, *mitzvah*, are *mem* and *tzaddi*, which equal *yud* and *heh* when read in the alphabet of *ATBaSH*.

[Translator's note: The alphabet of *ATBaSH* is a method of exchanging the first letter of the Hebrew Alphabet, *alef*, with the last, *tav*; the second letter, *beth*, with the last but one, *shin*; etc.—hence the name *ATBaSH*. Sheshach (Jeremiah 25:26) represents Babel by this rule.]

The last two letters of the word *mitzvah* are *vav heh*, the last two letters of God's name openly revealed, as we said above. The reason why the name is partly revealed and partly hidden is because the light that man brings down from above in the performance of the *mitzvah* comes also from that Divine, hidden light. So, when a person first fulfills a commandment, there is the initial connection to the hidden light, which comes from He, blessed be He, Who commands, Who is hidden beyond human grasp. A person could never have brought down this light alone, no matter how hard he tried.

This also explains the significance of the Bar Mitzvah. Even though an underage child is able to observe commandments before his Bar Mitzvah, once he becomes legally obligated to fulfill the commandments—and does so—the supernal light, much greater than that which he alone was capable of drawing down, begins to flow to him. Thereafter, every time he observes a commandment, he is able, with the addition of his individuality and originality, to bring down a light much greater than his alone.

Returning to our text, R. Isaac asked: "The Torah should surely have commenced with the verse 'This month shall be the head month to you,' which is the first commandment given to the Jewish people. Why, then, does it commence with the account of the Creation?" R. Isaac meant that the Jewish people should have been given the account of Creation immediately after the giving of the first commandment, because the first commandment is their first real connection to God. It initiates the flow of supernal light, which comes from a place much higher than that which the Jewish people alone could have grasped. If they had been given the commandment first, they would have been able to draw down greater light and holiness to their understanding of the Torah, to the account of Creation that they would be learning, and to the commandments that they would be observing. And yet, R. Isaac says, the commandment is not given before the account of Creation, because of the thought expressed in Psalms 111:6: "He declared to His people the power of His works, that He might give them the heritage of nations." In addition to the simple explanation of this verse, which we have already given, there is another possible meaning. The verse could be hinting to us that even before receiving the commandments, before connecting with the flow of light coming through the commandments, man is already capable of bring down light much greater than that which his own ability would allow. By giving over his "power" to God, man can connect to the supernal light and sanctify himself beyond his own capability. Thus, God's "declaring the power of His works" shows how a person can become deserving of the great light. By "declaring the power of His works," says R. Isaac, by submitting to the power of God and turning one's will over to the service of God, one may become worthy of receiving the "heritage of nations."

When God created the world, He revealed a particular sequence. First He created the force of light and holiness, which became the matter and energy that is manifest in the physical world. In its description of God's power revealed and recounted in the books of Genesis and Exodus, the Torah is telling people how to sanctify their physical strengths, and in so doing how to draw down upon themselves the first commandment and all the light and holiness that comes with it. Because it is nearly impossible for a person to sanctify his body and his strengths while in a state of distress, God forbid, God gave His people the Land of Israel, a land flowing with milk and honey. This explains the second part of the verse quoted above, "To give them the heritage of nations."

This also explains why, when God gave the first commandment—to sanctify the new moon of the first month—He immediately gave them the second commandment: to take a lamb for each extended family. The second commandment was needed immediately because it contains within it the promise of redemption and salvation, which are prerequisite to the fulfillment of any commandment, as we have just said.

The liturgy for this Sabbath describes the Hebrew month of Nissan as "the month with extended salvation in it." My father, my teacher, of blessed memory, said that in this context, "extended" is used in the way the Mishnah (*Avoth* 3:16) uses it. As we might say of a shopkeeper that he "extends" credit, so in the month of Nissan salvation is extended to all, even to those who are not deserving of it.

Because there are seventy faces to the Torah, it is possible to add yet another interpretation to the expression, "the month with extended salvation in it." The expression "to extend" is used in the Talmud (*Hullin* 7a): "Scholars are not suspected of tithing food not immediately extended." In this context "extended" means "at hand." Thus, in describing the month of Nissan as "the month with extended salvation in it," the rabbis meant "the month with salvation immediate, and very close to hand."

# *Shabbat HaGadol* (The Great Sabbath)—April 20, 1940

*"Draw, and take yourselves a sheep . . ."* (Exodus 12:21)

The Midrash (*Mechilta, Bo* 11:2) teaches that "draw" in this verse—concerning the commandment to prepare a Paschal Lamb—means "withdraw your hands from idol worship, and then take yourselves a sheep . . ."

In his holy book *Imrei Elimelech* (p. 183) my father asks, "Does this mean that our teacher Moses, up until that moment, did not order the Jewish people to desist from idolatry?" The *Imrei Elimelech*, in the context of this question, also refers to another question posed by the *Prisha*.

The *Prisha*'s commentary on the *Tur, Shulhan Aruch, Orach Chaim* cap. 402 asks, "Why is the Sabbath before Passover referred to by our sages as *Shabbat HaGadol* and not *Shabbat Rabbah*? If the decision to name this Sabbath specifically was made by the Rabbis of the talmudic era, it should reflect their preference for Aramaic nomenclature. The Hebrew word *gadol* is hardly ever used by the Rabbis to designate something 'great.' Hence, Yom Kippur is called *Tzoma Rabbah* (The Great Fast) by the talmudic sages." The *Prisha* infers that the "greatness" in the name of this Sabbath refers not to a specific miracle, as was previously believed, but to something more classical and general.

A possible explanation may be as follows. In the Talmud (*Berachoth* 33b) we learn; R. Chanina said: "Everything is heaven–sent except the fear of heaven, as it is written (Deut. 10:12), 'And now, Israel, what does God want of you? Only that you fear God your Lord . . .'" Is the fear of God then such an easily discharged endeavor? Has not R. Chanina taught in the name of R. Simeon b. Yochai that God has nothing in His treasurehouse but His vaunted hoard of the Fear of Heaven, as it is written (Isaiah 33:6), "Fear of God is His treasure." O Yes! For Moses it was a very small matter indeed. As R. Chanina explained, "A parable: If a man is asked for something big and he has it, it takes on very small dimension; if, on the other hand, he is asked for something small, but does not have it, it grows in stature."

Behold, God is close to every Jewish person, even when the person is not fit. As it is written (Deut. 4:7), "What nation is so great that they have God close to them, as God our Lord is to us, whenever we call Him?" Besides its commonly accepted meaning, this verse, with its use of the Hebrew word *gadol* for greatness, also hints to us that even though the Jew may, God forbid, not merit God's closeness and His salvation, nevertheless the Holy One, blessed be He, is close to that person and saves him.

When Moses calls the Jewish people *gadol*—great—he is referring to a particular greatness whereby God is still very close to them even when if asked "Are you close to God?" they would have to answer, "No." At such times the Jewish person is like anyone who when asked about a small matter that he lacks considers it a great matter, as was illustrated in the parable from R. Chanina above. So Israel's greatness is that even when they lack closeness to God—and this closeness seems overwhelmingly great to them precisely because they have so little of it—God is still very close to them. God's closeness is their greatness, and this is what Moses meant when he said, "What nation is so great . . . ?"

There is a famous midrashic teaching (*Yalkut Shimoni* vol. II cap. 355) quoting R. Mathia b. Chairaish: "God saw that a day would come when the Jewish people would not merit redemption. He gave them, therefore, the two blood commandments, the blood of the Paschal Lamb and the blood of their circumcision, as it is written (Ezekiel 16:6): 'I passed over you and saw you wallowing in your blood and I said to you: "Through your blood shall you live."'"

From this teaching we learn that by the time the Jewish people were redeemed, they had acquired merit through their observance of the two above-mentioned commandments. But on the Sabbath before Passover, they had not yet acquired any merit, as the two observances were still in their future. Though they were without merit, God was close to them; and they were given the commandments to take a lamb for the Paschal sacrifice and to circumcise themselves. They were bereft of closeness to God, and so they considered it at the level of "a great thing," as was discussed in the parable above. Therefore this Sabbath is known as the Great Sabbath—*Gadol*, Great—in memory of their closeness to God.

The verse (Psalms 147:19) says: "He teaches His words to Jacob, His statutes and laws to Israel. He did not do this for every nation, nor did He teach them His laws." We need to understand why the verse says first "His statutes and laws to Israel," regarding the Jews, while regarding the nations it says only "nor did He teach them His laws." Why is it not written that God denied the nations knowledge of His statutes as well?

A person may think that he understands logical concepts because of their intrinsic comprehensibility, but he is mistaken. The truth is that the capacity to understand is complicated by one's personality. One's essential, individual self puts limits on every attempt at pure intellectual objectivity. Even such "self-evident" laws as those prohibiting robbery and murder are not logical, rational, or natural "laws"—for as we see now, there are nations whose objective and self-evident reality necessitates and clearly proves that it is right to rob any man of his wealth, and even to murder people.

That is why Maimonides, of blessed memory, notes in the sixth chapter of his work "The Eight Chapters," that our holy sages were very particular in their choice of language when they made the following statement (*Torath Cohanim, Kedoshim*): "A person should not say, 'I have no desire to eat forbidden mixtures of milk and meat,' or 'I have no desire to wear forbidden admixtures of wool and linen,' or 'I have no desire for forbidden sexual relationships.' Rather a person ought to say, 'I would like to do any of these things, but how can I, when my Father in heaven has forbidden me?' The sages chose for this dictum only those commandments that are statutes. They did not say that a person ought to say that he desires to rob or murder. Obviously, any person who refrains from robbing and murdering only because he is forbidden to do so, and not because he is repelled by the act itself, is a perverse and corrupt human being."

A perverse and corrupt person does desire robbery and murder even though they are everywhere considered rationally, logically, or naturally forbidden acts. A corrupt person can justify and rationalize anything. Only someone who is essentially good understands that these acts are intrinsically wrong.

Consequently, when a Jewish person draws himself close to the Holy One, blessed be He, and to Torah, then even those commandments that are statutes, and not intrinsically comprehensible, also begin to seem obvious. This understanding does not come from intellectualizing or from logic or from any particular reasoning. Only those things that are essentially unnatural or counterintuitive are understood through these reasoning processes. Things that are an integral and essential part of a person, however, are understood and grasped with the same kind of simple cognition as that with which a person perceives himself.

Returning to Psalm 147:19, the verse says: "His statutes and laws to Israel." The "statutes" of the Torah are also natural, logical, and rational "laws" to the Jewish people because the Jewish people are so intrinsically connected to the Torah. The psalmist goes on to say, "He did not do this for every nation, nor did He teach them His laws," because the nations cannot comprehend that "statutes" are as natural as "laws." Only a Jew has this level of understanding.

Although the actual first commandment in the Torah was "This month shall be the head month to you," (Exodus 12:1) it was observed only by Moses and Aaron at that time. So the first commandment given to the Jewish people was the commandment relating to the Pascal lamb, which is essentially a statute. To understand a statute as naturally as a law, one must become united with the Torah. Therefore, when the Jewish people came to observe their first commandment, and God was drawing very close to the Jewish people even though they did not have any merit, the verse that opens this chapter told the Jewish people, "Withdraw your hands from idol worship." The Hebrew words for "idol worship," *avodah zarah*, may also be translated as "strange worship." Moses was saying, "Let not the worship of God, the Torah, and the commandments be strange to you." They must become part of your essential being.

# *Pesach* (Festival of Passover)—April 23–30, 1940

*It happened that R. Eliezer, R. Yehoshua, R. Elazar b. Azariah, R. Akiba, and R. Tarfon were reclining (at the seder) in B'nei Brak. They discussed the Exodus all that night until their students came and said to them, "Our teachers, it is [daybreak,] time for the reading of the morning* Sh'ma.*"* (From the Passover *Haggadah*.)

Let us try to understand this story. The rabbis could have seen for themselves that it was time for the morning reading of the *Sh'ma*. If we offer the explanation that they continued with their seder, reclining to discuss the Exodus, because they knew that there would still be time to read the morning *Sh'ma*, why then did they stop when their students came to them? It would seem from the text that the rabbis continued talking only until their students came, and that when the students came, they stopped.

One possible explanation could be, as we learn in the Talmud (*Berachoth* 28b): "When R. Yochanan b. Zakkai fell ill, his disciples went in to visit him. When he saw them he began to weep. His disciples said to him, 'Lamp of Israel, pillar of the right, mighty hammer! Why do you weep?' He replied, 'If I were being taken today before a human king who is here today and tomorrow in the grave, whose anger if he is angry with me does not last for ever, who if he imprisons me does not imprison me for ever, who if he puts me to death does not put me to everlasting death, and whom I can persuade with words and bribe with money, I would still be weeping with fear. Now that I am being taken before the supreme King of Kings, the Holy One, blessed be He, Who lives and endures for ever and ever, Whose anger if He is angry with me is an everlasting anger, Who if He imprisons me imprisons me for ever, Who if He puts me to death puts me to death for ever, and Whom I cannot persuade with words or bribe with money—nay more: when there are two ways before me, one leading to Paradise and the other to Gehenna, and I do not know by which I shall be taken—shall I not weep?'"

We need to understand why, if R. Yochanan ben Zakkai was crying because of his fear of the future, did he only begin to weep when his disciples came in to visit him and not before?

Perhaps it may be understood with the following quote from the Talmud (*Makkoth* 10a): "A person should not teach a disciple who is unworthy." Similarly, we learn elsewhere (*Yoma* 87a): "Whosoever causes a community to do good, no sin will come through him." The reason, we are given to understand, is lest he be in Purgatory and his disciples in Paradise. A similar reason is given to explain the following quote (ibid.): "Whosoever causes the community to sin, no opportunity will be granted him for repentance," lest he be in Paradise and his disciples in Purgatory. This is why a person should not learn from a teacher who is unworthy.

Let us analyze the text: Surely, if the disciple is unworthy and the teacher does not learn anything with him, then the disciple will most certainly end up in Purgatory. Why then should the teacher refrain from teaching his disciple? Conversely, why should one not learn from an unworthy teacher? How could this possibly make things worse? The answer is that student and teacher are tied to one another, both in this world and the next. Therefore, a person who is in Paradise is damaged when his teacher or his student is in Purgatory, God forbid. This is what the Talmud means when it says, "Lest he be in Paradise and his disciples in Purgatory." The teacher in Paradise will sustain damage when his student is in Purgatory, and vice versa.

R. Yochanan ben Zakkai was tremendously humble about himself, and so he said, "I do not know by which (of the two ways) I will be taken, whether to Paradise or Purgatory." As soon as his disciples entered, however, it was clear to him that these were saints upon whom the world depends. Therefore, when he saw them he started to cry. Of himself he said, "I do not know by which road I will be taken," and in his humility he feared that he might go to Purgatory and his disciples to Paradise, and that because of him they would be damaged in Paradise, God forbid.

Returning to our text in the *Haggadah*: Even though R. Eliezer, R. Yehoshua, R. Elazar b. Azariah, R. Akiba, and R. Tarfon had discussed the Exodus from Egypt all night, they thought, in their humility, that they had not even begun. When they saw their disciples before them, however, they saw how their disciples' faces shone after the seder night, and they realized how much they had affected their disciples with their telling of the Exodus from Egypt. They knew then that they had done enough, and so they stopped.

~⁂~

> "Blessed is the Omnipresent; Blessed is He. Blessed is the One Who has given the Torah to His people Israel; Blessed is He. The Torah speaks concerning four sons." (from the Passover *Haggadah*)

Let us try to understand why we need to bless God, when the Torah speaks about the four sons. We have already discussed in the past how the response of the Torah to the Wicked Son appears to resemble the response to the One Who Does Not Know How To Ask. The answer to both sons is (Exodus 13:8): "You shall tell your son on that day, saying, 'It is because of this, that God did so for me when I came out of Egypt.'" It is obvious that the Torah never intended for even the wicked son to be excluded. Both sons are in the category of not knowing how to request, or access, holiness. One son is totally unable to ask—has no idea at all of what to ask—while the wicked son is filled with unhelpful knowledge—and as far as virtues are concerned, he also has no idea of what to ask.

Therefore, the Torah answers both with one verse, for this is how to open them both to holiness, to draw them close. To the one who simply has no idea what to ask, it is enough to say, "It is because of this that God did so for me when I came out of Egypt." That is why the *Haggadah* precedes his response with the phrase "You should open (the subject) for him." The wicked son, however, is filled with useless and negative knowledge that prevents him knowing how to open up and ask for holiness, and so, regarding him, the preceding line says "blunt his teeth," for only then can you open the subject and involve him.

In the morning liturgy (*Shacharis*) we say: "Our Father, merciful Father, Who acts mercifully, have mercy upon us; instill understanding in our hearts." The Holy Blessed One observes the entire Torah, as we learn in the Talmud (Jerusalem Talmud, *Rosh Hashanah* 7G, and Exodus Rabbah, *Mishpatim* 30:9). "Teaching Torah to one's children" is a Torah commandment, and so in this prayer we say to God: "Our Father, You are commanded, as it were, with the commandment to 'teach Your children,' so please, instill understanding in our hearts."

This is why in the *Haggadah* we say: "Blessed is the Omnipresent; Blessed is He. Blessed is the One Who has given the Torah to His people Israel; Blessed is He. The Torah speaks concerning four sons."

It is a scriptural commandment to help all kinds of children—wise, wicked, simple, and those unable to ask—to turn around and draw close to the Torah. Even of the wicked son it is not said "Do not answer the fool," (Proverbs 26:4) or, as the Talmud (*Sanhedrin* 38b) says, "Do not even respond to a Jewish heretic (*epikoros*) for this will only make his heresy more pronounced."

On the contrary, with regard to the commandment to teach Torah to our children, all children respond and draw close. This is why God must observe this commandment as well, even reaching out to a person who is, God forbid, wicked. The first part of the commandment, to "blunt his teeth," has already been sufficiently fulfilled among us. What remains is for God, blessed be He, to draw us close to Him with mercy.

This may be the reason why the *Haggadah* begins with the recitation "Originally our ancestors were idol worshippers, but now the Omnipresent has brought us near to His service." The reference to the four sons follows immediately. The *Haggadah* is telling us that this has always been the case—that we were so far, far away, and the Omnipresent brought us close to serve Him.

*"We cried out to God, the God of our fathers, and God heard our voice and saw our affliction, our burden, and our oppression." (From the Passover Haggadah)*

When a person merits to have his prayers accepted, then God hears in these prayers all the person's troubles, and all his affliction. In the *Haggadah* we are saying that in Egypt, we were at a very low level and did not merit that our prayers should rise up to heaven, but God listened to our prayers in the merit of our fathers. Once God listened to our voices, however, He drew close to us and could see for Himself our affliction, our burden and our oppression, and He saved us.

*"Therefore, the organs that You set within us, and the spirit and soul that You breathed into our nostrils, and the tongue that You placed in our mouth—all of them shall thank and bless, praise and glorify, sing about, exalt and revere, santify and declare the sovereignty of Your Name, our King, continuously." (from the Passover Haggadah)*

We enumerate in detail each one of these—the organs, the spirit, the soul, the tongue, the mouth, and so on—individually. The text does not say that we thanked and blessed generally, altogether, because it is telling us that even after a person has lived in this world, when his limbs, spirit, soul, tongue, mouth, and so on have each separated, he will still continue to thank God. We end by saying, "All my bones shall say: 'God, who is like You?'" That is, even if there is nothing left of me except the bones, they will also continue to say, "God, who is like You?"

# Shabbat Chol HaMoed (Sabbath During the Week of Passover)—April 27, 1940

*"'Please let me have a vision of Your glory,' begged [Moses].*

*"God replied, 'I will make all My goodness pass before you, and reveal the Divine Name in your presence. I will have mercy and show kindness to whomever I desire. But, you cannot have a vision of My face. A man cannot have a vision of Me and still exist. I have a special place where you will be upstanding on the rocky mountain. When My glory passes by, I will place you in a crevice in the mountain, protecting you with My hand until I pass by. I will then remove My hand, and you will have a vision of what follows from My existence. My essence itself, however, will not be seen.'"* (Exodus 33:18–23)

We need to understand why our teacher Moses asked to be shown God's glory only now, after the incident with the golden calf, and not before the Jewish people had sinned.

Rashi's opinion (ibid.) is well known. According to Rashi, Moses saw that this was a propitious time when God was acceding to his requests, so he took leave to request to be shown even God's glory.

But what did the response that God gave to Moses mean? God said, "I will have mercy and show kindness to whomever I desire." To whom does this refer?

The Talmud (*Rosh Hashanah* 17b) quotes the verse (Exodus 34:6): "God passed by before [Moses] and proclaimed, 'God, God, Omnipotent, merciful and kind, slow to anger, with tremendous love and truth . . .'" The Talmud explains that the Holy One, blessed be He, drew his robe around him like the reader of a congregation and showed Moses the order of prayer.

Let us attempt a simple understanding of this verse, at least according to our limited intellect. Why did God show the order of prayer to Moses at that time, and not at any other time? Another question is this: Why does God say, "You will be upstanding on the rocky mountain?" The Hebrew word for upstanding is *nitzavta*. The Talmud (*Nedarim* 64b) says: "Wherever the words *nitzim* or *nitzavim* are used in the Torah text, it is not a good sign, for they usually mean contention or uprising."

And yet, as the verse in Psalm 82:1 says, "God stands (*nitzav*) among the congregation of God." God is upstanding because this is appropriate for Him, blessed be He, as it is written (Psalms 93:1): "The Lord reigns: He is clothed with majesty." For humans, however, it is not fitting. Man has no right to arrogate such a pose. Why, then, did God say to our teacher Moses, "You will be upstanding (*nitzavta*)?" And why did God go on to say, "I will then remove My hand?" Could God not have arranged things so Moses would not see God's honor until after God had passed? Surely, only something that would naturally be visible needs to be hidden by the hand. This is not the case with God's honor, which cannot be seen, in and of itself, until God reveals it.

Even though we have no way of even attempting to understand God's revelation of Himself to Moses, we may still try to learn what it suggests to us. (Sanhedrin 103a) Perhaps it is similar to what we have learned in the sacred literature—I believe I heard this teaching in the name of the Great Maggid (R. Dov Ber of Mezeritch), commenting upon the following, well-known saying of the sages, of blessed memory: "R. Yohanan said in the name of R. Simeon b. Yochai, 'What is meant by the verse (II Chronicles 33:13) "And he, Manasseh, prayed unto God, and God responded to him?" The text of R. Simeon had the Hebrew *VaYechtar* substituted for the word *VaYe'etar*. The meaning was changed. Instead of the verse reading "God responded to him," it now reads "God tunnelled toward him." This teaches that the Holy Blessed One made a kind of opening in the Heavens in order to accept his contrition. It was a ruse to avoid the Attribute of Justice, which was urging that his repentance not be accepted.'" The Maggid's holy teaching is this: From this talmudic passage we learn that God's acceptance of the sinner's repentance is actually beneath His honor, beneath the throne of glory.

The Maggid's teaching needs interpretation. In the liturgy of the High Holidays we praise God, saying, "It is Your way, O God, to have long patience toward the wicked and the righteous, and that itself is Your praise." If God's honor and glory are bound up with the very fact that He forgives, what then did the Maggid mean?

It may be, however, that the Maggid's teaching is only with respect to the Attribute of Judgment. There are accusatory angels, and it is only according to their values that it is beneath God's honor to accept the sinner's repentance. This is not the case, however, with respect to the values of Jews. On the contrary, because the Holy Blessed One and the Jewish people are one, if God were not to accept a penitent's contrition, it would be not only the Jewish person who remained sullied and degraded with sin, but also that part of him that is divine. Therefore, it is God's glory to forgive and to accept repentance. The Torah goes so far as to command: "When a man is legally sentenced to death and executed, you must then hang him on a gallows. However, you may not allow his body to remain on the gallows overnight, but you must bury it on the same day. Since a person who has been hanged is a curse to God, you must not [let it] defile the land that God your Lord is giving you as a heritage." (Deut. 21: 22–23) Rashi explains this verse with a parable, saying, "It may be compared to the case of identical twin brothers: One became king and the other was arrested for robbery and was hanged. Whoever saw him on the gallows exclaimed that the king was hanged." So the Torah commanded us to bury the hanged man because of his resemblance to God.

This explains why God said to Moses, after the events surrounding the golden calf, "I will send an angel before you to safeguard you on the way, and bring you to the place that I have prepared. Be careful in his presence and heed his voice. Do not rebel against him, since My name is with him. He will not pardon your disobedience." (Exodus 23:20–21) As we said above, according to the values of the angel, it is beneath God's honor to accept the sinner's contrition.

Perhaps, after being informed that God Himself, and not an angel, would continue to lead the Jewish people into the Promised Land, Moses then asked, "Please let me have a vision of Your glory," meaning "Is it Your glory to forgive, or is it beneath Your dignity, as the angels contend?" To which God responded, saying, "I will have mercy and show kindness to whomever I desire," meaning: "Even though the sinner is unworthy, this is My glory—and moreover, every Jewish person is in part divine."

In addition to this, God also said to Moses, "I will remove My hand," and "You will be upstanding on the rocky mountain." We learn in the Talmud (*Ta'anith* 4a): "Israel said before God, 'O God, set me as a seal upon they heart; as a seal upon thine arm.' (Cant. 8:6) Whereupon the Holy Blessed One replied to her, 'My daughter, you ask for something that at times can be seen and at other times cannot be seen. I, however, will make of you something that can be seen at all times, as it is said, "Behold I have carved you upon the palms of My hands." (Isaiah 49:16)'" This hints to us that even when we experience, God forbid, God's hiddenness (*hester*) and endure physical and spiritual troubles, we should not allow into our hearts the thought that we are really hidden, God forbid, from God. For even when it is the palm doing the concealing, there is still that level of "on the palms of My hands," because we are carved into the palms themselves. It is the ultimate closeness, such that we can never be utterly hidden.

"And you will be upstanding on the rocky mountain" also hints that one can be strong and upstanding even at a time of hiddenness (*hester*), because the soul knows that it is already carved, and always seen at the level of "I have carved you upon the palms of My hands."

With these two together, you will find naturally, within yourself, the power to be upstanding. This is also a commandment; God is commanding you to strengthen yourself and be upstanding.

# *Shevi'i Shel Pesach* (The Seventh Day of Passover)—April 29, 1940

*"Israel saw the great power that God had unleashed against Egypt, and the people were in awe of God. They believed in God and in His servant Moses. Then Moses and the children of Israel sang this song to God."* (Exodus 14:30–15:1)

We need to understand why the text refers to the Jewish people first as "Israel" and then later as "the children of Israel." Even though both terms appear frequently in the Torah, there must nevertheless be some meaning for each usage, which we should try to understand.

The special *Hallel* ("Praises") that we chant during the Festival services ends with the following sentence: "It is good to give thanks to You, and it is proper to sing praises to Your name, because You are God from this world to the next." According to this text, it would appear that the reason why it is "good to thank" and "proper to sing," is because "You are God from this world to the next." What does this mean?

An explanation may be as follows: Whenever we are about to recite Psalms, we first say a special prayer: "May it be Your will that just as we sing Your praises in this world, so should we merit to speak, to sing, and to praise You in the world to come." Now we can understand the sentence "It is good to give thanks to You, and it is proper to sing praises to Your name, because You are God from this world to the next." It means that what we say and sing here in this world may also be what we say and sing in the world to come, because You are God, both here and there.

There may be another explanation. As we know, everything the Holy Blessed One created, He created for His glory. There is a revelation of His glory when He redeems us and we thank and praise Him with songs and praises. There is also a revelation of God's glory when He punishes the Jewish people and we cry and pray to Him to save us. Then through God's might and our prayers to Him, blessed be He, His blessed glory becomes evident.

It is true that we may not yet deserve to be saved, God forbid. We may not yet deserve to have His blessed glory revealed through us in songs and praise, but only, God forbid, through our punishment and cries. Still, why should those Jewish souls who have already gone to the next world have to suffer?

Rashi says (Numbers 19:15): "The Patriarchs suffer in their graves when punishment comes upon Israel." In the holy Zohar, where a great deal is written on this subject, we learn that it is not just the souls of the Patriarchs that suffer, but also the souls of all departed or murdered Jewish people. They have pain in our pain and they worship together with us in our worship of God, with tears in times of pain, God forbid, or with songs in times of redemption. Why should they have to suffer?

This is why we say, "It is good to give thanks to You . . ." It may perhaps be true that we deserve only to worship God with suffering and to pray with tears, God forbid. Nonetheless, we say to God, "It is better that You save us, and we thank You and sing praises to Your name, because You are God from this world to the next." We say this because in the next world there are Jewish souls (singing and praising) worshipping with us, and why should they have to suffer and have pain, God forbid, with us?

With this idea in mind, we can answer a question raised by my father (*Divrei Elimelech*, p. 154), my teacher, of blessed memory about the Talmud (*Berachoth* 9a). The Talmud refers to a verse in Exodus (11:2): "Speak, please, in the ears of the people. Let each person request of his friend vessels of silver and gold. . . ." In the school of R. Jannai they said: "The Hebrew word *Na*, 'please,' always means 'I beg of you.' The Holy Blessed One said to Moses, "I beg of you, go and tell the children of Israel to request from the Egyptians vessels of silver and gold, so that Abraham the Righteous should not have cause to complain, saying, "You promised that my descendants would be slaves in a strange land, and fulfilled Your promise. But You also promised that they would leave with great wealth, and have not kept Your promise."'" About this talmudic teaching, my father asked: If Abraham had not complained, would then the Holy Blessed One not have been required to keep His promise?

There is a well-known debate about the great wealth we brought out of Egypt with us. The question is asked: While it was promised to Abraham that his descendants would leave Egypt with great wealth, it was also promised that they would be slaves for a period of four hundred years. The reward they were promised was in return for their four centuries of labor as slaves. If we assume that to compensate for the severity of their exile in Egypt, the four hundred years was reduced and they were redeemed one hundred and ninety years earlier than specified, then surely they no longer deserved to leave with great wealth—for had they not already been recompensed for the severity of their exile by not having to complete the full term of exile?

Based on what we have said above, it is possible to explain away the whole question. God begged the Jewish people to leave Egypt with great wealth, "so that Abraham the Righteous may not have cause to complain." It may be true that those who actually left Egypt did not deserve to come out with great wealth. They had sunk so low into the corruption and defilement of Egypt, they could not possibly have completed the entire four-hundred-year exile period and still remained recognizable as Children of Israel. God was therefore forced to shorten the exile. He compensated for the remaining time by taking into account the severity of their labor. Nevertheless, why should our father Abraham have to suffer because of our circumstances? If the Jewish people had left Egypt without any wealth and suffered poverty, then our father Abraham would have had to suffer with them, as we explained above. This is what is meant by "so that Abraham may not have cause to complain."

It is possibly true that the Jewish people did not deserve wealth, since, after all, the reason they left Egypt early was because God was forced to redeem them immediately because they had sunk so low. They were unable to play their full part in the exile, and so the severity of their labor had to be used as mitigation for the shortened time. Nevertheless, God begged them to collect silver and gold from the Egyptians, "so that Abraham may not have cause to complain . . ." that God did not fulfill the promise to redeem His descendants and lead them forth with great wealth.

This is what is hinted at in the verse with which we began this chapter, "Israel saw the great power that God had unleashed against Egypt . . ." The holy Zohar teaches us that when the Torah speaks of "Israel" it is referring to "Patriarch Israel," our father Jacob. The text continues, ". . . and the people were in awe of God. They believed in God and in His servant Moses. Then Moses and the children of Israel sang this song to God." They sang the song because they knew that even though the accuser rightfully charged them with having sunk as low as the Egyptians, they were still the "Children of Israel." The Accuser called calamity down upon their heads, saying, "They [Egyptians] are idol worshippers and so are these [Israel] idol worshippers." Yet, because they were the children of Israel, they were saved in the merit of the Patriarch Jacob, who did not deserve the pain he would have suffered in heaven because of them. And so, "Moses and the children of Israel sang this song to God," and "It is good to give thanks to You, and it is proper to sing praises to Your name, because You are God from this world to the next."

# *Acharon Shel Pesach* (The Last Day of Passover)—April 30, 1940

*"O bring them and plant them*
  *On the mountain You possess.*
*The place You dwell in*
  *Is Your accomplishment, God.*
*The Temple, O God,*
  *Your hands have founded.*
*God will reign for ever and ever."*
(from the "Song of the Sea," Exodus 15:17–18)

Let us understand: The whole point of the Exodus from Egypt was to bring the Jewish people into the Land of Israel. So why did they still need to pray for it to happen, when surely God would protect them and bring them into the Land of Israel and to the holy Temple? Also, why do we say of the Temple, "The Temple, O God, Your hands have founded," when the Temple was built by the Jewish people?

Rashi's explanation (ibid.) is well known: The Temple is an object of great affection to God because, while the Universe was created using one hand—as it is written (Isaiah 48:13): "Yea, My hand hath laid the foundation of the earth"—the Temple was built by two hands—as it is written here in our text, "The Temple, O God, Your hands have founded." When will God, using two hands, build it? At the time when "God will reign for ever and ever."

It may perhaps be as follows. We learn in sacred literature on the verse (Psalms 119:89) "Forever, O Lord, Your word stands in heaven," that the world of Speech is higher than the world of Action. Therefore, even when God bespeaks salvation of the Jewish people, and it has been called into being, it may yet happen that salvation remains out of reach. It is still above this world, in the world of Speech, and so there can exist some delay before it is drawn down into this world, the world of Action. The verse "Forever, O Lord, Your word stands in heaven" is taken to mean that there is some delay—that even when salvation has been commanded, it may yet be standing in heaven, above the world of Action. This is why the holy prophets sometimes performed metaphorical actions. An example of this is described in the prophets (II Kings 13:15–19), when the prophet Elisha commanded the King of Israel to shoot a bow and repeat three times "Smite Aram," and so forth. The action resembles the salvation it is trying to bring about, and is performed to draw the salvation down into the world of Action more immediately.

In these times, although we have neither prophet nor seer, our observance of the commandments is also a drawing down of the word of God, because God's word is in the commandments. To physically perform the commandments is to draw them down into the world of Action, and when this happens God's words of salvation are also drawn down to the world of Action. How much more is this so now, during Passover, when the practical commandments we observe are God's words of salvation. One instance of this is our observance of the commandment to eat unleavened bread (*matzo*) because our ancestors' dough did not have time to rise before the King of Kings, the Holy Blessed One, revealed Himself to them and redeemed them. The four cups of wine and the recitation of the four divine promises of redemption, etc., also serve to draw down the redemption immediately and straight away, that it should not, God forbid, be delayed.

With this understanding, we can answer a well-known question. How can we say, as quoted above from the *Haggadah*, that the reason for *matzo* is because the Jewish people did not have time for their dough to become leavened before they left Egypt, when we know that they had already been commanded to eat *matzo* before leaving Egypt (see Exodus 12:15)?

From what we have said above, it can be explained as follows: When God first gave the commandment to eat *matzo* with the Paschal Lamb, He was commanding the Jewish people to perform an action resembling the salvation they were trying to bring about. The reason for this was to enable them to visualize and act out a speedy salvation, and thus bring it about immediately.

Thus, at the end of the Song of the Sea, when the Jewish people prayed to be brought to the Land of Israel they were praying for something immediate. While they knew that God would eventually bring them to the Land of Israel and to the holy Temple, they were praying that it not be a long and drawn-out process. "O bring them and plant them on the mountain You possess. . . . The Temple, O God,

Your hands have founded." God's expressed promise to bring them to the Land of Israel had been tied to the promise of redemption from Egypt. The Exodus and the Crossing of the Red Sea had already, so successfully, been brought down into the world of Action through the active visualization of the observance of commandments. And so, they prayed that God's promise to bring the people into the Land of Israel should also be manifest in the world of Action, also brought into being by the observance of God's commandments. The world of Action is, so to speak, the world of God's hands. "The Temple, O God, Your hands have founded."

# *Metzorah*—April 13, 1940

*"When you come to the land of Canaan, which I am giving to you as an inheritance, I will place the mark of the leprous curse in houses in the land you inherit."* (Leviticus 14:34)

    Rashi (ibid.) explains: "This amounted to an announcement that the plague would definitely come upon them. The Emorites concealed all their treasures in the walls of their houses during the forty years the Jewish people were in the wilderness. They hid it there so that when Israel conquered Canaan, they would find no treasure. As a consequence of the plague of leprosy befalling their houses, Jews would be forced to demolish the stricken walls and discover the treasure."

    Let us try to understand. If the plague is purely beneficial, why does the Torah (Leviticus 14:38–40) command that a house first be locked up for seven days, and only afterwards, if the leprous spot persists, are the stones of the wall removed and replaced? Surely, once the leprous mark becomes visible it should be obvious that treasure is buried there. This should be even more obvious when, as Nachmanides explains, and as is quoted in the holy writings of his holiness, my teacher, my father, of blessed memory, (Divrei Elimelech, p. 275) the leprosy that affects houses and garments is an unnatural occurrence. If this was so, then the leprous plague existed only for the benefit of the Jewish people, in order to reveal the whereabouts of buried treasure. Why then does the Torah tell us that the house is *tameh*, ritually unclean for seven days?

    We cannot conceive of what the Torah intends with its commandments, but it is possible that it hints the following: We know and have faith that everything

God does to us—even when, God forbid, He is punishing us—is for the good. There are times, however, when we are smitten not only with physical suffering but also with things that, God forbid, distance us from Him, blessed be He. There is no *cheder* (schoolroom) for our children, no yeshiva, no synagogue in which to pray with a *minyan* (quorum), no *mikveh* (ritual bath), and so forth. In times such as this, God forbid, uneasy doubts may arise within us, asking how it is possible that even now God's intention is for our benefit. If it were for the good, surely He would be punishing us with things that draw us closer to Him, and not with the annihilation of Torah and prayer and, God forbid, the end of almost all the Torah. Is it possible that this is the kind of suffering about which it is written (Deut. 29:27), "God drove them from their land with anger, rage, and great fury, and He exiled them to another land, where they remain even today"?

Therefore, it is explicitly taught in the Torah that even though the leprous mark on the houses was *tameh* (unclean) and could make people *tameh*, God still made of it an instrument for the good of the Jewish people. First it was *tameh* for seven days, and only then was the treasure revealed. And so the law states: A person must say, "It looks to me as if there is [something] like a [leprous] mark in the house." (Leviticus 14:35) Even if he is a scholar and knows the exact definition of a leprous mark, he must still use the phrase "like a leprous mark."—for, as we said above, a person is never able to tell whether what is happening to him is a curse or an event. All he can say is that it looks like a curse. The truth however, as the Torah announces, is that what God is doing with us is for the good of Israel.

# *Kedoshim*—May 4, 1940

*"You must be sanctified and be holy, because I am God your Lord."* (Leviticus 20:7)

We learn in the Talmud (*Berachoth* 28b): "When R. Yohanan b. Zakkai fell ill, his disciples went in to visit him. When he saw them he began to weep. . . . They said to him, 'Master, bless us.' He said to them, 'May it be God's will that the fear of heaven be upon you like the fear of flesh and blood.' His disciples said to him, 'Is that all?' He said to them, 'If only you can attain this! You should know, when a man wants to commit a transgression, he says, "I hope no one will see me."'"

Let us understand. Is it possible, God forbid, that R. Yohanan b. Zakkai's exalted and holy disciples, the holy *tannaim* (teachers) of the Mishnah, did not fear heaven more than flesh and blood? How are we to understand R. Yohanan b. Zakkai's words to them, "You should know, when a man wants to commit a transgression, he says, 'I hope no man will see me'"? What connection could such a statement have to such holy disciples as R. Eliezer the Great, R. Joshua b. Hananiah, and R. Eleazar b. Arach, as is detailed in the Mishnah (*Avoth*. 2:8)? We have heard of the saints of the generation, and especially of my holy grandfather the Rebbe, Reb Elimelech of Lyzhensk and his holy brother the Rebbe, Reb Zusia of Anipoli, of blessed memory, that they felt the fear of God that angels have.

It is difficult to understand how R. Yohanan b. Zakkai could have blessed his disciples that God grant them fear of heaven. How can this be, when we have learned in the Talmud (*Megillah* 25a) "Everything is in the hands of heaven except the fear of heaven?"

It is well known that no Jewish person is ever utterly excluded from the totality (II Kings 14:14). When a person comes to a nadir, God forbid, and is about to commit some transgression—especially if this will cause his exclusion, God forbid—then God does not abandon him. We have learned in sacred literature that the *miluy* of the three Hebrew letters *yud-tzadi-resh* comprising the word *yetzer* (inclination) are (*Y*) *vav daleth*, (*Tz*) *daleth yud*, and (*R*) *yud shin*. The last letters of the *miluy* are the three letters of the name of God, *Shaddai* (*shin daleth yud*). In order that the person does not succumb entirely to his inclination, God forbid, the Holy Name *Shaddai* is there at the end. When the person reaches the end, God does not allow him to fall any further.

Therefore, it is conceivable to bless a Jewish person with the fear that, God forbid, he not succumb completely to sin, because the prevention of such a tragedy is indeed in the hands of the Holy Blessed One. However, it is not possible to bless someone with exalted fear, because such fear is entirely in the hands of the person himself; he must rise to it. So when his disciples said to R. Yohanan b. Zakkai, "Master, bless us," he saw their intention, which was that he should bless them with the fear of heaven. He replied that he could only bless them with fear that they not commit a low transgression, and that they themselves would have to rise to a higher, more elevated fear.

This is the meaning of the verse (Deut. 10:12), "And now, Israel, what does God want of you? Only that you remain in awe of God your Lord, so that you follow all His paths and love Him, serving God your Lord with all your heart and with all your soul." God can give you fear that you should not commit a low transgression, but what does God want of you? Fear that you will follow all His paths and love Him, serving Him with all your heart and with all your soul, which means rising much higher in all spiritual matters.

Similarly, when God punishes the Jewish person, God forbid, His intention is not that the person be excluded, but that he repent and return to Him. But because suffering makes it difficult for him to rise higher, the person must therefore arouse within himself the desire and the longing to elevate himself; he must try his best, and make an effort to raise himself. Then, whether he succeeds or whether, God forbid, he does not succeed, he still sweetens the judgment. This is because God's intention is not that the person should remain in this lower state of fear that he not sin, as we have already said. The intention and purpose of the Holy Blessed One is not just that the Jewish person not be damaged, but that, through this lower fear, he should rise to an exalted fear. The question is: Is he being elevated, or is the opposite happening—through suffering he becomes broken and sinks, unable to rise?

We can now understand our original text, "You must sanctify yourselves and be holy, because I am God your Lord," to mean that you must always long for a greater holiness, and indeed make a greater and greater effort even if you are already holy. You will then find that "I am *YHVH*, God (*Elohim*)"—that *Elohim*, Judgement, has already become *YHVH*, Mercy.

# *Emor*—May 11, 1940

*"You shall then count seven complete weeks after the day following the Sabbath; from the day you brought the* omer *as a wave offering until the day after the seventh Sabbath, count fifty days."* (Leviticus 23:15–16)

There is a well-known teaching in the Talmud (*Menachoth* 65b): "The Sadducees, who rejected the Oral Torah, asserted that according to the text quoted above, the Counting of the *Omer* should always begin on the day after the first Sabbath following Passover. Our Rabbis taught 'the day following the Sabbath' means the day following the first day of the Passover Festival."

We need to understand what the verse is hinting when it calls the Passover Festival "Sabbath."

It is possible, as we learn in the Talmud (*Avodah Zarah* 29b); R. Judah said: "R. Ishmael put this question to R. Joshua as they were on a journey. 'Why,' asked he, 'have they prohibited the cheese of heathens?' He replied, "Because they curdle it with the rennet of *nevelah* (a nonkosher animal). He retorted: "But is not the rennet of a burnt-offering more strictly forbidden than the rennet of *nevelah*? [And yet] it was said that a priest who is not fastidious may suck it out raw?' 'The reason then,' [R. Joshua said,] 'is because they curdle it with the rennet from calves sacrificed to idols.' Said he, 'If that be so, why do they not extend the prohibition to forbid any benefit derived from it at all?' He, however, diverted the topic to another matter, saying, 'Ishmael, my brother, how do you read this verse (Cant. 1:2): "For his love is better than wine," or do you read it "For her love is better than wine"? R. Ishmael replied, 'For her love is better than wine.' 'Not so,' he retorted, "as is proven by the adjacent verse (Cant. 1:3), "His ointments have a goodly fragrance.""

It is taught later in the Talmud (*Avodah Zarah* 35a) that R. Joshua "diverted the topic to another matter" because the prohibition against the cheese manufactured by heathens was a new ordinance, about which one should not particularize. When an ordinance was passed in Palestine, its reason was not revealed before a full year passed, lest there be some who might not agree with the rationale and who would therefore treat the ordinance casually.

The Talmud also explains the subtlety in R. Joshua's diversion of the topic to another matter. R. Ishmael interpreted the verse from "Song of Songs" to mean the following: "The Congregation of Israel begs God for more Torah, saying, 'Kiss me with kisses of Your mouth,' adding, 'Because You, God, have said about us, the Congregation of Israel, "for her love is better than wine."'" R. Joshua uses the verse to imply that the teachings of the Rabbis, their rulings and prohibitions, are more authoritative than the rulings of the Torah itself. He takes the Hebrew word *dodecha*, usually translated to mean "love," and translates it as "friends." He then interprets the verse as follows: "The Congregation of Israel says about the Holy Blessed One, 'For His friends are better than wine,' i.e., sweeter are the words of His friends, the sages, than the wine of the Written Torah itself."

Let us try to understand. If the reason for a new ordinance is not to be revealed before a full year passes, why did R. Ishmael ask his question immediately upon hearing of the new ordinance? If he was asking only because he personally wanted to know the reason, and did not intend to reveal it to others, why then did R. Joshua not enlighten him? If it was permissible for R. Joshua to know the rationale, should not R. Ishmael also have the right to know? Why, in order to change the subject, did R. Joshua use this particular verse from the "Song of Songs"? The Talmud (*Avodah Zarah* 35a) says that R. Joshua was actually hinting to the beginning of the verse, "Kiss me with kisses of Your mouth," saying, "Ishmael, my brother, press your lips one to the other and do not be so eager to ask for an answer." But if that is so, we still need to understand why he quoted the end of the verse, and not the beginning.

We observe unquestioningly, as statutes, all the commandments of God that are taught in the Torah. Even laws that appear to have a rational explanation are observed not because we understand them but in order to fulfill the decree of the King, as is explained in sacred literature. It might, however be thought otherwise regarding the ordinances of the rabbis, which are a fence around the Torah to guard us from breaking its laws. It might be argued that a person should only fulfill a rabbinical ordinance when he understands the reason for it, because if he does not understand it, its very purpose is defeated. Since its purpose is only ever to guard against infringement of a scriptural commandment, if a person does not understand the reason for the ordinance (to observe the scriptural commandment) how then can we say that he has fulfilled the rabbinical ordinance?

The truth, however, is quite different. God teaches Torah to His people Israel—and not only does God teach it, He actually gives away the Torah to them, giving them the power to enact commandments. Scriptural commandments are segments as it were, of the body of His Majesty the King. Since the Jewish people are connected to the body of the King—the Holy Blessed One, the Torah, and the Jewish people are One—therefore, when they are bound up with the Holy Blessed One, their desire and knowing and soul can also become commandments.

As the Talmud (*Rosh Hashanah* 25a), quoting R. Akiba, says: "The text (Leviticus 22:31, 23:2, and 23:4) repeats the words 'you,' 'you,' 'you,' three times, to indicate that 'you,' the Jewish people, determine the Festival dates even if you err inadvertently; 'you,' even if you err deliberately, and 'you,' even when you are misled."

And so, we make the blessing, "Blessed are You, God, King of the universe, Who has sanctified us with His commandments . . ." even over rabbinical commandments. We have already discussed how ordinances, although enacted from the outset by the sages in order to put a fence around the Torah, nevertheless become Torah commandments themselves once decreed. An example is the observance throughout the Diaspora of the additional days of Festivals. Even though we know perfectly well how to calculate the calendar, and we know on which day the Festival is observed in the Land of Israel, we still observe the added Festival day. We refrain on those days from donning *t'fillin* (phylacteries) even though *t'fillin* are a Scriptural commandment. Even though it was only enacted as an exigency during a period of difficulty in communicating decisions of the High Court, which adjusted the calendar for Jews living in the Diaspora, once the sages decreed the additional Festival day, the decree itself became a commandment, as we have explained above.

This may be what is being hinted at in the Talmud quoted above: R. Ishmael wanted R. Joshua to reveal the reason for the ordinance forbidding the consumption of the cheese of the heathens, because if people do not know the reason for the ordinance they are not observing the commandment properly, as we said above. R. Joshua answered him with the verse (Song of Songs 1:2) "For His friends are better than wine," meaning "Sweeter are the words of His friends, the sages, than the wine of the Torah itself."

The ordinances enacted by the sages are valid not simply because they put a fence around the Torah; they themselves become commandments, and are even sweeter than the wine of the Torah itself. So, even if a person does not understand the reason for a rabbinical ordinance, and how it creates a fence around the Torah, observance of the ordinance in and of itself fulfills a commandment.

The rule just concluded applies to every Jew, proportionate to his level of worship. His knowing, his desire, and his soul generate commandments.

In the name of his holiness, my teacher, my grandfather, the Rebbe of Magolnitze we have learned the following. "Whatever *kavanot* (meditative intentions) a Jew decides upon for use in his worship of God, those *kavanot* become the proper and appropriate ones."

Even if a person cannot integrate into his worship the *kavanot* specified by the Arizal (R. Isaac Luria), nonetheless if his thoughts come from his heart and soul to God, at his level of knowing and with his desire, then these are the proper and appropriate thoughts. Everything is dependent upon the level to which he negates and nullifies himself before God. The more he feels the nothingness of himself before God, blessed be He, the more divine his very essence becomes, until divine commandments actually flow from him. This is why when, God forbid, there is a time of suffering, we wonder what good can come of it, for (to the contrary) people are not busy with the Torah as they once were, and even those commandments that are observed are no longer performed with *kavanot* (pure intentions). It is understood however, that at such times the self-abnegation before God is greater, because it is obvious that no one but the Holy Blessed One can save us. So, provided everything that can be done to fulfill our obligations is done, this nullification brings about closeness to Him, until all our deeds and words and thoughts to God become commandments.

Now, even though with the observance of every commandment we say, "Blessed are You, God, King of the universe, Who has sanctified us with His commandments . . ." with the Counting of the *Omer*, our sanctification is special and unique. First of all we sanctify ourselves in the details of each of the seven *Midoth* (Divine Attributes), which are Loving, Fearing, Truth, Beginning, Ending, Joining, and Being (in Hebrew *Gedulah, Gevurah, Tifferet, Netzach, Hod, Yesod,* and *Malchut*). We sanctify ourselves in each of the *Midoth* during each of the seven weeks of the *Omer*—but we do not stop there, for just as there is a commandment to count weeks there is a commandment to count days, and so we sanctify ourselves in the specifics of all *Midoth*. During the first week, which is the week of the Divine Attribute of Loving, we sanctify all seven facets of Loving: Love of Loving, Fear of Loving, Truth of Loving, Beginning Loving, Ending Loving, Joining of Loving, and the Being of Loving. The second week of the *Omer* is a sanctification of the second of the Divine Attributes, Fearing: Love of Fearing, Fear of Fearing, Truth of Fearing, etc. All of this sanctification makes the Jew so holy that every part of him becomes a commandment.

This explains why the Torah calls the Passover Festival "Sabbath." Generally speaking, the Jewish Festivals are holy only because the Jewish people sanctify them, making them holy. But the Sabbath is fixed and eternal because God sanctifies the Sabbath, as we say frequently in the Liturgy of the Sabbath, "Blessed are You, God, Who sanctifies the Sabbath." Through our sanctification with the Counting of the *Omer*, the Festival of Passover that we sanctify also merits to be called "Sabbath."

# B'Har—May 18, 1940

"God spoke to Moses at Mount Sinai, telling him to speak to the Israelites and say to them: 'When you come to the land that I am giving you, the land must be given a rest period, a Sabbath to God. For six years you may plant your fields, prune your vineyards, and harvest your crops, but the seventh year is a Sabbath of Sabbaths for the land. It is God's Sabbath, during which you may not plant your fields nor prune your vineyards. Do not harvest crops that grow on their own and do not gather the grapes on your untrimmed vines, since it is a year of rest for the land.'" (Leviticus 25:1–5)

Rashi (ibid.) asks, "What has the matter of the *sh'mittah* (sabbatical year) to do with Mount Sinai?" He answers: "Just as all commandments—their general rules and all their specific details—were ordained on Mount Sinai, so, the law of *sh'mittah*, its general rules, specific proscriptions, and minute details, were all ordained on Mount Sinai."

In the "Song of Songs" the verse twice says, ". . . and my Beloved is mine," (Cant. 2:16, 6:3) while a third verse later states, ". . . and His desire is for me." (Cant. 7:11) Surely, it ought to say first, "His desire is for me," the desire of the Holy Blessed One is for me, and only afterwards ". . . My Beloved is mine," not just that His desire is for me, but that He, God, is mine?

When a Jew throws himself upon the Holy Blessed One even though he may not merit that God, as it were, give Himself in return, and even though God was not longing for him, nevertheless God gives Himself to that person. God does this because of the covenant He made with our fathers and with us at Sinai. But when a person gives himself over to God again and again, saying, "I am my Beloved's . . ." then God, blessed be He, draws close not only because of the covenant that binds Him to the person at the level of "My Beloved is mine," but also because "His desire is for me." God's longing for the individual grows. The same applies to the individual Jew who may not yet feel desire at the level of "His desire is for me." Even though his desire has not yet reached the level of longing to give himself to the Holy Blessed One, nevertheless when he gives and then gives himself again, his longing for God is awakened.

When, God forbid, the Jewish people are suffering, and especially in the agony that currently prevails, when it is apparent that neither they themselves nor anyone else can save them—that only He, blessed be He is able to save them—then it is obvious that they have already given themselves over to God wholeheartedly and with longing.

Nonetheless, we must inculcate into our memories and our very selves remembrance of the awesome situation we are enduring in our distress. We must never forget how we tremble with longing, saying, "If only God would save me, I would worship him, I would pray, and I would learn so much Torah," and so forth. We are not referring to fools who think, "If only God would save me, I might do successful business and eat more." While it is true that God must send salvation to the Jewish people even in matters of commerce and nutrition, it is not for the sake of these things that one longs for salvation. The agony with which God chastises us is not for the purposes of commerce or nutrition. We must long for salvation so that we may worship Him more than before. We need to take the great anguish and bitterness we endure, together with our longing to be saved and to worship, and fasten them inside ourselves, for the rest of our lives and the lives of our children.

This might explain why even before leaving Egypt we ate bitter herbs with the Paschal lamb. Today, in the liturgy of the Passover *Haggadah*, we say that the bitter herbs are in memory of the embittered lives our ancestors led in Egypt, but at first, we were still there in Egypt. Why before leaving Egypt did we need any reminders? The answer is simply this: They who experienced slavery and redemption needed to consume their bitterness, to integrate it into themselves, so that they would remember forever, long after being redeemed, the bitterness they endured and the yoke of heaven to which they submitted at that time.

It is true that there are people who say to themselves, "How have I sinned, and why should I submit to any more? Do I not put on *t'fillin*, God forbid? Or do I not observe the Sabbath, God forbid?" However, we need to remind ourselves that it also depends upon how we put on *t'fillin*, how we pray, how we spend the Sabbath, and how we occupy ourselves with Torah. We must remember that it was also about the fine details of the commandments that God held the mountain like a barrel over the Jewish people, saying, "If you accept the Torah, 'tis well; if not, there shall be your burial." (Talmud *Shabbath* 88a)

We learn in the Midrash (*Tanchuma*, Noah:2) that when God held the mountain over the Jewish people, His concern was with their committing to strict observance of the Oral Torah, even though they had already announced (Exodus 24:7), "We will do and we will listen." This was because the Oral Torah contains so many exacting details. Furthermore, God's holding the mountain over the people cannot have been just about the parts of the Oral Torah that explain the Written Torah in detail, for those are in essence the Written Torah. How would we know how to observe the commandment to "bind them as a sign upon your arm" (Deut. 6:8) if the sages had not explained for us in the Oral Torah that it refers to *t'fillin*? How could we have said "We will do and we will listen," if a detailed explanation of our obligations was not included? No, it was the decrees and fences the sages added, those not mentioned at all in the Written Torah, that were intended when God held the mountain over the people. We see how strict are the demands about this matter.

The Talmud teaches that in this world, there is no reward given for observing the commandments. But I have seen somewhere in the sacred literature—I seem to remember it was in the writings of the Maharsha, of blessed memory—that a reward is given for those additional fences and barriers around the Torah that a person might take upon himself to observe, in order to protect it.

This is why the Torah hints that all the details and minutiae of the Torah are from Sinai, and it was about these details that Mount Sinai was held over the people like a barrel. If they would observe and fulfill all the details of the commandments, then, the Torah promises, "For six years you will plant your fields, prune your vineyards, and harvest your crops." The Torah promises field and vineyard, work, sufficient bread, and all good things, because reward is assured in this world for observance of the details.

## B'Chukothai—May 25, 1940

*"Turning toward you, I will increase you . . . I will lead you forth with your heads held high."* (Leviticus 26:9–13)

On the previous Sabbath, we examined the verse from "Song of Songs" (Cant. 6:3) in which the Children of Israel say of God, "I am my Beloved's and my Beloved is mine." The question we asked was why we first assert a number of times, "My Beloved is mine," and only later in the text (Cant. 7:11) do we say, "His longing is for me." In the earlier assertion the Children of Israel seem to be saying, "God already belongs to us." The later verse would thus seem to belong more appropriately before the earlier one, indicating as it does that while His desire is for us, He has not yet given Himself to us.

Aside from what we said last Sabbath, there is another way of interpreting the song. First though, one must point out another matter requiring clarification. In saying "His longing is for me," the verse uses the Hebrew word *ally*, usually translated as "upon me." Why not use the more appropriate Hebrew word *ay-ly*, which translates as "toward me" or "for me"? It would make more sense to say "His longing is for me," as in the words of God to Cain (Genesis 4:7), "Sin crouches by the door. Its longing is for you. . . ."

It is thus: When "I am my Beloved's and my Beloved is mine," it is our human longing for God that brings our Beloved close. The level of intensity of our desire for God and our adequacy, are all that determine the extent of our closeness to Him. When, however, we give ourselves to God again and again, this calls forth

God's longing for us, and then it becomes "His longing is upon me." The desire becomes God's desire, and not merely a connection brought about through our longing. This is why the text says "upon me" rather than "toward me." When His desire for us is aroused, it goes beyond the simple reflection described in the verse (Proverbs 27:19), "For as water reflects the face to the face, so reflects the heart of man to the man." God's longing is not simply "for" me; it is now also "upon" me, much greater than I. And not only is God's longing now greater than mine, but I, myself, have grown greater than I was. God's longing is upon me, and His desire is so much greater than I, that I become greater than myself.

This might be the meaning in the event described in the Talmud (*Berachoth* 61b): "Rabbi Akiba was reciting the *Sh'ma*, accepting upon himself the yoke of heaven, while his flesh was being raked with iron combs. His students called to him, asking, 'Thus far?' Rabbi Akiba replied, 'All my days I have been at pains over this verse in the *Sh'ma* (Deut. 6:5) "Love God your Lord with all your heart, with all your soul, and with all your might." "When will I ever have the opportunity to fulfill it properly?" I asked myself. Right now, when I have the opportunity to love God with all my soul, should I not realize it?'"

Why was Rabbi Akiba at pains, longing for his martyrdom, to give up his soul for the love of God? If all he wanted was to do the will of God all the days of his life, he could do so by learning Torah, through worship, through observance of the commandments, and so forth. Even if he believed that martyrdom is the greatest commandment of all, if God does not bring about the circumstances of martyrdom in a person's life, life nevertheless presents so many other opportunities to fulfill Torah commandments and to worship God, so why be at pains over it?

Together with what we have said before, the explanation may be as follows: Rabbi Akiba is quoted in the Mishnah at the end of *Yoma* (*Yoma* 8:9), "Lucky are you, Israel! Before Whom are you purifying yourselves, and Who is purifying you? Your Father in heaven. . . ."

The meaning is clear. There is a sequence: First the Children of Israel must attempt to purify themselves, and then God purifies them. So ardent was R. Akiba's desire to have God sanctify and purify him that he attained the level of "His longing is upon me." When this happened, R. Akiba became much greater than himself. He began to experience a longing to worship more powerful than that which he alone could attain, to the point where his longing became pain—pain that he was not able to give his life and soul completely to God.

R. Akiba also said something important with his statement "All my days I have been at pains . . ." During his lifetime, every Jew has moments, even hours, of great devotion. R. Akiba told his disciples that for him, intensity of worship and the longing to give over his soul were not momentary and fleeting, but "All my days."

A person must imbue everything with "I am my Beloved's." Before anything else, he must observe the Torah and the commandments in thought, speech, and deed. He must know and understand that his main purpose and function in this world is to observe the Torah and the commandments; to be a Jew—that it was for this that God created him. This does not apply just to a person who can make Torah his vocation but to anyone, even one who spends most of his day engaged in business and worldly activities and can only find a few hours for study and prayer. That person can still make study and prayer his reason for being, though he has only a few hours to engage in it. If he puts his whole self into it, it becomes the focus and function of his whole life. A person spends only about an hour each day eating, and most of his time working and doing business, and yet eating is a focus of his life.

We must give ourselves entirely over to God with all our energy, especially in a time of great distress, God forbid. We need to be aware that salvation is not just necessary for us as people, but that as Jews we also desperately need help. Everything depends upon God, and without God there can be no salvation. So when a Jew gives himself over to God again and again, he arouses God's longing and reaches the level of "His longing is upon me." "Upon me" refers to God's longing, which elevates us to become greater than ourselves, both physically and spiritually, as people and as Jews.

This is why the verse in our weekly portion first says "I will turn to you," meaning "I will face you, 'as water reflects the face to the face.'" God is saying: "As much as you are drawn toward Me, so will I be drawn toward you, at your level." Then comes the second part of the verse, "I will lead you forth with your heads held high," because once God desires us, we grow to be much greater than we were, at the level of "upon me."

# *Naso*—June 8, 1940

*"God spoke to Moses, telling him to speak to Aaron and his sons, saying:*
*'This is how you must bless the Jewish people. Say to them:*
*"May God bless you and keep watch over you.*
*"May God make His presence enlighten you and grant you grace.*
*"May God direct His countenance toward you and grant you peace."*
*They will put My name upon the Jewish people and I will bless them.'"*
(Numbers 6:22–27)

We need to understand what this is hinting to us. Why must Aaron and his descendants bless the Jews with the blessing that God bless them? As the verse states, "They will put My name upon the Jewish people, and I will bless them," it is obviously God Who blesses the people. Furthermore, what is the meaning of "They will put My name upon the Jewish people"? What needed to be added, after the blessing was so specifically spelled out?

Rashi's explanations (ibid.) are well known: "And I will bless them" means "I will give my approval to the priestly blessings." Another explanation quoted from the Talmud (*Hullin* 49a) says, "And I will bless the priests."

The Tosaphists (*Shabbath* 88a) ask: "Why at the giving of the Torah did the Jewish people need to have the mountain held over them, when they had already said 'We will do and we will listen'?" The Tosaphists answer: "Perhaps they might recant, because of their fear at seeing the fire." We need to understand why, if this was so, the mountain was not held over them before they said, "We will do and we will listen." Surely there was more reason to suspect they might not accept the Torah in the first instance, than to recant for fear of the fire, after already having said, "We will do and we will listen"?

A simple interpretation, applicable to our situation, is that it was only during the actual event, at the receiving of the Torah, that their innate corruption, the self-seeking brought about by the original sin of Adam and Eve, was removed. Only at that moment, when their bodies and their lives were as nothing, were they able to fully accept the Torah, even while a mountain was held threateningly over them and they were told, "If you accept the Torah, 'tis well; if not, there shall be your burial." (*Shabbath* 88a) Before the events at Sinai however, because they were not yet relieved of their innate corruption, they were still physical, human beings. No matter how saintly they were, even when saying in the manner of angels, "We will do and we will listen," they were yet unable to accept the Torah when frightened to death. So, God did not hold the mountain over them beforehand. It was only later, when their taint was removed and they were completely nullified as human beings, when their bodies did not matter to them at all, that they were able to accept even as they were being coerced.

We have already spoken about the teaching from the holy book, *Tanna D'Bai Eliyahu*, that says that the Torah is for the sake of Israel. What this really means is that by observing the commandments alone the Jew does not fulfill his obligation. His duty is done only if the observance transforms him into a Jew, as it is written, "And you will be for Me a kingdom of priests and a holy nation." (Exodus 19:6) The real meaning of the verse is that you, your essential self, will be entirely given over to God. This is why the Jewish person must serve God by putting all his attributes, his nature, and his disposition into the service of holiness.

My grandfather, the righteous, holy Rabbi of Lublin, of blessed memory, cites the following parable in his book *Zot Zikharon*, in the name of the Great and Holy Maggid of Mezeritch, of blessed memory. "When a person, before praying, seeks to awaken within himself love for God, he should remind himself of the love that he already has—for example, for his children or his possessions. When he feels his love is aroused, he should remind himself of God, of His greatness and of the goodness of all that God has done for him, and then his love for God, blessed be He, will also be awakened." This means that even mundane love, such as that which a person has for his material possessions, can be elevated to become love of God.

In the sacred literature on the verse (Exodus 10:26) in which Moses speaks to Pharaoh regarding the livestock of the Jewish people, "We must also take of them to serve God our Lord," we learn that in order to serve God, we must take also from the animal in ourselves, as this transforms darkness into light and bitter into sweet.

It is impossible to do this when we are suffering, God forbid. And this is why we pray to God that He redeem us with loving-kindness.

My holy, sainted father of blessed memory, comments on the verse from the daily liturgy, "Requite us with loving-kindness." "Everything the Holy Blessed One does for us is kindness, but we pray 'Requite us with the sort of kindness that will also seem loving to us.'"

We pray for this because even though we keep commandments, if we are crushed, God forbid, then an essential part of ourselves is not observing the commandment. For how is it possible to study the Torah when every head is stricken? Is it possible to be inflamed with passions of the heart when every heart is broken, God forbid?

"My strength and song is God, and this is my deliverance. This is my God; I will enshrine Him. My father's God; I will exalt Him." ("Song of the Sea," Exodus 15:2) Because He has delivered me totally, because I feel so good and can savor the redemption, it is possible for me to sing, "This is my God," the God whom the essential self of me wants to worship. He is "my father's God; I will exalt Him." At this level of joy and freedom, I am not satisfied with the holiness and worship that was given to me as an inheritance from my fathers, but more than this, "I will exalt Him."

This could be the meaning of the well-known saying: Every generation is appropriate to its leaders, and the leaders are appropriate to the generation. Why must the leader be appropriate to the generation? So that he can be close to them in their desires and needs, in order to help them devote their essential, individual selves to the worship of God. Then the salvation that God causes to flow upon them will not be suspended above their level, pertaining only to spiritual matters, but will become concrete, and appropriate to them and their essential, individual, and physical needs.

As we learn in the writings of my father, (*Divrei Elimelech*, p. 154) about the talmudic teaching (*Berachoth* 9a) on the verse (Exodus 11:2), "Speak, please, in the ears of the people. Let each person request of his friend vessels of silver and gold," the Holy Blessed One said to Moses: "I beg of you, go and tell the Children of Israel to request from the Egyptians vessels of silver and gold, so that Abraham the Righteous should not have cause to complain, saying, 'You promised that my descendants would be slaves in a strange land, and fulfilled Your promise, but the promise that they would leave with great wealth, You have not kept.'" About this talmudic teaching, my father asked the following: What if Abraham had not complained, would then the Holy Blessed One not have had to keep His promise?" He answers, "God could have given them great wealth without monetary value; it could have been spiritual riches. But because of his promise to our father Abraham, and so that Abraham should not have cause to complain, He also made sure we left Egypt with gold and silver."

Returning to the original text we quoted, "This is how you must bless the Jewish people . . .": It is true that the *cohen* (priests) must bless them, but the blessing must become concrete. So God commanded, "Put My name upon the Jewish people." This was to ensure that the blessings not remain abstract and good only in a heavenly sense, but that they also take care of their physical needs, because they are human and need physical salvation. This is explained by Rashi, in his commentary on this verse: "Bless them with children, bless them with money, etc."

# *Shavuoth* (Festival of Weeks)—June 12, 1940

*"May Your loving-kindness be my comfort, like Your words to Your servant. May Your mercies come to me, that I may live; for Your Torah is my joy."*
(Psalms 119:76–78)

The phrase "like Your words to Your servant" in this context means God speaking to King David directly or through the prophets. But, since every Jew recites psalms, we need to understand exactly what for us, personally, is the meaning of "like Your words to Your servant."

In the account of the revelation on Sinai, it is written (Exodus 20:15): "And all the people saw the sounds." Rashi explains: "They saw that which should only be heard, which would be impossible on any other occasion."

Let us understand: For what purpose did God show them this miracle? It is easier to understand God's reason for showing fire and smoke, as it is written in the verse (Exodus 20:17), "His fear will then be on your faces." That, however, is not why God showed us what should only be heard.

According to our limited understanding, it might be suggested as follows. God, blessed be He, is the teacher of Torah to His people Israel. The giving of the Torah was not only a giving or a saying, but also a teaching. Our teacher Moses taught the whole Torah, while God, blessed be He, taught the Ten Commandments. As we learn in the Midrash (*Mechilta, Yithro* 20:1), when God said "yes" we said "yes" and when He said "no" we said "no." But because the Ten Commandments are the Written Torah, and we know from the Talmud (*Gittin* 60b) that it is forbidden to teach the Written Torah orally, God showed them the sounds so that it would not be an oral teaching.

The giving of the Torah was also a teaching that God learned together with us. This is hinted at in the last verse of *Parshat Naso* (Numbers 7:89), "When Moses came into the Communion Tent to speak with [God], he heard the Voice speaking to him from between the two cherubs on the ark cover over the Ark of Testimony. [God] thus spoke to him." Commenting on the phrase, "He heard the Voice speaking to him," Rashi (ibid.) says: "The Hebrew word *medaber* (speaking) in this context is the same as *mitdaber* (spoken), and so the verse reads, 'He heard the Voice spoken.'" "Out of respect for Heaven," the Torah is saying, "God was speaking to Himself and Moses overheard it."

A simple explanation could be, as we learn in the Talmud (*Megillah* 16a) on the verse (Esther 7:5), "Then spoke the King Ahasuerus, and he spoke to Esther the queen." "The word 'spoke' appears twice, because first he spoke to her through an intermediary. This was because he thought Esther was a commoner. When, however, Ahasuerus heard that Esther was a scion of the royal house of King Saul, he spoke to her directly." Even though he had taken her to be his wife and queen, she did not merit being spoken to directly until he discovered that she also was of royal lineage.

There is a teaching from the Baal Shem Tov, of blessed memory, on the verse (Cant. 5:6) "My soul went out when he spoke," that part of the soul of the speaker leaves at the time of speaking. It follows, then, that there must be some reciprocity between the essential soul of the speaker and that of the listener, because it is not just speech that is issuing from the mouth of the speaker, but also part of the essence of his soul. Therefore, so long as Ahasuerus did not know that Esther was of royal lineage, that not only was she a queen now but was quintessentially aristocratic, he did not speak to her. Since temporal royalty is but a reflection of the Heavenly Kingdom, therefore, despite the greatness of our teacher Moses, God was still speaking between Him and Himself, and Moses only overheard Him. This is the explanation of the phrase quoted above, "Out of respect for Heaven . . ."

Often the Torah will begin with the phrase "God said to Moses," "Speak to the children of Israel," or "Say to Aaron." How can God have been speaking to Himself? It may perhaps be as follows: Just as the creation of the world was done through the Torah, so all God's speech to our teacher Moses was also done through the Torah. So, when the Torah writes, "God spoke to Moses, saying, 'Speak to the children of Israel,'" and so forth, the Holy Blessed One was repeating these verses in the Torah between Him and Himself, while our teacher Moses overheard it and understood.

This means that there was a difference between those times when God was teaching Moses together with the whole Jewish people and those times when

God was learning only with Moses. When the Holy Blessed One learned the Torah with Moses together with the Jewish people, He did not just learn it between Him and Himself, but spoke with them and directly to them. God spoke between Him and Himself for Moses to overhear only when He was learning with Moses alone. When He learned with the people, however, He spoke to them, and herein is the greatness of the connection between God and the Jewish people at the time of the receiving of the Torah. Because God spoke to them, and connected Himself to them, it was the essence of the Speaker connecting with them. It was the very essence of "I" in the phrase "I am God your Lord." The Hebrew word for "I" in the first of the Ten Commandments is *Anochi* rather than *Ani*. *Anochi* is a *notariqon*, an Aramaic acrostic, reading *Ani Nafshai Katavit Yahavit*, "I My Soul have Written and Given." God has, so to speak, written and given His Soul. "My soul," so to speak, is revealed to the Jewish people through the Torah that God taught us.

There are times when the accusers grow strong, God forbid, and overpower the Jewish people, and it is difficult for the Jewish people to be rescued. At such times God, blessed be He, reveals His essence, and all accusations are silenced. This is what happened on the night of the Exodus from Egypt during the Slaying of the Firstborn (Exodus 12:12), when God said, "I will pass through Egypt this night, and I will smite every firstborn in the land of Egypt from man to animal. I will do judgments against all gods of the Egyptians. I am God."

Therefore, at Shavuoth, the anniversary of the giving of the Torah—and whenever we learn Torah—it is a time of salvation. At such a time, no accuser, God forbid, can overpower Israel, because God, blessed be He, is speaking with us, and the very essence of "I" (*Anochi*) is being revealed. This, then, is the meaning of the verse from Psalms with which we opened the chapter, "May Your loving-kindness be my comfort, like Your words to Your servant." The phrase, "Like Your words to Your servant" means not as God speaking between Him and Himself, but "as You spoke at the Revelation on Sinai when you spoke to me directly,"—"for Your Torah is my joy," and You are speaking to me.

※

>"A Song of Ascents. I will lift up my eyes unto the mountains. From where will come my help? My help comes from God, Who made heaven and earth."
>(Psalms 121:1)

Let us try to understand what it means to ask, "From where will come my help?" We know that He, blessed be He, is the One Who saves. Why do we need to qualify the answer with the phrase "Who made heaven and earth?"

The simple meaning is this: When the Jewish people are in danger, God forbid, when they cannot see any opening through which salvation can come, God forbid, they ask, "From where will come my help?" The answer is: "My help comes from God, Who made heaven and earth." God created heaven and earth out of nothing, and so for them also there was no opening through which, or basis upon which, they could come into being. So now, God can save us out of nothing and nowhere.

It may also be as follows. Why is it written, "I will lift up my eyes unto the mountains"? We learn in the Talmud (*Sanhedrin* 81a) on the verse (Ezekiel 18:6), "But if a man be just, and do that which is lawful and right, and has not eaten upon the mountains . . ." R. Acha b. Hanina said, "The Hebrew word *harim*, 'mountains,' can also be read *horim*, 'ancestors,' so 'has not eaten upon the mountains' means that he did not eat through his forbears' merit."

What could this Talmud be teaching, when we pray all the time that God should save us in the merit of our ancestors?

It could be, as I learned from my holy father-in-law, of blessed memory, who repeated a teaching in the name of a *tzaddik* (saint) about the saying of the sages, that every person must say to himself: "When will my deeds reach the level of my ancestors'?" He explained that to "reach" is also to "touch." It is sufficient for your actions to touch upon theirs. (Rebbe Reb Bunim on teaching from *Tana D'bei Eliyahu, Rabbah* cap. 25)

The reason for this is because if a person's actions do not in any way, shape, or form touch upon the deeds of his ancestors, it is as though the deeds of his ancestors are vastly higher, like a mountain peak or a vaulted roof. So if he is eating on their credit, in merit of his ancestors, it is not good. This is what the Talmud quoted above is hinting, that "has not eaten upon the mountains" means that he has not eaten in merit of his ancestors, who are as far above him as mountain peaks.

With this we can understand the Talmud (*Shabbath* 88a): "At Sinai, God covered them with the mountain like a barrel, saying, 'If you accept the Torah, 'tis well; if not, there shall be your burial.'" Why "like a barrel"? And why say "covered them," as though with a lid? Why not say "held the mountain above them"? We learn in the holy Zohar, on the verse (Exodus 19:2) "Israel camped opposite the mountain," that the mountain refers to our ancestor, the Patriarch Jacob.

This is why God covered them (sic.) like a barrel (sic.): He actually hollowed out the mountain and turned it upon them like an overturned barrel. God was saying, "If you accept the Torah in such a way that your ancestors do not remain out of reach like mountains above you but surround you everywhere like this barrel that you can reach out and touch, it is good. If not . . ." The Talmud (ibid.) says: "This furnishes a strong protest against the Torah. Yet even so, they reaccepted it in the days of Ahasuerus." Rashi (ibid.) explains: "They reaffirmed their prior acceptance of the Torah at Sinai, out of love for the miracle that had just occurred."

As the verse (Deut. 4:37) says, "It was because He loved your fathers, and chose their children after them, that God Himself brought you out of Egypt with His great power." For us to touch and connect with the deeds of our fathers, we need to pray that the love that God showed our fathers He should also show us.

When Rashi wrote, "They reaffirmed their prior acceptance of the Torah at Sinai, out of love for the miracle that had just occurred," he means that with this love shown them by God, they could even accept the mountain being held over them like a barrel. With this love they could reach out and connect to the deeds of their fathers.

This is the meaning of the verse we quoted at the outset, "I will lift up my eyes unto the mountains." To begin with, I see myself so far from the deeds of my fathers that they are as distant to me as mountains, such that I must "lift up my eyes" to them—and so, "from where will come my help?" I am disconnected from them, and the love that God showed them is hidden from me. Then, "My help comes from God, who made heaven and earth," heaven above and earth below. For though they are so far apart, God still created them as one, as the Midrash says, "God created heaven and earth like a vessel and its lid." Similarly, God should show us His love and draw us close with mercy, so that we may reach to the level of the deeds of our ancestors.

# *B'Ha'aloth'cha*—June 15, 1940

"*When the ark went forth, Moses said, 'Arise O God, and scatter your enemies! Let your foes flee before You!'*
   "*When it came to rest, he said, 'Return O God, [to] the myriad of Israel's thousands.'*" (Numbers 10:35–36)

Regarding the unique textual symbols that appear before and after these verses in the Torah scroll, Rashi, referring to the Talmud (*Shabbath* 115a) explains: "God made dividing marks in front of and behind this section in order to indicate that this is not its proper place. A more appropriate place would be in the section dealing with the travels of the people, after Numbers 2:17." Why then, Rashi asks, is it positioned here in the text? He answers: "In order to make a break between the narrative of one punishment and that of another punishment."

Let us attempt to understand. Why must the symbols chosen as a dividing mark, separating this passage from those before it and after it, be the Hebrew letter *nun*? And why are they written upside down?

Moses said, "Arise O God." Rashi (ibid.) explains that because the Ark was traveling in front of them at a distance of three days' march, Moses was praying, "Stay God, wait for us, and do not travel farther away from us."

If this is so, why then did Moses continue with his prayer, saying, ". . . and scatter Your enemies?"

In the *Mussaf* service on Festival days, in the liturgy recited as the *cohen* (priests) prepare to bless the congregation, we read the following: "May our service be sweet before You, God, like a burnt offering or a sacrifice. . . . Bring back Your service to Zion Your city, and the order of service to Jerusalem, and we will worship You there, with fear."

What is the meaning of "and we will worship You there, with fear"? Surely in a time of exile and great trouble we have a greater fear. Why then do we pray to God that when He rescues and redeems us, "we will worship You there, with fear"?

While it is obvious that in our present circumstances we have great fear because of our pain and distress, it is still difficult for us to worship God with this fear. Firstly, for the simple reason that they do not allow us to worship, and also because our hearts are so broken and our spirits are so low. When, however, God has saved us and redeemed us, then we will be able to fulfill our desire to worship Him with fear.

A person who even when in great distress worships God with all His ability has longing and desire for God to rescue him from his distress, so that he will be able to worship God even more. His desire then, changes the wrath into mercy, and draws down the salvation.

Jews bless God's holy Name in both the *nochach* (immediate) and *nistar* (third) persons. In the phrasing of each blessing we say, "Blessed are You, Lord our God, Who has sanctified us . . ." The first part is said in the immediate, second person, *nochach*, while the end is in the third person, *nistar*. The prayer "Blessed is He Who spoke and created the world . . ." opens in the third person, *nistar*, and ends "Blessed are You . . ." in the second person, *nochach*.

Angels, on the other hand, may only bless God in the third person, *nistar*, as in "Holy, holy, holy, is the Lord of Hosts: The world is full of His glory." (Isaiah 6:3) This is because the Jewish people arose in God's Thought before the creation of the world, existing when everything was *nistar*, hidden. But they also exist in the physical world, the world of Action, and so they bless God, Who is above any attempt at understanding, in the third (hidden) person—and also when He reveals Himself in the world of Action. This is not the case with the angels, who only belong in one world, the world that is above any revelation of God, and so they bless God only in the third person.

This explains why the Jewish people have the power to change mercy into wrath against wicked people, and then to change this wrath into mercy for the Jewish people. They can take the revealed Face of God representing Love and Mercy and turn it into the *Hester Panim*, Hidden Face of God, which is by definition a punishment. They can likewise take *Hester Panim*, the Hidden Face of God, which is by definition a punishment, and transform it into revelation, i.e., Love and Mercy. This is all because they exist in both the hidden and revealed worlds.

When our teacher Moses ascended the mountain to receive the Torah, the Talmud (*Shabbath* 88b) tells us, "He argued with the angels and won them over. They came to love him, and each one of them gave him a gift." We need to understand: If Moses only managed to convince the angels to change their minds and agree that the Jewish people deserved to receive the Torah, why then did they give him presents? It is true that in the holy Zohar much is written on the matter of the gifts, but this concerns another aspect. The angels referred to in the Zohar writings were the lords of the nations of the world, who actually thought that the receiving of the Torah by the Jewish people was not in the best interests of the Jews, God forbid. The angels who are mentioned in the Talmud, however, apparently did not intend any evil toward Israel. Nonetheless, this does not explain why they were so inclined to love Moses that they gave him gifts. According to what we have said above, this in itself was part of the argument. The angels said to God (Psalms 8:5), "What is man, that You should even consider him?" Our teacher Moses was able to change their wrath into mercy with the power of Israel. The fact that Moses with the power of Israel could change wrath into mercy, even in angels, showed the angels the greatness of Israel, and so they gave him gifts.

To return to our earlier question: Why do we pray "Bring back Your service to Zion Your city . . . and we will worship You there, with fear"? Although we have fear even now, it is difficult to worship God wholeheartedly with it.

This brings us back to our original quote. The verse "When the ark went forth . . ." is enclosed in special symbols to indicate to us that this is not its proper place. What that hints to us is this: It is not just this place that is not its place; it has no place anywhere. Worship such as this, worship that comes out of pain, has no place at all. And so the dividing marks, the inverted *nun* letters, were made for it. We learn in the Talmud (*Shabbath* 104a) about the shapes of the Hebrew letters: "Of the bent *nun* and the long, straight [final] *nun* it is said, *Nun* is *Ne'eman*, the faithful. The faithful starts out bent and humbled, but will ultimately be the faithful, straight and tall."

So, when the Jewish person has everything he needs, he bows and humbles himself before God in service. But when he is beaten down through suffering, God forbid, then he is not like the bent *nun*; he is an upside-down *nun*. When this happens, the Ark and the Torah are hidden and distant from the Jewish people. And so our teacher Moses prays, "Arise O God, and scatter Your enemies! Let Your foes flee before You!" "Foes of God" means those who hate the Jewish people.

If the Ark and the Torah will not be hidden then the *nun* will not be upside-down. There will be only worship of God, and closeness to Him that comes out of joy, and all good things.

# Sh'lach—June 22, 1940

*"'We must go forth and occupy the land,' [Caleb] said. 'We can do it!'"*
(Numbers 13:30)

Let us attempt an understanding of this episode. If the spies spoke with reason, saying, "the people living in the land are aggressive, and the cities are large and well fortified," (Numbers 13:28) why did Caleb not enter into a debate with them, trying to demolish their argument and their reasoning? Why did he limit himself to the simple statement "We must go forth . . ."?

This is how the faith of a Jew must always be. Not only when he sees reasonable openings and paths for his salvation to take within the laws of nature must he have faith that God will save him, and take heart—but also, God forbid, when he sees no way for salvation to come through natural means, must he still believe that God will save him, and strengthen himself in his faith and his belief. In fact, at just such times it is better not to look for natural paths for salvation to take, for if such a way is not apparent and, God forbid, a person's faith should become damaged, a blemish in the person's faith and in his belief in God may actually prevent the salvation from happening, God forbid.

A person needs to say: "Yes, all the logic and facts may indeed be true. The people who inhabit the land may be very strong, and their cities well fortified, and so forth, but still I believe in God, who is beyond any boundaries, and above all nature. I believe that He will save us. We must go forth and occupy the land. We can do it!" He must say this without rationalizing or theorizing, for it is this kind of faith and belief in God that brings our salvation close.

# *Balak*—July 13, 1940

*"Glimpses no wrongdoing in Jacob, and sees no vice in Israel, God their Lord is with them."*

*"This is a nation that rises like the king of beasts, and lifts itself like a lion. It does not lie down until it has devoured its prey and drunk the blood of its kill."* (Numbers 23:21, 24)

The Talmud (*Berachoth* 7a) discusses the following verse (Psalms 7:12): "God rages every day." How long does this rage last? But one moment. And how long is one moment? One fifty-eight thousand eight hundred and eighty-eighth part of an hour (1/58,888th). No creature has ever been able to identify precisely the moment of God's rage except the wicked Balaam, of whom it is written (Numbers 23:8): "He knows knowledge of the Most High." How could Balaam, who did not even know the mind of his animal, know the mind of the Most High? The meaning is, therefore, that only he knew how to identify precisely the moment in which the Holy One, blessed be He, is enraged. This is just what the prophet said to Israel (Micah 6:5): "O my people, remember now what Balak king of Moab devised, and what Balaam the son of Beor answered him . . . that you may know the righteous acts of the Lord."

What does "that you may know the righteous acts of the Lord" mean? R. Eleazar says: "The Holy One, blessed be He, said to Israel, 'See, now, how many righteous acts I performed for you, in not being angry during the period of the wicked Balaam. For had I been angry, not one remnant would have been left of [the enemies of] Israel.'" This too is the meaning of what Balaam said to Balak (Numbers 23:8): 'How shall I curse, whom God has not cursed? And how shall I execrate, when the Lord has not execrated?' This teaches us that God was not enraged at all during that period. And how long does his rage last? But one moment. And how long is one moment? R. Abin (some say R. Abina) says, 'As long as it takes to say *rega*, "moment."' And how do you know that God's rage endures only for a moment? For it is written (Psalms 30:6): 'His rage is but for a *rega*, moment, while His favor lasts a lifetime.'"

Let us understand what R. Abin meant when he said that a *rega* (moment) is as long as it takes to say *rega*. He argues with the opinion cited earlier in the passage, that a moment is one fifty-eight thousand eight hundred and eighty-eighth part of an hour, which is a very small amount of time. To maintain that a moment is as long as it takes to say *rega* means that it all depends on the speed of an individual's speech. There are those who speak quickly, and those who speak slowly.

God rages every day, but for how long does this anger last? Only a moment. It is an example of God's loving-kindness that He is angry only for a moment, for who could possibly stand before the wrath of God?

In *Parshath Bereshith*, the first chapters of Genesis, on the verse (Genesis 1:27) "God created man in His image," Rashi (ibid.) explains: "Everything else was created at God's verbal command, while man was brought into existence at God's hand."

We have already pondered the meaning of this teaching, for to create with speech seems to be a higher form of creation than to create by hand. How is it that everything else was created at God's command, while man, who is higher than everything, was created by His hand? As we have explained, the holiness from above does not enter into the essence of the rest of creation but remains in the words of God's verbal command. With the Jew, however, the holiness reaches into his every action. He is created, so to speak, at the very hands of God, and he is essentially and entirely holy.

This also explains the eternity of the Jewish people. Everything else was created with a verbal command, with God's speech that is high above, shining upon them only from a great distance. The light is not fixed inside them and does not exist within them; it is like a flash of lightning that illuminates them for a short time. This is not the case, however, with the Jewish people. They were created at God's hands, and so their holiness is in their makeup. Wherever they are, it exists within them, and so they are eternal. The very physical corpus of the Jew is eternal, because when a person expends his strength for Torah and worship, and he makes a part of Torah and worship out of his body's energy, his whole body is elevated to the eternal world, existing forever. Only the food he consumed during his lifetime, which was added temporarily to his body, is subsequently lost.

This is the meaning of "God rages for as long as it takes to say *rega*." It is all part of God's loving-kindness that it is just momentary, affecting only those parts of the body that were created by God's verbal command. The wrath is only in order to purify, whereas if, God forbid, the suffering were drawn out, it would also touch upon that part of the Jew that was created at God's hands.

This is why the Jewish people have the ability to sustain themselves in their suffering. Right from the beginning, the Jewish person does not fall; he merely lays himself down. But even with the act of laying himself down, he brings down his enemies, because the Jew is created at the hands of God, blessed be He, and His holiness persists into the essential core of the Jewish person. This is what the verses quoted above are hinting at: "God their Lord is with them. . . ."

"This is a nation that rises like the king of beasts." It gets up again, buttressing and encouraging itself. "It does not lie down until it has devoured its prey and drunk the blood of its kill." The Jew never falls utterly. At most he will lay himself down, and even then, as he does so, he does more damage to his enemies than to himself. This is why "He rises like the king of beasts." Even when he is in the most terrible distress, "He lifts himself like a lion."

# *Pinchos*—July 20, 1940

*"Moses spoke to God, saying, 'Let the Omnipotent God of all living souls appoint a man over the community. Let him come and go before them, and let him bring them forth and lead them. Let not God's community be like sheep who have no shepherd for them.'"* (Numbers 27:15)

We learn in the Talmud (*Berachoth* 28b); our Rabbis taught: "When R. Eliezer fell ill, his disciples went in to visit him. They said to him, 'Master, teach us the paths of life so that through them we may merit the life of the world to come.' He said to them, 'Be solicitous for the honor of your colleagues. Keep your children from *higayon* (rationalizing) and set them between the knees of scholars. When you pray, know before Whom you are standing. This is how to merit life in the world to come.'"

We can see from this that even though the first and most important thing is to learn Torah, nevertheless this alone is not enough to merit the world to come. Without a doubt, the students of R. Eliezer had learned a great deal of Torah from him, yet they still asked to be taught how to merit life in the world to come. Also, we see that in response R. Eliezer did not admonish them to learn more and more Torah. Instead, he taught them other things.

It might be asked, however, why the students waited until R. Eliezer was dying before asking their question, and did not ask earlier. Is not a full lifetime's labor required to merit a place in the world to come? And why did the students say, "Show us ways to live so that we may achieve life in the world to come," when we learn in the Mishnah (*Avoth* 1:3): "Be not like servants who serve their master in order to gain a reward"?

These students had been disciples of R. Eliezer all their lives, and they learned from him ways to live, as students do from their rabbis. However, when it was time for R. Eliezer to leave this world, his disciples, realizing that they would now have to become the leaders of their generation, asked him for advice on how to teach others. How were they to educate those beginners who are still at the low spiritual level of working only in order to gain a reward? In response he told them things that might also, to our simple understanding, be suitable for beginners.

As well as this, it is possible that with his advice to "keep your children from *higayon* (rationalizing)," R. Eliezer was teaching something that we, now, may also find useful.

We learn in the Talmud (*Berachoth* 6a): "Weak knees are the work of the Other Side." If it is the forces of evil that make the knees grow tired, why is it specifically the knees that evil concentrates upon?

The friends of Job, when they saw his spirit broken by the trouble and pain that had befallen him, said to him (Job 4:4): "Your words have upheld him who was falling, and you have strengthened the bending knees." Until then, it had been Job who strengthened and encouraged others with his words, bolstering a person whose knees were tiring.

A person whose spirit has broken is described as having "bending knees," and this is what the Talmud is hinting to us. The knees give way when a person's spirit breaks, when he finds the load of suffering that heaven has placed upon him unbearable. When this happens it is the *Sitra Achra*, the Other Side, that is undermining him. It is the work of the evil inclination.

As we see, the principal method used by the evil inclination to bend the knees of the Jewish people is with questions raised in people's minds. Not only now, in this time of great trouble, but also previously, if one of our young men stumbled, forsaking his friends with their Torah, becoming instead a tradesman or a businessman—or crossing the line, God forbid—the reason was that his faith had been damaged. He had begun questioning, wondering where it would all end? How would he earn a living? And so forth. He had these thoughts even though it is plain for all to see that "neither poverty nor wealth come from trades or skills" (*Kiddushin* 82b). Aside from this, whether or not a man has a livelihood he does not live forever. When his allotted day arrives, the rich man who has not behaved properly knows that he has nothing with which to boost his spirit other than the fact that he ate well or had nice clothes—and from the moment of his passing not one bit of it remains his. The Torah Jew, however, and one who has behaved well, knows that at least he lived a pure life, a Torah life.

Just as it was then, so it is now. Any weakness of the knees comes from questioning and thinking. If convinced that tomorrow would bring salvation, all would be able to find the strength within them to carry on. Instead they raise questions in their minds: How long will this go on? Who knows whether we will be able to bear it? Etc. As a result of the doubts, fears grow, the body is weakened, and the knees buckle. This is why it is most important to strengthen our faith to reject the questions and the thoughts, and to believe in God, that He will extend benevolence to us, help us, and save us.

If we refer to Genesis Rabbah, at the beginning of Chapter 12 in *Bereshith*, we find that in-depth studies and analyses of purpose are called *higyonot*, as it says: "The clever ones analyze thunder, understanding its implications and *higayon*." This is the meaning of R. Eliezer's advice to "keep your children from *higayon* (rationalizing)": Do not teach your children to rationalize the purpose of events, for then you will be able to put them between the knees of Torah scholars. If you do not prevent them from pursuing this kind of reasoning, then you cannot be sure that they will remain Torah scholars, and that their knees will not buckle, or that they will be able to withstand hardships. But if you can prevent them from debating God's purpose, and if they can have faith in God, then you can put them between the knees of Torah scholars—specifically knees, because you can be sure that their knees will not buckle.

R. Eliezer taught this to his disciples as they themselves were about to become leaders of their generation. The first reason for this was simply to explain to them how to show their students that there is no profit in rationalizing, that a person cannot use his intelligence to know what is going to happen, and he cannot do himself any good with his intelligence. Secondly, when the leader of the generation is really bound up in his faith, then the students who are tied to him are also able to reject speculation and quiet their questioning minds. They too are able to strengthen their faith, because of that piece of their Rebbe that they have absorbed.

This is the hint in the quote, "Moses spoke to God, saying, 'Let the Omnipotent God of all living souls appoint a man over the community. Let him come and go before them. Let him bring them forth and lead them. Let not God's community be like sheep who have no shepherd for them.'" Rashi (Exodus 21:1), on the verse "These are the laws that you must set before them," explains that "before them" means "like a table, set out before them." And so the phrase "before them" always applies to any clear and unambiguous understanding.

This is the meaning of Moses' plea for a leader who can ". . . come and go before them . . .": one who can set out before them what they need to understand. ". . . And let him bring them forth and lead them": a leader who will be able to bring out their best understanding from within them, and lead them showing them how best to use their intelligence safely.

"Let not God's community be like sheep who have no shepherd for them." The extra emphasis placed on the phrase "for them," means lest each person inside himself not have a shepherd. The shepherd must enter inside, into the depths of each person, and strengthen his faith in God, and through this also draw salvation close.

# *Ki Thetze*—September 14, 1940

*"When you wage war against your enemies, God your God will give them into your hands, so that you will take captives."* (Deut. 21:10)

We learn from the holy Rabbi, the Godly man, the great Maggid of Mezeritch, of blessed memory, on the verse (Psalms 110:4), "You are a *cohen* (priest) forever," that *cohen* is the attribute of *chesed* (loving-kindness). The meaning of the verse, therefore, is as follows: "You are loving-kindness forever." The ability of a Jew to address God as "You" when saying a blessing—"Blessed are You"—is due to the *chesed* (loving-kindness) of God.

"You" is *nochach*, the second person accusative, whereas "He" is *nistar*, the third person. In Hebrew, *nistar* means "hidden." When the men of the Great Assembly determined the precise language of the prayers and blessings in which we say to God "You," explicitly uttering God's name, they surely succeeded in bringing about an immediate revelation of God. When we utter the blessing "Blessed are You, Adonai, our God . . . " surely God is truly facing us, and we can actually say "You," and the blessing is not in vain, God forbid.

We learn in sacred literature (*Tikunei Zohar* 21) that just as prayer needs Torah, as it is written in the verse (Proverbs 28:9), "He who turns away his ear from hearing Torah, even his prayer is abomination," so also does Torah need prayer. We can understand this with the help of what we have said above. We say the blessing, "Blessed are You . . . our God . . . King of the Universe, Who teaches Torah to His people Israel." This is a general statement in *nistar*, the third person. It means that God teaches Torah to all of Israel. However, teaching of an individual person, where God speaks to that one person alone, can be achieved only by that person individually.

In his commentary on the verse beginning the Book of Leviticus (1:1), "[God] called Moses and God spoke to him . . .", Rashi, quoting the Midrash (*Sifra, VaYikra* 1:2) says: "The redundant use of the phrase "to him" implies that the Voice went and reached Moses' ears only, but no one else could hear it." End quote. Our teacher Moses was special in that he could also hear the voice that was speaking only to him, individually and privately. Although God teaches Torah to the entire Jewish people, this is not a teaching that is personal and individual to every person. Rather, God teaches Torah to His people in general, to all Jews as one. So, it is up to each and every Jew to work to achieve that level where God speaks to him individually, as we said above.

How do we achieve this? With prayer. By saying "You" to God, a person achieves a revelation of God, imminent. God speaks directly to him, teaching him Torah individually, directly and immediately. God says "you" to the individual in return. When this happens, each person can see and comprehend a part of the Torah that is uniquely his. This is because the Torah that God teaches someone individually and personally cannot be grasped by anyone else, while another person, in his turn, may comprehend what the first cannot.

We learn in the holy book *Maor V'Shamesh,* on the verse (Psalms 25:14) "God's secrets are with those who fear Him," that it is not the study of Kabbalah alone that is a secret. After all, the Kabbalah is written in books, available to anyone who wants to learn it. The mystery, rather, is in the understanding and perception of God that each person may achieve and that no one else can acquire. That which each person perceives of God and which cannot be explained or related to someone else comprises the real secret and the mystery.

A person can achieve this knowledge of God through prayer when he stands facing God, addressing Him directly as "You," and when God speaks to him in return, addressing him individually, immediately, and directly, as "you," as we explained above. However, if our direct and immediate words to God are to create a revelation of Him that is direct and immediate, the person who is uttering words of prayer must, himself, first be revealed through his prayers. His own essential self must be found in his words of prayer. Then "like water reflecting the face to the face," (Proverbs 27:19) the revelation of God will be reflected in the revelation of himself that is in his prayer. Even when a person's prayer issues from the depths of his heart only because he is in great distress, God forbid, nevertheless, because he is pouring forth his soul and his soul is there in the words of his prayer, there is in the reflection an immediate and direct revelation of God for that individual.

This is the meaning of the verse with which we opened this chapter, "When you wage war against your enemies, God, your God will put them into your hands, so that you will take captives." Even though it is because of war, and even though it was you who decided to declare war in the first place, nonetheless you are in pain and praying from the depths of your heart. So God will do this much for you: He will put it right into your hands; He will be "your God"—your unique and individual God.

The phrase "You will take captives" is written *V'shavitha shivyo* in Hebrew. It may also be translated as "You will restore his restoration." The Jewish people ask (Lament: 5:21), "Restore us to You, and we will be restored," praying for God to kindle in us the desire to repent. And God, blessed be He, says (Malachi: 3:7), "Return to Me and I will return to you," as is well known. But, with the individual revelation achieved through personal prayers, you will succeed in "restoring His restoration." That is to say, you will have "repented with His repentance." This is the repentance for which we have been praying, "Restore us to You, and we will be restored," because God will draw you back to Him.

# *Ki Thavo*—September 21, 1940

*"Look down from Your holy dwelling in heaven, and bless Your people Israel."*
(Deuteronomy 26:15)

We learn in the Talmud (*Sanhedrin* 59b); R. Simeon b. Manassia said: "Woe for the loss of a great servant. For had not the serpent been cursed, every Jewish person would have had two valuable serpents, sending one to the north and one to the south to bring him costly gems, precious stones, and pearls."

It is difficult to understand why the serpent, from whom all evil devolves, would have been such a good messenger for Israel, and why this good could not have come from other beasts and animals. If the reason is that when the serpent was cursed all the other animals were cursed with it, why then does the Talmud not say that if only the serpent had not been cursed, then all the beasts and animals would bring us gems and precious stones? Why does it say this only and specifically of the snake?

It may perhaps be as follows: We learn in the Jerusalem Talmud (*Peah*, 5a); R. Shmuel b. Nachmeni said: "We ask the snake, 'Why must your tongue flicker as you move?' The snake replies, 'My tongue caused me all this trouble.' We ask, 'What pleasure do you derive from biting? The lion rends and eats, the wolf rends and eats, but what pleasure do you get?' The snake replies, '"Will the snake bite without venom?"' In Hebrew the word for 'venom,' *lachash*, also means 'whisper.' 'If Heaven did not whisper in my ear to bite,' says the snake, 'I would not bite.'"

All other animals and beasts kill and rend to satisfy their hunger and for pleasure, while the snake does not bite to satisfy its hunger or for pleasure. This hints to us that when an action is altruistic, great things can come of it. Thus, only as a consequence of being cursed was the snake prevented from being useful. If not for the fact that it was cursed, it would bring gems and precious stones to the Jewish people.

The meaning could also be as follows: We can see that when God punishes man, using a carnivore as His instrument and simply substituting, God forbid, man for the meat of another animal, then the heavenly judgment is clothed in a natural event. The nature of every carnivore is to eat and satisfy its hunger. When, however, punishment is meted out using a snake, the judgment is a revealed one. It is not clothed in a natural event because the snake is not satisfying a hunger and takes no pleasure from biting, and so this is naked justice, administered "as is." This is the meaning of the passage in the Talmud, "Woe for the loss, etc." As the snake after being cursed has become an instrument of unclothed revelation of judgment, we can deduce that if it had not been cursed, the good it would have brought would have been an equally great good. It would have been supernaturally good. Similarly, when we see that, God forbid, we are being tortured and tormented in ways that are clearly of no benefit or profit to the person torturing us, but simply to cause pain, it is a revelation of naked judgment, unclothed in a natural event—and we can deduce from it that when we return to God and pray, then God will rescue us supernaturally, with a salvation not clothed in natural events.

It is possible that this is what is being hinted in the verses where our teacher Moses said: "O Lord, why do You mistreat this people? Why did You send me? As soon as I came to Pharaoh to speak in Your name, he made things worse for the people. You have done nothing to help Your people." (Exodus 5:22–23)

We know that the style of leadership of our teacher Moses was a miraculous one, unclothed in natural events. He brought water up from below ground and bread down from above, and so forth. After becoming the messenger to Pharaoh to redeem the Jewish people, Moses saw that Pharaoh's fresh decree against them—namely, that he would no longer give them straw with which to make bricks—was one from which he derived no benefit or profit. Moses thought that he was responsible, that the new decrees and the torture that necessarily preceded the salvation were happening precisely because he was the messenger and his leadership was supernatural. He felt responsible for the suffering because the salvation that he, Moses, wrought would also not come clothed in natural events.

So he said to the Holy Blessed One, "Why do You mistreat this people; why have You sent me?" Moses also pointed out to God that Pharaoh had made things bad for the people, that the evil was directed solely at them and served no purpose, for even Pharaoh derived no benefit from it. "So," Moses pleaded, "even though it will be followed by great and supernatural salvation, do the Jewish people have the strength to withstand this much suffering?" Then God said to Moses, "Now you begin to see what I am doing to Pharaoh. With a strong hand he will be forced to let them go, and he will be forced to drive them out of his land." (Exodus 6:1) "Therefore say to the Israelites, 'I am God.'" (Exodus 6:6) God explained that henceforth there would be a total, complete, and unclothed judgment of the Egyptians and enemies of Israel, while for the Jewish people God would reveal supernatural mercy and loving-kindness.

This is what enables the Jewish person to bolster himself in times of such awesome suffering. The troubles are not clothed in nature, the judgment is not natural, and so also the buttressing of faith is not naturally achieved, because in the natural course of events it would be impossible to understand how to strengthen ourselves. Therefore, this strengthening of our faith works to change judgment to mercy, because it is a revelation beyond anything clothed in natural events.

This is what is hinted at in the verse that precedes our opening quote: (Deut. 26:14) "I have not eaten [the second tithe] while in mourning. I have not separated any of it while unclean, and I have not used any for the dead. I have obeyed You, God my Lord, and have done all that You commanded me."

Even though, as hinted at in the verse, I had cause—death and mourning, God protect us—nevertheless I did all that You commanded me. Rashi (ibid.) explains the phrase "I did all that You commanded me" to mean "I was happy, and I made others happy with it." That is, "I achieved this, even though in the natural course of events it would be impossible to understand how I could have strengthened myself, and how as well as this I also made others happy."

And perhaps "I made others happy" may also be hinting that when others saw how even in my troubles I strengthened myself, then they who watched were also able to strengthen themselves in their pain, *a fortiori*, saying their own suffering is not as bitter as mine. This is the meaning of "I was happy, and I made others happy with it."

So, we pray, "Look down from Your holy dwelling in heaven, and bless Your people Israel." Our sages say (Exodus Rabbah 41:1) that whereas in the Torah the Hebrew word *hashkafa*, "look down," generally implies something bad, here the meaning is inverted to denote something good. It is the strengthening of faith that succeeds of itself in turning bad into good, and to bring blessings to "Your people Israel."

And bless Your people Israel.

# *Nitzavim*—September 28, 1940

*"The hidden things belong to God, and that which has been revealed, to us and our children for ever. [We must therefore] keep all the words of this Torah."* (Deut. 29:28)

Every Jewish person prays to God and cries out to Him, blessed be He, regarding any calamity [that it should not occur]. And when, God forbid, the trouble is even greater, he cries out even more, as it is written (Esther 4:1), "And Mordechai cried a great and bitter cry." Even when there is no impending calamity, we pray to God because prayer itself is closeness to God. When we pray, we pray with a full voice, as it is written in sacred literature, "The voice awakens the intention, (*kavannah*) the intention awakens the voice." But what can we do when they do not permit us to cry out, or even to congregate for prayer, and we are forced to pray in hidden places, and every Jewish heart must lament this alone? At least in the depths of his heart, every Jew must shout out to God about it.

This is the meaning of the verse (Psalms 130:1), "From the depths I called to You, O God. God, hear my voice. Let Your ears bend to the voice of my supplications."

Simply put, it is difficult to understand why we need both "Hear my voice" and "Let Your ears be attentive to the voice of my supplications." God, blessed be He, has no physical body, and is not touched by any of the things that appertain to the body. The concept of "ears" does not apply to God, for everything above is spiritual. We use physical descriptions only as figures of speech. When we speak quietly to someone, he is usually forced to stop and bend his ears in order to hear what we say.

This is what we mean when we pray, "From the depths I called to You, O God." I can call only from the depths of my heart, and not with a loud voice; therefore I say, "God, hear my voice. Let Your ears bend to the voice of my supplications." What I mean is, "Please, You must bend Your ears, as it were, to listen, to hear my voice. And please, see how they have forbidden me to pray, and how I am forced to pray in hiding, whispering. If only for the pain that I suffer because of this, please save me."

This is the meaning of the phrase we quoted at the beginning of the chapter, "The hidden things belong to God our Lord. . . ." The verse refers to both kinds of worship. "The hidden things"—the words that rightfully belong to God, the words of Torah and prayer, which we are forced to hide—still ascend unto God, on condition that the other half of the verse is also fulfilled: "That which has been revealed, to us and our children for ever."

In the Torah text, *nikud* points appear above each of the letters in the words "to us and our children." The *nikud* points mean that in the innermost part of our hearts we must be absolutely convinced that this is forever—that when God saves us and we will be rescued, the worship of God for us and for our children will be open, in public, in full voice, and with all the *kavanah* (intention) of our hearts.

*The Jewish Year 5701:
October 3, 1940–
September 21, 1941*

# *Rosh Hashanah* (New Year)—
# October 3, 1940

*"You heard my voice; please be not deaf to my plea for well being."* (Lament. 3:56, from the liturgy recited before blowing the *shofar*.)

We are able to understand this with the help of a well-known parable from the holy book *Imrei Elimelech* (p. 330). A prince began to stray from the proper path, giving his life to vain, empty things and to the company of base and reckless people. Courtiers complained to the king about the prince and his behavior. They claimed that he disobeyed the king's decree and did nothing to glorify his father, the king. Furthermore, it was charged that the prince had become so insensible and capricious that he did not even acknowledge his father as sovereign, and could not distinguish between his father and a commoner.

The prince was exiled from the king's presence and sent to live among vulgar people who maltreated him, making him suffer, until in his great anguish he began to ask himself, "Why am I in this predicament, in so much pain?" He started to heed the decrees of his father, and to plead, "Please, Father, have mercy on me, save me. Take me back to you and I will do your bidding. Heal me from all my hurt, for how can I do all that needs to be done when my hands are broken, my heart is broken, and my head is full of wounds?"

But the prince had many enemies in court at that time. There was no shortage of accusers to maintain the deceit that the prince still lacked respect for his father and his father's sovereignty, and that all his cries were simply a response to being exiled from his father's house. They pretended that the prince's cries were due only to the pain of being hurt and beaten; that his cries of "Father, Father!" were simply a conditioned reflex, nothing more than childhood memories of his father chastising him; that seeing the faces of people he recognized had jolted his memory somewhat, because the king, his father, had been in the habit of sending trusted advisors to help rehabilitate his son. His accusers offered the king other proofs of their words, saying, "Even now he has no intention of accepting upon himself the king's decree; otherwise, why does he listen to those vulgar people, and take their advice as well? Obviously he doesn't truly recognize your majesty's sovereignty." The accusers' indictment succeeded so well that despite his pleas and supplications the prince remained in exile and misery, God forbid.

Once, the king passed by the windows of his son's room at a time when his thoughts were composed, and the prince started to yell out all the cries that he was accustomed to shouting: "Woe, I am in pain! I have no food, Father! Take me back, bring me close to you . . ." The prince shouted with a voice so piercing and bitter, it caused the doorposts to tremble. His father ran to him, embracing him and taking him close unto himself. When the accusers began muttering their customary charges, that the prince had only been crying because he was accustomed to doing so and that even now he did not really recognize his father or his sovereignty, the king thundered at them: "Now I see that all this time it was only because you hated my son that you denounced him. For who can not instantly hear when cries are genuine? It was obvious he recognized me. He cried when he saw me because he recognized me: he knows that I am the king, and that his destiny is in my hands. His repentance came from his acceptance of my sovereignty over him. Even his pleas for his physical needs came from his recognition and acceptance of my sovereignty."

In our current situation we can understand the parable as follows: When the prince strayed from the proper path, bringing damage and ruin to the royal palace and acting in ways that were harmful to the affairs of state, he was punished once or twice. Every time he was punished he promised not to revert to his wicked deeds, but when the punishments ended he did revert. When the ministers of the king took him and imprisoned him in order to prevent him from doing more damage, he was in great pain, especially since he was being tortured while in prison. He cried a great cry unto the king, who heard it and came to save him.

The rule is that "The King, with justice, upholds the world." (Proverbs 29:4) So the ministers asked the king why he rescued his son. How many times had his son promised to repent of his evil ways and then not kept his promise? Just because he was not currently doing any damage, did the king really think he had repented or was he obedient merely because was being prevented from doing any damage? The king replied, "I am convinced that from now on, after this bitter punishment, he will behave in the proper way. But even if you are right—that he has not really forsaken his sinful ways, that the repentance is not real—nevertheless, his voice, the gut-wrenching screams of pain from your beatings, were indisputably his. My body reaches out to him, because it is impossible for a father to hear the sounds of his son being punished, and not rescue him."

The analogy is that we, the Jewish people, children of the King, are in great distress. It may perhaps be true, as the accusers say of us, that even though we are now repenting with all our hearts and each one of us has stopped his evil ways, this does not come from the goodness of our hearts but only because we are under such duress. However, God sees into our hearts, that our intentions are truly to repent. What is more, even if we were not truly repentant, nevertheless, "You heard my voice." The screams that come of our tremendous bitterness and pain is indisputably our own voice. How could You bear to hear our pain and not have mercy, God forbid? You hear our voice: therefore, "Please be not deaf to [our] plea for well-being."

~~~

*"The beginning of Your word is true, and for ever, every one of Your righteous judgments endures."* (Psalms 119:160, from the liturgy recited before blowing the *shofar*.)

Rashi (ibid.) explains, in the name of the Midrash (*Yalkut Shimoni*, Psalms 887:138), which asks: "What is the meaning of this verse? That 'The beginning of Your word is true' but not the end of Your word? The meaning is this. From the end of Your words it may be seen that the beginning is true. When the nations of the world heard the beginning of the Ten Commandments (Exodus 20:1), 'I am God . . . Do not have any other gods before Me' and so forth, they said, 'Look, everything God does is for His own pleasure and glory.' Only when they heard the later Commandments (Exodus 20:12), 'Honor your father and mother' and so forth, did they admit that the Commandments were wholly true. Hence, 'The beginning of Your word is true.'"

Even the best among the nations of the world think that truth exists in and of itself, and that God commanded the truth because the truth can be nothing but true. This is why they admit the verity of the rational commandments. They assume that God commanded them precisely because they are intrinsically true. It is self-evident, for example, that one really ought not steal or rob, etc. It follows, however, that regarding any commandments that they do not hold to be intrinsically true, the nations mock the Jewish people, saying, "What is this commandment?" and so forth (see Rashi, Numbers 19:2).

The Jewish people, on the other hand, say repeatedly in the liturgy of the High Holy Days, "You, God, are true." God, blessed be He, is true, and nothing else is true. Any truth that exists in the world is only true because God commanded it so, and wanted it so. Because God, blessed be He, is true, therefore it also is true. We are forbidden to steal because God, Who is the Truth, so commanded. Because of God's commandment, this prohibition became the truth. When God commands the opposite, and the Jewish court (for example) declares property ownerless, making it legally ownerless by removing a person's title to his own property, then this also becomes true. When He commanded our father Abraham to sacrifice his son Isaac, then the binding of Isaac became the truth, and if He had not later commanded Abraham not to harm him, then the truth would have been to slaughter him.

Jews, therefore, could never have said anything like the words of the stupid, evil, idolaters—namely that God seeks His own pleasures, God forbid. On the contrary, we say (Mishnah *Avoth* 6:11): "Everything that the Holy Blessed One created, was for His glory." It is true that a person should not seek his own glory, but this is not a self-evident truth. The reason for it is because God commanded that we should not be glory seekers.

The truth is that God, Who created everything for His glory, must seek His own glory, even if for humans the opposite is true and we must not be glory seekers. We do not question Him, blessed be He, or argue that He demands everything for Himself, and only afterwards reconcile this by looking to the later Commandments. (If God created the world for His own glory, then this must be the truth.) We do not measure truth and righteousness with our minds, nor do we stop and ponder upon God, God forbid. We do not ask if this is how it should or should not be, or whether something is or is not true.

The will of God, blessed be He, is true and right, and even when we are tortured, God forbid, we do not deliberate. What is happening may not meet with our approval, but it does not depend upon our approval, and so we do not merely dismiss the problem as unanswerable, explaining that we cannot reconcile it because it is beyond our grasp. On the contrary, we know that nothing is true or right unless it is what God wants and commands and does.

Thus we say in the High Holy Day liturgy, "Your throne is established in *chesed* (loving-kindness) and You will sit upon it in truth." By definition, *chesed* extends even to the person who does not deserve it. While it might seem an untruth that people receive loving-kindness they do nt deserve, there is no such thing as intrinsic truth; there is only God's will and His deeds, and these are the truth. Therefore we say, "You have established Your throne in *chesed* and You will sit . . ." because when God sits upon the throne of loving-kindness, extending loving-kindness over and above what is deserved, it becomes the truth.

This, then, is the meaning of "The beginning of Your word is true, and forever. . . ." As our sages said in the Midrash quoted above, while the nations of the world say that it is only from the end of the Ten Commandments that we can recognize that the beginning is also true, we Jews know that "Forever . . . Your righteousness"—that is, the real truth is that all judgments depend solely upon Your righteousness." Whatever You consider right, is right and true. That is why the prayer continues: "Guarantee for good Your servant," (Psalms 119:122) meaning that whether we are truly righteous or not whomever You validate is, rightly and truly, righteous and true. So if You, God, guarantee that we are righteous, then even if we are not worthy it will still be true and just.

⊰✽⊱

*"Guarantee for good Your servant; let not the wicked oppress me."* (Psalms 119:122, from the liturgy recited before blowing the *shofar*.)

"Guarantee Your servant for good," because the main principle of repentance is to never return to the sin. But two things are needed for repentance: "Turn away from evil, and do good." (Psalms 34:14) We will not do again the evil that we have done, and we will do the good that we have not yet done.

At present we can only promise to "turn away from evil," that we will not continue to act badly. But about "doing good" we cannot make promises, because we are so broken with bitter suffering, which takes almost all we have away from us. How then can we promise to learn Torah, and act charitably? Therefore, we beg of God, "Guarantee for good Your servant." We can guarantee and take responsibility for turning away from evil, but on the injunction to "do good," You will have to be the guarantor. Aside from which, if only You would "let not the wicked oppress me" we would also be in a position to do well.

⊰✽⊱

*"Our Father, our King, return us in full repentance to You."* (From the High Holy Day liturgy.)

When we repent out of fear, the intentional sins we have committed are weighed as unintentional transgressions. This, though, is not full repentance, as the unintentional sins remain in place. Full repentance is when we repent out of love, which changes intentional sins to merit.

However, as we learn in the holy writings of his holiness, my teacher, my father, of blessed memory, when a person is suffering great pain, it is very difficult for him to worship God out of love. Therefore, we ask God, "Return us in full repentance." Usually, when we ask of God, "Return us to You and we will repent," (Lament. 5:21) God answers, "Return to Me and I will return to you." (Malachi 3:7) Nevertheless, we have the right to ask, "Return us in full repentance." It is not in our power to achieve full repentance on our own, for even when we do repent, it is only out of fear. Therefore, we pray, "Save us," and we will be able to return in full repentance.

# *Shabbat T'shuvah* (The Sabbath of Repentance)—October 5, 1940

*"When I proclaim God's name, give greatness to the name of God."*
(Deut. 32:3)

Rashi (ibid.), quoting the *Mechilta* (*Bo*: 13:3) explains this verse as follows: "The text is saying, 'It is incumbent upon you to give greatness to God, and bless His name.' From here the Rabbis derived the law that people make the response, "Blessed be the Name of His glorious Kingdom forever and ever," upon hearing God's name recited in the Temple."

We learn in the Talmud (*Shabbath* 89a); R. Joshua b. Levi also said: "When Moses ascended on high, he found the Holy One, blessed be He, tying crowns on the letters of the Torah. Said God to him, 'Moses, is there no greeting of peace in your town?' 'Can a servant extend a greeting of peace to his Master!' replied Moses. 'Yet you should have assisted Me,' said God. Immediately, Moses cried out to Him (Numbers 14:17), '"And now, I pray, let the power of the Lord be great, just as You have said."'"

From this talmudic quote we learn that by saying "And now, let the power of the Lord be great," Moses was assisting God, as it were. And here, in our opening quote, Moses said to the Jewish people, "When I proclaim God's name, give greatness to the name of God." Moses was telling them to magnify and help God, as it were, by giving honor and glory and by saying "Blessed be the Name of His glorious Kingdom forever and ever."

The essence of a sacrifice is described in the Talmud (*Hagigah* 12b): "The firmament called *Zebul* is that in which the heavenly Jerusalem, the Temple, and the Altar are built. The angel Michael, the great Prince, stands and offers thereon a sacrifice." The Tosaphists conclude that Michael offers as a sacrifice the souls of the departed righteous (Talmud, *Menachoth* 110a, Tos. cit. *Michael*).

It is only through a person's worship in this world—when he gives all his strength and soul in his worship of God, in his study of Torah, and in his prayers to God—that he sacrifices part of his soul to Him, blessed be He. Thereafter, when the person dies and he ascends to the upper world, Michael sacrifices his entire soul to God. This is the essence of a sacrifice. The sacrifice of an animal is only, as with the *Akeidah* (Binding of Isaac), "in place of his son." (Genesis 22:13) Only when a person is in a state of total penitence, when he is ready to give away his soul entirely, is the animal sacrifice realized at the level of "in place of his son." Nowadays, when there are no animal sacrifices, the study of Torah, prayer, and intense worship has become the essential sacrifice, determined by the extent of the soul invested in them.

This is what our teacher Moses meant when he said, "Give greatness to the name of God." Help God, as it were, through blessing His name, and by offering up your soul in your blessing as a sacrifice to God. These sacrifices then become "the bread of God" (cf. Levit. 21–22). (Sacrifices are referred to as "bread of God" because just as bread gives a person strength, so our sacrifices give, as it were, strength to God.)

When a Jew shouts out to God from pain, even though it is only pain and not his desire to worship God that causes him to shout, nevertheless, since suffering washes away sins and he is crying out to God, this also is counted as a sacrifice. The Talmud (*Berachoth* 5a) explains the verse (Psalms 94:12) "Happy is the man whom You O Lord, chasten, teaching him out of Your law": Do not read it *t'lamdenu* ('teaching him') but *t'lamdeynu* ('teach us'). You, God, have taught us this from Your Torah: that we are lucky to have You chastise us. This is concluded *a fortiori* from the law regarding the tooth and the eye (Exodus 21:26–27). Tooth and eye are only single limbs, and yet should a master damage the tooth or eye of a slave, the slave obtains thereby his freedom. How much more liberating, then, are painful sufferings that torment the entire body of a person!"

That it is a sacrifice when a person cries out to God is also hinted at in the verse that we recite before the blowing of the *shofar*, "May the gifts of my mouth find favor before You, O God, and teach me from Your judgments." (Psalms 119:108) There are different ways of offering a sacrifice. One can make it an obligation by saying, "Behold, I will bring a burnt offering," or one can make a voluntary offering by saying, "This I will offer, as a sacrifice."

My words "the gifts of my mouth" are a voluntary sacrifice, in the category of "This I will offer . . .", and since they are filled with my soul, God, please accept them as a voluntary sacrifice. Even though they issue only as result of my pain, please "Teach me from Your judgements." The Torah teaches me that this is also considered a sacrifice, as the Talmud quoted above shows from the verse in Psalms, "Happy is the man whom You O Lord, chasten, teaching him out of Your law." This we learn from the Torah: that pain cleanses and atones for sins.

In the *Haftorah* reading for this week (Hosea 14) we say, "Return, Israel, to God your Lord for you are ensnared in your iniquity. Take with you words and return to God, saying to Him, 'Forgive all our sins and take the good, we will pay You oxen with our lips.'" The primary thing is to repent and return to God—"Take with you words and return to God, saying to Him . . ." And you should pray to God to remove your sins and to "take the good, we will pay You oxen with our lips." Why must we bring sacrifices of pain and suffering, God forbid, offering "oxen with our lips" by crying in pain? God might rather "take the good," and then the offerings we make—"the oxen we pay with our lips"—would come from the good, and salvation from our singing and praising of God.

# *Yahrzeit* (Sixteenth *Tishrei*)—
# October 18, 1940

On the first *yahrzeit* of my holy, pious son, the Rav, of blessed memory, the second day of the Festival of Sukkoth. The verse associated with his name, Elimelech, recited by my holy, pious son, of blessed memory, after the silent *Amidah* is:

> "Say unto God, You are my Lord: My prosperity is not Your charge. But for the holy who are in the earth and the heroes in whom all my longing dwells."
> (Psalms 16:2)

We learn in the Talmud (*Sanhedrin* 47a): "It is written (Psalms 79:1–2), 'A psalm of Asaf. O God, heathen nations are come into Your inheritance; they have razed Jerusalem to rubble; the corpses of Your servants are given as food to the birds of the sky, the flesh of Your saints to the beasts of the earth.' To whom is the psalmist referring when he says, 'Your servants,' and whom does he mean when saying, 'Your saints'? Surely, *chasidim*—'saints,' must be understood literally, while 'servants' are those who deserved death, but having been slain are elevated to the status of 'servants.'"

There needs to be some elucidation. *Chasidim* (saints), who were already saints before they died and whose "flesh was fed to the beasts of the earth," were surely elevated through their martyrdom, yet they are still called *chasidim* after the fact. Those, however, who were not originally servants of God but were elevated to the level of "servants" through their martyrdom at the hands of idolaters, have their status changed and are no longer called by the names they had before their deaths. Why, then, are "Your servants" newly named?

A simple explanation might perhaps be that, with respect to worship of God, there simply is no title higher than *chasid* in the entire Scriptures. So while after martyrdom, *chasidim* do rise to higher levels by virtue of their deaths, there is no other name by which they can be called. All that can be said is that they have become greater *chasidim*.

It may also be as follows. We learn in the holy Zohar (vol. II, 42a) that the epithet *chasid* (saint) is derived from the Hebrew word, *chesed* (loving-kindness), as is well known. Now, *chesed* always implies kindness toward others. We learn in the Talmud (*Sanhedrin* 110b): "The Generation of the Wilderness has no place in the world to come. This was the opinion of R. Akiba. . . . Rabba Bar Channa in the name of R. Yochanan said, 'It was an instance when R. Akiba abandoned his *chasid* qualities.'" The talmudic reference to the *chasid* qualities of R. Akiba was to his universally acknowledged love for Jews, his defense of them, and his prayers for the happiest of fates for them. Clearly, only someone of a benign disposition, who is benevolent and transparent in his dealings with others, can become a *chasid*. If someone is not by nature a good person, he will have to work hard to turn himself into someone of service to Jews, and only then can he become a *chasid*.

From this we can understand why at the *Simchath Beth HaShoevah* (Water-Drawing Celebrations) in the Temple, which began on this, the second night of the Festival of Sukkoth, only *chasidim* (Men of Piety) and *anshei maaseh* (Men of Stature) used to dance before the crowds (see Mishnah, Sukkah 5:1–4). The holy Rav, in his *siddur*, discusses the reasons why.

Let us try to answer another question. Why is it that the Water-Drawing Ceremonies in the Temple, which celebrated God's *chesed* (loving-kindness), began precisely on the second night of the Festival of Sukkoth, whose *ushpizin* (symbolic guest) is the Patriarch Isaac, the paradigm of *gevurah* (withholding)?

This can perhaps be understood with the help of what was said above. In the world to come, Isaac will be the champion of Jews and the chief advocate for Israel. He will attempt to atone for them even with his body and his life. As we learn in the Talmud (*Shabbath* 89b), Isaac will say to the Holy Blessed One, "Behold! I offered my up soul as a sacrifice to You." The characteristic *gevurah* (withholding) of Isaac manifests itself here as the desire to take upon himself the judgment that was intended for all Israel. Such *gevurah* is actually the highest level of *chesed*, and so it was specifically on this second day of Sukkoth, when the *ushpizin* is the Patriarch Isaac, that the Celebration of the Water-Drawing, which is *chesed*, began. The *chasidim* and *anshei maaseh* were dancing in response to the outpouring of *chesed* that was flowing to the Jewish people at that time.

We need to understand, however, why it is only in the world to come that Isaac will say to the Holy Blessed One, "Behold! I offered up my soul as a sacrifice to You." Why did he not intercede during the destruction of the Holy Temple, or during any of the calamities that have befallen the Jewish people? Why at such times does Isaac not beg God to let him atone for the Jewish people, saying, "Behold! I offered myself up to You"?

The deeds of the Patriarchs are templates for their children. The *Akeidah* (Binding of Isaac) was only a commencement of Jewish forms of worship. In all of our present-day worship, we say, "God of Abraham, God of Isaac, and God of Jacob . . ." to express our connection with their ways if worshipping God. And so, the *Akeidah* was not only a test of Isaac, but also the commencement of a form of worship that requires total self sacrifice for God and for Jewish people.

The *Akeidah* was a test of the desire and intention of Abraham and Isaac. It was never actually accomplished or completed because the angel said to Abraham (Genesis 22:12) "Do not harm the lad." For this reason, the murder of a Jew by idolaters, which as an action devoid of worshipful intention is in absolute antithesis to the *Akeidah*, actually consummates the *Akeidah*. The *Akeidah* was just the beginning, the expression of intent and desire, while the murder of a Jew is the conclusion of the act. Thus, the *Akeidah* and all the murders of Jews since are components of one event.

That is why it will only be in the world to come, may it happen speedily and in our days, when the last of those to be murdered in order to complete the *Akeidah* process will have been martyred for God, that Isaac will say: "Behold! I offered up my soul to You, in an act that has been completed by all the martyrs who consummated my sacrifice." This could not have been said at any earlier time, because only in the world to come will the sacrifice have been completed in fact. Before the completion of the *Akeidah* of Isaac and his children, before the last sacrifice of murdered Jews, Isaac cannot say "Behold! I offered up my soul to You."

This is what is hinted at in the verse (Genesis 22:1) "After these events, God tested Abraham." The test refers not only to the events directly relating to the *Akeidah* at which only Abraham and Isaac were tested, but also, as the text says, "After these events," because all murdered Jews comprise the final act of the *Akeidah*. Their martyrdom turns God's wrath away from the Jewish people, and so the murdered ones die for all the Jewish people, in an act that rises to the level of the *chesed* (loving-kindness) of Abraham. This is why the verse quoted above does not call murdered *chasidim* (saints) by any other name, as was the case with "servants." Even though they do attain a higher level, the chief desire and purpose of *chasidim* is ever the *chesed* that they can perform for the Jewish people, as opposed to a desire to be elevated themselves. As stated earlier, *chasidim* are so called because of their *chesed* for Jewish people.

Therefore, on an anniversary day such as this, and on all days like this, we need to repent. It stands to reason, for if every animal sacrifice in the Temple needed to be accompanied by repentance, how much more so now, with these holiest of sacrifices, must we repent. And if, God forbid, we do not accompany their deaths with our repentance, and we do not take it upon ourselves to worship God from now on, it is possible that the martyred souls in heaven will ask, "If this is so, why then were we sacrificed?"

With this, we can understand the Talmud (*Yoma* 66b) that relates the following description of the Scapegoat ritual of Yom Kippur in the Temple: "They made an elevated causeway over which the scapegoat was led, because the Babylonians would pull its hair, shouting, 'Take our sins and go. Take our sins and go.' R. Judah said, 'They were not really Babylonians, but Alexandrians. But, since the Palestinians hated the Babylonians so much, they called the Alexandrians in this instance, Babylonians.'"

Even at a simple level, this is difficult to understand. One normally associates an enemy with something bad, and yet in this instance the Babylonians are credited with a good thing. That is, it would certainly appear to be a good thing, for surely the desire to have the scapegoat hurry along was motivated by the desire to be rid of their sins. That is why they shouted "Take our sins and go. Take our sins and go." And why did R. Jose, whose family was from Babylon, react in the way the Talmud recounts when R. Judah said, "They were not actually Babylonians, but Alexandrians"? He said, "May your mind be relieved even as you have relieved my mind!" End quote. What was so bad about their behavior that R. Jose, a Babylonian, was relieved to hear that they were actually Alexandrian?

When we see how the people of Jerusalem behaved, it becomes obvious why the Alexandrian behavior looked so bad. We learn subsequently in the Mishnah (*Yoma* 6:4): "The nobles of Jerusalem would walk with the priest leading the scapegoat. At every booth they would say to him, 'Here is food and water.' They accompanied him from booth to booth." This is the essential teaching to be learned from this story: When a Jew attempts to atone for the sins of Israel, even if he is not atoning with his own life but with the life of a goat, he should still not go alone while we stay in our places without doing anything. So, as the Mishnah recounts, the nobles of Jerusalem accompanied him, walking a little in his holy footsteps. Their behavior was the opposite of those who said, "Take our sins and go," and this is why they attributed this conduct to their enemies, the Babylonians.

From now on, we must repent, elevating our worship. Aside from the fact that we ought to do it for our own sake, it is also for the sake of the holy martyrs that we need to enlarge upon our worship of God and to repent still more. Then God, blessed be He, will save us. Even though we do not deserve to be saved, God forbid, He will do it for the sake of the holy sacrifices. For shall it have been in vain, God forbid, that their blood has been spilled like water?

This explains the verse with which we began the chapter, "Say unto God, You are my Lord: My prosperity is not Your charge. But for the holy who are in the earth and the heroes in whom all my longing dwells." The name *Adonai*—God—is the paradigm of Judgment. What we are saying to God is this: Your Judgment upon the holy ones of Israel, who have been murdered, has been done. Now, though I do not merit salvation and "My prosperity is not Your charge," nevertheless, "For the holy who are in the earth," for their sake, rescue us swiftly.

# Sh'mini Atzeret (The Eighth Day Festival)—October 24, 1940

*"The eighth day shall be a time of retreat for you when you shall do no mundane work. As a burnt offering, for an appeasing fragrance to God, you shall sacrifice one bull, one ram . . ."* (Numbers 29:36–39)

We learn in the Midrash (*Tanchuma*, *Pinchos* 16); A parable: "The king commanded a banquet for seven days, to which he invited all his subjects. Upon completion of the seven days of feasting, he said to his loved ones; 'Enough! We have done our duty by our subjects. Now let us, you and I, revel and feast with what remains, on a measure of meat, or fish, or vegetables.' So the Holy Blessed One speaks to the Jewish people, saying, 'All the sacrifices that you brought during the seven days of the Festival of Sukkoth were brought on behalf of the nations of the world. But now, on the eighth day, let us, you and I, feast with what remains—one bull, one ram.'"

We need to understand what the Midrash is hinting to us with its injunction to revel and feast with just a measure of meat, fish, or vegetables. Why, on the eighth day of Sukkoth, a Festival day of rejoicing for all Israel, do we not, in fact, bring an abundance of sacrifices, as we do on the other days of the Festival?

The explanation may perhaps be as follows. We learn in the Talmud (*Sanhedrin* 91b); R. Hiyya b. Abba said in R. Johanan's name: "Whence do we learn that upon the resurrection of the dead, all prophets will sing in one voice? From the verse (Isaiah 52:8), 'All Your seers shall raise their voice; together will they sing.'" What does this prediction—that the prophets will eventually sing in one voice—have to teach us personally?

Another, more obvious, question is this: The verse in Isaiah refers not to prophets but to seers. Rashi (Isaiah 52:8) explains that "seers" are lookouts standing on the walls and watchtowers, whose job it is to watch for visitors and announce their arrival to the town. Why does the Talmud use the verse to predict what prophets will do? This question is not so difficult to reconcile, because the Talmud often refers to prophets as seers. An instance of this is the Talmud (*Megillah* 2b) that states: "*M'NaTZ'PaCH* were said by the seers." The five, final, Hebrew letters *mem-nun-tzaddi-peh-chaf* were drafted into the Hebrew alphabet by the seers, i.e., the biblical prophets. As for why the Talmud sometimes refers to the prophets as seers, one assumes that every time the appellation "seers" is used, it is done intentionally.

It is possible that both the talmudic reference to the verse in Isaiah using the word "prophet" instead of "seer" and the quote from the Talmud in *Megillah* are hinting at the same teaching. It is well known that the five, final, Hebrew letters *M'NaTZ'PaCH* (*mem-nun-tzaddi-peh-chaf*) are manifestations of the divine attribute of *Din*, Judgment. They restrict the written word, preventing it from growing any further. After a final letter has been written, nothing more can be added to the word—and yet, the difference between the simple and final forms of these letters can be observed only in the written word. In pronunciation and speech, there are no differences between the simple and final forms of the Hebrew letters.

Perhaps the reason for this is because written words are capable of absorbing more of the Divine Light than spoken words. As we see in the Talmud (*Pesachim* 50a); R. Abina taught: "The verse (Exodus 3:15) says, 'God said . . . this is My name forever, this is My notice for all generations.' God was telling Moses, 'Not as I am written am I pronounced; My name is written as *YHVH,* and pronounced *Adonai.*'"

So we see that even now the written form can contain within itself the revelation of the tetragrammaton, *YHVH*, while speech is currently incapable of doing so. Only within the precincts of the Temple or in the future world to come can the name of God, *YHVH*, be uttered.

This could be why the Talmud says, "*M'NaTZ'PaCH* were invented by the seers." Or rather, as the Talmud confirms, the five, final letter forms were actually the original, ancient Hebrew forms that had been forgotten. The prophets merely reinstated them, reestablishing them in common usage.

It is well known that the revelation of Divine *Din* (Judgment) is above the revelation of Divine *Rachamim* (Mercy). We know that Divine *Din* is difficult to accept and to grasp, because the revelation of Divine Judgment manifests itself as Law and Punishment, God forbid, although this situation endures only temporarily, as we have learned (Rashi, Genesis 1:1): "In the original Thought, there arose to create and rule the world with *Din* (Judgment). Only because God saw that the world could not exist under such conditions, He first introduced *Rachamim* (Mercy) and made it a partner with *Din* (Judgment). In the future, in the world to come, the tribe of Levi, which represents the attribute of *Din*, will perform the Temple service. All rulings on *Halachah* (Law) will be decided according to the School of Shamai, at the level of *Din*, as is found in the writings of the Arizal (R. Isaac Luria), of blessed memory. In this world, however, the *cohen* (priests) perform the Temple worship, and the *Halachah* is decided according to the school of Hillel, at the level of *chesed* (loving-kindness).

This is why the prophets—who are called seers because they stand like watchers, gazing outwards and looking down from their elevated position—looked down from their holy heights and drafted the final letters *M'NaTZ'PaCH* into the written Hebrew alphabet. They did this because the written form has greater scope for the revelation of God, and can contain and absorb the great revelation of the world to come that is in *Din* (Judgment). Outside of the written form, this revelation would be impossible.

So, what the prophets revealed is that in all the suffering of the Jewish people, the *Din* and punishment are really a tremendous revelation of God. It is only because the world cannot yet absorb or grasp the great revelation, which belongs to the world to come, that *Din* manifests itself in this world as strict judgment and harsh punishment. Therefore, the prophets did what they could to bring about this tremendous revelation. They succeeded in having the final letters *M'NaTZ'PaCH* reintegrated into the Hebrew alphabet, to facilitate a drawing down of this great revelation, and through this to bring about a sweetening of the *Din* upon Israel.

However, it was only because the prophets could look down upon the suffering of the Jewish people as from above, like watchmen, that they were able to see the tremendous Light within it. This is not possible for someone who is looking from below. He sees only the suffering, and it is difficult for him to see the Divine Light within the pain. Our teacher Moses said to God (Exodus 5:5), "Why do You mistreat Your people?" because at that time, the Jewish people walked around with the same thoughts and talked as we do now, saying, "We watched for salvation, saying, 'Another moment, and we will be rescued,' but the result has been a worsening situation and greater pain." And so Moses said to God, "I know and I can see that everything is for the good, but why do You mistreat Your people? They cannot bear the suffering, and because of it they are unable to see the good in it."

While it may have appeared once that there were prophets who both rebuked and sang, and others who spoke only words of rebuke, revealing all the punishments that were coming, God forbid, in the future this will clearly be perceived as an illusion. In the future it will be obvious that all the words of all the prophets were only ever one song, because then the Divine Light within *Din* will be revealed, sweetening everything to *Rachamim* (Mercy). This is the meaning of the verse "All Your seers shall raise their voices; together will they sing." They will all sing the same song, because the verse refers to them as seers, who look out and down from high above—who therefore are looking from above where *Din* are the highest revelation, to below, where *Rachamim* reigns—so, they can reveal *Rachamim*, Mercy, out of *Din*, Judgment.

*Sh'mini Atzeret*, the Eighth Day Festival, corresponds to the moment when Bride and Groom are completely alone together for the first time. The Holy Blessed One and the Jewish People are united, as is well known. And so God says, "Let us revel and feast, You and I alone, with a measure of meat, fish, or vegetables." You must bear in mind that it is not only when things are going well, but also in times of restriction and withholding, God forbid, that the Holy Blessed One is alone and united with the Jewish people. From this there should come about a revelation of salvation, speedily.

# Be'reshith—October 26, 1940

*"In the beginning of God's creation of heaven and earth . . ."* (Genesis 1:1)

Rashi (ibid.) explains: "God created the world for the sake of the Torah, which is called *Reshith* (Beginning)—'The beginning of His way' (Proverbs 8:22)—and for the sake of Israel, who are called *Reshith* (Beginning)—'The beginning of His increase' (Jeremiah 2:3)."

We learn in the Talmud (*Sanhedrin* 101a); Our Rabbis taught: "Whoever recites a verse of the 'Song of Songs' treating it as a secular tune, or recites verses in drinking houses, brings evil upon the world, because the Torah girds herself in sackcloth and standing before the Holy Blessed One laments, 'Sovereign of the Universe! Your children have made me into a harp upon which they play frivolously.' God replies, 'My daughter, while they are eating and drinking, what would you rather have them do?' To which she replies, 'Sovereign of the Universe! If they have mastered Scripture, let them occupy themselves with the Torah, the Prophets, and the Writings; if they are students of the Mishnah, with Mishnah, Laws, and Legends; if students of the Talmud, let them engage in the laws of Passover, Pentecost, and Tabernacles on the respective Festivals.'"

On the simplest level, it is difficult to understand why the Holy Blessed One asks the Torah, "When they are eating and drinking, what would you rather have them do?" God surely knows how they should occupy themselves. And why does the Torah answer, "If they have mastered Scripture, let them occupy themselves with the Torah, the Prophets, and the Writings; if they are students of the

Mishnah, with Mishnah, Laws and Legends; if students of the Talmud, let them engage in the laws of Passover, etc."? Why does she not simply answer that they ought to study Torah? Surely, it is obvious to every person that they should learn what they are able to learn. When the Torah commanded (Deut. 6:7) "Teach them to your children and speak of them . . ." it was not necessary to explain in detail what each person should study, because everybody knows what he ought to be learning.

It may perhaps be that when the Holy Blessed One asked the question, He was asking rhetorically, to apologize for the Jewish people. He was suggesting to the Torah that they were quoting verses in drinking houses and while eating and drinking because this is a time when the evil inclination has most control over them. As the Talmud notes (*Berachoth* 32a): "Will a lion roar over a pile of straw as over a load of meat?" Thus God asked, "But with what else should they occupy themselves at such times?" To which the Torah replied, "If they have mastered Scripture, let them occupy themselves with the Torah, the Prophets, and the Writings . . ." and so forth. As we have already said elsewhere, a person who learns Torah but is not transformed thereby into holiness and Torah is merely a bookshelf containing books. He remains what he was before beginning to study—a piece of wood. We find this also in the Midrash (*Yalkut Shimoni*, Proverbs: 950): When R. Meir wanted save his teacher Elisha b. Abuya from Gehenna, he quoted the Mishnah (*Shabbath* 15:1), "We rescue the cover of the book, together with the book on the Sabbath. We can rescue Elisha b. Abuya because of the Torah that is in him." There, R. Meir compared Elisha to the cover of a book, which can be saved when we rescue the book. The case, however, is quite different with a real *Talmid Chacham* (pious scholar), of whom the Talmud says (*Makkoth* 22b), "How stupid are the people who stand up in deference to a scroll of the Torah but do not stand up in deference to a great personage." It is clear that a righteous person is himself compared to a scroll of the Torah—and even more than that—and not merely to the cover alone.

This is why the Torah replied, "If they have mastered scriptural knowledge," meaning if through learning the Scriptures they have really internalized the Scriptures, then even when they are eating and drinking they will not be at the mercy of their desires. If they are students of the Mishnah, then the same applies through learning Mishnah, and so forth. If a person has absorbed the Scriptures, Mishnah, or Talmud properly, then even if his evil inclination is at war with him he will nonetheless overcome his inclination. The Torah also said, "Let them engage in the laws of Passover, Pentecost, and Tabernacles on the respective Festivals," because time itself would then act to remind them of their obligations. This is why it is so important to have fixed times for studying Torah: so that when a person forgets, or is prevented, time itself reminds him and gives him strength to ignore and overcome all obstacles.

At the present time, when we face so many obstacles, it is not eating and drinking but our pain and suffering, may the Merciful One protect us, that prevents us from learning Torah. Nevertheless, in the past, all people, including tradesmen and businessmen, set aside fixed periods for Torah study so that the times set for the classes should themselves help them not to abandon them. Now, when we have so much more free time, we must from the outset assign ourselves even more fixed times for study than we did before. Then God will have mercy and save us, and we will be able to busy ourselves with Torah and worship out of abundance.

To return to what we have discussed above: Because they have absorbed the Scriptures and the Mishnah, this gives them the strength to overcome all obstacles, whether the obstacles arise from a surfeit of eating and drinking or whether, God forbid, they come of suffering.

"In the beginning of God's creation of heaven and earth . . ." The creation was for the sake of the Jewish people and the Torah, as Rashi said. The reason for the whole world is the Jewish people and the Torah, and so, even though there are times when, God forbid, the world is against the Jewish people and the Torah, we hope that God will again swiftly reveal the true meaning of the world. Then God will rescue the Jewish people and the Torah, and reveal the Original Thought, in which everything is for the Torah and for Israel. Amen.

# *Noah*—November 2, 1940

*"With God did Noah walk . . ."* (Genesis 6:9)

Rashi (ibid.) comments: "Noah required support, but Abraham had the strength in his righteousness to walk alone."

We learn in the Talmud (*Sanhedrin* 104a); Our Rabbis taught: "It once happened that two Jews were taken captive on Mount Carmel, and their captor was walking behind them. One captive said to the other, 'The camel walking in front of us is blind in one eye. It carries two flasks: one of wine, and the other of oil. There are two men leading it: one a Jew, and the other a heathen.' Their captor said to them, 'Hey! You stiff-necked people, whence do you know this?' They replied, 'Because the camel is nibbling at the foliage only on that side where it can see, but not on the other side where it is blind. And because it is laden with two flasks, one of wine and the other of oil, because we see the drops of wine absorbed by the earth while the drops of oil remain on the surface. And of the two men leading it, one a Jew and the other a heathen, because a heathen obeys the call of nature on the roadway while a Jew modestly turns aside.' The slave driver hastened onward and found that it was as they had said. Returning, he kissed them on the head, brought them into his house, and prepared a great feast. Dancing before them, he exclaimed, 'Blessed is He Who chose of Abraham's seed and imparted to them of His wisdom. Wherever they go they become lords to their masters!' Then he freed them, and they went home in peace."

R. Shlomo Eidels (Maharsh'a), in his commentary on the Talmud (ibid.), explains why the slave driver chose to ridicule the two captive Jews by calling them "stiff-necked people." The reason, he says, is that although conditions of exile and slavery are likely to dull people's senses, making them lose their wisdom, the slave driver observed these two captives being so obstinate they could still try to be clever, despite their suffering.

As there are seventy faces to the Torah, I may add another explanation. The slave driver did not call the Jews "stiff-necked" merely because they were stubbornly trying to be clever, by obstinately extolling their own wisdom. He was in fact admitting that the captives were wise—outstandingly so.

We need to understand: God said to Moses (Exodus 33:2–4), "I will send my angel ahead of you. . . . However, I will not go with you, as you are a stiff-necked people and I may destroy you along the way." God's given reason is clear and unambiguous: The Jewish people are too stubborn, and God will therefore send an angel instead. Yet later in the same text (Exodus 34:9) Moses said to God, "If you are indeed pleased with me, O God, let my Lord go among us, because the nation are a stiff-necked people, but forgive our sins and errors and make us Your own." How is it possible for the same reason to be given in support of an action and for its opposite? God refused to go with the Jewish people because they were obstinate, and proposed sending an angel instead, while Moses argued that God alone should go with them precisely because of their obstinacy.

The point is that being stiff-necked is one of the most transcendent virtues. Whoever is not stubborn and obstinate is inconstant and irresolute. In dealing with a person who cannot make up his mind, it may be impossible to arrive at any conclusion. Now he says he wants to worship God, while an hour later he may be a different person altogether. In particular, when faced with temptation or a test of his resolve the inconstant man will fail, God forbid. An obstinate person, on the other hand, is straightforward when spoken to. Once he has decided to worship God, he can be trusted to remain firm in his conviction. The more stiff-necked and stubborn the person is, the more he will endure, even if his conviction is tested in some way.

The evil aspect of obstinacy becomes manifest only when a person uses it in the service of evil, or stubbornly holds on to his character flaws, God forbid. But this is true of all the virtues; they can all be perverted and used for something bad. For example, the virtue of loving-kindness, *chesed*, can be used in the service of sinful love, God forbid. A well-known teaching from the Great Maggid of Mezritch explains the following biblical verse (Leviticus 20:17) "If a man take his sister, or half sister, in a consensual sexual act, it is an extremely shameful perversion." The Hebrew word *chesed* is used to describe the act, but *chesed* is more often used as a description of loving-kindness. The Maggid explains that the love between brother and sister is love on a plane far beyond sexuality. A brother and sister who are sexual with each other are depraved because their love, which ought to be transcendent, is corrupted, and *chesed* is being used for something bad, God forbid.

In the same way, the virtue of stubbornness can also be corrupted. After the sin of the golden calf, God said to Moses (Exodus 33: 2–4), "I will send my angel ahead of you. . . . However, I will not go with you, as you are a stiff-necked people and I may destroy you along the way." God was saying that the Jews had taken the virtue of stubbornness and used it to do wrong. Then God told Moses, "I will have mercy and show kindness to whomever I desire," (Exodus 33:19) and subsequently revealed to Moses the Thirteen Attributes of Mercy (Exodus 34: 6–8) through which Jews could draw down forgiveness for their sins. Moses realized that he had been given a way of saving the situation, and said, "Now I have a solution. Really, the Jewish people are noble, righteous, and heroic, capable of withstanding tremendous challenges as befits their spiritual stature and great resolve. Problems arise only when their character flaws, added to their tremendous obstinacy, are put to no good use. So, forgive our sins and errors, our deliberate and accidental transgressions, for then [as Rashi explains] we will be Your very singular possession, putting our stubbornness always in Your service, and then it will be appropriate for You to walk with us."

We learn in the Talmud (*Shabbath* 88a): When the Jewish people proclaimed (Exodus 24:7), "All that God has said, we will do and we will listen," giving precedence to "we will do" over "we will listen," a heavenly echo went forth and exclaimed, "Who revealed this secret to My children, a secret employed only by the Ministering Angels?"

Moses argues as follows: If when acting like Ministering Angels the Jews are so praiseworthy, then when they utilize a characteristic such as stubbornness for the service of God they deserve more than an Angel. They deserve that God Himself should go with them.

We have learned that an angel who is sent down to this world needs seven days of purification before it can return to its previous exalted state. For Jews this is not so. On the contrary, the Jew is actually capable of worshipping and bringing God's dwelling place down into this very world, as was clearly the case with our patriarchs, and again at Mount Sinai, in the Tabernacle, and in Jerusalem's Holy Temple. Indeed, the heart and body of every Jew is the most fitting place for the dwelling of God. This means that while angels are altered by contact with the world, the Jew remains unaffected; he resists change. The Jew who worships God with obstinacy is acting out the consequence of our connection to God—of whom the prophet spoke and said (Malachi 3:6), "I am God; I have not changed." It is another way of saying (Psalms 139:13) "Light and darkness are the same to Him." It means that all states of being, *sephirot*, or physical forms have no effect whatsoever upon God.

Therefore, Jews who are connected to the Sovereign Body are also connected to this attribute of immutability, through which they remain unchanged by contact with the physical world and are able to withstand all stresses or pressures. Not only are we able to withstand any and all challenges, we are always, no matter what the external circumstances, capable of bringing God into this world. This is what it means to be stiff-necked and obstinate at the level of "I am God; I have not changed." This is a much higher level than that occupied by the angels, and explains why Moses asked God to walk with us, rather than sending us an angel in His stead, precisely because we are a stiff-necked people.

To be stiff-necked and continue functioning as worshipping Jews, to endure and to perform the duties incumbent upon us, involves the high level of stubbornness described above. In addition to this, to actually engage fully in study of the Torah, entering deeply into the knowing of it, is an even greater challenge—for regardless of the troubles besetting us, there is no great difficulty in putting on phylacteries (*t'fillin*) or fulfilling other practical Commandments. But to study Torah, and especially to enter into the depths of the Torah, is extremely difficult.

To return to the story from the Talmud quoted above, when the slave driver said, "You stiff-necked people, whence do you know this?," the slave driver had already been aware that the Jews were a stiff-necked people, but he had not known that they were so stiff-necked that they could still think clearly and cleverly even in the midst of slavery and pain. As we said above, the virtue of being stiff-necked is connected to the divine attribute of "I am God; I have not changed." When the slave driver realized this, he was moved to free the two Jews, as was related in the Talmud.

Noah had many enemies, as Rashi (Genesis 7:13) comments: "The men of Noah's generation had made plans, saying, 'When we see him entering the ark, we'll smash it open and kill him.'" It is reasonable to assume that among such a generation of evildoers, Noah must have suffered greatly. There were many barriers to Noah's worship of God, and he needed support. Abraham the Patriarch also faced many tests and trials, especially from King Nimrod, who threw him into the fiery furnace. So, Rashi explains, "This was the difference between Noah and Abraham: Noah required assistance in order to remain upright." Who needs support? Obviously, only someone who is jeopardy of falling. Noah did not have the resolve to overcome the tests and challenges alone, he needed God to support and maintain him in his worship. But, Rashi continues, "Abraham could brace himself and continue on his spiritual journey." He took strength from his connection to God, without ever stumbling or halting. He empowered himself to carry on because he was an archetype, modeled upon the Holy Blessed One, Who says, "I am God; I have not changed."

# *Toldoth*—November 30, 1940

*"And may God give you the dew of heaven and the fat of the earth, much grain and wine. Nations will serve you; governments will bow down to you."* (Genesis 27:28–29)

We need to understand, at least to the extent our limited minds are able, what this story is hinting at. Why was it fated that the blessings that Isaac our patriarch bestowed upon Jacob were really intended for Esau?

We learn in the Talmud (*Hagigah* 15b) in the name of R. Meir: "When a person suffers, to what expression does the *Shechinah* give utterance? 'O woe! My head, O woe! My arms.'"

Why did R. Meir ask, "When a person suffers, etc.," and not, as we find elsewhere, "When the Jewish people suffer . . ."? Secondly, how valid is the inquiry? How can we ask, "To what expression does the *Shechinah* give utterance?" when there is no indication that the *Shechinah* says anything at all? Why should it speak? It has already been said, quoting God (Psalms 91:15), "I am with him in his distress." This does not imply that God gives utterance to any particular expression, and so the question "To what expression does He give utterance?" is irrelevant.

R. Meir's original quote in the Mishnah (*Sanhedrin* 6:7), asking what the *Shechinah* says, is in respect of a person who has been sentenced to death by hanging. R. Meir's point is that even when it is just one individual who is in pain the *Shechinah* still says, "O woe!" He makes this point because it was possible to interpret the verse "I am with him in his distress" to mean that God is with us only when all the Jewish people together are in distress. In the Midrash (Exodus Rabbah 2:5) on God's appearance to Moses at the burning bush, where the connection between God's suffering and that of the Jewish people is made, the verse "I am with him in his distress" is quoted, and our sages explain that God appeared to Moses from inside the burning bush to show him that He was with all the Jewish people in their distress. Here, however, R. Meir is adding that the *Shechinah* also suffers when even a single Jew is in distress. He does this by singling out a single individual who was sentenced to death for his own crime.

This is why in R. Meir's question it is the *Shechinah* who speaks, because in talking of the Holy Blessed One, we usually refer to *YHVH* (God), Who animates the *sephirah* of *Tifferet* (Glory). Another name for the *sephirah* of *Tifferet* is *K'neseth Israel* (The Congregation of Israel). The Congregation of Israel is by definition a group. The *sephirah* of *Tifferet* (Glory) is also known as "Mercy," because it synthesizes the two antithetical *sephirot* of *Chesed* (Loving-Kindness) and *Gevurah* (Judgment). Thus the *sephirah* of *Tifferet* is also by definition a grouping. This is why it represents the Congregation of Israel, a group. The *Shechinah*, on the other hand is the *sephirah* of *Malkhut* (Sovereignty), which, even though it is also equated with *K'neseth Israel* nonetheless also includes singularity and individuality. This is because individuation, separation, counting, and numbering are possible only in the *sephirah* of *Malkhut*, as is well known.

Therefore, regarding even the individual who worships God, the *Shechinah* (i.e., *Malkhut*) says to the Holy Blessed One (i.e., *Tifferet*), "Look at this child whom I bring to You," as is well known. That is, not just the entire Jewish people are good, but also this individual person is righteous and saintly.

With his question, R. Meir is hinting that the *Shechinah* suffers not only when the entire Jewish people are in trouble, but that the pain of an individual person also ascends upon high. This one is murdered and that one dies from his suffering, may the Merciful One protect us. This one's mind gives out and his heart and whole body becomes weak from the suffering—for as the Talmud states (*Hullin* 35b), "What difference does it make if I kill all of him, or only part of him?" Even though the Jewish people as a whole are eternal, when one individual dies, both he and his life are lost, and until the resurrection of the dead his life is cut off, may the Merciful One protect us. This, then, is the meaning of the particular choice of wording, "'When a 'person' suffers," as we learn in the Talmud (*Sanhedrin* 38a), "A 'person' was created solitary." This is why even over the pain of a single individual the *Shechinah* says, "O woe! My head, O woe! My arms." It is specifically the *Shechinah* who speaks up when an individual suffers because she embodies the concepts of singularity and individuality, as we said above.

Let us return to our original question about the circumstances surrounding Isaac's blessing of Jacob. Rashi, quoting the Midrash (Leviticus Rabbah 4:6) comments on the verse (Genesis 46:26), "All the soul that came with Jacob to Egypt": "Esau's family consisted of only six (himself and his five sons) and Scripture refers to them in the plural as 'the souls of his house.' This is because they worshipped many gods. Now, the family of Jacob coming to Egypt consisted of seventy people and Scripture calls them 'soul,' in the singular, because they all served One God."

The truth is that the Jewish people are always united because they share one holy soul. Therefore if Isaac had blessed Jacob directly, he would have blessed the Congregation of Israel only as a whole. The will of God, blessed be He, was that Isaac should also bless every single Jew individually, and so God brought it about that Isaac thought he was blessing Esau, who epitomizes separation and "souls," while actually blessing Jacob. Thus, he also blessed each individual Jew.

On the verse "*And* may God give you . . ." with we which we opened the chapter, Rashi's explanation (Genesis 27:28) is: "*And* may God give you, and then return and give you again." From what we have said above, it may be explained thus: If Isaac had blessed all Jews together as one group, it would have sufficed to say, "May God give you." However, since each individual is also blessed separately, it is necessary to give and then to return and give again—now to this one, and later to that one, and so for each and everyone; now this need, and then later a different need.

# *VaYishlach*—December 14, 1940

*"I am unworthy of all the kindness and faith that You have shown me. With [only] my staff I crossed the Jordan, and now I have enough for two camps. Please, rescue me from the hand of my brother—from the hand of Esau. I am afraid of him, for he can come and kill us all—mothers and children alike. And You once said, 'I will do good things with you, and make your descendants like the sand grains of the sea, which are too numerous to count.'"*
(Genesis 32:11–14)

  Rashi (ibid.) explains Jacob's fear thus: "I fear that my sins have doomed me to be abandoned to Esau's clutches, and yet You said 'I will do good things with you.'"
  We need to understand: If Jacob was afraid that through his sins he had brought ruin upon himself, how would it help for him to remind God of His promise, "I will do good things with you"?
  It is perhaps as follows: We learn in the Midrash (Exodus Rabbah 2:12) about the verse describing the meeting of Moses and God at the burning bush, "When God saw that [Moses] was going to investigate, He called to him from inside the bush. 'Moses Moses!' He said." (Exodus 3:4) The Midrash notes: "At the critical moment in the *Akeidah* (Binding of Isaac) when we hear God calling Abraham, we find the words "Abraham, Abraham!" (Genesis 22:11) There is a comma between the two words. When God calls to Moses, however, there is no comma: "Moses Moses!"
  Why is this so? asks the Midrash, answering, "The answer may be found in the example of a man foundering beneath an unbearable weight. He calls to whom-

ever is nearest, 'Hey you you come quick and help me shed this load!'" God calls urgently, "Moses Moses!" twice in quick succession without any punctuation between the words because God has, as it were, an unbearable burden upon Him. He calls to Moses, who is closest to Him, to help relieve Him of the burden.

This is the difference: At one level, the verse (Psalm 91:15) "He will call on Me and I will answer him; I am with him in his distress . . ." means that when Jews are in pain, God forbid, there is a point at which God bears the distress together with us. Another level, however, is when the pain of the Jews is so great that they have no strength to bear it. Then the strength to resist, to continue to endure, to remain alive in the midst of such terrible hardships and merciless affliction, is provided solely by the Holy Blessed One. In this case the brunt of the burden is, as it were, upon God. It is not human Jewish strength that bears and withstands such agony, but God's strength that He gives to Jews. It is by far the greater burden of pain that is borne by God. So God is praying to the Jewish people, as He prayed then to Moses, "Please relieve me of this unbearable burden."

In the midst of such terrible anguish, how can we possibly help relieve God of His unbearable burden? We can do it with repentance, with prayer, with charity, and also with the compassion we show one another.

When the pain was not in itself so unbearable, and He, God, was only at the first level of "I am with him in his distress . . .", then we might conceivably have asked ourselves whether we were worthy of redemption and salvation. But in the present circumstances the pain is so great, may the Merciful One help us, that a level has been reached where all the burden of the pain is really, as it were, upon God Himself. At this time, in heaven above, there must be great haste with the mercy and the redemption, because He, God, is guiltless, and why should God, our Father, our King, have to suffer, God forbid, so much pain?

Jacob is saying, "I am unworthy of all the kindness, and perhaps the sins that I have committed have doomed me to be given over into the hands of Esau. However, You said, 'I will do good things with you.'" Besides the obvious meaning, there is also the deeper meaning contained in the word "with." God promised Jacob, "I will be with you." Now that the main burden of Jacob's doom is upon God, as it were, Jacob prays, "Even if, due to my sin, I do not merit salvation, God forbid, and I am not worthy of redemption, You, God, are worthy. Please save me, immediately and straight away."

is written (Ezekiel 16:6), "When I passed over you, I saw you wallowing in your blood."

Let us try to understand the meaning of Moses' question (Exodus 3:11), "Who am I that I should go to Pharaoh? . . . and how can I possibly get the Israelites out of Egypt?" Rashi (ibid.) explains that Moses was asking how the people of Israel would merit the miracles that would have to be wrought for them to bring them forth from Egypt. To which the Holy Blessed One replied, "In merit of the purpose I have in mind for them, for they are destined to accept the Torah upon this mountain in the third month after leaving Egypt."

But if their destined acceptance of the Torah made them worthy of redemption, why did the Jewish people also need the merit of observing the two commandments, the blood of the Paschal lamb and the blood of circumcision?

We learn in the holy book *Imrei Elimelech* (p. 114) that the verse (Exodus 14:15) "God said to Moses, 'Why are you crying out to Me? Speak to the Israelites, and let them start moving'" teaches us that the Creator, Blessed be He, cares more for the honor of the Jewish people than for His own honor. This is so because He does not forgive anyone who impugns the honor of His people, the Children of Israel. When our teacher Moses prayed to God, blessed be He, to save the Jewish people for the sake of Heaven's honor, God said to him, "Why are you crying out to Me?" meaning "Why are you crying out for Me, on My behalf? Rather, 'Speak to the Israelites.' Pray on their behalf, because I care much more for the honor of my people, the Children of Israel, and I will certainly help them in all their troubles."

This may be the reason why the angel Michael offers Jewish souls on the heavenly altar before the Holy Blessed One, as we learn in the Talmud (*Hagigah* 12b and *Tosaphot*, ibid.). Why is it specifically the angel Michael who offers up the sacrifice? Michael is the defender and advocate of the Jewish people, as is mentioned in the Book of Daniel (10:21). With every act of sacrifice he champions the cause of the Jewish people, saying, "Master of the Universe, even if You can bear Your own pain and look patiently upon the desecration of Your honor, how can You bear the pain of Your children for so long? How can you bear with patience the desecration of the honor of the Jewish people? After all, You care more about the honor of Your children than for Your own honor." This is why Michael offers Jewish souls upon the altar before the Holy Blessed One, as though to say, "Please have pity on these." Most particularly he pleads for those souls that departed the world in great pain and suffering—and not just those who are completely dead, but parts of souls that have departed due to the pain of the Jewish people are also offered up. Offering them to God, he says, "Please have pity on these," for how much strength and how many bits of the soul of Jewish people have died—even from those who are still living in this world—due to their own pain and the pain of others?

With this we can understand, reflecting our own situation, the words of our teacher Moses to God (Exodus 5:23): "As soon as I came to Pharaoh to speak in Your name he made things worse for the people, and You have done nothing to help Your people."

What is God's reply? "Now you will see what I will do to Pharaoh. . . ." (Exodus 6:1) The response seems to indicate that God was spurred to action precisely because of the complaint Moses made.

Rashi's (Exodus 6:1) explanation is well known. Quoting the Midrash (*Tanchuma, Vaera*:1), he considers it a failure on Moses' part. God said, "Because you criticized My methods of guiding the world, you may see what happens to Pharaoh, but you will not live to see what happens to the kings of the seven nations of Canaan when I bring the Jewish people into the Holy Land." But if, as Rashi says, our teacher Moses sinned when saying (ibid. 5:21), "O Lord, why do You mistreat Your people?" the verses that follow immediately, are out of context. "God spoke to Moses and said to him, 'I am God (*YHVH*). I appeared to Abraham, Isaac, and Jacob with the name Merciful Almighty (*El Shaddai*), but my name, *YHVH* (God), I did not reveal to them.'" (ibid. 6:1) If Moses had sinned with his question, how did he earn the privilege of this revelation of the name of God, *YHVH*? If you argue that the Holy Blessed One only revealed this divine name for Moses to convey it to the Jewish people, why then is it written twice?—once in "God spoke to Moses and said to him, 'I am God (*YHVH*),'" and then "Therefore tell the Israelites, 'I am God (*YHVH*).'" (ibid. 6:6) It would seem that the first time the name was revealed, the revelation was for Moses alone.

The fact is that even the words Moses spoke to Pharaoh made a great impression in heaven. At first he told Pharaoh to let the Jewish people go for the sake of Heaven, as it is written (Exodus 5:1): "so that they may sacrifice to God in the desert." Subsequently, however, Moses thought that perhaps this was why God had so much patience with Pharaoh: because God has patience with those who dishonor Him. If he demanded that Pharaoh meet the needs of the Jewish people, however, then God, Who has even more care for them than for Himself, would have greater pity upon them and this would arouse in Heaven a far greater impetus for God to save them immediately. Therefore, even though God had previously said to Moses (Exodus 3:7), "I know the pain of the Jewish people," which made it obvious that He was going to redeem them because of their suffering, God nevertheless also commanded Moses to say to Pharaoh, "Let us sacrifice to God." So Moses had no choice but to say to Pharaoh, "Let us sacrifice to God," which essentially means, "Let us leave for Heaven's sake." That is why he later said to God, "As soon as I came to Pharaoh to speak in Your name . . ."—emphasizing "Your name" as though to say, "Because I didn't speak up on behalf of the Jewish people,"—

"Pharaoh has made things worse for the people." To this God replied, "Now you will see what I will do to Pharaoh. . . ."—i.e., "because you have aroused an awareness of the pain of the Jewish people, therefore I will no longer have patience with Pharaoh and 'Now you will see.'" Thus Moses was granted the revelation of the name God, *YHVH*.

Let us return to the quote from my holy father's book, *Imrei Elimelech*, (p. 114) on the verse "Why are you crying out to Me? Speak to the Israelites, and let them start moving." When Moses prayed on behalf of Heaven's honor, the Holy Blessed One told him, "Pray on behalf of the Jewish people," because He is more caring of their honor than of His own. This is really how it should be. The guiding principle of the Jew should be the desire to champion the honor of Heaven, while the principle desire of God, blessed be He, is to champion the cause of the Jewish people.

This is also the meaning of the *yahrzeit*, or anniversary of a person's death. While a righteous person is alive here in this world, he is a Jew amongst Jews and all his worship and his prayers are for the sake of Heaven. But once he has departed this world, he enters heaven and stands in worship of God, serving Heaven. He continues to pray his holy prayers, but, as he is elevated above this world and above the Jews of this world, and has come closer to God, his desires and prayers become the desires of God, which are for the sake of the Jewish people. And as we said above, these prayers are more effectual, for righteous people are greater in death than in life, and more able to draw down good things upon the Jewish people than when they were alive. This is especially so on the day of their death, when they ascend ever higher into Heaven.

This is why we see (Numbers 13:16), "Moses gave Hoshea b. Nun the name 'Joshua.'" Moses added the Hebrew letter *yud* to Hoshea's name in order to protect him from the evil council of the spies. As Rashi (ibid.) explains: "By giving him the name 'Joshua,' which is a compound of two Hebrew words meaning, 'May God save,' he in effect prayed for him, 'May God save you from the evil council of the spies.'" Caleb did not need a name change or prayers for special protection, because upon entering the Land of Canaan he immediately betook himself to the graves of the Patriarchs in Hebron and prayed. Moses, who was still in this world, needed to pray and intercede, on Heaven's behalf, that the spies not cause a blemish in heaven and desecrate God's honor. Caleb, however, prostrated himself at the graves of the Patriarchs, who were already in the upper world and do not always need to pray only on behalf of God, and so, when a Jew needs help, can pray on his behalf and assist him. Therefore Caleb did not need Moses' help.

Whenever God spoke to Moses about the salvation of the Jewish people from Egypt, He never told him exactly when it would happen. It is almost certain that there were at that time Jewish people in whose mind there arose the thought,

"Even when it appears that our rescue is imminent, it just seems never to happen." Therefore, when it arose in the will of God, blessed be He, that the time for redemption had finally arrived, He said, "On the tenth of this month, every person must take a lamb for each extended family, a lamb for each household." He gave them commandments they needed to observe, the Paschal lamb and circumcision. Originally, when God was considering redeeming them in the merit of their future acceptance of the Torah, that was sufficient for His purposes even though they had not yet accepted it; God already considered the Jewish people deserving of redemption without any effort on their part. Now, however, God, blessed be He, was about to do something not for His sake or the Torah's sake, but strictly on behalf of the Jewish people, for whose honor and needs He cares even more than for His own. In response to God's desire to champion their honor and arrange immediate salvation—on the tenth of the month—there had to be fresh merit, and so there was suddenly a need for commandments that they could fulfill.

The meaning of "This month shall be the head month to you" is "I am going to act for your sakes, so you must observe the commandments for Mine." Therefore, "from the tenth of the month, etc.," you must fulfill the commandments of "the tenth of the month," which is the date chosen for redemption, and then you will see it revealed.

# *Shabbat HaGadol* (The Great Sabbath)—April 5, 1941

The significance to us in our predicament of Shabbat HaGadol (the Sabbath prior to Passover) may perhaps be as follows. We learn in the Talmud (Yoma 69b): "The verse (Nehemiah 8:6) says, 'Ezra blessed God, the great Lord.' What does 'Great' imply? R. Joseph said in the name of Rav, 'He exalted God through the Ineffable Name.' R. Giddal said, 'He exalted God through the verse "Blessed be God, Lord of Israel, from time immemorial and forever." (I Chronicles 16:36)'"

Whether we accept one opinion or the other, both agree that the exaltation of God referred to in the book of Nehemiah was the result of something done by the Jewish people. R. Joseph suggested that Ezra uttered the Ineffable Name, while R. Giddal, for various reasons, thought the verse "Blessed be God . . ." was more likely to have been the means.

The only name God gives Himself is the four-letter name *YHVH—Yud, Heh, Vav, Heh*. "God spoke all these words, saying: 'I am *YHVH*, God your Lord . . .'" (Exodus 20:1); "God spoke to Moses and said to him 'I am *YHVH*.'" (Exodus 6:2) God Himself revealed this name. This is not the case, however, with other names of God, which are names that the Jewish people have given Him.

Adam, the first man, called God *Adon*, "Master" (Genesis Rabbah 17:4); our patriarch Abraham called God *Adonoy*, "Our Master" (*Berachoth* 7b); and Hannah referred to God as *Adonai Tz'vaoth*, "Lord of Hosts," as we learn in the Talmud (*Berachoth* 31b). The Jewish people call God by these names, and He responds to the names with which we call Him. God is revealed, adorned, and glorified by these names.

On the verse from the Sabbath liturgy, "You gave us, God our Lord, with love and desire Your Holy Sabbath." R. Shneur-Zalman of Liadi, in his book *Tanya*, taught (cap. 47): "It was God He gave us." Since God has given Himself to us, as it were, we are permitted to name Him. And the names we call Him become the holy names by which God then refers to Himself.

The Talmud we quoted above goes so far as to say that even the adjective "great" is used in reference to God only because the Jewish people make Him great. We are called "a great nation" because of our connection to God, blessed be He, as it is written (Deut. 4:7): "And what nation is so great that they have God close to it, as God our Lord is, whenever we call Him?" Conversely, God is called great because the Jewish people call Him great.

The Talmud asks, "What does 'great' imply?" The question itself is difficult to understand: Is it not obvious that God is great? Why even ask the question? The talmudic question, however, addresses the issue of the word "great" as an adjective used to describe God. The question is how can the word "great" be used to describe something totally unique? The word "great" is a relative term. For example, if one finds a grape as large as a small apple, the grape may be referred to as "great" because it is greater than other grapes, even though an apple of this size would be a small apple. Thus we can have a great grape, compared to other grapes, but how can one possibly say God is great, when He is One, Unique and Singular? The Talmud answers, "We can say God is great because Jewish people have exalted His honor and sovereignty in this world, making it greater than it was." God is called "Great" because we have made His sanctity and honor greater than they were.

With this we can now understand the argument between Rav and R. Giddal, in the Talmud quoted above. Rav said, "Ezra exalted God through the Ineffable Name," but R. Giddal was anxious to point out that exaltation of God is not restricted to great saints, nor is it a phenomenon confined to places of tremendous revelation such as the Temple's sacred precincts. The Ineffable Name was only ever uttered by the High Priest in the holy Temple, but according to R. Giddal, anyone at anytime can exalt God. God's greatness, said R. Giddal, was increased whenever people said "Blessed be God, Lord of Israel, from time immemorial and forever," even if they did not utter the Ineffable Name and were nowhere near the level of holiness of a high priest in the Temple. Nevertheless, by exclaiming, "Blessed be God, Lord of Israel," and by accepting the holiness of God upon themselves and upon all the Jewish people, they make the God of Israel greater than He had been. This is why God is called "Great." When any Jew, even the lowliest, assumes the yoke of heaven, sanctifying himself with holiness and the worship of God, he grows holier, and then God is called great through him.

The difference between the Jewish people and the nations in this respect is expressed in the verses (Psalms 113:4) "High above all nations is God," because God is high above all nations of the world. But about the Jewish people it is written (Psalms 135:5), "Great is God our Master, above all gods." God can be called great because God is our Master and has mastery of us. He is not above us, and over us, because in the sense that God is separate from and above us He cannot be called great, as we discussed above. In that respect, God is One, Singular and Unique. "Great," then, is the adjective we use when referring to God, Who is our Master, in this respect: He is ours and we can make Him great by magnifying our worship of Him.

This is the explanation of Ezra's blessing of God "from time immemorial and forever." The Hebrew phrase *Min haOlam ad haOlam* may also be translated "from the world to the world." The Hebrew for "eternity," *Olam*, also means "world."

We know from the holy Zohar (vol. II, p. 9b) that the First Temple in Jerusalem corresponded to the first Hebrew letter *Heh* in the four-letter name of God, YHVH (*Yud Heh Vav Heh*), while the Second Temple was second *Heh* of the tetragrammaton. These two letters *Heh* also correspond to Heaven and Earth, respectively. Since Ezra lived in the era of the building of the Second Temple, he said "from the world to the world." Ezra was drawing from Heaven, the first and supernal *Heh*, to Earth, the lower and final *Heh*.

It is well known that the supernal world, the upper *Heh*, is the *sephirah* of *Binah* (Understanding), while Earth, the lower world and final *Heh*, is the *sephirah* of *Malkhut* (Sovereignty). The upper world of *Binah* is the source of the supernal stream that flows to the Earth. The Hebrew word, *nachal*, "stream," is written with the three letters *nun cheth lamed*. It is a *notariqon*, an acrostic for one of the thirteen attributes of God's Mercy, namely, *Notzair chesed l'alafim*, beginning with the same Hebrew letters, *nun cheth lamed*. It translates as "He remembers deeds of love for thousands of generations." (Exodus 33:7)

The world of *Malkhut* (Sovereignty) the lowest *sephirah*, is the lower end of the supernal stream. In this case, *nachal* (stream) is *notariqon* (acrostic) for *Nafsheinu chiktha l'Adonai*, "Our soul longs for God." (Psalms 33:20) The stream flows both ways. From above it flows with thousands of generations of God's cherishing of our love, while from below it flows with our longing for God.

The wisdom and longing that elevates the lowest *sephirah* of *Malkhut* to the highest realms become the inundation of *Mayin Nukvin*, Feminine Flow, which draws downwards toward it the light flowing from the supernal world above.

The same connection is made when a Jew worships God to the best of his ability. If he feels his worship is good enough, then he remains where he is. But if through his worship he is filled with the longing to worship God with even greater strength and to acquire more of God's holiness, then he draws down upon himself more light from above and becomes greater than he was. When the person's spiritual self becomes greater, then God is also called "Great." The Talmud asked, "What does 'great' imply?" and answered, "They made God great when they blessed Him, saying, 'From time immemorial and forever.'" The phrase, as we said, can also be read "from one world to the other world," from the upper world to the lower world, from Heaven to Earth. With their longing in this world, which is the lower stream—"Our soul longs for God"—they drew down upon themselves the light from the upper world, the supernal stream. When the Jews were thus exalted, then God was called "Great."

Likewise in Egypt, as long as the Jews had not yet observed any Commandments, they had not felt a sense of the supernal light, and so they could not long for it. But by this Sabbath, which was the tenth of the month of Nissan, this was no longer the case. God had given them the Commandment of the Pascal Lamb (Exodus 12:3). The Jews, through observing God's Commandment, began to long for even more supernal light. Their longing made them greater, and God became "greater" because of it. That why this Sabbath is called The Great Sabbath, *Shabbat HaGadol*.

This may also be the reason why God hardened the heart of Pharaoh. In the verse God says to Moses, "You will be able to tell it to your children and your grandchildren how I made fools of the Egyptians. . . . You will know that I am God." (Exodus 10:1) The implication is that they would see the greatness of God and learn to believe in Him. But why did they need to be in Egypt to learn of God's great power? Surely, God could have taken them out and then shown great and wondrous miracles. Did God need Pharaoh in order to demonstrate even the smallest part of His greatness to us?

With what we have said earlier this may be understood to mean the following. God sought the longing of the Jewish people. Human nature dictates that when a person is depleted physically, emotionally, and spiritually—when, God forbid, things are really difficult for him—the longing for God is more readily aroused in him. So it was specifically when the Jewish people were in exile in Egypt that God revealed and showed them miracles, so that "You will be able to tell your children . . ." This served to increase their faith in and longing for God, so that the longing would bring down upon them the greater light from above.

This is why it is customary on *Shabbat HaGadol* to recite the Passover *Haggadah*, beginning with the passage, "We were slaves in Egypt and the Lord our

God brought us forth from there with a strong hand and outstretched arm." God did not wait until after He had brought us out of Egypt to show us His strong hand and outstretched arm; rather, while He was bringing us out, He showed us His strong hand and outstretched arm. As the text of the *Haggadah* states, the more we talk about our coming out of Egypt, the better it is. The main objective is to increase the light and holiness, and through it to generate an increase in Heaven, causing God to be called "great"—for as we said above, it is the Great Sabbath.

# *Pesach* (Festival of Passover)—
# April 12, 1941

*It happened that R. Eliezer, R. Yehoshua, R. Elazar b. Azaria, R. Akiba, and R. Tarfon were reclining (at the seder) in B'nei Brak. They discussed the Exodus all that night until their students came and said to them, "Our teachers, it is time for the reading of the morning Sh'ma." (From the Passover Haggadah.)*

In his holy writings, my brother-in-law, the holy R. Aharon Yechiel, of blessed memory, refers to the phrase "until their students came," asking where the students came from. His holy father, of blessed memory, answered him; it means: until the students also arrived at the exalted level of their rabbis.

Reflecting upon our situation, we may possibly explain this teaching as follows. There is a well-known question posed in the commentaries on the *Haggadah*. In the section on the Four Sons, each son has a verse from the Torah quoted to him, and both the Wicked Son and the One Who Is Unable To Ask are given the same verse (Exodus 13:8): "It is because of this that God did so for me when I came out of Egypt." The question is this: Why, when explaining the verse to the Wicked Son, do we say, "God did so for me"—i.e., exclusively for me, "and not for him,"—while when quoting this same verse for the One Who Is Unable To Ask, we do not stress any implied exclusion?

No Jew is a separate individual. He belongs to the entirety of the congregation of Jewish people. Thus when one person learns Torah and worships God, he thereby illumines all Jewish people. Similarly, regarding repentance, we learn in the Talmud (*Yoma* 86b): "On account of an individual who repents, the sins of the whole world are forgiven." Therefore, when talking to One Who Is Unable To Ask, we say, "God did so for me," and this naturally includes him as well. This is not the case, however, with the Wicked Son, who has excluded himself from the congregation. About him we say, "God did so for me, and not for him."

This may also be why the *Haggadah* says of the Wicked Son that we should "blunt his teeth." We learn in the Talmud (*Baba Kamma* 27b); Ben Bag-Bag said: "Do not steal into your neighbor's premises without his knowledge, even for the purpose of recovering what is rightfully yours, lest you appear, because of him, a thief. You may, however, break his teeth and tell him to his face, 'I am taking what is mine.'" Rashi (ibid.) explains that "break his teeth" means to take by force what belongs to you.

From this we can see that in the Talmud the expression "break his teeth" is used when a person recovers ownership of his property from someone. In the *Haggadah*, "blunt his teeth" has a similar connotation. The Wicked Son is entitled to recover his portion from you by force, because your worship of God contains some that is his. Since, however, he has excluded himself from the congregation, you have the right to "blunt his teeth"—to reclaim that part in your worship belonging to him and take it for yourself, saying, "God did so for me, and not for him."

Another answer to the question of the difference in our responses to the two sons may found in the text itself. In responding to the Wicked Son the *Haggadah* says, "Because he has excluded his self from the *clal* (entirety) he has rejected the first principle."

We have previously discussed the concept of *clal*. There is a *clal* comprised of separate parts, like a rule determined from details, e.g., a father gives his son money each day for a number of days, and so the son assumes it to be a *clal* (general principle) that every day his father will give him some money. This is a kind of *clal* inferred from details and separate events. In truth, however, the father may only give his son money for a period of time, after which he may stop giving.

There is another kind of *clal* that constitutes an essential, simple unity from which the details are branches that diverge outward and downward. When we reach the source and root of such a *clal*, everything has become one, and as we go higher and further the source and root are still more unified. An example of this is fruit that has fallen from a tree. When cut off from its source, we watch it decay. We already know that the germ of the tree unifies all the disparate parts, combining the leaves, branches, and fruit. As soon as the leaves, branches, or even bark are cut off from the root, they begin to decay, because it is only in the root, which is an expression of the germ, that they are truly unified. As with fruit, so all parts of the tree begin to decay when they separate from the root. The germ of the tree is not made up of isolated and disparate parts. The fruit and leaves and branches are not parts that are joined together to make a whole generic tree. On the contrary, the principal, essential tree is the germ. In it everything is unified, and from it diverge the details—the fruit, the leaves, and the branches.

This is how it is with the Congregation of Israel. The whole is not comprised of individuals. On the contrary, the individuals are branches of the whole. By this we mean that the Congregation of Israel exists not because of a decision to join together and unify, but because the germ is the Jewish soul that includes all Jews and from which all individual Jews branch out. This is why a person who is not connected to the Congregation of Israel, who has not elevated himself beyond his individual identity to join his soul with the soul of the Jewish people, will be unable to ascend higher to the Holy Blessed One. So long as he is just an individual, he is his own root and branch, his own germ. Only when he elevates himself to join the soul of the Congregation of Jews can he go further in holiness, rising to cleave to the Holy Blessed One.

The *tzaddikim* (pious ones) utterly nullify their persons and negate themselves, distilling everything into love for Jews and for the soul of the Congregation of Jewish people. The Midrash (*Sifra, Kedoshim* 2:12) quotes R. Akiba, saying, "'Love your neighbor as yourself,' (Leviticus 19:18) this is the great *clal* (entirety) in the Torah." To connect with the germ at this level, to fulfill the commandment to "Love your neighbor," is not just to connect with the Congregation of Jewish people. It was also the way in which R. Akiba connected to the Torah itself, enabling him to reach the soul of Torah. This is why he said during his martyrdom (*Berachoth* 61b), "All my life, I have been at pains to fulfill the commandment (Deut. 6:5) 'Love your God with all your heart and all your soul . . .' which I interpreted to mean, even if God takes my soul. I said to myself: 'When will I ever have the opportunity to fulfill it? Now that I have the opportunity shall I not fulfill it?'" R. Akiba had so completely nullified himself through fulfillment of the commandment "Love your neighbor" that he did not experience himself as an individual. He felt only a longing to be included in the unity of the "supernal source" or germ expressed in the commandment "Love your God with all your heart and all your soul. . . ."

Even someone at our level, who is not able to nullify his self completely, is still, at source, part of the Congregation of Jewish people. His awareness of this connection increases in proportion to the amount he strives to reduce his own desires and generally lower his bias toward himself, and in proportion to the amount of good he tries to do for other Jews, caring about their concerns and rejoicing in their joy. Then, his germ—that part of him rooted in the Congregation of Israel—is revealed to him, bit by bit. Even if he still experiences his own concerns and desires above those of others, because he has not quite succeeded in completely nullifying himself, nevertheless, with practice, the germ of the Congregation of Israel and the soul of the Jewish people in him surges higher and more powerfully within him. For example, when a person sees a Jewish child drowning in the river, God forbid, he yells and jumps in to save him. If the child was his own, perhaps he would yell even louder and run even faster to save him. Should we say, because of this, that therefore he does not care about other Jewish children, God forbid, and only for his own? Of course he cares for them and loves them, but the love he has for his own child is stronger, and so he feels it more. Even if his own child were not at the river, he would still run to save a Jewish child. So, even if he has not yet succeeded in nullifying himself completely, proportionate to his efforts to help other Jews, the germ and soul of the Jewish people surges in him and he is able to rise to the Torah and to God. The Wicked Son mentioned in the *Haggadah*, however, has excluded himself from the *clal* so his core identity is not that of the Congregation of Jewish people but rather of himself alone. He has rejected the core principle, the principle of the *clal* of the Congregation of Israel.

Returning to our original text: Among those reclining and discussing the Exodus all that night was R. Akiba, who devoted himself to loving Jews and joining the *clal* of the Congregation of Israel, and who declared this to be the most basic and general principle of Torah. A point was reached where "their students came." As we quoted above from my brother-in-law's holy writings, even the students reached this high level, for the effect of the Rabbi's achievement that night also elevated the students. R. Akiba was not conducting the Passover seder for himself, but for all Jewish people, and for his students in particular.

୧ৠ୨

> *"As for the Son Who Is Unable To Ask, you must open for him . . ."* (From the Passover *Haggadah*.)

Let us try to understand why here the Hebrew text uses the feminine form of "you," *at*, when saying "You must open for him," while in replying to the Wise Son and Wicked Son the masculine form, *ata*, is used. Secondly, why does the text suggest "You must open for him," rather than, "You should say to him"? Thirdly, in replying to the Wise and Wicked Sons, why does the text say "and you, also, should say to him," while in replying to the Simple Son the text merely says "you say to him"?

There is also the question, raised in holy literature, concerning the emphasis on the act of "questioning" that appears to be such an important element in the Passover seder. Why is it that we question the commandments for seder night more than we question other things at any other time? After all, we might just as well ask about the reasons for *t'fillin* (phylacteries).

It may perhaps be as follows. The Mishnah (*Avoth* 5:7) teaches: "Seven characteristics of a wise man: A wise man does not speak ahead of his academic or ranking superiors, does not interrupt when others talk, does not answer hurriedly, confines his questions to the topic, answers unequivocally, replies to questions in their proper order, professes ignorance where appropriate, and admits the truth." The Mishnah does not suggest that a wise man should not ask questions, or be expected to understand everything his teacher tells him without needing to ask. On the contrary, asking questions seems to be an essential element of a student's obligation. In the Mishnah (Avoth 6:5) among the forty-eight prerequisites for the acquisition of Torah, there is one that the student "make his teacher wiser." How does a person acquire Torah by making his teacher wiser? Only his teacher would appear to benefit from the process. What we really need to understand is how a student makes his teacher wise. What happens when a student asks a question that his teacher cannot answer, forcing the teacher to delve deeper, immersing himself, reaching for the source, until he comes up with something quite novel? Why was the new idea born only in response to the student's question, when the teacher's intellect was so much broader to begin with than that of his student?

The point is this: Whenever we learn Torah, our grasp of it is achieved only through the connection of our mind with the light and soul of Torah. This occurs in the *sephirah* of *Chokhma* (Wisdom), the highest level of the human mind. The Hebrew word *chokhma* combines two words, *koach* and *mah*—the "Power of What" or "Question Power." It is with *Chokhma* that the soul illuminates the mind, dispersing the ignorance of things. From the *sephirah* of *Chokhma*, information passes to the *sephirah* of *Binah* (Understanding), where perception is expanded upon and comprehension is integrated into consciousness, as is well known. We are unable to grasp *Chokhma* with our minds because comprehension surfaces only after information has been processed, expanded upon and integrated through the *sephirah* of *Binah*. Before this process of expansion and integration, *Chokhma*, the "Power of What," is beyond our comprehension. Nevertheless, while we first experience our conscious perception in *Binah*, it is in fact the "Power of What" in *Chokhma*, flowing through our mind from its source, that we are grasping (Zohar, vol. III, 220b).

This is why knowledge sometimes comes to a person in a flash, without thinking—it just seems so obvious, like anything that he knows. Subsequently, he may use his mind, his understanding, to study and explain what he already knows. Sometimes he cannot expand upon it, to explain what he knows, yet he still knows that it is so. This sort of knowing is far beyond the conscious comprehension that is provided by *Binah*. It comes from the source of *Chokhma*. When it occurs, it is the person's own *Chokhma* revealing itself to him.

This is the "anticipatory thinking," *kadmut ha-sechel*, often referred to in the holy writings of the Great Maggid, of blessed memory. It is how he explains the Talmud (*Berachoth* 55b): "He rose, and a scriptural verse came to mind." The Maggid explains: "'He rose' means that he ascended to the level of 'anticipatory thinking,' as is well known."

Therefore, although the student does not have the intellectual faculties of his teacher and, not understanding every facet of his teacher's ideas, is incapable of expanding upon them, if he is a worthy student he does, nonetheless, grasp some part of them. He comprehends at least the superficial meaning in his teacher's words. Then his mind, which cleaves to the mind of his teacher, also connects with the *Chokhma*, the "Power of Question," in his teacher. The student connects with levels of *Chokhma* in his teacher that are not even revealed to the teacher because they have not yet passed into his *Binah* for perception and comprehension. This is akin to the mind of the child that is born of the mind of the father. Even though the child does not have the breadth of understanding of his father, nevertheless his ideas are connected to those of his father, and his mind taps the same sources of wisdom as does his father's mind.

And so, the questions asked by the worthy student serve to draw the flow of *Chokhma* from his teacher. He is connecting to the *Chokhma*, the "Power of What," of his teacher, which can become manifest only through the asking of questions. If the student could really reach the most profound level of his teacher's "Power of What," he would not even be able to ask questions. It is because he reaches only a superficial layer of his teacher's *Chokhma*, touching upon its lowest part, comprising those elements that flow through his teacher's *Binah*, that he is able through his questions to reveal some of his teacher's *Chokhma*, as is well known.

We learn in the Zohar (intro., 1b); R. Elazar opened, saying: "In the beginning—God created the Beginning. 'Raise your eyes heavenward and see (*Miy*) Who created all this?' (Isaiah 40:26) Above, there are no questions. But because the question can be asked below, though God is hidden, it is called *Miy*—Who? There is another, further below, called *Mah*—What? The difference between the Above, in whose power everything exists, and the below is the following. Because the question can be asked, the truth can be sought and inquired after, going from level to level to the end of all levels it is called *Miy*—Who? But, upon leaving, and inquiring after and examining everything, it is all as hidden and mysterious as it was before. What do you know? What have you seen? It is therefore *Mah*–What?" Asking the question *Miy*—Who? implies previous knowledge. There must already have been some prior comprehension of facts, so the question *Miy*—Who? can be asked, even when it is only the question that can be understood and there is yet no way to understand the answer. The question *Mah*—What? however, cannot even be asked, because it asks at the levels beyond consciousness or comprehension, at the levels of *Chokhma* where there is not even sufficient comprehension for the question (*Miy*—Who? is usually understood to imply the *sephirah* of *Binah*, because vis-à-vis the *sephirot* in general, *Binah* is the one about which it is said that it can be questioned but not understood. This would seem to contradict our discussion of *Miy*—Who? in the *sephirah* of *Chokhma*. However, what we are discussing now is the relationship of student to teacher, where the teacher's *Binah* has already been exposed, so that the questioning and the explorations are now deeper and more profound.) Since the student's questions arise out of his connection to his teacher's most profound *Chokhma*, his teacher may be unable to find the answer immediately, until he connects with his source, drawing it along to flow through *Binah* for expansion and comprehension. This is how the student makes his teacher wiser, by helping him to draw out the *Chokhma* from its source. The student also benefits, acquiring Torah in the process, which is why it is one of the forty-eight prerequisites for the acquisition of Torah. The student has to climb to the source of his teacher's *Chokhma*, adding new Torah to that which has already been expanded upon.

From this it can be understood why the Talmud says (*Shabbath* 3b): "Said R. Hiyya to Rav: 'Son of illustrious ancestors! Have I not told you that when Rebbe is engaged in one tractate you must not question him about another, lest he be not conversant with it? If Rebbe were not a great man, you would have put him to shame, for he might have answered you incorrectly.'"

We want to understand at the simplest level why R. Hiyya calls Rav "son of illustrious ancestors." He uses this epithet elsewhere in the Talmud (*Berachoth* 13b) in a discussion of Rebbe's acceptance upon himself of the yoke of the kingdom of heaven. The intention there is obvious, but what is the purpose of the epithet here, in the Talmud? It may perhaps be understood in terms of what we have intimated above. The soul of a student who is not worthy cannot ascend to connect with the source of *Chokhma*, illuminating his teacher's mind. Therefore, even if the unworthy student asks his teacher a question, it can only relate to something that his teacher has already expanded upon and consciously revealed with his intellect, and so it is not difficult for his teacher to answer him immediately. This is not the case, however, with the "son of illustrious ancestors," for he is by definition a child of great people, of whom the Talmud says (*Bava Metzia* 85a): "The Torah always comes home to roost." So, the "son of illustrious ancestors" has within him Torah even beyond his own conscious comprehension, because the Torah resides in him in the merit of his ancestors. Thus, he is connected willy-nilly to the "Power of What" in his teacher. His questions create a revelation of *Chokhma*, of which the teacher himself may not have been aware. This is why R. Hiyya said, "If Rebbe were not such a great man himself, you might have put him to shame."

The Wise Son and Wicked Son are children, and, as we said above, the mind of the son reflects the mind of the father: so, when they ask a question they reveal something of the source of *Chokhma* in their fathers. And so the *Haggadah* says of the Wise Son, "You, also, should say to him . . ."—"you" because his question will have caused a revelation of your most essential self. Regarding the Wicked Son, who causes a revelation of a facet of wickedness, "You, also, should blunt his teeth . . ."—"you" because that newly revealed, essential part of you needs to blunt his teeth.

The instances of the Simple Son and the Son Who Is Unable To Ask are quite different. Because they have no idea how to ask, these two sons have no real grasp of your essence at all, and so they cannot draw anything out from the source of your wisdom. This is why the *Haggadah* does not suggest, "You, also, should say . . ." in your conversation with the Simple Son. It merely states, "Say to him. . . ."

The One Who Is Unable To Ask does not even ask, as the Simple Son did, "What is this?" For him the *Haggadah* says, "You (*at*) must open for him." Not only can he not raise any questions, he does not give you any opening, even by asking simply, "What is this?" and so you must open for him. This is why the *Haggadah* chooses to emphasize the feminine form of address. Moses also used the feminine *At* (you) when admonishing the Jewish people in the verses (Deut. 5:22–24) "And you said to me . . . 'If we hear the voice of God our Lord any more, we will die. You (*at*) can transmit to us whatever God our Lord tells you.'" Rashi (ibid.) explains the use of the feminine, *at*: "Moses said, 'You made me weak like a woman by refusing to hear the Torah directly from God.' Similarly, here, *at* (you) are weakened by the One Who Is Unable To Ask, because he does not give you any opening with his questions.

Passover is the source of all salvation and redemption, as is well known, but the salvation and the redemption are still as yet *in potentia*, not actualized, so we must draw them down, revealing them. This is why we are commanded to ask questions. By asking, we reveal the salvation and redemption that before were only conceptual. Our asking draws them out and actualizes them.

"In order that you remember the Exodus from Egypt, all the days of your life . . ." (Deut. 16:3) Quoting the sages, the *Haggadah* says, "this includes the Messianic era." The Hebrew word for "includes," *l'havi*, actually means "bring." So the sages were really saying that retelling the Exodus story and constantly learning something new from it "brings" on the Messianic era.

> "It is this that has stood by our fathers and us. For there has not just been one who rose against us to annihilate us, but in every generation they still rise against us to annihilate us. And the Holy Blessed One rescues us from their hands." (From the Passover *Haggadah*.)

A well-known question asked by the commentators on this text is: To what does the author of the *Haggadah* refer when saying, "It is this that has stood by our fathers?" What is "this," and how has it stood by us? A simple explanation might be that "this" refers to our experience of history, to the fact that the Holy Blessed One rescues us, and that he rescues us not only before we fall into the hands of our enemies but even after we have already fallen into their hands. It is this historical fact— that even when it appears certain to us that we are already in their hands, God forbid, He will yet rescue us—that has stood by us, giving us hope and encouragement.

Another explanation might be as follows. Isaac said, "The voice is Jacob's voice, and the hands are the hands of Esau." (Genesis 27:22) The Midrash Rabbah (*Eikha*, intro. 2) interprets this verse to mean: "So long as the voice of Jacob continues trilling with the sounds of Torah in synagogues and study houses, the hands of Esau will have no mastery." When we see Esau's hands in control, we must assume it has come about because we were not sufficiently diligent in our Torah studies and did not teach our children properly. How, then, will we be rescued? "It is this that has stood by our fathers and us . . . The Holy Blessed One rescues us from their hands." He rescues us even when Esau's hands are in control, so that in the future Jacob's voice may be heard trilling in synagogues and study houses. This explains the connection between this paragraph and the one immediately following; "The Holy Blessed One rescues us from their hands" is followed by "Go and learn . . ." So, from now on, go and learn Torah.

❧

> In the prayer *Nishm'at* (from the Sabbath and Festival liturgy, included toward the end of the Passover *Haggadah*) we say, *"From the world to the world, You are El—All Merciful. Other than You we have no king, redeemer, or savior."*

Rashi (Genesis 1:1) says: "Originally, there arose in the Thought the idea to create the world, to be ruled with the attribute of *Din* (Judgment). But, realizing that the world could not thus endure, God gave precedence to *Rachamim* (Mercy), allying it with *Din*. However, the world above and the future world are to be ruled with the attribute of *Din*, and every person will receive exact recompense for his worship and his deeds. We also learn in the teachings of the Arizal (R. Isaac Luria) that in the future world the *halachah* (Law) will be decided according to the school of Shamai, and Temple services will be performed by the tribe of Levi, who are proponents of *Din*, as is well known.

However, regarding the portion of the future world that we acquire solely through our effort in this world, God will always have to treat us with the attribute of *Rachamim*. This is because our portion in the future world comes only out of this world and this world cannot endure without *Rachamim*, as we quoted above: "But, realizing that the world could not thus endure . . ." With this we can understand the original quote, "From the world to the world, You are God. Other than You we have no king, redeemer, or savior." "From the world to the world" means from this world to the future world, which emerges from our experiences in this world. Not only have we "no other redeemer," but we also have "no other savior." So not only must God, blessed be He, redeem us from our suffering, He must do it with an abundance of goodness that saves us.

We have previously related a teaching from the holy book *Sha'ar Etz HaChayim HaKadosh*, by R. Chaim Vital, of blessed memory, that one of the transcendent virtues of the prophet was his ability to remain joyous even when suffering. Yet we learn of the prophet Elisha (II Kings 3:15), "Elisha said . . . 'Bring me a minstrel.' And it came to pass, when the minstrel played, that the hand of the Lord came upon him." Although he was always joyous, in order to bring down a flow of prophecy upon himself, he needed a still greater level of joy. That is why, even after God has rescued us, may it be immediately and forthwith, and after we have left our suffering behind us and are able to fulfill all our obligations, it will still not be enough to bring the light of the world above down into this world. To do that we will need an exceptional salvation, which will have to include abundance, peace of mind, and joy. This, then, explains our text. For although the world above is ruled with *Din* (Judgment), nevertheless "from this world to the world"—because the world above is reached only via this world—"You are *El*—All Merciful." Therefore, "Other than You, we have no king, redeemer, or savior." Not only will You have to redeem us, You will have to save us as well.

※

> "Neither do the dead praise God, nor they who descend into silence; but we will praise God from now unto the world. Hallelujah!" (Psalms 115:17–18, from the *Hallel* liturgy, included in the Passover *Haggadah*.)

Who are "they who descend into silence"? They who go silent and inarticulate to their deaths, who do not sing God's praises with their lives. But we who sing God's praises in this world "will praise God from now unto the world. Hallelujah!" because we will still be singing His praises in the future world.

# *Shevi'i Shel Pesach* (Seventh Day of Passover)—April 18, 1941

"... They had faith in God and in Moses His servant. Then Moses and the Children of Israel sang this song to God, saying, 'I will sing to God for He is very great... This is my God and I will glorify Him...'" (Exodus 14:31, 15:1–21)

We learn the following in the Midrash (Cant. Rabbah, cap. 2:4): "In former times, if one dared point a finger at an icon, punishment was sure to follow. But these days, someone may lay hands upon mention of the Divine Name numerous times and go unharmed." If a person pointed his finger at a representation of a human, flesh-and-blood monarch, he could expect to be punished for lese-majeste. Yet, today, when someone touches one of the Holy Names of God, he does not expect divine retribution. What this Midrash is suggesting is essentially this: The Names of God are, as it were, pictographs or icons of God.

It is taught numerous times in the Holy Zohar that both before the creation of a person and after his death, he stands before God in the very same physical shape and form that he occupies in this world. This is because the physical shape and form we inhabit is a reflection, revealing the shape of a divine soul, that has passed through a chain of *hishtalshelut*—the processes of transition from the purest, simplest, undifferentiated "Breath of God" into the complex biophysical matrix of the body.

The flesh and bones of the face are merely the media through which the shape of the face is expressed, while the shape of the face itself is the medium through which the shape of the soul is revealed. Think of pigments used to paint the portrait of a wise man. If, when looking at the finished portrait, we think they truly portray the wise man, we do not mean that it is merely a good likeness of that person's shape. What we mean is that even his wisdom can be seen in the picture of his face. The pigments used in the portrait actually convey to the viewer something profound about the soul and wisdom of the subject. Something about the shape of the wise man's soul is being revealed through the pigments, even though the colors themselves are just a medium.

The shape underlying the face and of which the face is a reflection, is the soul revealing itself. This is why a person's wisdom shines on his face, and as he becomes wiser his face changes. So before he is born and after he dies, when he stands in heaven it is in his own shape, because his physical form is the shape of his soul.

The case is similar with regard to the Holy Names of God. The ink used to write the letters is just a medium through which we depict the letters. Why are the letters these specific shapes and no other? What are these particular shapes? They are the specific shapes that convey the essence of God through the chain of *hishtalshelut*, the processes of transition whereby the Lights of Divine Holiness are revealed in this world. Thus the written forms of the Holy Names are, as it were, icons of God.

There is a well-known teaching found in the *Shaarei Orah* (Gates of Light, caps. 1 and 5) on the verse (Psalms 19:9) that says: "Commandments of God are perfect; they delight the heart." The *Shaarei Orah* notes that the Hebrew word for "commandments" used in the text of the psalm is *pikudei*, usually translated as "number," "count," or "point." It asserts that the whole text of the Torah is a series of permutations of the Divine Name of God. The whole Torah is a fabric woven from Holy Names in acrostic, anagram, *notariqon*, gematria, etc., form.

Perhaps from this, we can understand a little of the following. The Talmud (*Shabbath* 104a) says: "Children came and spoke, divulging mysteries the like of which were not revealed even in the days of Joshua b. Nun. 'Why does the Hebrew letter *gimmel* put out its leg toward the *daleth*?' they asked. 'Because *gimmel* means "to give" and *daleth* means "poverty," so the *gimmel* is giving something to the *daleth*.' 'Why then does the *daleth* turn its head away from the *gimmel*?' 'Because the *daleth* is ashamed of having to accept alms.' 'Why does it stick out its hand behind it?' 'So that the *gimmel* can give without having to look into the face of the recipient.' . . ."

The Talmud continues; "these children" went through the entire Hebrew alphabet revealing mysteries. Why does the Talmud call them "children" if they were indeed revealing Torah, unparalleled even during the days of Joshua son of Nun?

We know that God teaches Torah to His people Israel. We need to understand, however, whether this means that every time a person learns Torah he is being taught by God, or if God teaches him directly only on particular occasions.

Let us examine how God learned Torah with Moses our teacher, because we shall never find a greater Torah scholar than Moses. It appears evident from the Talmud (*Megillah* 21a) that it was only when Moses learned something for the first time that God taught him directly. When Moses revised what he had learned, he was studying by himself. The Talmud asks the following question: "One verse (Deut. 9:9) quoting Moses says, 'I sat upon the mountain forty days and forty nights,' while another verse (Deut. 10:10) quoting Moses says, 'I stood upon the mountain like those first days, forty days and forty nights.' Rav answered, 'Moses stood and learned, while when he sat, he revised.'" Rashi (ibid.) comments: "When Moses was learning, it was from the mouth of the Almighty. When he was revising, it was Moses revising alone what he had learned from God."

However, the Midrash (Exodus Rabba, *Ki Thissa*, 41:5) on the verse (Exodus 31:18) "When God finished speaking with Moses . . ." says as follows: "When Moses first ascended Mount Sinai into Heaven, he repeated the Torah verbatim, after his Creator. Once he was proficient in it however, God said to him: 'Come, you and I, let us say it together.' This is the real meaning of the phrase 'God finished speaking with Moses.' They repeated it together."

Rav in the Talmud and the Midrash in Exodus both agree that it was only while Moses was learning something new that God taught him directly, as a teacher would a student. When Moses was revising what he already knew, however, there is a dispute: According to Rav in the Talmud (*Megillah* 21a), Moses revised quite by himself, while according to the Midrash, Moses and God continued to study together as study partners.

It is therefore, exactly like this that God learns Torah with us.

In the Talmud (*Ta'anith* 7a, *Makkoth* 10a) Rebbe says: "I have learned much from my teachers, even more from my colleagues, but from my disciples, I have learned most of all."

Whenever we learn something new, and God as the "Teacher of Torah to Israel" is our teacher, then in heaven there is a greater revelation of Torah. Even though the whole Torah belongs to God, the greater revelation of Torah in the upper worlds occurs when God teaches something new to a human.

In the book *Pardes Rimonim* (Orchard of Pomegranates, cap. "Gates of the Clear Light"), R. Moses Cordovero discusses the difference between a thought that has been articulated and a thought that has not yet been articulated. "Once a thought has been made manifest in this world, then in heaven that idea stands revealed in a whole new way. Once a person has drawn a sketch, his grasp of the concept that the sketch depicts becomes much more powerful."

Therefore, when a child learns the shapes of the Hebrew letters for the first time, there is fresh revelation in heaven concerning these letters. And this fresh revelation, occurring in heaven through the child's learning of the letters, is drawn downwards, so the child draws down upon himself a fresh revelation as to the meaning of the shapes of the letters.

This is not the case with adults, who are too familiar with the shapes of the letters. When we look at them we are not learning anything new, so we do not have God teaching us anything directly. The only revelation we can inspire in the upper worlds is in the meaning of the text of the Torah, in the *P'Shat*. When the Talmud described "children" who explained the mystical meanings in the shapes of the letters, it was actually referring to holy people who could approach the text as children. They brought about revelation even in the shape of the letters, and not just in the meaning of the text. They could still learn like children, and so were able to look at the *alef* and *beth* and *gimmel* and ask, "Why is the leg of the *gimmel* stretched out toward the *daleth*?"

Therefore, every time a person revises Torah that he has already learned, he must learn something new from it, delving deeper into it so that God is given the chance to be the teacher again. Only when something new is learned—when one learns with God and directly from Him—can a fresh revelation occur in heaven, bringing down a new revelation upon the student who is learning in this world.

We must learn something from everything that God does. For example, if the Jewish Court sentenced someone to the punishment of a flogging, that sentencing was Torah. The decision to punish was made in the same way that all Torah is studied and decisions concluded. So, the suffering God punishes us with is also Torah, and if a person can learn something from his suffering, then God can be his Torah teacher for that period of time. We know that God learns most of all from His students, so there occurs a revelation above and below. In the fresh revelation there is a negation of *hester panim* (hiding of the Divine Face) and so all the judgments are sweetened.

What can be learned from pain? To begin with, we can learn faith in God and a continuing and powerful belief that God will save us. We can learn how far we need to go to brace ourselves, over and over again, to put our trust and hope in God in the midst of the pain.

We can learn from the fact that the Red Sea did not split for Israel until the whole tribe of Benjamin had jumped in. Nachshon b. Aminadav went into the water until it rose above his nostrils, as is well known from the Midrash. Why was such a leap of faith necessary? When the Jews stood before the sea, God said to Moses (Exodus 14:15), "Why cry to Me? Speak to the Jews, and tell them to start walking." Rashi (ibid.) explains: "'The faith the Jewish people have put in Me,' says God, 'in leaving Egypt and following Me into the wilderness, is sufficient to merit splitting the Red Sea for them.'"

Similarly, Rashi explains another verse (Exodus 14:1–4): "God spoke to Moses, saying, 'Tell the Jewish people to turn around and encamp in front of Pi Hachiroth. . . . Pharaoh will say, "They are trapped, the wilderness has them surrounded." I will harden Pharaoh's heart and he will pursue them and I will be glorified through Pharaoh and all his armies, and Egypt will know that I am God.' And they [the Jewish people] did so." Rashi comments: "They didn't say, 'How can we meet our pursuers head on? We need to run,' which shows even greater faith in God than simply following God into the wilderness."

From this we can learn that moments of great danger and trouble are also times when we are being tested from heaven. Can our faith redouble and take on yet more strength? The Jewish people had faith. We left Egypt and walked into the desert, then were told to go back and face the Egyptians, our pursuers, which tested our faith even further. Then to add to our troubles we were faced with the Red Sea, as a test to strengthen our faith, bolstering it with a trust even more powerful, until we could jump into the sea and into the danger, up to our nostrils. Only then did God save the Jewish people.

It is not just faith that we need to learn in a time of danger and a time of trouble. As it says in the Holy Zohar (vol. III, p. 168G), "If wood won't catch fire, then keep stamping on it until it does catch fire." As we have already said elsewhere, if a person faints, we pummel him and slap him to bring him back to life. It may be that the only way to strengthen and revive him is to belabor him still more. So must we respond when we are in trouble. Of course we must pray to God to help us immediately, but at the same time we must take encouragement and resolve to strengthen our worship of God from the very kicking and beatings we endure, because they come from heaven as a means of waking us up from our state of unconsciousness.

In the Midrash (Cant. Rabbah, cap. 4:6) we learn: God says, "The Temple in its destruction gave Me more holy people than it produced during the time that it stood." The destruction and suffering are a Torah that God is teaching us. This teaching brings about revelation above and below, a sweetening of the judgments, and a drawing down of mercy, as we have explained above.

This is the meaning of the verse with which we opened this chapter, "They had faith in God and in Moses His servant." We learn in the Midrash (Cant. Rabbah 4:2) about this verse, that it is the Torah testifying that the Jewish people had this faith even while they were still in Egypt. That is why they said, "I will sing to God . . ." They were prophesying about the future when they said "This is my God, and I will glorify him." They used the Hebrew name for God, *El-i*, which is the manifestation of loving-kindness. They had the right to say "This is my God," because the revelation of God as loving-kindness was drawn down through their faith in God even during the suffering in Egypt.

Now at this time, when our troubles are bitter beyond belief, God should have mercy on us and save us in the blink of an eye, when we continue to believe. Our belief creates an image of God that is a revelation above and below, and in God we will find strength, and we will believe, and we will hope, and in a moment He will save us. Amen.

# *BeHa'alothecha*—June 14, 1941

*"And Aaron did so; he lighted its lamps over against the face of the menorah, as God had commanded Moses."* (Numbers 8:3)

Rashi (ibid.) explains that the Torah considered it necessary to state that "Aaron did so . . . as he was commanded," in order to tell us the virtue of Aaron—that he did not deviate from God's instructions. A well-known question asks: What is so extraordinary and remarkable about Aaron the High Priest conscientiously obeying his instructions? Another matter requiring clarification is the phrase "over against the face of the menorah." In specifying that "He lighted its lamps over against the face of the menorah," the text would seem to be suggesting that Aaron's noteworthy obedience to God's commands was confined to this matter. Why does the text ignore Aaron's conscientiousness in all his other endeavors regarding the menorah lighting?

The explanation requires a better understanding of the Hebrew word *haggadah*, "telling." The Talmud (*Shabbath* 87a) discusses the verse (Exodus 19:9) "And Moses *higgid* (told) the words of the people to God." "Of what significance is the choice of *haggadah* (telling) in this context? But when Moses 'told' the Jewish people of the punishments for disobedience to the Torah, his words were as unpalatable to them as *gidin*." Rashi, on the Talmud (ibid.), translates *gidin* as "a bitter herb, wormwood."

[Translator's note: There are three types of address. The first, "saying" (*amirah*), is the gentlest form, and the most easily heard. The second, "speaking" (*dibbur*), is provoking and can be difficult to hear. The third, "telling" (*haggadah*), is disturbing and can be very painful to hear.]

Rashi says that "And Aaron did so" is stated in order to tell (*l'hagid*) us the virtue of Aaron, that he did not deviate from God's instructions. Rashi is implying that even when Aaron's life was bitter as *gidin*—wormwood—he continued to do his holy work without deviating in the slightest from God's command. This is what made it possible for Aaron to "light its lamps over against the face of the menorah." The Jewish people are "the face of the menorah"—firstly because they illuminate all the worlds, and secondly, as the Talmud (*Shabbath* 22b) notes: "Does God require the light, that He needs the menorah lit every evening, when surely the Jewish people travel by God's light? The menorah, however, is witness and testimony to mankind that the *Shechinah* (Divine Presence) dwells among Israel."

This means that the purpose of the menorah was, in fact, the Jewish people. In kabbalistic terminology "purpose" is synonymous with "face," as opposed to "back," as is well known.

Aaron's lighting of the menorah was so successful that the flame did not just rise to illuminate the Heavens above—it was not just in Heaven that he created light—but over against the face of the menorah he produced light for all the Jewish people.

# *Chukath*—July 5, 1941

Tammuz 10 (July 5), 1941\*

*"The Egyptians mistreated both our fathers and us. When we cried out to God, He heard our voices. . . ."* (Numbers 20:15)

We learn in the Mishnah (*Avoth* 1:3): "Do not be like servants who serve their master in the expectation of receiving a reward; but be like servants who serve their master without the expectation of a reward, and let the fear of heaven be upon you."

At first glance, this would seem to address only the saintliest people who are willing to forgo all expectation of reward, whether in this world or the next. Their worship of God is unconditional, and solely for God's sake. But what ordinary person can say that he never craves a reward, either in this world or in the next? It is also most unlikely that an ordinary person will not from time to time think about punishment, and in fear of retribution abstain from sinning or from contemplating sin, or that he will never feel a desire or a longing within him to learn more Torah and observe more commandments in the anticipation of a promised share in the world to come.

Rashi, commenting on the Talmud (*Avodah Zarah* 19a), "Like servants who serve their master without the expectation of a reward," explains it as follows: "Let

---

\*[Translator's note: The author in his manuscript notes the date. It corresponds to the *Yahrzeit* of the late Rebbetzin Rachel Chaya Miriam Shapira, of blessed memory, who died Tammuz 10, 1937.]

your heart be with God, as though to say, 'Even though in the end I may not receive a reward, I still love my Creator and desire His commandments.'"

According to this explanation then, every God-worshipping Jew worships without expectation of a reward. For although a person may want God to be good to him, he does not make this a condition of his worship, God forbid. Any person, even knowing that he will not be receiving a reward, would still be a God worshipper. This includes even people whose worship is a mixture of emotions, i.e., fear of being punished and longing for reward. Their worship is driven by fear of punishment and longing for only because they are self-centered, and while they fear punishment and long for reward, the reality is that even if they were not promised a reward, they would still worship God.

A person who yearns for a more highly evolved worship, for a greater connection to God, must overcome this self-centeredness. He must accustom himself to worshipping God not for himself, but for God alone. He must reach for a level where the fear of failure is not a fear of being punished and the joy of success is not the satisfaction of being rewarded, but where all emotion is for God. The ability to achieve this depends on how prepared to minimize his ego a person is. Everyone can achieve some level of proficiency at living less self-centeredly. Even if this goal cannot be achieved always, a person can accustom himself to the level of this purest worship for a number of days or hours. The main components of this kind of worship are the study and physical practice of Torah. Through practice of the Torah and its study, which is also a physical activity—as the Talmud (*Sanhedrin* 65b) says, "Movement of his lips is also action"—the entire body becomes Torah. A person learns to feel the needs of Torah and of worship no less than he feels his own needs and desires. He no longer feels only his self, and so his learning and worship are no longer performed for himself.

With this, we can understand the connection made in the Mishnah quoted above, "Do not be like servants who serve their master in the expectation of receiving a reward; but be like servants who serve their master without the expectation of a reward, and let the fear of heaven be upon you." Why does the Mishnah juxtapose the unconditional worship of God and the fear of heaven?

The Talmud (*Shabbath* 88a) asks: "What is the meaning of the verse in Psalm 76:9, 'You caused judgment to be heard from heaven; Earth took fright, and was still'? If the Earth was frightened, why was it still; and if it was still, what was it afraid of?" The Talmud answers: "First it was afraid and then it grew still, in accordance with the teaching of Resh Lakish. For it was Resh Lakish who said: 'God made a condition with Creation, saying, "If Israel accepts the Torah, you will have permanence. But if they refuse, I will turn you back to void and chaos."'"

We need to understand why it was that only Earth took fright. Why did Heaven not take similar fright? Heaven is also part of Creation, and was therefore included in God's condition. If Israel chose not to accept the Torah, was not Heaven also doomed to void and chaos?

The fright that Earth took was self-centered; it was frightened at the prospect of its own destruction. But only Earth experienced this self-centered fear. The Word of God had passed through the Heavens, purifying them, as in "You caused judgment to be heard from Heaven." Therefore Heaven was not afraid for its own existence, but only that Israel might not accept the Torah. Heaven's fear was for God's sake. This is the fear of a servant serving its master without thought of reward or punishment.

The truth is that all Jews worship God without expectation of a reward, as Rashi explained in the passage quoted above. It is just that they tend to feel their needs and their fears on their own behalf first and foremost. This is why the Mishnah ends with the words "let the fear of Heaven be upon you," emphasizing the phrase "fear of Heaven." It is admonishing us to practice Heavenly fear—fear purified by the word of God passing through it; Godly fear, and not Earthly fear, which is nothing but fearful self-centeredness. The difference between these two is a result of the Word of God having passed through Heaven. We can learn a lesson from this: If we occupy ourselves by learning Torah and practicing it, we too will be purified because we will have become the medium through which the word of God passes. Then, like Heaven, we will become servants who serve their master without the expectation of a reward.

Although in times filled with trouble for Jewish people our suffering atones for our sins, it is unfortunately also true that we become more self-centered. We become obsessed with the daily litany of our hurts and needs. This is understandable: Is it possible for a person to be hit and not feel physical pain? The response of any person forced to spend every tormented, agonized day anxious for the life hanging by a thread before his eyes is to become obsessed with self. His worship of God also falls to the lowest level of worship, that which is centered upon himself.

With this we can understand the words of the Talmud (*Nedarim* 10a): "R. Eliezer HaKapar says that Nazirites, who take an oath to forgo wine, are sinners because they cause themselves pain when forswearing wine."

Taken at face value, this makes no sense. If taking the oath of a *Nazir* is a sin, why does the Torah give us the Nazirite laws? If the Torah had not given us these laws, there would be no *Nazirim* denying themselves wine and sinning thereby. The truth is, however, that there is always something good that comes out of pain, because experiencing pain can be cleansing, and it can help a person to distance himself from his evil inclination. This is elucidated in the story told by a *Nazir* to

Simeon the Just (Talmud, *Nedarim* 4b): "Simeon the Just said, 'Only once in my life have I eaten of the trespass offering brought by a defiled *Nazir* (see Numbers 6:18). On one occasion a *Nazir* came from the south country, and I saw that he had beautiful eyes and was of handsome appearance, with thick, dangling, pendulous locks of hair. Said I to him, "My son, what possessed you to destroy your beautiful hair?" He replied, "I was shepherding for my father in my town. Once I went to draw water from a well, and I was caught by the sight of my reflection in the water, whereupon my evil desires rushed upon me and sought to drive me from the world, through sin. I said to my evil inclination, 'Wretch! Why do you vaunt yourself in a world that is not yours, with one who is destined to become worms and dust? I swear that I will shave off my beautiful hair for the sake of Heaven.'"' R. Simeon said, 'I immediately rose and kissed his head, saying, "My son, may there be many *Nazirim* like you in Israel. Of you it is written: 'When either a man or a woman shall separate themselves to vow an oath of a *Nazir*, to separate themselves for God.'" (Numbers 6:2)'"

Even though pain atones and helps to distance one from sin, nevertheless when the atonement comes about through the pain of Jewish people, there is in that transaction itself a blemish and a sin, because pain causes a person to become self-absorbed, as explained above (see Talmud, *Baba Kama* 91b, *Tosaphot*, cit. *Ellah*).

In order to awaken mercy in heaven for Israel and to sweeten all the judgments, we must arouse within ourselves compassion for our fellow Jews. Not only must we give them everything we can; we also need to arouse our compassion for them, because when we arouse mercy within ourselves, mercy is aroused in heaven. We must resist becoming accustomed to the fact that Jews are suffering. The sheer volume of Jewish suffering must not be allowed to blur or dull the compassion we feel for each individual Jew. On the contrary, our heart must all but dissolve, God forbid, from the bitter pain. When we awaken within ourselves compassion for Jews, we can accomplish two things: First, our own prayers will issue with more soul and more heart. Second, as is well known from the sacred literature, there are occasions when salvation has already been decreed from heaven on Israel's behalf, but tarries because it is abstract and cannot come down to this world and clothe itself in physical, practical reality. So, when a Jew not only knows intellectually but also feels with the very core of his body that he must support and help his fellows, then mercy becomes a part of his body. When next he prays on behalf of his fellow Jews, he prays with a body full of compassion. Then the salvation that was stopped for want of a channel through which to flow finds in this person a perfect conduit and broadens to meet physical needs as well.

This is exactly what is meant in the Talmud (*Megillah* 14b): When King Josiah was in trouble, he sent for Chulda the prophetess (II Chronicles 34:22) even though the leading prophet of that era was Jeremiah. "But how could Josiah himself pass over Jeremiah and send to her?" the Talmud asks. The members of the school of R. Shila replied, "Because women are more compassionate."

Women have more compassion than men because their physical bodies are more compassionate, and so women can more swiftly bring salvation down into this world. So great is the power and merit of pious women, that we learn in the Midrash (Ruth Rabba, cap. 7:14): "The women said to Naomi, 'Blessed is the Lord who helped Naomi and gave her salvation.' R. Hama said, 'Because those women blessed Naomi, the seed of David was not exterminated in the days of Athaliah.'"

How mighty is the kingdom of King David, and yet it survived only because of the blessings of those pious women. There are two reasons for this: First, as we learn in the holy Zohar, all pious women are at the level of *Malkhut*, Sovereignty (the tenth and final *sephirah*), which is also known in Kabbalah as *K'nesseth Israel-Esheth Chayil Atereth Ba'alah*, Congregation of Israel—The Warrior Bride—Crown of Her Husband. Thus the House of David, which is also *Malkhut*, is given permanence by the blessings of pious women, who are *Malkhut*.

Second, the Talmud quoted above says, "Women are more compassionate." The Hebrew word *rachmaniyoth*, "compassionate," has the root *rechem*, "compassion" or "womb." It is written with the three Hebrew letters *resh*, *cheth*, and *mem*. The letter *resh* represents *Rachamim,* which is *Tifferet*, the *sephirah* of Divine Compassion. The letter *cheth* represents *Chesed*, the *sephirah* of Divine Loving-Kindness. The *mem* represents *Malkhut*, the *sephirah* of Divine Sovereignty.

As is well known, when the *sephirah* of *Gevurah*, Divine Withholding, influences *Malkhut*, then judgments come into the world. When the *sephirah* of *Chesed*, Divine Loving-Kindness, influences *Malkhut*, then loving-kindness is revealed to the world. Since those pious women were at the level of *Malkhut* and were deeply compassionate, they opened up *rechem*, compassion-womb, as we said above, and compassion was revealed in the world of *Malkhut*.

"The Children of Israel, the entire congregation, came to the Tzin Desert in the First Month. The people settled in Kadesh. Miriam died there and was buried there. . . ." (Numbers 20:1) Rashi (ibid.), interpreting the repetition of the word "there," comments: "It is as though it was written that Miriam died 'at the Mouth of God.'"

In a description of the mystical, primal, human body, the holy Zohar, in Elijah's introductory speech (*Tikunim*:1), correlates the seven lower *sephirot* with various limbs and parts of the torso. The right arm is *Chesed*, Loving-Kindness, while the left arm is *Gevurah*, Withholding, etc. The *sephirah* of *Malkhut* is the Mouth, and as we said above pious women are *Malkhut*-Mouth. It was unnecessary to state explicitly that Miriam died at the Mouth of God.

Similarly, Rashi (ibid.) explains: "Why is the story of the death of Miriam adjacent to the chapter concerning the Red Heifer? Just as animal sacrifices atone for sin, so the death of the pious is an atonement."

But why is the death of Miriam associated particularly with the law of the Red Heifer and not some other animal sacrifice mentioned in Leviticus, such as sin offerings or guilt offerings, etc.?

Rashi (Numbers 19:2) explains the law of the Red Heifer thus: "'Let the mother come and clean up the mess made by her child.' The Red Heifer is the symbolic mother, atoning for our sin of worshipping the Golden Calf."

In what possible symbolic respect was the Red Heifer mother to the Golden Calf, especially in light of the fact that there were many more Red Heifers in the course of history than just the one they made in the desert? (See Mishnah Parah.)

In light of what we have said above, we can explain as follows: The death of Miriam directly follows the law of the Red Heifer because women are compassionate, and Miriam was like a mother even to Jews who were not her children. She is an archetypal mother, and this role did not end with her death. In heaven she is still our mother, continually arousing mercy on behalf of all Israel, even for those who are not directly her descendants—just like the Red Heifer cleaning up after the Golden Calf, atoning for it, even though the calf is not actually her child.

To return to the original quote: "The Egyptians mistreated both our fathers and us. When we cried out to God, He heard our voices. . . ." (Numbers 20:15) Rashi (ibid.) explains that our ancestors experience pain in their graves over the suffering of Israel. This is why it says, "He heard our voices . . ." He heard not only the voices of the Jewish people, but also the cries of our fathers and mothers, because they also feel our pain. If a person does not feel compassion for Jews, it is very difficult for him to pray for them and it is very unlikely that his prayer will have any effect. "The Egyptians mistreated both our fathers and us," and so our fathers also suffered and also cried out with us—and in addition to our voices, God also heard the voices of our fathers in heaven, and He saved us.

# *Massay*—July 26, 1941

*"Moses recorded their forays as they journeyed at God's Mouth; and these are their journeys according to their forays."* (Numbers 33:2)

In his holy writings, my brother-in-law, of blessed memory, mentions the following well-known question: Why does the verse first say "their forays as they journeyed," and then reverse the order, with "these are their journeys according to their forays"?

We learn in the Talmud (*Sanhedrin* 98b); Ulla said: "Let the Messiah come, I will not see it." Ulla foresaw the terrible suffering accompanying the birth pangs of the Messiah, and preferred not to be a witness to it.

Let us attempt to make sense of his attitude. It may well be true that there are things more terrifying than death, may the Merciful One protect us, as the Talmud (*Kethuboth* 33b) points out regarding torture: "If they had tortured Hananiah, Mishael, and Azariah (cf. Daniel 3), they would have worshipped the idol." It is also true, however, that torture is worse only while it endures, but before or after the suffering, which person would not rather suffer the pain than face certain death? Once the pain has passed, the person is himself again and his sins are atoned for. This is why King David praised the Holy Blessed One (Psalms 118:18) saying, "God has chastened me exceedingly, but He did not let me die." Why then did Ulla, in anticipation of the time of suffering, say, "Let the Messiah come, I will not see it," so that he would not have to endure the pain of the birth pangs of Messiah?

By his comment, Ulla did not mean that he wished to avoid his own suffering. He wanted to avoid witnessing all the pain of the Jewish people, because he knew he could not bear to see other people suffer so much. This was the case for Ulla in particular, because Ulla was so pious that for him Jewish suffering was unbearable. The more a person adores himself, the less love he has for fellow Jews, as he is always thinking only of himself. He is the paradigm of "I am, and none else but me." (Isaiah 47:8) The degree to which a person can love his fellow Jews and worry about their suffering is proportionate to the degree to which he can nullify himself. A person who is full of selfish desires and self-adoration wants only to fulfill his own desires, so he cannot truly love Jewish people. Conversely, when a person nullifies himself and his desires on his own behalf, he is able to love Jews. As the *Tosaphists* in their commentary on the Talmud (*Shabbath* 13a) explain: "Ulla was a *tzaddik gamur*—a wholly pious man who could not even contemplate sinning or acting on his selfish impulses—and was therefore used to kissing his sister." His love for the Jewish people was great, and so he said, "Let the Messiah come, I will not see it."

There is another explanation. Let us attempt to understand, even at our low level of comprehension, the concept of *chev'lay Mashiach*, birth pangs of the Messiah. It can be explained simplistically as a way of cleansing sin before the great revelation that constitutes the coming of the Messiah. The question that asks itself, however, is why must the generation of people greeting the Messiah have to suffer for all the sins of previous generations?

After humankind's first sin, God said to Eve (Genesis 3:16), "In despair will you give birth to children." This was not just retribution, a punishment for sin. It is well known that all the different worlds, great or small, at all the levels that God creates them, come into being through *hishtalshelut*—a chain process of birth and becoming, of cause and effect. Before the sin, everything was nullified before God, and the identity of each object in the universe was not that of individual extant objects. Identity more closely resembled that of objects in the world of *atzilut* (archetypes), in that it was conceptual. An example of this idea continues in the *sephirot* in the world of *atzilut*. There, the *sephirot* have names and appear to possess some sort of identity, even though they have no existence beyond the presence of God, blessed be He, for in the world of *atzilut* God and His creatures are One, as is well known.

The Holy Blessed One miraculously created all the worlds, each revealing an identity that does not require individual existence, and so it was in this world also, before Adam's sin. In the future world, as we know from the writings of the Arizal (R. Isaac Luria), this world will be elevated again to the level of *atzilut*. Since Adam's sin, however, the world has been physical in an entirely selfish way, so that everything in creation experiences its own individual existence. It is therefore impossible for anything new to be born without something dying, because for something to give birth to a new revelation of God, drawing new light down into this word, it must go through a process of nullification. It is impossible for anything to reveal the Divine Light while retaining the illusion of existence, as is well known. We can watch this process in the germination of any seed that we plant. A tree's branches, leaves, and fruit cannot be discerned in the seed, and they may be thousands or millions of times larger than the seed—but before the new tree can be revealed, the seed itself must cease to be. That is why every seed decomposes in the earth before it germinates. It is a kind of death. This is what is meant by the phrase "In despair will you give birth to children." A woman experiences a painful process in which she relinquishes some of her physical powers, before she can give birth to a new creation. As we learn in the Midrash (*Tanchuma, Tazria* 6): "While squatting upon the birthing stool, ninety-nine of her groans despair unto death, while only one calls out for life." Through the nullification of the existence of parts of herself, she prepares for God, blessed be He, to bring forth a new creation.

This would seem to explain, to the limits of our comprehension, the concept of the birth pangs of the Messiah. The redemption will be the revelation of God, when God reveals of His Light and Holiness through the Jewish people. This is why the redemption and its timing are dependent upon the Jewish people. For the Jewish people to merit that such Light be revealed through them, there has to be a nullification of their power, and these are the birth pangs of the Messiah, as it is written (Isaiah 66:9), "'Shall I labor, and not give birth?' says God."

The Holy Blessed One is laboring to give birth through the Jewish people, and so the Jewish people suffer the birth pangs, losing their powers as part of them dies, for this is how they give birth to the Light of the Messiah. For us, it is the same as with a woman squatting on the birthing stool. We know that the strongest contractions indicate that the delivery is progressing, that the child has been revealed a little more. So also, when seeing a Jew suffering greatly with the birth pangs of the Messiah, we know that a greater part of the Light of the Messiah is being revealed through that person.

Ulla, who was a *tzaddik gamur*—wholly pious man, seems to be hinting to us with his words "Let the Messiah come, I will not see it" that the Messiah's coming and Ulla's not seeing it are not two separate issues. Ulla predicted that he himself would endure such great birth pangs, giving birth to such a large part of the Messiah, that he would expire and pass away.

It is not only the individual who dies, or the one who suffers tremendous pain, that gives birth to the great Light of the Messiah. If many people are united in pain or in fear, and one of them dies from his suffering, may the Merciful One protect us, then great Light is revealed out of all of them, because they were all together in pain, and in fear they suffered together.

This is the meaning of "Moses recorded their forays as they journeyed." Rashi (ibid.) quoting the Midrash (*Tanchuma, Massay* 2), says, "A parable: The king had a son who took ill. So the king brought him to a sanitarium for treatment. On their way home, the father began enumerating all the stages of the journey to his son, saying, 'Here we spent the night . . . here we caught cold . . . here you had a headache... etc.'"

All of the tribulations mentioned in the text, however, were birth pangs revealing the Divine Light. And so it is written "their forays as they journeyed at God's Mouth" because the *sephirah* of *Malkhut* (Sovereignty), the revealed world, is synonymous with the mouth, as Elijah the prophet taught in his speech (*Tikunei Zohar*, intro. 1). The stages passed through—"here we spent the night, here we caught cold, etc."—were forays of the Messianic Light, revealing the *Malkhut*—Sovereignty of Heaven, the Mouth of God. This, though, is the difference: When Moses was recording the events after the journeys and the tribulations were over, everyone could see what had issued from their journeys at the Mouth of God. The purpose was obviously to bring the Mouth of God, *Malkhut*, Sovereignty of Heaven, into this world through their journeying, and so it is written "their forays as they journeyed at God's Mouth." However, while the journeys were happening the issues were not obvious, because during the journeys they felt only the pain, so the text says "their journeys according to their forays."

Perhaps there is yet another hint. "Moses recorded their forays as they journeyed at God's Mouth . . ." As our teacher Moses continues to suffuse every generation, his presence grows and develops. In the future he will also be the Messiah. There is a well-known teaching from the Zohar (*Raya Mehemnia*, vol. II, 120b) that the first letters of the Hebrew words *mah she'haya hu*—"Whatever has been, is what will be"—in the verse from Ecclesiastes (1:9) spell Moses' name, *MoShHe*. The implication is that Moses redeemed us once and will, no doubt, do so again. So Moses, with his writing, succeeded in achieving for every generation, and particularly for the generation of the Messiah, an immediate revelation of God's purpose. We will endure the journey and the pain, for it will also be revealed that these issue from the Mouth of God, and the name of God will be sanctified and magnified through the salvation of the Jewish people.

# *Shabbat Nachamu* (Sabbath of Consolation)—August 9, 1941

*"Console, console you My people, says Elohim your God. Bid Jerusalem take heart, and declare unto her that her battle is ended. Her iniquity is pardoned, for she has undergone at YHVH's (God's) hand double for all her sins."* (Isaiah 40:1–2)

Let us try to understand: Why does the prophet use God's name *Elohim* (Judge) when referring to God's consoling of us, and then the name *YHVH* (All Merciful) in reference to our punishment?

There are calamities for which it is possible to accept consolation. A person may have had an illness from which he recovered. Although he had been in great danger and in tremendous pain, when with God's help he was healed, he was immediately consoled for all the pain he endured. Similarly, if money was lost, then when God restores the lost fortune, consolation follows quickly. But when lives are lost, it is impossible to accept solace. It is true that when the pain is due to the loss of family and loved ones, or to the loss of other Jewish people because they were precious and are sorely missed, it is possible to take comfort in other surviving relatives and different friends. But any decent person mourns the loss of others not simply because he misses them; it is not only his yearning for them that causes pain and distress. The real cause of his grief is the death of the other—the loss of life.

Yes, we are assured that the dead are much better off in the next world, but is it not equally true that God created every person to live a full lifespan of seventy or eighty years in this world? And how many blessings are there in the Torah bestowing a full life and lengthy days?

Of the Torah itself it is said (Prov. 3:16): "Long life is in her right hand," and (Prov. 10:27) "Fear of God lengthens life." Regarding this latter verse, the Talmud (*Yoma* 9a) says that it refers to the High Priests in the First Temple who enjoyed longevity. It follows, then, that the long life promised in the Torah as a reward is enjoyed in this world and not in just the next world. The Midrash (Cant. Rabbah 6:6) compares a person's life to a lamp: If the lamp goes out because all the oil is consumed, "It is good for the lamp and good for the wick, but when it goes out before its time it is good for neither lamp nor wick." It is over this very tragedy that we cry so bitterly, that our souls weep. We grieve for those souls who were snuffed out in the prime of life. How can we ever be comforted; what possible consolation can there be if they no longer live? Our original verse addresses this very point when it says, "Console, console you My people, says *Elohim* your God." Only *Elohim*—God the Judge, blessed be He—can comfort us because He, *Elohim*, will speedily bring those lost to us back to life, with the resurrection of the dead.

This explains the difference between this text and that of Job (42:10), where it says, "*YHVH* reinstated the return of Job." *YHVH* (All Merciful God) comforted Job, giving him other children, but those children upon whom Judgment had already fallen remained dead, and the Judgment remained in place. It was only with different mercies and other children that Job was consoled. But here in the text it says, "Console, console you My people, says *Elohim* your God," because it will be the very same Judge that punished you who will come to console you when God brings the dead back to life. How can Judgments possibly become Mercy? The prophet explains, "For she has undergone at *YHVH*'s (God's) hand double for all her sins." With this it becomes clear that the punishment was only ever at the hand of *YHVH*, All Merciful God. The punishment was only ever Mercy disguised as Judgment.

Our sages of blessed memory have said as follows (*Yalkut Shimoni*, Lament: Chapter 10): "Why so is it written, 'For she has undergone at God's hand double for all her sins?' (Isaiah 40:1–2) But because it is written (Lament. 1:8), 'A sin did Jerusalem sin,' she sinned doubly (Jeremiah 2:13): 'Two evils have My people done Me.' Therefore was she punished doubly, and therefore will she be doubly consoled, as it is written, 'Console, console you My people, says your God.'"

Now, what is meant by "sinned doubly"? Does it mean she committed one sin twice? Sins are reckoned according to the number of times they are committed, so what does "sinned doubly" signify? And what is meant by "she has undergone at God's hand double for all her sins"? If she sinned twice, then surely there was no double punishment but one punishment for each sin?

The ten Jewish martyrs who died at the hands of the Romans were killed to atone for the sale of Joseph by his brothers (Genesis, cap. 37). R. Akiba, the tenth martyr, died in place, so to speak, of God. This is a teaching of R. Shimshon Ostroplia on the verse (Levit. 27:32), "The tenth one shall be holy to God." Each of the martyred rabbis was in place of one of the tribes, the brothers who sold Joseph, but the tenth one, R. Akiba, was "Holy to God." In fact, only nine of the brothers were involved in the sale of Joseph. Rabbi Akiba was the tenth martyr, sanctified for God, in place of God, as it were. This is because when the brothers sold Joseph, they implicated God, including God in their quorum when they swore an oath not to reveal to Jacob what had occurred, as is well known.

Since God dwells within every Jew, when a person commits a sin, God forbid, he forces God, the Divine in himself, to sin also. Thus every sin is actually a double sin, and when the person is punished, it is not only for his own sin, in order to repair his soul, but also for that part in him of God, so to speak, which also sinned, as we learn regarding the martyrdom of Rabbi Akiba. This, then, is the meaning of "punished doubly."

But how can it be that God, the Divine in man, remains with him and does not depart even when he sins? After all, it is written (Psalms 5:5): "Evil does not sojourn with You." So how is it possible that God, the very source of holiness, remains with a person even as he sins?

We learned in the Talmud (*Ta'anith* 4a): "The Jewish people begged of God (Cant. 8:6), 'Place me as a seal upon Your heart, as a seal upon Your arm.' God replied, 'Daughter, you asked of Me that which is only sometimes seen and sometimes concealed, but I will make you something that can be seen forever,' as it is written (Isaiah 49:16), 'For behold, I have engraved you upon the palms of My hands.'" Rashi (ibid.) explains: "Like the palm of the hand, the Jewish people are always in God's sight."

So we are always in God's sight, even when we are sinning. We are engraved upon the palms of His hands, and so we are not like something that can be seen only at certain times.

This, then, is the meaning of the verse, "Console, console you My people, says your God." The double consolation is for the double sinning that was doubly punished when the Divine part in them was also punished. This is the meaning of the verse, "For she has undergone at God's hand double for all her sins." Why doubly, and why at God's hand? Because the Jewish people are engraved upon the Hand of God, and are always connected to God, even when sinning. Therefore, "She has undergone at God's hand double for all her sins." For this same reason, our salvation will also be double, as it is written, "Console, console you My people."

At the end of Lamentations (5:21) we pray, "Return us to You, O God and we will return." How dare we ask of God that He return us? We sinned, we strayed, and He should bring us about? Note that the text says ". . . and we will return." Let us both return, as it were. We both need to repent, because if we humans have sinned, then the part of us that is God has also sinned, as explained above.

In agony such as ours it is difficult to repent properly, as we ought to do. So we beg of God, "Return us to You, O God, and we will return."

# *Ekev*—August 16, 1941

*"It will come to pass when you listen to these judgments, safeguarding and keeping them, that God your Lord will keep and guard the covenant and the kindness with which He made an oath to your fathers."* (Deut. 7:12)

We learn in the Talmud (*Zevachim* 53b); R. Levi b. Hama said in R. Hama b. R. Hanina's name: "A strip of land issued from Judah's tribal territory and penetrated Benjamin's tribal territory, whereon the Temple altar was situated. The pious Benjamin grieved over it every day, wishing it were in his domain, as it is written, 'Fretting over Him, all day long.' (Deut. 33:12). Therefore Benjamin was privileged to become a host to the Holy One, blessed be He; the Holy of Holies was situated in his territory, as it is written, 'And between his shoulders He dwells.' (ibid.)"

Because Benjamin experienced longing, and because his desire to be a part of the holiness of the Temple was so powerful that he suffered pain, he attained his desire. Through the power of his yearning, he became a host to the holiness. We know from sacred literature that it is a Jew's desire that draws holiness down from heaven. The Hebrew word *ratzon* (desire) comprises the very same letters as the Hebrew word *tzinor* (conduit). The pious Benjamin's longing was so powerful, causing him so much pain, that he was able to draw the holiness down. This is how he became host to the *Shechinah*, the Dwelling Presence of God.

It is also possible that it was not just a more powerful desire—one that caused him pain—that made Benjamin successful. More likely the cause was twofold: Desire and pain both produced separate, complementary effects that together resulted in the drawing down of holiness. While desire connects with and draws down the love and the light, the pain of longing overcomes any withholding or judgments that block, hide, restrict, or prevent the flow of holiness from heaven. The longing is for the flow and connection to the light, while the pain is at the absence of this flow.

Therefore, a Jew's ability to draw down the holiness of God upon himself is determined equally by both the measure of his desire to worship God—to be sanctified with His holiness—and the measure of the pain he feels when he finds defects in himself that are not sanctified. These two aspects determine his ability to eliminate any withholding and restrictions from inside himself, so that he can truly draw God's holiness upon him.

Extrapolating from this it is possible to understand, even at our level, the answer given by R. Akiba to his students (Talmud *Berachoth* 61b): "While his flesh was being raked with iron combs he recited the *Sh'ma*. When they asked him, 'Our Teacher, thus far?' R. Akiba answered them, 'All my days I have been at pains over this verse in the *Sh'ma* (Deut. 6:5) "Love God your Lord with all your heart, with all your soul, and with all your might." "When will I ever have the opportunity of fulfilling it properly?" I asked myself. But, right now, I have the opportunity to love God with all my soul. Should I not realize it?'"

We need to understand: What did R. Akiba's students mean when they asked him "Our Teacher, thus far?" Were they suggesting he had brought the whole calamity upon himself, and that it was his fault? What could R. Akiba possibly have done to change anything? Was there anything he could do to prevent the unfolding of his martyrdom? If his dying was to atone for the selling of Joseph by his brothers (Genesis 37) as is proposed in kabbalistic literature, then surely it was impossible for him to have prevented the events from unfolding. If he was being killed for teaching Torah in public and his students were asking whether teaching Torah is worth going "thus far," R. Akiba was still powerless to effect any change because he was being punished for something that had already happened. We know that from the time of his imprisonment and interrogation by the Roman authorities R. Akiba was no longer teaching Torah, as he had refused to teach even R. Simeon b. Yochai Talmud (*Pesachim* 112a): "R. Simeon b. Yochai said to R. Akiba while in prison, 'Master, teach me Torah.' 'I will not teach you,' he replied. 'If you will not teach me,' said he, 'I will tell my father Yochai and he will turn you over to the state.'"

We are forced to conclude that when the students asked "Our Teacher, thus far?" they were not referring to the matter of R. Akiba's death at all. We learn in the Talmud (ibid.) that R. Akiba was meditating on the word "One" ("Hear O Israel, God our Lord, God is One") when he died. The students were watching him submit to the yoke of heavenly dominion, even while he was dying. They were not asking him a question at all, but were wondering aloud how it was possible for R. Akiba to concentrate on reciting the *Sh'ma*, accept upon himself the yoke of heaven, and meditate on the word "One" in the midst of such agony, while his flesh was being raked with iron combs.

He answered them, "All my days I have been at pains over this verse in the *Sh'ma*. . . . 'When will I ever have the opportunity of fulfilling it properly?' I asked myself. . . ." R. Akiba was saying, "Not only did I desire to fulfill this commandment properly, I was also in pain at being unable to fulfill it." Therefore, "it was both my desire and my pain," says R. Akiba, "that brought down so much Divine Light that even under torture I am not disconcerted. I am able to don the yoke of heavenly dominion while concentrating and meditating."

We also need Divine Mercy and an outpouring of light and holiness upon us in order that our pain and anguish not impede our worship of God, and especially to prevent our minds and our hearts from becoming flustered. This we can only bring about when we live at the level of "All my days I have been at pains," as we said before. It is exactly the Jew's measure of desire and longing to worship God truthfully, without allowing difficulties to deter him, and the measure of pain he feels upon finding himself nowhere near the level of holiness and worship that he desires, that determine his success. We are not talking just about the desire and pain that we had before all the troubles began. Even now, the desire a Jew feels for himself and all Israel to worship God without interference, and the pain he feels over the destruction of our bodies and souls, have the effect of removing the hindrances and clearing away all difficulties. As we said earlier, pain defeats the judgments and restrictions, and when this happens we will find ourselves worshipping God amidst joy, salvation, and goodness.

Who can avoid pain when seeing such suffering of body and spirit? Who is it whose heart does not break when he sees the lack of schools and yeshivas—no places of Torah and no gathering of students to learn Torah? This is not just pain over the current situation, and it is not just now that the houses of God are destroyed. What is happening now will effect the future, because from now on there will be a shortage of young men to learn Torah. How many of them are gone, incomprehensibly murdered or starved to death, may the Merciful One protect us? How many have been forced to concentrate only on their physical survival? Where will we find young men to learn Torah in the future if they do not learn now? How many of them have been unable to withstand the test, and have been driven by hunger to go out on the Sabbath to do business in the marketplace? What can we expect of the children and young men who spent years in the markets and on the streets doing business, knocking at doors, begging for crumbs of bread during the week and on the Sabbath? Will they take advantage of the opportunity to return to the schools and yeshivas, and will everything be as it once was?

Everyone knows that for a number of years before the advent of the current trouble, many children of observant families were heartbreakingly distanced from Torah and from the ways of their parents, becoming freethinkers, may the Merciful One protect us. To balance this, however, God put into the hearts of children from unobservant families the desire to come closer to the Torah, and these newcomers withstood tests, because all they wanted was to be pious children of Torah. These young people who came from outside filled the spaces that were left by those who had abandoned the homes of the observant and the camp of worshippers of God.

This is not the case now. There are many young people who, out of pain and poverty are distancing themselves, but not even a single young person from an unobservant family is taking their places. The reason for this is simple: We no longer have any places or people left for gatherings of Torah scholars. The study houses and *shtib'lach* (prayer houses), which used to draw and arouse the children of the unobservant to Torah, worship, and *hassidut* (piety) are gone. It is self-evident that the cause of people's abandoning Judaism at this time is the bitter, almost unbearable trouble that has fallen upon us, may the Merciful One protect us.

So when God does have mercy and saves us, with whom will we be left? God forbid, there won't be anyone remaining to fill up the schools, and there won't be enough students left to make the founding of a yeshiva worthwhile, and the congregation of those who tremble at the word of God will be, God forbid, pitifully small. It is not just the mass of ordinary Jews, young people, and children learning Torah who will be missing. All of Jewry, even great Jews, will be damaged by this.

In the book *Tol'doth Yaakov Yosef* we learn two interpretations of the verse from Psalm 12:2, "Save me O God, for the pious have ceased to be; the believers have disappeared from among the children of man." One interpretation is that simple people have stopped believing because the pious have disappeared. The leaders of the Jewish people have been damaged, and this has caused the simple people to fall away from their spirituality. The second interpretation is that the pious have disappeared because the belief of the simple people has been damaged. The fact that people in general have lost faith has caused the disappearance of the great spiritual leaders."

For a deeper understanding of this idea, we will examine a passage from the Talmud (*Moed Katan* 17a), "The lips of the *cohen* guard knowledge. They should seek the law at his mouth, for he is an angel of the Lord of Hosts. " (Malachi 2:7) This has two aspects: "Only if the teacher resembles an angel of the Lord of Hosts," says the Talmud, "should we seek the law at his mouth. But if not, we should not seek the law at his mouth."

With that talmudic dictum in mind, let us examine what it says elsewhere in the Talmud (*Shabbath* 25b): "This was the practice of R. Judah b. I'lai. On the eve of the Sabbath a basin filled with hot water was brought to him; he washed his face, hands, and feet; and then, wrapping himself in fringed linen robes, he sat, looking like an angel of the Lord of Hosts."

It would appear from the theme of this quote that R. Judah b. I'lai resembled an angel only on the eve of the Sabbath, when he had finished his ablutions. What about all the other days of the week, and especially when he was learning with his students? Did he not then also need to resemble an angel?—because "If the teacher resembles an angel of the Lord of Hosts, then we should seek the law at his mouth, and if not . . ." then not.

It appears that the meaning of the Talmud quoted above is this: Even when a teacher does not always resemble an angel, but only does so from time to time, we should still seek Torah from his mouth even during those times he does not resemble an angel. If, however, he never resembles an angel, we should not learn Torah from him. Why is it that even if the teacher only rarely resembles an angel, his students should ask him to teach them Torah? Why must they request the Torah from him at those times?

They need to request the Torah from him then, because when the teacher does resemble an angel, he is already a messenger of God and students do not need to ask anything of him; as an angel, his job is to teach them Torah. However, when he does not resemble an angel, then his students have to ask him for Torah so that the level of angel, which is dormant in the teacher, will reveal itself. If the students do not ask the teacher for Torah then the teacher suffers damage, because he is not aroused to teach. In addition, it is even possible for the degree of angel in the teacher to be dulled, and to disintegrate. This is what the verse (Psalm 12:2) quoted above means when it says, "The pious have ceased to be; the believers have disappeared from among the children of men."

When Jews contemplate their physical and spiritual destruction, and the annihilation of the Torah and the Law that will result from all of this, God forbid, obviously their pain is great. But, through our longing for Torah and worship, and with the pain we feel at the destruction and the withholding of Torah and worship, we can sweeten all judgments and bring about a connection that constitutes a spiritual and physical salvation and a total redemption for all Israel. But this will only happen if people, even at this time, remain resolute and continue to worship God and study Torah with all their capability.

True, at a time when every head is sickened and every heart is breaking, it is difficult to study or pray as we ought to. On the other hand, it must be admitted, there are people today who make too much of the troubles, doing nothing but wasting time and words all day. Is it too much to demand that they use their spare time to learn things that do not require too much concentration, or at least to recite psalms?*

Returning to the original quote: "It will come to pass when you listen to these judgments, safeguarding and keeping them, that God your Lord will keep and guard the covenant and the kindness with which He made an oath to your fathers." (Deut. 7:12) *Ekev tishm'un*—When you listen to these laws. The Hebrew word *ekev*, "when," also translates as "heel." Thus, when you hear and comprehend how the Torah and the Law are being crushed and ground beneath the *ekev* (heel) of judgment and decree; when you suffer pain as a result of that realization; and if you can keep bright the hope, "guarding" it in your hearts (see Genesis 37:11: "Jacob 'guarded' the matter") and longing for the day when you will be able to worship God and fulfill His Commandments, then "God your Lord will keep and guard the covenant and the kindness with which He made an oath to your fathers. He will love you and bless you . . ." because it is through this process that you will sweeten all the judgments and decrees, bringing down the flow of goodness and salvation for Israel.

---

*[This note was added by the author in 1943.] The above was said and written in 1941. Then—however bitter were the troubles and suffering, as is apparent from the text above—it was at least possible to lament, to find words to describe a handful of events, to worry about the survivors, and to grieve for the future—how will they rebuild the schools and yeshivas, etc.? We still had the wherewithal to admonish, and inspire those who remained, with the desire for Torah and worship. This is no longer the case, now at the end of 1942, when the holy congregations have been annihilated in a radical excision. Those individuals who survive, pitiful and few, are broken in slavery and Egyptian bondage, downtrodden and terrified for their lives. There exist no words with which to lament our woes. There is no one to admonish, and there is no heart to awaken to worship and to Torah. How many trials must one undergo as the price of a prayer, and how many tests must be withstood, just to observe Sabbath, even for those who genuinely long to observe it? There is certainly no spirit or heart left to grieve for what the future holds, or to plan reconstruction of the destroyed edifices at such time as God will have mercy on us and save us. Only God, He will have mercy and save us in the blink of an eye. As for the rebuilding of all that has been destroyed, that will only happen with the final redemption and the resurrection of the dead. God, alone, can build and heal. Please, O God, have mercy; please do not delay rescuing us.

# Re'Eh, Rosh Chodesh Elul—August 23, 1941

*"Behold, I set before you this day a blessing and a curse. A blessing, if you obey the commandments of God your Lord, which I command you this day, and a curse, if you do not obey the commandments of the Lord your God, but turn aside from the way that I command you this day."* (Deut. 11:26–28)

A Jew must believe and perceive that everything happens at the hand of God, and that the Holy Blessed One does not execute judgment without justice, God forbid. This is fundamental. It is one of the Thirteen Principles of the Jewish Faith, enumerated by Maimonedes in his commentary on the Mishnah (*Sanhedrin* 10:1): "I believe without a doubt that the Creator, blessed be His name, rewards those who observe His commandments and punishes those who violate them." Besides this, it is also a source of strength and joy in times of suffering, as is written in the *Tanya*: "If a person, while in pain, acknowledges his sins (because everyone knows the blemishes of his own heart) and sees why this particular punishment was justly dealt him, he will not complain, God forbid. On the contrary, he will assume that just as God has punished him so will He nurture him when he repents of his sins, and like a father reconciling with his son God will comfort him. In these reflections, a person may take courage and joy."

Aside from that, sufferings are *hester panim*, concealment of the Divine Face. When a person perceives within his suffering the Hand of God, and His justice and truth, he abolishes the *hester* (concealment). He reveals God even out of the *hester* and *dinim* (judgments). Then, as the concealment evaporates, it becomes *chesed* (loving-kindness), which reveals the Divine Light that is the Face of God.

How could we ever have said that the pain concealed God's Face? Not only does God say (Psalms 91:15), "I am in pain with him," but God, blessed be He, endures the brunt of our pain. On the contrary, it is the person who does not accept suffering with acquiescence, God forbid, and thinks that his suffering is unjustified, God forbid, who creates the concealment. It is as if, God forbid, he was doing away with God, as it were.

This is why God says, "Behold, I set before you this day a blessing and a curse . . . a blessing if you obey . . . and a curse if you do not obey. . . ." He is showing us the justice and truth in all things—the blessing if you obey and the curse if you do not. The result of this perception will be "Behold, I set before you this day" for you will see that it is "I Who am set before you." God, blessed be he, is giving Himself, as it were, to us, and so this becomes a revelation of God, Himself, to us.

Furthermore, it is specifically now—in the month of Elul, marking the start of the days of *Din* (judgment)—that we say, "I am my Beloved's, and my Beloved is mine."

# *Shoftim*—August 30, 1941

*"Be guileless with God your Lord."* (Deut. 18:13)

Rashi (ibid.) explains: "Walk before Him without guile; wait upon Him without projecting into the future. Simply accept whatever happens to you, and then you will be with God—to be His portion."

On the simplest level, "without projecting into the future" can be understood to mean that almost everyone is prepared to commit to worshipping God sometime in the future, saying, "tomorrow or the day after will be the right time." However, the evil inclination will seduce anyone who makes the decision to worship God immediately. This is what is hinted at by "Be guileless with God your Lord," to which Rashi added: "Without projecting into the future." Be guileless with Him right now, in the present.

There is another explanation. Moses our teacher said to God (Exodus 6:12), "If the children of Israel did not listen to me, how then will Pharaoh hear me, and I of uncircumcised lips?" In his holy writings, (Divrei Elimelech, p. 145) my father, of blessed memory, asks, "What logic is there in Moses' argument? The Israelites had a perfectly good reason for not listening, as the Torah tells us (Exodus 6:9): 'They listened not to Moses, for they were dispirited.' On the contrary, Pharaoh, who was not enslaved, might well listen to him?"

One might also ask: Why did Moses initially say of himself (Exodus 4:10), "I am clumsy of speech, and lumpish of tongue"—Onkelos, in the Aramaic *Targum*, translates this as "Speaking with difficulty"—while in the later text Moses says, "I am of uncircumcised lips," which Onkelos translates as "stopped lips," indicating that he could not speak at all.

My father, of blessed memory, in his holy writings asks another question: Why do we learn that the reason they did not listen to Moses was "because they were dispirited, and because of the hard work," when the opposite would make more sense? If they were suffering so much, they should have listened and been overjoyed to hear the good tidings. Besides my holy father's response, there may also be another explanation.

A person who is in distress yet still has some spirit left in him may respond to good news with joy and credulity. But if he has been so beaten and tortured that he is utterly broken and effaced by pain and poverty, then even if he is cognizant and believes that everything will turn out well, there is no longer a person capable of rejoicing. There is no one left to be convinced or encouraged. I have actually seen something like this happen. Therefore, the Torah informs us, "They did not listen to Moses," even though they believed in him. "Because they were dispirited and because of their hard work," there was no one left to be encouraged or to pay attention to the good tidings.

This is what our teacher Moses was saying to God: "If the children of Israel did not listen to me, even though I was bringing them good tidings, because they and their spirits were already so broken, then I am of uncircumcised lips. If the Jewish spirit is so broken, then my mouth is stopped shut, because any greatness that You gave me, God, was only ever for the sake of the Jewish people." The Talmud (*Berachoth* 32a) says the following about the verse (Exodus 32:7), "And God said to Moses, 'Go down.'" "What did God mean when He told Moses, 'Go down?' R. Elazar explained, 'The Holy Blessed One said to Moses, "Moses, stand down from your heights of greatness. I only ever granted you greatness for the sake of Israel. Now that Israel has sinned, why do I need you?" Immediately, Moses became weak and lost all power of speech.'"

"How will Pharaoh listen to me," Moses asked, "now that I am no longer that same Moses who could speak to him?"

It is clear, amidst all this suffering, that if only everyone knew that they would be rescued tomorrow, then a great majority—even of those who have already despaired—would be able to find courage. The problem is that they cannot see any end to the darkness. Many find nothing with which to bolster their spirits, and so, God forbid, they despair and become dispirited. This is how Rashi explains the meaning of "Be guileless with God your Lord." Even if you are broken and oppressed, nevertheless be artless and whole. Take strength in God your Lord because you know that God your Lord is with you in your suffering. Do not attempt to project into the future, saying, "I cannot see an end to the darkness," but simply accept whatever happens to you, and then you will be with God—to be His portion. Then, naturally, your salvation will draw close, for, as Moses said (Deut. 9:29), "They are Your people and Your inheritance."

# Ki Thavo—September 13, 1941

*"The Egyptians were cruel to us, making us suffer and imposing harsh slavery on us. We cried to God, God of our ancestors, and He heard our voice, saw our suffering, our harsh labor, and our distress."* (Deut. 26:6–7)

We need to understand why our sages in the Midrash (*Tanaim*, ibid., quoted in the Passover *Haggadah*) interpret each of the latter phrases—"our suffering," "our harsh labor," and "our distress"—while ignoring the first part of the text—that which says, "The Egyptians were cruel to us, making us suffer and imposing harsh slavery on us." The second part is interpreted as follows: "Suffering" refers to the separation of men and women, "harsh labor" refers to the killing of our children, and "distress" refers to our stress. Why did our sages explain only the latter part of the text in which "God heard our voice" and not the first part of the text where it says, "The Egyptians were cruel to us"?

Now, in our present circumstances, we can see that by comparison with the way we used to feel we have become numb to all pain and suffering. In the past, we suffered every hurt, no matter how minor. But if we were capable of responding to all the pain of our current suffering with emotion and distress, as we once did, it would be impossible to survive, God forbid, even for a single day. The reason is simple, as our sages said in the Talmud (*Shabbath* 13b): "Dead flesh of a living person does not feel the scalpel." We can feel only a bone-crushing sensation throughout our body. The universe is blacked out for us. Day and night have ceased to exist. There is nothing but disorientation and confusion. It seems as if the whole world is pressing down on us, squeezing, squashing, and stressing us, God forbid, to bursting point. We cannot feel the details of each torment or gauge the degree of its pain. The sages did not interpret the first part of the text, "The Egyptians were cruel to us," because Jews did not experience every harsh decree individually. Still God, blessed be He, "heard our voice," and saw the smallest detail of every torment, as our sages explained. Then God had mercy, and saved us.

*The Jewish Year 5702:
September 22, 1941–
September 11, 1942*

# *Rosh Hashanah—*
# September 22–23, 1941

*"You heard my voice. Please be not deaf to my plea for well-being."* (Lament. 3:56)

*"The beginning of Your word is true, and for ever, every one of Your righteous judgments endures."* (Psalms 119:160)

*"Guarantee for good Your servant; let not the wicked oppress me."* (Psalms 119:122) (From the liturgy recited before blowing the *shofar*.)

If the first verse is to be understood literally, why does it begin with the phrase "You heard," implying that God has already heard us, and then follow with the request, "Please be not deaf to my plea for well-being"?

The Midrash (Genesis Rabbah 65:20) interprets the verse (Genesis 27:22), "The voice is Jacob's voice, but the hands are the hands of Esau," as follows: "So long as the voice of Jacob continues trilling with the sounds of Torah in synagogues and study houses, the hands of Esau will have no mastery."

The Torah and the commandments are our very life and times. Even prayer requires Torah study, as we learn in the verse (Proverbs 28:9), "Whosoever turns his ear away from Torah, even his prayer is an abomination."

Oh! When we remind ourselves of how we used to pray in previous years . . . how our prayers would rise to heaven during the Festivals and High Holidays . . . the sounds of Torah learning issuing from study houses, yeshivas, and schools, crowning our prayers . . . and Torah that every person privately learned in his house all year, especially the Torah of the month of Elul, surrounding our prayers during these holy days. Together, the holy sounds of Torah and prayer broke through all the heavens and rose before the Throne of Glory. And it is not just we who were sanctified more each time, and it was not just to us that salvation flowed, for the Torah and prayer also fixed the Kingdom of Heaven.

God said (Exodus 20:2), "I am God your Lord, who brought you out of Egypt, from the place of slavery." The name of God—*YHVH*, the tetragrammaton— was revealed only when the Jewish people left slavery for freedom, and sorrow for joy. When the Jewish people are in pain, the name of God—*YHVH*, is hidden and God is called *Elohim*, as is explained in the holy Zohar (vol. III, 84b). It is only when the Jewish people are redeemed and free, and able to worship God that the Kingdom of Heaven is also revealed: "I am *YHVH*, God your Lord, who brought you out of Egypt, from the place of slavery." The redemption was the revelation of *Anochi* ("I am") and of *YHVH* (God).

This is why, in the verses recited before blowing the *shofar*, we pray, "You heard my voice," in the past. That is, You heard the sounds of my prayers and of the *shofar* because they were surrounded by the sounds of Torah that pierced the heavens. Now, even though the sounds of my prayer are feeble, unable to rise on high—as though heard from afar, as a sound to which one must bend one's ear—nonetheless, "Please be not deaf to my plea for well-being." Not only does the outcome affect us, it also affects You, God, as it were, as the next verse recited before blowing the shofar states, "The beginning of Your word is true." Our sages in the Talmud (*Kiddushin* 31a) explain, regarding this verse: "What does this verse imply; that the beginning of God's word is true, but not the end of His word? The meaning is this. The psalmist said, "From the end of Your words it may be seen that the beginning is true." When the nations of the world heard the Ten Commandments (Exodus 20:1), 'I am God. . . . Do not have any other gods before Me,' and so forth, they said, 'Look, everything God does is for His own pleasure and glory.' Only when they heard the later Commandments (Exodus 20:12), 'Honor your father and mother,' and so forth, did they admit that the Commandments were wholly true. Hence, 'The beginning of Your word is true.'"

We see that the quote "The beginning of Your word is true" refers to "I (*Anochi*) am *YHVH*, God your Lord, who brought you out of Egypt," the first words of the Ten Commandments, revealed on Sinai.

According to what we said above, the revelation of "I am *YHVH*, God," came about precisely because "I am God your Lord who brought you out of Egypt, from the place of slavery." The revelation of God happens only when the Jewish people are redeemed and able to worship God. Therefore the next verse is, "Guarantee for good Your servant; let not the wicked oppress me," for it is not we who have caused the desecration of the Torah and prevented the worship of God this way. Therefore, we beg God to have mercy, and "Guarantee for good Your servants," for if You will save us and not allow the wicked to destroy us, then with the help of God we will renew the Torah, the prayer, and the worship with even greater strength.

～✣～

> "Blow a shofar at the month, at the hidden moon on our feast day. For this is a statute for Israel, a judgment for the God of Jacob." (Psalms 81:4)

This is the Festival during which the moon is hidden so that there cannot be two witnesses to testify against the Jewish people in their hour of judgment, as is well known. However, in the Rosh Hashanah liturgy we say that the Holy Blessed One "knows and bears witness." If this is so, then the Holy Blessed One might bear witness and testify against us. This is why the verse says, "a judgment for the God of Jacob." The judgment that will be passed this day not only affects the Jewish people, it also concerns the Holy Blessed One. On this day, Jews repent and with the act of blowing the *shofar* accept upon themselves the sovereignty of heaven, for, as is well known, the blowing of the *shofar* announces the coronation of the King and a renewal of His sovereignty. Thus, whatever concerns us also concerns Him.

Therefore, "Blow a *shofar* at the month, etc." means "Return, repent, and accept the yoke of heaven upon yourselves," during this Festival day when the moon is hidden so that there will not be two witnesses to testify against you. If you wonder whether God, who knows and witnesses, will testify, remember that "It is a statute for Israel, a judgment for the God of Jacob." The statute is that the judgment concerns not only the Jews, but also the God of Jacob. God will be affected one way or another by the outcome of the trial, so He, God, cannot bear witness against Himself, and other witnesses are required. Since the moon is hidden there are no other witnesses, and we will surely be acquitted in the judgment.

～✣～

> "If You, Yah (God), should mark iniquities, Adonai (Lord), who could stand?"
> (Psalms 130:3, recited in the High Holiday liturgy.)

We need to understand why the verse uses the name *Yah* for God. Why specifically *Yah*? And why does it not then go on to say "*Yah* (God), who could stand?" instead of *Adonai* (Lord)?

We learn in the Talmud (*Menachoth* 29b) on the verse (Isaiah 26:4) "Trust in *YHVH* (God) for ever; for *Yah* (God) is rock of worlds," that the world to come was created with *Yud* and the world we inhabit was created with *Heh*. Even though we cannot really understand these lofty issues, nevertheless inasmuch as it affects our worship, we may try to understand, at our level, why the worlds were created with *Yud* and *Heh,* the first two letters of the tetragrammaton (*YHVH*), and not with *Vav* and *Heh,* the last two letters.

*Vav* and *Heh* are dependent upon the Jewish people, who create worlds with them. We have learned that everything created by the Holy Blessed One was created for His glory (Talmud, *Yoma* 38a). So this world and the world to come, which were created by the Holy Blessed One with *Yud Heh,* were created to reveal His glory. When Jews worship God with the physical and psychological attributes identified with the Hebrew letter *Vav*—the six lower *sephirot*—and then accept upon themselves the yoke of the sovereignty of heaven, which is identified with the final *Heh*—the *sephirah* of *Malkhut*—as is well known, they are also creating something of God's glory. In the holy Zohar (Intro., 4b) we learn that when a Jew creates something new in Torah, a new heaven is created. Thus, the Jewish people's worship is also a kind of creation. Through it, part of God's glory is created and revealed, so that even above, new heavens are created.

With *Yud Heh* God created the worlds, beginning with *Atzilut* (Archetypes); then *Briyah* (Creation), in which God's glory is revealed; then *Yetzirah* (Formation), in which more is revealed; and then *Assiya* (Action). The Jewish people, with their worship, create at the level of *Vav Heh* further revelation in the world of *Assiya*. Their physical deeds reveal God's light and holiness in the physical part of the world of *Assiya*. The practical commandments that a Jew fulfills physically, with his flesh, his blood, his strength, and even with the psychological characteristics that come from his animal soul and comprise his physical vitality, draw the holiness of God and of the Torah into the world.

That is why every Jew, in his mind, wants to worship God, even though in practice it may be very difficult for him to do so. The difference between thought and action is that thought is at the level of *Yud Heh*, where there is already a revelation of God that has been brought about by God. This is not so, however, with practical actions, at the level of *Vav Heh*. Here, the person himself must bring about a new creation, and that is a difficult thing.

With this we can understand, in our situation, the Midrash (Genesis Rabbah 17:4): "R. Acha said, "When the Holy One, blessed be He, came to create man, He sought the advice of the ministering angels. He said to them, "Let us make man." And they asked Him, "What good is he?" God answered, "His wisdom is greater than yours." God made all the animals pass before the angels, asking whether the angels knew their names, but they could not answer. Then He passed them before man, who spoke their names, saying, "This is an ox, this is a donkey, this is a horse, this is a camel." Then God said to man, "And you, what is your name?" Man replied,

"It seems to me that a fitting name would be *Adam*, because I am created out of *Adama*, Earth." God said, "And I? What is My name?" Man said, "It would be fitting to call You *Adonai*, Lord, because You are Lord of everything You created.'" R. Acha continued, 'God said (Isaiah 42:8), "I am God; this is My name." God was saying, "This is the name by which Adam called Me."'"

At the simplest of levels it is difficult to understand why it is that man should be the one to give names to everything in the world. Not only that, but also why is it that man names the Holy Blessed One *Adonai*, Lord? Why should this be the final argument, against the angels, in the decision to create man?

We know that the name of each thing is its source of vitality. It is written (Genesis 2:19): "Whatever the man called the soul of each living thing remained its name," because the name of a thing is its vital soul. There are instances, however, when something is called by a name after its life has been created, as when God called light "day," giving the day its name only after it had already been created. Then there are instances whereby, through naming, the thing itself is called into being, as it is written (Exodus 30:2), "I have called Betzalel son of Uri son of Chur, of the tribe of Judah, by name. I have filled him with a divine spirit, with wisdom, understanding, and knowledge." By calling upon Betzalel by name, God actually filled him with wisdom, etc. On the verse (Numbers 13:16) "Moses gave Hoshea son of Nun the name Joshua," Rashi (ibid.) explains: "By giving him the new name, which is a compound of two words, *Yah* and *Hoshua* 'May God save,' he in effect prayed for him: 'May God save you from the evil counsel of the spies.'" By naming Joshua in this way, Moses managed to put extra holiness inside him, in order to protect him.

Because the angels counseled God not to create man, the Holy Blessed One replied, "His wisdom is greater than yours." The verse (Genesis 1:1) "In the beginning God created heaven and earth," is translated in the Jerusalem *Targum* as ". . . with wisdom created." Thus, God said to the angels, "Man's wisdom/creativity is greater than yours, because he can be creative through his worship of God. Proof of it is that he can name things, which is also a way of creating their vital souls." But what kind of creativity is it when that which is named has already been created? It is the creativity of man using everything already extant in the world to call upon the name of God, thereby making God sovereign over all of them. This is why he named God *Adonai*, Lord, as Adam said in the Midrash quoted above, "Because He is Lord over all." Through serving God with all living things, man makes God their sovereign.

The time for repentance is Rosh Hashanah, the anniversary of the creation of the world. This is because repentance, whose definition is the commitment to worship God henceforth, is also a kind of creativity, because renewal and creativity are similar. The Midrash (Leviticus Rabbah 29:6) explains the verse "Blow a *shofar* (ram's horn) at the *chodesh* (month) . . ." (Psalms 81:4): "Don't read it as 'month'; *chodesh* also means 'renewal.' Renew your actions. Don't read it as 'ram's horn'; *shofar* also means 'beautification.' Beautify your actions." That is, renew your actions like God does every day, as the Talmud says (*Hagigah* 12b): "God renews the creation of the world, daily."

At the creation of the world, God created worlds and destroyed them, as we learn in the Midrash (Genesis Rabbah 3:7). The creation and destruction of worlds refers to the concept of "Shattering of Vessels," from which God made this, the "World of Fixing," as is well known. We know from the writings of the Arizal (R. Isaac Luria, *Likutei Shas Berachoth* 61a) that the Ten Holy Martyrs murdered by the Romans were killed because at that moment in history there was about to be a repetition of the destruction and creation of worlds. This was due to the proliferation of *k'lipoth* (husks) obscuring the Divine Light. The worlds stood ready for destruction, as they did at the time of the original Shattering of Vessels, and this instability was fixed by the martyrdom of the ten Rabbis at the hands of the Romans.

We should remember this when watching the suffering that we are presently enduring, when we see so many Jewish souls, scholars, saints, and God worshippers being snatched away, may the Merciful One protect us. Every Jew is suffering so much now, especially those who are killed, may the Merciful One protect us, but God is Righteous; He will have mercy and say "Enough" to our woes and to the suffering of His people, the House of Israel. When looking at this situation, we know that now is such a time, at the level of "Shattering of Vessels." Therefore, we must strengthen ourselves more and more, with repentance and the "renewal of our deeds," to make a fresh creation.

The first thing that we must renew with our repentance is this: Not only will we merely refrain from repeating all the mistakes we have made up to now, and do only good, but we will also become, with our whole being, new and better creations, as worshippers and servants of God. For then, all the worlds will be fixed, as we said above. When a Jew worships, he creates worlds at the level of *Vav Heh*. When calling the names of God, the Jews call *Adonai*, Lord, and God is revealed in His sovereignty and reveals His Divine Majesty.

This is the meaning of "If You, *Yah*, should mark iniquities, *Adonai*, who could stand?" If God, with the name *Yah,* comprising the letters *Yud Heh*—which God Himself created, and which does not depend upon Israel—should mark our sins, refusing to overlook them, then the name *Yah* might still endure. But the name *Adonai* will not survive because God needs the Jewish people to name Him thus, for, as we learned in the Midrash above, it was Adam who named God *Adonai*. In the Talmud (*Berachoth* 7b) we learn that it was our father Abraham, the first Jew, who named God *Adonai*.

In the High Holiday liturgy we pray (Psalms 130:5), "My hope is *YHVH*. My soul hopes; I wait upon His word. . . . Israel prays to God, because lovingkindness is with God and there is much salvation with Him. He will redeem Israel from all its sins."

Because *YHVH* is expressed only through the existence of the Jewish people, therefore *YHVH* is the hope of the Jewish people, and He will redeem Israel from all its sins.

༺❀༻

*"Out of my straits I called upon God. With divine alleviation He answered me."* (Psalms 118:5, from the liturgy recited before blowing the *shofar*.)

The teaching found in the *Tikunei Zohar* (*Tikun* 6) is well known: "Those who pray on Rosh Hashanah for their own needs are like dogs howling, 'Give! Give! Give us life! Give us food!'" But when a person is in terrible suffering and agony, it is hard not to scream out in pain, unless one is numbered among those great saints who are stripped of physical attachments and unabsorbed in themselves. For people like us, however, especially in such terrible, bitter anguish, it is impossible not to cry out and pray to God, even on Rosh Hashanah and Yom Kippur, about our pain and suffering. This in itself is a source of distress, and our soul cries out bitterly that even during such holy days as these we are reduced to praying "Give us life! Give us food!" instead of loftier, altruistic prayers for the needs and sake of heaven.

We have already commented on the verse (Exodus 2:23) ". . . And the Israelites groaned from their work. They cried out, and their cries went up to God from the work." We said that the Jews groaned only because of their slavery and pain, but their cries and prayers arose out of their desire to be able to pray other, loftier prayers, to be able to cry to God rather than from the work. This in itself was the prayer: that from the work, their prayers rise to God. They prayed that their prayers should be about God, rising beyond prayers about work.

This is the meaning of the verse "Out of my straits I called upon God. With divine alleviation He answered me." At present, I am calling out of my straits about my pain, but please, God, respond with divine alleviation, so that I can pray from comfort and plenitude, so that I can pray properly, unselfishly, for the sake of God.

# *Shabbat Shuva* (Sabbath of Repentance)—September 27, 1941

"Return O Israel to God your Lord, for you have stumbled in your iniquity. Take with you words, and turn to God: say to Him, 'Forgive all iniquity, and receive us graciously, and our lips will offer oxen.'

"Ashur cannot save us; we will not ride upon horses, nor will we say any more to the work of our hands, 'You are our gods,' for in You the orphan finds mercy.

"I will heal their backsliding, I will love them freely: for My anger is turned away from him." (Hosea 14:2–6, from the *Haftorah* reading for this Sabbath.)

Let us try to understand: Why does the verse open in the singular *Shuva*—"Return O Israel to the Lord your God," and end in the plural, *K'chu*—"Take with you words"? Also, why in His response does the Holy Blessed One first use the plural, "I will heal their backsliding," and then go on to say, "For My anger is turned away from him," in the singular?

We learn in the Talmud (*Hullin* 7a): "Once, R. Pinchas b. Yair was on his way to redeem captives, and came to the river Ginnai. 'O Ginnai,' said he, 'Split your waters for me, that I may pass through you.' The river refused, saying, 'You are trying to do the will of your Maker; but I, too, am trying to do the will of my Maker. You may or may not accomplish your purpose. I am sure of accomplishing mine.' He said, 'If you will not split, I will decree that no waters ever pass through you again.' It thereupon split for him. There was also present a certain man who was carrying wheat for the Passover, and R. Pinchas once again addressed the river:

'Split for this man, too, for he is engaged in a religious duty.' It thereupon split for him too. There was also an Arab who had joined them [on the journey], and so R. Pinchas once again addressed the river: 'Split for this one, too, that he may not say, "Is this how they treat a fellow traveler?"' It thereupon split for him too. R. Joseph exclaimed; 'How great is this man! Like Moses and the six hundred thousand of Israel!'"

At the simplest level, we need to understand the answer R. Pinchas gave to the river, for the argument of the river appears to be a stronger one: "You are trying to do the will of your Maker; but I, too, am trying to do the will of my Maker. You may or may not accomplish your purpose. I am sure of accomplishing mine." There is a treatment of the question in the Agadic Novellae (ibid.) of the Maharsha (R. Shmuel Eidels). He points out that there is no moral weight attached to the action of a river, whereas the actions of R. Pinchas have moral weight and thus override the instructions given the river.

Aside from this explanation, the following is also possible. R. Pinchas was going to save a Jew, for, as the text notes, he was on his way to redeem a captive. For the sake of saving a soul, we know that God is ready to negate as it were, His own intentions. The Law states clearly that even in a case with only the remotest possibility of saving someone's life, we must desecrate the Sabbath (Mishnah, *Yoma* 8:7). The river was doing the will of the Creator and was certain of accomplishing its purpose, whereas the outcome of R. Pinchas b. Yair's mission was in doubt. Nonetheless, if there was even a remote possibility of saving a Jew, the river had to void its commission and split. The mandate of the river to flow in obedience to the will of God was never of greater importance than God's command concerning the observance of the Sabbath. The Sabbath has to be desecrated even if there is only the remotest possibility of saving a life.

In the High Holiday liturgy (*Selichot* for the Fast of Gedaliah), we pray: "Holy Torah, beseech with prayers." Aside from the simplest meaning, the prayer means the following. Since God observes the entire Torah, He should also observe the Torah ordinance demanding that the Torah be set aside for even the remote possibility of saving a life. How priceless is the soul of a Jew, if the Law contains within it the caveat that it must be set aside even on a slender chance of saving a Jewish life? And how much more so now, at this time, when so great a portion of the Jewish people is in such trouble and danger, may the Merciful One protect us. Therefore we ask the holy Torah to plead on our behalf, in the name of the law demanding that Jews must be rescued.

Returning to the Talmud quoted above: We need to understand what R. Joseph adds to the ending of the story, when he says: "How great is this man! Like Moses and the six hundred thousand of Israel!" He appears to be stating something obvious, since the river split for R. Pinchas as the Red Sea split for Moses and all the Jewish people. There is another more general difficulty in the talmudic story of R. Pinchas b. Yair, arising out of a Midrash (Genesis Rabbah 5:5) on the verse (Exodus 14:27) "And the sea returned to its original condition." The Midrash concludes that its 'original condition' was the conditional terms originally imposed upon the sea, by God, at the creation of the world: "God created the sea on condition that the Red Sea would split for the Jews when they came out of Egypt." According to the Tosfos Yom-Tov in his commentary to the Mishnah (*Avoth* 5:6), the Midrash supports the general thesis expounded by Maimonedes as a theological axiom: that God never changes His mind, nor can there ever be any change in God's knowing. This explains the Mishnaic saying, "Ten things were especially created at twilight on the sixth day of creation: The mouth of the earth [that swallowed Korach and his co-conspirators], the mouth of the wellspring [that followed the Jews through the wilderness], the mouth of [Balaam's] ass, etc. The ten supernatural phenomena were pre-determined by God at the creation of the world so that God should not later appear to have changed His mind. Since God foresaw the need, He created the vehicle."

If it is true that all supernatural phenomena must be preordained, then it must also be true that God made a condition with the river Ginnai to split its waters for R. Pinchas when the time came. Why then, did the river start arguing with R. Pinchas b. Yair and refuse to split, when splitting was an agreed upon precondition of its creation?

The river may have been arguing that only for the entire Jewish people, Moses and the six hundred thousand together, was it obliged to split, because only in their entirety, not as individuals, are the Jews important and valuable to God. God made a condition with the sea that it would split before Moses and the six hundred thousand, and the river Ginnai argued that it too would split its waters if the whole of Israel came before it. But, the river argued, for an individual it should not disobey its commission to keep flowing, because by flowing it was doing the will of its Maker.

However, as explained above, this argument is erroneous, because even for the possibility of saving a single Jew it is obligatory to desecrate the Sabbath. Now we can understand the meaning of R. Joseph's concluding words. Seeing that R. Pinchas b. Yair had won the argument with the river, because every Jewish life is precious beyond price, R. Joseph's remark was directed not at R. Pinchas, but at the individual R. Pinchas went to save: "How great is this man! Like Moses and the six hundred thousand!" And if one individual is of such great importance, imagine the value to God of a group of Jews! It is not only the nation as a whole that is precious.

The issues are simple, and easily understandable, even for people of our limited intelligence. The Hebrew word *Yisrael*, written *Yud-Shin-Resh-Alef-Lamed*, is a *notariqon* (acrostic) for the Hebrew phrase *Yesh shishim riboah otiot l'Torah*, There are six hundred thousand letters in the Torah. Another *notariqon* reads *Yesh shishim riboah anashim l'Israel*, There are six hundred thousand Jewish people.

If even one single letter is left out, the entire Torah scroll is invalid and has no sanctity. We learn the following from the introduction to the book *Shaarei Orah*, in reference to the verse (Psalms 19:9) "Commandments of God are perfect; they delight the heart": "The entire text of the Torah is a series of permutations of the Divine Name of God. It is a fabric woven from Holy Names in acrostic, anagram, *notariqon*, or gematria, etc. form." Therefore when, God forbid, one Jew goes missing, the whole Torah becomes invalid and the imperfection touches upon the name of God, because the Torah is woven from Names of God. This could be what is meant by the *Hallel* prayer (Psalms 115:1) "Not for our sake, God, not for our sake, but for Your Name's sake bestow glory." When God does things for "our sake," we are a whole entity, and perhaps the boon will be granted to the entire Jewish people. Thus we pray, "Not for our sake, God," meaning not in the collective sense, for all of us together, but "for Your Name's sake," because if it is for Your name's sake then every individual counts, in order to prevent a blemish in the Name of God.

Just as we beg and plead of God to have mercy and compassion for every individual, that He should save and rescue every Jew, so likewise, every Jew has to repent individually and not depend on the whole nation. It is not enough to say, "Well, the Jewish people as a whole are good, and in general they repent, so that should be sufficient for me to be included with the whole." Besides, every person has his own failings and character flaws that only he can fix.

It is not just because they need fixing that we must look at our character flaws. The issue goes far beyond the negative aspects. We learn in the *Etz HaChaim* (Gate 3:2) that even saints are individuals, and no two are alike. No creature is like its neighbor, and so when an individual Jew worships God, there is a revelation of God's light and holiness that is peculiar to that individual and that cannot be revealed through anyone else. Even now, in this time of distress, during the annihilation of Israel, there may be revelation coming through us that would not be revealed in comfortable times, as we have already explained concerning the talmudic story (*Berachoth* 3a): "R. Jose entered into a ruin in Jerusalem to pray, whereupon he heard a heavenly echo cooing like a dove, 'O Woe to me that I have destroyed my house and exiled my children. . . .'" Why did R. Jose not hear the heavenly echo until he entered the ruins? Why did he hear it only when he was in the ruins of Jerusalem? The Talmud says that Elijah the prophet told him, "It is not just now that the Divine Voice is heard so to exclaim, but three times every day. And more than that, whenever Jewish people go into the synagogues and schoolhouses. . . ."

We explained that perhaps it was precisely because R. Jose was in one of the ruins, in the destroyed city of Jerusalem, and his heart was even more broken within him than usual, that he was more capable of hearing the Divine Voice.

Let us return to the quote from the prophet Hosea with which we began the chapter. The prophet began by speaking in the singular, *Shuva*—"Return O Israel"—meaning that every individual must repent and return to God, each reflecting his individual, characteristic requirements. Then the prophet spoke to the whole nation as one entity. God, in His response, also spoke to them as a whole—"I will heal their backsliding; I will love them freely"—and as individuals—"For my anger is turned away from him," and I will rescue and save the individual.

At *Kiddush*, after services on the holy Sabbath, I remarked, "I would have thought that in such troubled times as these, when Rosh Hashanah comes around, the prayers of Jewish people would be shouted, and the outpourings of the heart would gush like a torrent of water. But although we trust in God that our prayers have been effective, everyone can see that before the war, our prayers were louder and more passionate and offered with a greater outpouring of the heart than the prayers that were uttered during Rosh Hashanah this year. This is simply because our bodies are so weakened, and Jews have no more strength. But, in addition, we observe that in general Rosh Hashanah and Shabbat Shuva, the Sabbath of Repentance, lack the trepidation and passion with which they were celebrated previously." [Now, as I am writing this, I can add that others have told me they agree: They have observed it too.]

What has caused this to happen? Firstly, as King David said (Psalms 138:3), "On the day when I called, You answered me, and strengthened me with strength in my soul." When a Jewish person prays, and his prayers are answered, his subsequent prayers are even stronger and stimulated to greater passion. But when he prays and then sees that not only are his prayers not answered but his troubles actually increase, may the Merciful One protect us, a person's heart falls and he cannot arouse himself to passionate prayer.

The second reason is, as we have already said, for anything to really happen, for faith and for joy, there needs to be a real person to experience the faith and the joy—but when the person has been wholly crushed and squashed, there is no one left to rejoice. The same applies to passion and arousal in prayer. The Jew is falling now, lying prone and crushed, and there is no one to be aroused in prayer.

However, King David said (Psalms 118:5), "Out of my straits I called upon God." That is, I called not just from one straitened circumstance, but from straits—plural. Though I called upon You when I fell into my first crisis, and not only was not answered and rescued but plunged even deeper into crisis—straits within straits—nevertheless, I take strength and call upon You again.

# *Sukkoth* (Festival of Tabernacles)—October 6–12, 1941*

King David (Psalms 16:2–3) said, "Say unto God, 'You are my Lord: My prosperity is not Your charge. But for the holy who are in the earth and the heroes in whom all my longing dwells.'" Regarding this verse, we learn in the Talmud (Menachoth 53a): "The Congregation of Israel said to the Holy Blessed One, 'Lord of the universe, give me credit for making You known in the world.' God replied, 'Have you not said: "My prosperity is not Your charge?" I credit none but Abraham, Isaac, and Jacob, who first made Me known in the world. Hence, "But for the holy who are in the earth and the heroes in whom all my longing dwells."'"

We learn in the Talmud (Berachoth 7b): "From the day that the Holy Blessed One created the world there was no one who called God *Adonai*, Lord, until Abraham came and called Him *Adonai*, as it is written (Genesis 15:8): And he said, '*Adonai*, how do I know that I will inherit it?'"

However, we learn in the Midrash (Genesis Rabbah 17:5) that while Adam was naming all the animals in creation, God asked him, "And Me, what is My name?" He answered, "It would be fitting to call You *Adonai*—Lord—because You are Lord of everything You created." R. Acha continued: "God said (Isaiah 42:8), 'I am God; this is My name,' meaning, 'This is the name by which Adam called Me.'" If this is so, then contrary to the Talmud quoted above, Adam named God *Adonai* long before the Patriarch Abraham called Him by that name.

---

*(The second day of the Festival of Sukkoth, upon the *yahrzeit* of my holy, pious son, Rav Elimelech Benzion, of blessed memory.)

The explanation may be as follows. When the Patriarch Abraham called God *Adonai*, he was told that his descendants would go into exile, as it is written (Genesis 15:12–13): "Abraham fell into a trance and was struck with a deep, dark dread. God said, 'Know for sure that your descendants will be foreigners in a land that is not theirs for four hundred years. They will be enslaved and oppressed.'" We learn in the Talmud (*Nedarim* 32a) that the exile was a punishment for Abraham having previously asked, "*Adonai*, how do I know that I will inherit it?"

This is what the Patriarch Abraham added to the sense in which Adam called God *Adonai*: Adam said, "It is fitting to call You *Adonai*—Lord," when it was clear and obvious to everyone that God is Master of everything. As Adam put it, "It is fitting to call You *Adonai* because You are Lord over all Your creatures." To this, our father Abraham added that also in times of exile, darkness, and suffering, God is *Adonai*, Lord, and will always be called by the name *Adonai*. Not only when it is evident that God is Master of all will the Jewish people call Him *Adonai*, by worshipping, connecting, and cleaving unto God, blessed be He; but, we will also make it a point of worship to call God *Adonai*, accepting His mastery and ownership over us, even in times of concealment when all the good is hidden.

The paths to worship and revelation of God's majesty are manifold. There is the revelation of His majesty that depends upon periods of clarity and prosperity for the Jewish people, and then there is worship and revelation that depends upon periods of *hester* (concealment) and exile, when all the world sees how tremendously the Jews suffer for the sake of His blessed Name, accepting upon themselves the sovereignty of heaven with total self-abandon.

Besides the fact that pain and exile bring their own revelation, we have the following teaching from the holy Arizal (R. Isaac Luria). With their deaths, the holy souls of *tzaddikim* (saints) ascend to heaven, becoming the *mayin nukvin* (feminine flow) that rises from the *sephirah* of *Malkhut* (Sovereignty) to inundate the six *sephirot* of *Ze'er Anpin* (Small Faces). From there they ascend together to inundate the two supernal *sephirot* of *Ima* (Mother) and *Aba* (Father), *Chokhma* and *Binah*. This ultimate ascension brings about the true and complete union and is equivalent to the teaching in the Talmud (*Menachot* 110a, Tos. cit. *Michael*) describing how the angel Michael, the great Prince, stands before the heavenly altar and offers up the souls of the righteous before God, as is well known.

Even though the Talmud speaks only of the death of pious people, whose deaths enable the angel Michael to make a whole sacrifice of their souls upon the altar, the sacrifice is not confined to death of the body or to martyrdom. The concept applies equally to all agony suffered by the Jewish people, to the fragmentation of self and the forfeiture of self when it is lost to anguish and exhaustion. We learn in the Talmud (*Berachoth* 17a): On fast days, we pray, "May the fat and blood I lose as a result of this fast be accepted as a sacrifice upon the altar before You." How much more so should the loss of fat, blood, strength, and mind—the result of bitter suffering that is much worse than fasting—be accepted as a sacrifice offered by Michael upon the heavenly altar to God. With his offering, he brings about the unification and the revelation of God's light and holiness and His salvation, "And your Guide will not hide His face any more." (Isaiah 30:20)

With this, perhaps we can explain the following. Why when the Patriarch Abraham called God by the name *Adonai* was it written into the Torah (Genesis 15:8), while Adam's original naming of God, *Adonai*, is not recorded in Scripture but only in the oral Torah (Genesis Rabbah 17:5)?

We know that the Hebrew word *Yisrael*, written *Yud-Sin-Resh-Alef-Lamed*, is a *notariqon* (acrostic) for the Hebrew phrase *Yesh shishim riboah otiot l'Torah*, There are six hundred thousand letters in the Torah. Another *notariqon* reads *Yesh shishim riboah anashim l'Israel*, There are six hundred thousand Jewish people. Our father Abraham called the name *Adonai* out of the suffering of Jewish people, who offer up parts of themselves as a sacrifice. These parts of Jews—their blood, fat, strength, and mind—are letters of the Torah, and so out of them the name *Adonai* is written into the Torah. This was not the case with Adam, who did not call *Adonai* out of exile and suffering. He offered up no sacrifice that might shape the letters, and so his naming of *Adonai* was not written into the Torah.

This is hinted at in the Talmud quoted above, on the verse "Say unto God, 'You are my Lord: My prosperity is not Your charge. But for the holy who are in the earth and the heroes in whom all my longing dwells.'" From the day the Holy Blessed One created the world there was no one who called Him *Adonai* until Abraham came and called Him *Adonai*. The name *Adonai* was handed down by the Patriarch Abraham and his descendants to the Jewish people so that they might call upon *Adonai* even out of their suffering. This is why the Congregation of Israel said to the Holy Blessed One, "Lord of the universe, give me credit for making You known in the world. Give me credit, because I offer my heart and soul, my strength and my mind—and even my whole life—to make You known in the world. The whole world is simply astonished to see us die so willingly for You, and Your name is magnified thereby in the world. By doing what we do, we facilitate the completion of the Supernal Union, so the concealment is transformed and the Divine Light is revealed." The Holy Blessed One replied, "Truly, the worship of every Jew is precious to Me, especially worship involving total self sacrifice. Nonetheless, credit is due not to you, but to Abraham, Isaac, and Jacob, who were *t'chilah* (first) in making Me known in the world, because they initiated a worship of God that is wholly self-sacrificial."

It is entirely possible that the midrashic concept of "Abraham, Isaac, and Jacob were *t'chilah* (first) in making Me known in the world," does not preclude a

Jewish person from taking the initiative and being creative and original in his worship of God. Rather, the inference is that the Patriarchs blazed the creative trail, enabling other Jews to be *t'chilah*–first, original, and creative in worship. We learn in the Midrash (Leviticus Rabbah 22:1): "Even those insights that are newly discovered by a veteran student at some time in the future, were all given to Moses at Sinai." Even though it was all given to Moses, the student can still be creative—for if all had not been given to Moses, the student would not be able to be creative. The same applies in matters of worship. R. Simeon b. Yochai was the initiator of his holy path, and the Arizal (R. Isaac Luria) and the Ba'al Shem Tov, of blessed memory, opened their holy paths. But all their achievements were due to the might of the Patriarchs, who made it possible for any worshipper to be *t'chilah*—first, new, and innovative—in his forms of worship.

This may also be the hint in the famous last words of R. Simeon b. Gamliel, first of the ten Rabbis martyred by the Romans. The Talmud describes the scene (*Avot d'Rebbe Natan* 38:3): "When they arrested R. Simeon b. Gamliel and R. Ishmael b. Elisha, R. Simeon was much distressed. 'Woe to us,' he said, 'Are we to die like Sabbath desecrators, idolaters, adulterers, or murderers?' 'Shall I tell you something?' said R. Ishmael. 'Speak,' said R. Simeon. 'Perhaps,' said he, 'While you were eating one day, some poor people were turned away from your door, and were not invited inside to share your meal with you?' 'As heaven is my witness, it never happened,' replied R. Simeon, 'I paid men to stand at my gate, with instructions to bring anyone who wanted to eat, inside to share my food with me.' 'But perhaps,' said R. Ishmael, 'Once, as you were speaking on the Temple Mount with tens of thousands of Jews sitting at your feet, you were a little self-satisfied?' Said he to him, 'Brother Ishmael, man is ready to meet his destiny.'

"They beseeched the Roman Speculator, begging to be the first to die. R. Ishmael said, 'I am a priest, son of the High Priest. Kill me *t'chilah*, first, that I should not have to watch the death of my friend.' R. Simeon b. Gamliel begged, 'I am a prince, son of the Prince of Israel. Kill me *t'chilah*, first, that I should not have to watch the death of my friend.'

"'Draw lots,' said the Roman Speculator. They cast lots and it fell upon R. Simeon. Immediately they took a sword and cut off his head. R. Ishmael, crying and screaming, picked it up and held it to his bosom, 'O holy mouth, trusted mouth, holy mouth, trusted mouth, pearls dropped from these your lips. Who buried them in dust? Who filled your tongue with dust and ashes . . . ?' He was not allowed to finish his speech before they chopped off his head too."

Besides the simple wish to be the first to die and not have to watch his friend's death, perhaps R. Simeon b Gamliel meant something more when he said, "Please, kill me *t'chilah*." It could be that he wanted to initiate the new pathway in worship that was being worked out. The new pathway requires someone to have such profound love for Jews that he would rather die first than watch his friend die, even though the friend would gain no reprieve from his death.

Nature dictates that people strive to prolong life as much as possible, even if only for a few hours. According to the Law (Mishnah, *Yoma* 8:5), even if it means prolonging someone's life for only an hour, we must still desecrate the Sabbath to do so. R. Simeon might thus have conjectured that it was his duty to live, if possible, to allow for a miracle to occur, to have his death sentence commuted perhaps. Still he begged, "Kill me *t'chilah*, so that I not have to watch, etc." In this form of worship, in total self-abandonment for the love of another Jew, R. Simeon was *t'chilah*, first.

It is not just those who explicitly express the sentiment, the desire to die rather than watch a Jew be killed, who are included in the category of those walking the path of R. Simeon b. Gamliel. Many among those who have died or been killed in these last years, and also among those who died in the pogroms that occurred earlier, may God have mercy and say, "Enough," were saints who walked this very path. They were people whose love for Jews was so great, they were always in the most profound readiness to give up their life rather than watch a Jew in pain. Therefore it was arranged in heaven that they should die first. This kind of love for Jews comes of loving God with a powerful, self-sacrificial, self-abandoning love.

That is why it is the Patriarch Isaac, he who stretched out his neck upon the altar for God, who will in the future be the advocate for the Jewish people. He will offer to atone for all their sins himself, and so draw down salvation upon them. For this reason, on the second night of the Festival of Sukkoth—whose *ushpizin* (symbolic guest) is the Patriarch Isaac—the rejoicing begins, with the water-drawing ceremonies in the Temple: "And you will draw water in joy from the wellsprings of salvation." (Isaiah 12:3)

## *Hoshanna Rabbah* (Seventh Day of *Sukkoth*)—October 12, 1941

On Hoshanna Rabbah we pray, "Save the only ones who unify You, Hoshanna! Save the ones who are trapped in exile, Hoshanna!" In order to unify the name of God, the Jewish people worship Him and bear the brunt of suffering, and even physically give their souls for the Oneness of God. What does God, blessed be He, do in order to unify His name? While the Holy Temple in Jerusalem existed, the Jewish people enjoyed a very high standard, and He, God, collapsed constellations, performing supernatural miracles and wonders for them. That was how the Holy Blessed One unified His name and showed the whole world that He is One. Now, however, when the Jewish people are in exile, the Congregation of Israel is the only one unifying God. Therefore, we pray, "Save the ones who are trapped in exile, Hoshanna! God, please do something for the sake of the unity of Your name, and reveal the glory of Your majesty upon us all."

# Sh'mini Atzereth (Eighth Day Festival)—October 13, 1941

*"The eighth day shall be a time of retreat for you when you shall do no mundane work."* (Numbers 29:35)

Rashi (ibid.) explains this verse in the name of the Midrash (*Tanchuma, Pinchos* 16): "During the seven days of the Sukkoth Festival, Israel offered seventy sacrifices for the seventy nations of the world. Now, however, as they propose to set forth on their way home, God says to them, 'I beg of you, make Me a small banquet so that I may take some pleasure exclusively with you.'"

Let us attempt to understand why God commanded only "a small banquet." If He had commanded us to offer up many sacrifices, we would have gladly done so. Also, why should the "small banquet" be on Sh'mini Atzeret, after we offered the seventy bullocks, and not on some other festival day?

Our situation may have the following hint to give us. As is well known, the seventy bullocks that were sacrificed for each of the seventy nations of the world were brought so that divine abundance would also flow to the seventy nations, because all divine abundance flows to the world through the Jewish people.

But it can happen, God forbid, that our sins upset the balance, and the nations receive so much of the abundance that they are able to constrain us thus. Then, we are left with no more than what is by any definition a very meager feast, meager in physical sustenance and meager in spiritual content. Still, our hearts must not give way; we must take courage and bolster ourselves, offering to God at least the "small feast" that we do have, and from which the Holy Blessed One can derive some pleasure.

And similarly, when we remind ourselves of the holiness of the days of Rosh Hashanah, Yom Kippur, and Sukkoth, and even of the Sh'mini Atzeret and Simchat Torah Festivals that we celebrated years ago, we may think to ourselves, "Of what account are these Festivals we celebrate now?" But our hearts must not fall and we must take the courage to make a small feast for God, as well as we are able to in the circumstances. This applies not only to Shemini Atzeret and Simchat Torah but also into the future. Right from *Bereshith* (The Beginning) we must establish fixed times for Torah study, as well as we can in our situation—in straits, in pain, howsoever—and God will have mercy and rescue us immediately and forthwith.

# *Be'reshith*—October 18, 1941

*It is well known that the Torah has its end rooted in its beginning, and its beginning in the end. In sacred literature, we learn many reasons for the connection between the last words of the Torah (Deut. 34:12) "Before the eyes of all Israel," and its first words (Genesis 1:1) "In the beginning . . ."*

In our current situation, we could say that the connection hints at the following. When *chesed* (loving-kindness) is of the revealed sort, meaning that God is bestowing an abundance of kindness, meeting all the needs of the Jewish people, this is *chesed* "before the eyes of all Israel." However, when *chesed* is *nistar* (concealed), then to begin with it is *chesed* only in the eyes of God, as it were. Later, when God rescues the Jewish people, it becomes *chesed* in their eyes also, because then they can see the *chesed* that was hidden in the *hester* (concealment).

But look, we lack the strength to bear this kind of *chesed*. Therefore, our teacher Moses brought it about that "all the signs and miracles . . . and all the mighty acts" (Deut. 34:11) should be "before the eyes of all Israel . . . In the beginning." That is, from the outset, at the beginning, and immediately, there would be *chesed* "before the eyes of all Israel," meaning good, revealed *chesed*.

It may also be, as we learn in the Talmud (*Shabbath* 88b); R. Samuel b. Nahmani said in R. Jonathan's name: "What is meant by the verse (Cant. 4:9) 'You have ravished my heart, my sister-bride; You have ravished my heart with one of your eyes.'? In the beginning, you do so with one of your eyes; but when you are fulfilled, with both your eyes." Rashi on the Talmud explains that "In the beginning" refers to when we received the Torah.

At the time of our receiving the Torah, God held the mountain over the Jewish people like a barrel, as the Talmud describes (*Shabbath* 88a), whereas the Tosaphists in their commentary on the Talmud (ibid.) ask: "Why did God need to hold the mountain over them like a barrel, when the Jewish people had already declared, 'We will do and we will listen'? They answer, 'Because the people might renege upon seeing the great fire.'"

Because God was showing them fire, He could not be certain that they would adhere to the commitment—"We will do and we will listen"—that they had made upon first being offered the Torah. It was only much later, in the days of Ahasuerus when God rescued them from annihilation in the plot of Haman, that they "confirmed, and took upon them," (Esther 9:27) committing to abide by the original covenant to "do and listen." Then, out of love of the miracle and the salvation, they took it upon themselves, voluntarily, to commit to observe the Torah.

This means that when God is leading the Jewish people using pain and fear, it is not certain that they will honor their original agreement to observe the Torah, as taught in Tosaphot above. They could turn back and renege upon seeing the great fire, simply because it is so difficult to fulfill all the commandments in times of suffering. Also, the Jewish soul cleaves more to God when He leads them with love and good deliverance. Then, they are more certain to observe, because they are acceding to the Torah and accepting it with love, as they did in the times of Ahasuerus, when they "confirmed, and took upon them."

We find that when God leads the Jewish people with punishment, then, as R. Samuel b. Nahmani said in R. Jonathan's name, "You have ravished my heart with one of your eyes." As Rashi explained, "with one eye" refers to the receiving of the Torah. It is only afterwards, when fulfilled, that it will be "with both eyes."

But when God leads the Jewish people with love, then He can trust from the start that their commitment to the Torah will hold. Then, right from the very beginning it is "with both eyes." Then, "all the signs and miracles . . . and all the mighty acts" are "before the eyes of all Israel"—In the beginning. For then, right from the outset it will be "before their eyes"—in the plural: both eyes.

## *Toldoth*—November 22, 1941*

"*And God will give you . . .*" (Genesis 27:28)

Rashi (ibid.) explains the word "And" at the beginning of the verse to mean "God will give you, and then return and give you again." The question is well known: Why did Isaac's blessing to Jacob state that God would give and "return and give again"? Surely, his blessing was intended to be permanent: That God would unceasingly give? Furthermore, later in the narrative we read that when Esau discovered the deception, he protested the blessing of Jacob, whereupon Isaac said of Jacob (Genesis 27:33), "He also will be blessed." What is the meaning of the word "also" here, and why did Isaac not simply say, "He will be blessed"?

When King Hezekiah was healed from his illness, he sang, as it is written (Isaiah 38:9): "The song of Hezekiah King of Judah when he had been sick, and was recovered of his sickness.'" At the end of his song, he said (Isaiah 38:19), "All who live shall praise You, as I do this day. The father to his children shall make known Your truth."

King David said (Psalms 3:2), "How my troubles have multiplied! Many are they who say of my soul, there is no salvation for her in God *sela* (Eternal)."

---

*After God in His Mercy healed me and my son-in-law, R. Yechezkel Ha-Cohen, from our dangerous illnesses.

What does the Hebrew word *sela*, expressing eternity, mean in this verse? It would have sufficed to have said, "How my troubles have multiplied! Many are they who say of my soul, there is no salvation for her in God." The psalm continues, "But You, God, are a shield for me," ending with, "Salvation is God's; Your blessing be upon Your people, *sela*." Here again we find the word *sela*.

We are given to comprehend these verses within the context of our current suffering. For now, when so many Jews are fallen—as casualties of various actions or killed by disease, may the Merciful One protect us—the person whom God does rescue and does heal cannot even find it in his heart to rejoice in his salvation. Though he is a Jew—and why should he not rejoice when a Jew is saved from death?—nevertheless he dare not rejoice. In his heart, he thinks, "If I rejoice in my life, I am no better than the person described in the verse (Isaiah 47:8) 'I, and no one else but me.' I would be ignoring the destruction of the entire Jewish people, the multitude of men, women, and children who with long lives ahead of them have filled so many graves in the earth, as though they had plunged alive into the abyss." Even aside from such personal reflections upon the destruction of our people, a person may find it impossible to rejoice in his own survival regardless of the circumstances. A number of years ago, when the troubles began, with round-ups and shootings, and many of our brothers and friends were killed, may the Merciful One protect us, those who survived rejoiced. Then their joy was curtailed, as so many died later in the typhus epidemic, may the Merciful One protect us, and in the dangerous conditions prevailing at the time. And while those who were healed from their illnesses and who survived other sufferings rejoiced, their joy was curtailed because they perished later from hunger, may the Merciful One protect us. So it has been, from one suffering to the next, until now, when the stage has been reached such that when God saves a person from pain and illness, the person does not even know if he should rejoice in his salvation.

This is hinted at in the verse "How my troubles have multiplied! Many are they who say of my soul, there is salvation for her in God *sela* (eternal)."

The enemies of the Jewish people, who are trying, God forbid, to annihilate us, are saying that all the Jews will eventually fall into their hands, God forbid. Even those individual Jews who may escape one particular danger are not saved *sela*, forever, but, God forbid, will fall prey to some other danger. "But You, God, are a shield for me," and You can save me, *sela*—eternal, forever and ever—because "Salvation belongs to God." Thus the Psalm ends, "Your blessing will be on Your people, *sela*, eternal." You are *sela* (eternal), and Your salvation is *sela* (eternal).

The secret to salvation is: "Your blessing should be upon Your people *sela*." Our thanks must be *sela*. We must thank God, blessed be He, and sing before Him over each salvation, for the singing and praise bring down still more salvation, as is well known. The main principle of the song, besides the words that we sing, is our commitment to worship God with greater zeal, as the Jewish people said ("Song of the Sea," Exodus 15:1): "I will sing to God . . . This is my God, I will beautify Him," meaning, as the Talmud says (*Shabbath* 133b), "I will beautify myself before God with His commandments."

Someone who commits himself to additional worship in only one particular aspect brings down upon himself salvation only in one respect, and rescue from only one danger. A person who is saved from trouble, especially if he is healed from a life-threatening illness, must take to heart the thought that if God had not saved him, he would not have survived, God forbid. Thus, it is not enough to accept upon himself additional worship in only one area, in his thanks and his praise. He owes his whole life to God, and so must worship God with his whole life, knowing that even those hours that he spends eating and drinking and sleeping are stolen from the holy hours in which he could be worshipping God. Therefore even those hours must also be holy, a form of worship. He must eat and drink and sleep in order to strengthen himself to worship the Holy Blessed One, as Maimonides of blessed memory, writes. Then, when he gives his whole life to God with song and added worship, the salvation that is drawn down by his singing is not just salvation in a single aspect, whhich may be followed by another trouble, God forbid; it is comprehensive salvation, salvation that is not followed by more suffering.

This is the meaning of the verses quoted above, "How my troubles have multiplied! Many are they who say of my soul, there is no salvation for her in God *sela*," and "But You, God, are a shield for me . . . Salvation belongs to God; Your blessing be upon Your people, *Sela*." The blessings with which we bless You are *sela*, so our salvation is also *sela*, eternal. This was what King Hezekiah meant when he said, "All who live shall praise You, as I do this day. The father to his children shall make known Your truth." He will praise You, God, not just in one particular detail, but in his whole life and with his whole life. Thus, his salvation should also not be in one particular or merely temporary, but—"the father to his children shall make known Your truth"—it will be an ongoing salvation, extending even to his children. If this is the case, then the person is permitted to rejoice, for this is not joy in the category of "I, and no one else but me." He has given his life over to God, and he rejoices in God's joy.

"And *Elohim* (God) will give you." Our father Isaac blessed Jacob that when, God forbid, governance is by the divine attribute of *Din* (Judgment), in the category of *Elohim* (God), and various sufferings befall him, then still God will give, and return and give salvation again. There will not be more suffering following upon the salvation.

Esau, when he heard that Isaac had blessed Jacob, wanted to be able to harm Jacob again, even after he had been saved, God forbid, but Isaac preempted him by saying, "He also will be blessed," or rather, "He also will be a blessing."

The secret to salvation is this: The person should not only bless and praise His blessed Name over his rescue from suffering, but his entire person must become a "blessing," as in "All who live shall praise You, as I do this day." He should put his whole being into song and worship for God, and then the salvation will be forever.

# *VaYishlach*—December 6, 1941

*"Jacob sent* malachim *(messengers) ahead of him to his brother Esau."*
(Genesis 32:4)

The question concerning this verse is well known. Rashi (ibid.), quoting the Midrash (Genesis Rabbah 75:4), says: "Jacob sent actual *malachim*—angels—ahead of him." Why did he need to send actual angels? Another question is this: In praying to God, Jacob said (Genesis 32:12), "[I am afraid] lest he come and kill us all—mothers and children together." Why did Jacob need to explain what it was that Esau could do? Why was it not enough to say, "I am afraid of him"? Jacob might have said either "I am afraid of him," or "He might come and kill us all." Why did he need to say both?

We learn in the Talmud (*Hullin* 7b): "While R. Pinchas b. Yair was on a mission to redeem captives, he stopped at an inn. To accommodate him, the innkeeper tried feeding R. Pinchas's donkey, placing some barley before it, but it would not eat. He tried winnowing the barley, but the animal still refused. The barley was carefully sifted, but still the donkey would not eat it. 'Perhaps,' suggested R. Pinchas, 'it is not properly tithed?' It was at once tithed, and the donkey ate it. Thereupon he exclaimed, 'This poor creature goes to do the will of the Creator, and you would feed it untithed produce?'" Regarding this anecdote, the Talmud (ibid.) comments: "If the previous generation were people, then we are like animals, and not even like the donkey of R. Pinchas b. Yair."

Because R. Pinchas b. Yair rode on the donkey while fulfilling a commandment, the animal was elevated to a very lofty spiritual plane. If this is the case, we need to understand the following talmudic teaching (*Kiddushin* 68a) regarding the verse (Genesis 22:5) "He saw the place from the distance, and Abraham said to the young men with him, 'Stay here with the ass. The boy and I will go yonder, bow down, and return to you.'" The Talmud comments, "*Im ha'chamor*—with the ass—should actually be read *am ha'chamor*—people of the ass," comparing the people to the ass.

Why does the Talmud, in making a derogatory statement about the young men who traveled with Abraham and Isaac, support the comment with a reading from the text that compares them to the ass? In that particular instance, the ass was going to do the will of its Creator; Abraham was riding it to the *Akeidah* (Binding of Isaac). Why was the animal of such little worth that it was used as a basis of comparison for people who were considered to be of very low stature?

At a simple level it could be understood as follows. R. Pinchas b. Yair had already observed the commandment to redeem captives, as the Talmud narrative implies, and so the animal was elevated to a high level because it had been sanctified by the commandment. This was not the case in the narrative of the *Akeidah*. There, when Abraham said, "Stay here with the ass," prior to the *Akeidah*, he had not yet performed the commandment. Therefore, his words *im ha'chamor* contain the hint "people of the ass." There is some validity to this idea because, as is well known, the verse (Zachariah 9:9) "A poor man, riding on the ass," refers to the Messiah, who will ride the very same ass. So we see that after the *Akeidah* the status of the ass was elevated, and the Messiah will ride upon it.

In general, we need to understand why Abraham abandoned the two young men while on his way with Isaac to the *Akeidah*. The Midrash (Leviticus Rabbah 20:2) explains it as follows. It became apparent to Abraham and Isaac that the young men could not see the cloud suspended over the mountain, while they could see it. The Patriarch Abraham understood this to be sign that he should continue on without them. His saying to them, "Stay here *im ha'chamor* (with the ass)," can be read *am ha'chamor* (people of the ass)" for it is as though Abraham had said, "The ass cannot see the cloud and nor can you, so stay here with the ass." But why was their inability to see the cloud taken by Abraham as such a strong indication that he ought to part with them?

We also need to understand the reason why the Patriarch Abraham saw the cloud over the mountain only on the third day (Genesis 22:4). If the cloud were a natural phenomenon, it is understandable that he could not see it earlier, as he was too far away. However, what he saw was a holy, supernatural vision, one that the young men and the animal could not see. If only Abraham and Isaac could see it, why did they not see it from a greater distance, and prior to the third day?

One could argue that the reason was simply because Abraham first had to pass through a variety of tests encountered on the way, as we learn in the Midrash

(Genesis Rabbah, cap. 55–56). But there may be another more fundamental reason. God said to him (Genesis 22:2), "Take your son, the only one, the one you love—Isaac—and go away to the Moriah area. Bring him as a burnt offering on one of the mountains that I will designate to you." God had not yet told Abraham which particular mountain it would be; the holy place that was designated for the *Akeidah* was still, as it were, a thought in the mind of God. If it had not yet been revealed in the universe of Speech, how much less, then, had it been revealed in the universe of Action, and on the actual protrusion of the mountain. The Divine Light had not yet come to rest in any way upon the physical form of the mountain. It was only when the Patriarch Abraham elevated himself, drawing close to the mind of God, that he could sense the holiness of that particular place. By doing this, he brought the holiness down into the universe of Action, and onto the mountain, until he could actually see the cloud over the mountain. How did our father Abraham draw himself close to the mind of God? By drawing closer to the commandment with the physical act of walking to fulfill it. As is well known, the reason why a Divine Commandment is a command is only because it is the will of God, having so arisen in His thought. Therefore, when a Jewish person observes the commandment, he cleaves to God, blessed be He, to the commandment of God, to God's mind, and to His desire. The degree to which a person cleaves unto God, soaring to His thought, exactly reflects the degree to which His thought is revealed below, in this world. Therefore, only Abraham and Isaac, acting of their own free will and desire and elevated thereby to the desire of God, were able to see the cloud. The opposite, however, applies to the ass, for, while it did perform part of the commandment—in the words of R. Pinchas b. Yair, "It was going to do the will of the Creator"—nevertheless, its actions were not of its own volition or choice, and so it was not drawn to the desire of God. The desire of God was not revealed to it, and so it did not see the cloud.

    This is one of the fundamental principles of prayer, and of Torah, which itself is a requirement of prayer, as it is written (Proverbs 28:9): "He who turns away his ear from hearing Torah, even his prayer is an abomination." Truly, it must be said of all trouble and suffering that in the mind of God they are nothing but *chesed* (loving-kindness). Therefore, by elevating himself and merging with the thought of God, blessed be He, the Jew draws God's thought down into the universe of Speech and the universe of Action. Then, the *chesed* is also revealed in this world, and there is no more *Din* (Judgment) and *Hester* (Concealment) of *chesed*. In his prayers, a person enumerates requests for health or for sustenance with all the desire in his heart. He also learns Torah, which is the desire and will of God, and through it, he is elevated into the *chesed* that is hidden inside the *Din* of his illness or poverty. He draws it down into the universe of Speech with his words of Torah and prayer, and hence into the world below. Thus, the *chesed* is also revealed below, in the universe of Action.

We learn in the Talmud (*Berachoth* 61b): "When they took R. Akiba out to kill him, it was time for recitation of the morning *Sh'ma*. They tore his flesh with iron combs, while he took upon himself the yoke of heaven. His students said to him, 'Our rabbi, this far?' He replied, 'All my days, have I been at pain over the verse in Scripture (Deut. 6:4–5) "Love God your Lord with all you heart, all your soul, and all your might." "When will I ever have the opportunity to fulfill it?" I asked myself. And now that I have the opportunity, should I not fulfill it?' He was drawing out the word 'One' and meditating upon it when his soul departed." With total self-abandonment, and through the elevation of his thoughts, he unified the name of God as he meditated upon the word "One." He did not continue onward with the next words of the *Sh'ma*, "Love God your Lord with all your heart," but if he had, this would have connected God's thought of love with the words, thereby drawing them down into the universe of Speech and further into the universe of Action, so that the *chesed* would have been revealed in the world below. And so his students asked him, "Our rabbi, this far?" meaning "This far and no further?" They were asking why he did not continue with "Love God your Lord . . ."

This explains the teaching in the Talmud (*Menachoth* 29b): "When God showed Moses the martyrdom of R. Akiba, Moses cried, 'Lord of the Universe! Is this Torah, and this its reward?' God replied, 'Be silent, for so it arose in the Thought before Me.'" He, R. Akiba, arose in the Thought, but did not want to draw it down into the universe of Speech. Therefore, the *chesed* was not revealed below and the Concealment and Judgment remained.

Let us return to our discussion above. By specifying the details of our requests in our prayers, we draw the requests and the *chesed* into the universe of Speech and the universe of Action. Then, the kindness and the salvation and the healing are also revealed below. This explains the significance of the Torah we say in times of suffering. For when we say Torah, some of the pain and the prayers and the salvation enter into the words of Torah, in the same way that they enter into the words during our prayers, thus drawing down and revealing the *chesed* in the universe of Speech, as we explained above. Therefore, by allowing all the things that Esau might possibly do to enter into the words of his prayer, the Patriarch Jacob drew down the salvation into the universe of Action, and God saved him.

# *Chanukah*—December 15–22, 1941

*"In the days of the Hasmonean High Priest, Mattityahu b. Yochanan, and his sons—when the evil Hellenic empire conquered Your people Israel, compelling them to neglect Your Torah and stray from Your desired statutes— at that time of distress, You in Your great mercy stood up for them. You took up their grievance, avenging their wrong. You delivered the strong into the hands of the weak and the many into the hands of the few. You put the corrupt into the hands of the undefiled, the wicked into the hands of the pious, and the savage into the hands of diligent students of Your Torah, making Yourself a great, holy name in Your world. For Your people Israel, You wrought great victory and salvation as clear as the day. So Your children went into the holy sanctuary, cleansing and purifying the Temple, and kindling lights in Your holy courtyard. They fixed these eight days of Chanukah as a festival to express appreciation and to praise Your great Name."* (From the Chanukah liturgy.)

Let us try to understand: When the evil Hellenic empire was compelling Jews to neglect the Torah, it was not just the Jews who were in trouble. It was also, so to speak, God's problem. So why do we say, "You in Your great mercy stood up for them," when God was really standing up for Himself?

Let us try to understand at least a little, with our limited intelligence, why, when speaking of the faith of Abraham the patriarch, the Torah says, "Abraham believed in God, and He considered it righteousness." (Genesis 15:6) Why was it that with our father Abraham, faith was considered an act of righteousness, while the faith of the Jews who were in Egypt was not considered righteousness, though the verse says (Exodus 4:31), "The people believed and heard that God had remembered the Jewish people"? This is even more difficult to comprehend when we consider that for the Jews in Egypt, faith was more challenging than it was for Abraham. God did not speak directly to them, nor did they even know God's name. Moses said to God (Exodus 3:13), "When they ask me what Your name is, what shall I say to them?" The Jews of Egypt were in such pain and distress that, as it is written "Because of their broken spirit and the hard work, they could not listen to him" (Exodus 6:9).

It may perhaps be understood as follows: It is often taught in sacred literature that faith is not simply confidence substituting for certainty. Faith is the Light and Holiness of God inside the Jew. This Inner Light resonates to the holiness of God's brilliance and is tied and bound to it. Faith is intrinsic to Jews; it is an inheritance passed down to us from our ancestors, and therefore we say in our prayers, "God, our God, God of our Fathers, God of Abraham, Isaac, and Jacob . . ." (From the silent *Amidah*.) The fact that He is our God and that we believe in Him has nothing to do with reason or logic. He is God, our God, because we are tied to Him through our ancestry. Only Abraham the Patriarch did not inherit faith, and so of him it is said, "Abraham believed in God, and He considered it righteousness." It is not said of the Jews of Egypt that their faith was considered an act of righteousness because faith was already instilled inside them as an inherited trait. Even for our Patriarch Abraham, the Torah tells us, it was only his faith that was considered an act of righteousness. It is not written that God considered his meeting other challenges, such as the *Akeidah* (Binding of Isaac), acts of righteousness. Even though the *Akeidah* was the sternest of tests, it depended on the level of Abraham's faith. The greater and more powerful the faith, the stronger and more capable of self-sacrifice is the worshipper. Only Abraham's faith was remarkable, and considered a righteous act. His sacrifice of Isaac in the *Akeidah* was nothing more than the natural consequence of his faith.

Because worship depends on faith, a Jew's faith must be wholehearted; for it is only total, selfless faith that enables Israel to give its life for God. If the faith is flawed, and only half hearted, how can it empower anyone to self-sacrifice? Total, selfless faith means continuing to believe in Him even in times of *hester panim* (concealment of God's face) with faith that everything comes from Him, that everything is beneficial and just, and that all the agony and anguish is filled with God's love for the Jewish people.

To our grief, we see that even amongst those whose belief was always wholehearted, there are now certain individuals whose faith has been damaged. They question God, asking, "Why have You forsaken us? If we are being tortured in order to bring us closer to Torah and worship," they argue, "then why, on the contrary, is the Torah and everything holy being destroyed?"

Now if a Jew utters these words in a form of prayer or supplication, as an outpouring out of his heart before God, it is a good thing. But if, God forbid, he really is questioning—even if not God directly but his internal faith, God forbid—then may God protect us!

Faith is the foundation of everything. If the faith of a person is, God forbid, damaged, then the person is torn asunder and distanced from God. Souls condemned to Gehenna emerge purified and cleansed after having repented. We hope to God that all those suffering these tortures now will rise, cleansed, purified, and closer to Him. But the soul of someone whose faith is damaged is like a soul enduring Gehenna while continuing to add offenses to its sins. After a time, upon examining itself, the soul sees the situation and asks itself, "What have I achieved with all this suffering, if I am just as sullied now as I was before?"

In all honesty, what room is there, God forbid, for doubts or questions? Admittedly, Jews endure suffering of the sort with which we are currently afflicted only every few hundred years. Still, how can we expect or hope to understand these, God's actions, and then allow our faith to be damaged, God forbid, upon finding that we cannot understand them? If one blade of grass created by God is beyond our understanding, how much more unfathomable is the soul; and if we do not understand a soul, how much less do we understand an angel, and how much less even than this can we understand the mind of God? How could we possibly expect to grasp with our mind what God knows and understands?

What excuse does a person have to question God and have his faith damaged by this prevailing suffering more than all the Jews who went through suffering in bygone times? Why should a person's faith become damaged now, if it was not damaged when he read descriptions of Jewish suffering from antiquity to the present day in Scripture, the Talmud, or Midrash? Those who say that suffering such as this has never befallen the Jewish people are mistaken. There was torture comparable to ours at the destruction of the Temple and at Beitar, etc.* May God have mercy and call an end to our suffering; may He save us now, immediately, forthwith and forever.

---

*[Note added by author on the eve of the holy Sabbath, Kislev 18–November 27, 1942.] Only such torment as was endured until the middle of 1942 has ever transpired previously in history. The bizarre tortures and the freakish, brutal murders that have been invented for us by the depraved, perverted murderers, solely for the suffering of Israel, since the middle of 1942, are, according to my knowledge of the words of our sages of blessed memory, and of the chronicles of the Jewish people in general, unprecedented and unparalleled. May God have mercy upon us, and save us from their hands, in the blink of an eye.

The reason why today's suffering can damage someone's faith more so than it did in the past is only because he is more self-centered than he used to be. His pain affects him more than it once did. If someone says that he flinches only at seeing the torture of others, it may in fact be true that he is feeling compassion for his fellow Jews, but the truth is also that deeper down, inside himself, his compassion is really terror of being forced to go through such terrible torture himself. It is this that damages his faith and feeds his doubts, God forbid. As we have already said, a person must relinquish his life, his self-centeredness, and his bias, for only then will his faith be undamaged. He will be able to continue affirming with perfect faith that everything happening is just and a manifestation of God's love for the Jewish people.

With our limited perspective, we suggest that there may be a hint of this in the Talmud (*Berachoth* 61b): "R. Akiba was reciting the *Sh'ma* while his flesh was being raked with iron combs. His students asked, 'Our Rabbi, thus far?' He answered them, 'All my days I have been at pains over this verse in the *Sh'ma* (Deut. 6:5) "Love God with all your heart, with all your soul, and with all your might." "When will I ever have the opportunity of fulfilling it properly?" I asked myself. But right now, I have the opportunity to love God with all my soul. Should I not grasp it?'"

If we approach this at the simple level, then the well-known question arises, why would the students of R. Akiba—who were themselves remarkable for their individual piety—have asked, "Our Rabbi, thus far?" They were well aware that every Jew is prepared to give his life for God. Furthermore, why did R. Akiba answer them by referring to himself when he might have answered more directly by simply quoting the verse "Love God with all your heart, with all your soul," even if God demands your soul?

With what we have said above, this can perhaps be explained in a way that teaches us something about our own plight. The terrible tortures R. Akiba endured caused such great suffering in his disciples that they were provoked to ask the same question that was asked by Moses when he was shown this same event (Talmud *Menachoth* 29b): "Is this Torah and this its reward?" The disciples were afraid that, God forbid, they might have doubts, however fleeting, as a result of their emotional and visceral response, and that their faith might be damaged. They wanted their teacher, who was so powerful in his faith, to speak of his belief, so that his faith might inundate them. When they asked, "Our Rabbi, thus far?" they were saying, "Can you be our teacher thus far, even into the circumstances of this terrible death?" Perhaps they did not articulate their question fully, or make it more specific, but merely hinted at it in order to avoid invoking the response that the Talmud (ibid.) says had already been given to Moses: "Be silent."

R. Akiba understood that the students were not questioning God but rather begging him to bestow upon them some of his faith, and so he told them something about himself and his own aspirations to faith: "All my life I was in pain over this verse . . . Right now I have the opportunity to love God with all my soul. Should I not grasp it?"

At that time, in R. Akiba's epoch, when the divine decree was against only the ten martyrs who were put to death by the Roman Emperor, the students sought a bolstering of their faith through the words of R. Akiba. Now, however, when the decree of martyrdom is upon the whole Jewish people, God forbid, we must look to strengthen our faith by looking at the decree of martyrdom itself.

It is a well-known teaching from the Rav (R. Shneur Zalman of Liadi, *Tanya* I. 25) that even the least sincere Jew, who commonly finds himself unable to resist the urge to sin, is nevertheless prepared to give his life for God when tested. This is because when his enemies try to extinguish the spark of his soul with their heresy, may the Merciful One protect us, the tiny spark bursts into flame and grows stronger and more powerful, as is well known.

If only people would bear in mind that it is not because we robbed or did anything wrong to anyone that we are being persecuted, but because we are Jews—children of Israel, bound to God and to His holy Torah. Firstly, it would explain why our enemies are not satisfied with just killing us or extinguishing the divine spark inside us but feel they have to annihilate simultaneously both body and soul of the Jew. Then, if we could only bear it in mind, our faith and our cleaving to God and to the Torah would, on the contrary, burgeon and strengthen. But because we tend to feel only our physical pain and not the spiritual pain, and because we fail to remind ourselves that what we are enduring is actually a war upon God and the Torah, therefore there are certain individuals who experience a weakening of their faith.

The Hellenes in Hasmonean times also tried "compelling them to neglect Your Torah and stray from Your desired statutes." They did this with the torture and oppression of Israel, as is recorded in the writings of Josephus, and through the spread of Hellenic culture among the Jews. It reached a point where they said to Jews, "Write upon the horn of your ox that you have no portion in the God of Israel," as is known from the Midrash (*Tanchuma, Tazria* 11). At that time the Jews knew that the purpose of all the physical suffering was to make them forget the Torah, to make them "stray from Your desired statutes." This was what they worried about, it was the chief cause of their pain, and so their faith grew stronger and God's salvation came to them in merit of their faith. Thus the liturgy reads: "At that time of distress, You in Your great mercy stood up for them. You took up their grievance, avenging their wrong." The distress of the people of Israel was not at their physical pain but at the efforts of the Hellenes to destroy God's Torah and worship. That is why "You stood up for them, and You saved them."

# *VaYigash*—December 27, 1941

"Judah approached him and said, 'Please, my lord, let your servant say something to my lord personally. Let not your anger burn against your servant, though you are as Pharaoh.

"'My lord asked if we still had a father or another brother. We told you, "We have a father who is very old, and a small child of his old age. His brother died, and he is the only one of his mother's children still alive. His father loves him."

"'You said to your servants, "Bring him down to me, so that I may set my eyes on him." We said to my lord, "The lad cannot leave his father. If he left him, his father would die." And you said to your servants, "If your youngest brother does not come with you, you shall not see my face again."

"'We went to your servant our father and told him the words of my lord. When our father told us to go back and get some food, we replied, "We cannot go. We can go only if our youngest brother is with us. If he is not with us, we cannot even see the man."

"'Your servant our father said, "You know that my wife [Rachel] bore me two sons. One has already left me, and I assume that he was torn to pieces by wild animals. I have seen nothing of him until now. Now you want to take this one from me too! If something were to happen to him, you will have brought my white head down to the grave in evil misery."

"'And now, when I come to your servant our father and the lad is not with us, his soul is bound up with his soul! When he sees that the lad is not there, he will die! Your servants will have brought your servant our father's *white head down to the grave in misery. Besides, I offered myself to my father as a guarantee for the lad, and I said, "If I do not bring him back to you, I will have sinned to my father for all time."'* (Genesis 44:18–33)

We need to understand why the opening verse says only "Judah approached him," and not "Judah approached Joseph." We could answer that this chapter is merely a continuation of the previous one, which makes it obvious that Judah was speaking to Joseph, but if that is the case, why does it need to say, "Judah approached him and said"? Also, why does the form of speech keep changing from the second to third persons, and back, until the end of the speech when he speaks only directly, in the accusative?

We learn from the holy rabbi, the man of God, the Rebbe, Reb Ber of Mezritch, of blessed memory, on the verse (Psalms 110:4) "And You are *cohen* (priest) forever," that *cohen* represents *chesed* (loving-kindness). The *chesed* of God is in the fact that the Jewish person addresses God as "You."

According to our limited understanding, the explanation could be as follows. One can speak directly, in the second person accusative, only when the listener is facing the speaker and vice versa, but not when they have turned their backs on one another. Therefore, when the members of the Great Assembly determined in the wording of the prayers that we say "You" to God, in the second person accusative, it is because the Holy Blessed One is there in front of the Jewish person. God is face-to-face with the Jew, at the level of (Psalms 52:3) *chesed El*—Loving-Kindness of God. He is so clearly revealed that the Jew can address God as "You." For this to happen, though, the person who prays also must not turn his back on God. He must present himself before God in thought, desire, and heart, so that he may say to God, "You." Even if he cannot bring himself to face God throughout the entire prayer, at least he can achieve it at certain parts of his prayer.

There are those who feel as if they are leaping toward the Holy Blessed One, and in that moment their whole being is drawn toward Him. Then there is the person who may feel only a desire to be drawn towards Him, and prays (from the liturgy comprising the blessings of the *Sh'ma*), "Unify our hearts to love and fear Your name," without actually feeling the love and fear of God. He may feel only the longing to have a powerful love and fear of God, but this longing can increase until he feels, even momentarily, as we described above, that his whole being is drawn toward God, through his longing to come close to Him in love and fear. And so, at least momentarily, the person cleaves unto God.

We learn in the sacred writings of my brother-in-law, the holy R. Aharon Yechiel, of blessed memory, on the verses (Deut. 30:11–14) "For this commandment that I teach you today is not too wonderful or too distant for you to fulfill. It is not in heaven, so that you might say, 'Who will climb to heaven for us, to bring it and teach it to us, so that we might do it?' It is not over the sea, so that you might say, 'Who will pass to the other side of the sea to bring it back and teach it to us, so that we might do it?' It is something that is very close to you. It is in your mouth and in your heart, so you can do it." R. Aharon Yechiel says that it is a miracle that first it is written "in your mouth" and then afterwards "in your heart," for if it were imperative that it be first "in your heart"—that from the outset the commandment must be fulfilled with the desire in your heart—who would ever have achieved such a level? But because it is first written "in your mouth," then even if at first your prayer is not from your heart, if you continue speaking with your mouth only, this will eventually arouse your heart.

    This is hinted at in the verse "Judah approached him." We learn in the Midrash (Genesis Rabbah 93:3) on the verse (Proverbs 25:11) "Apples of gold in silver trays," that each of the phrases spoken by Judah to Joseph is rich with meaning. According to what we have said above, one of the meanings hints at an approach to prayer: "Judah approached him." Even though at the beginning of his prayer a person may not feel he can speak directly and immediately to God, but only indirectly in the third person, nevertheless moments of revelation and closeness will enter his prayer, so that it becomes direct and immediate. Hence Judah continued, "Let not your anger burn against your servant," speaking directly, in the second person accusative. Then he again lost his sense of connection and encountered concealment, and so he said, "My lord asked," in the third person, after which he once again returned to direct, immediate speech: "We told you, 'We have a father.'" By the end, he had come to a revelation and intimacy with God that was immediate and direct, and his speech ends, "And now, when I come to your servant our father, and the lad is not with us, his soul is bound up with his soul! When he sees that the lad is not there, he will die! Your servants will have brought your servant our father's white head down to the grave in misery." This, however, can happen only when a person makes the initial "approach," and his prayers are not incidental or delivered solely from force of habit. He should be deliberate in his approach to God. Before starting to pray, he concentrates on the fact that prayer is a cleaving to God, and that at the very least it should be as if he were approaching a human king. This is how Judah "approached" his prayers in his thoughts—with the knowledge that prayer is an "approach" to God. So in the end he achieved a revelation of God that is direct and immediate. Thus, he cleaved, bringing down salvation upon him and all the Jewish people, Amen.

# Sh'moth—January 10, 1942

*"'Who am I that I should go to Pharaoh?' said Moses to God. 'And how can I possibly get the Israelites out of Egypt?' 'Because I will be with you,' replied God. 'Proof that I have sent you will come when you get the people out of Egypt. All of you will then worship God on this mountain.'"* (Exodus 3:11)

Let us try to understand: When God said to Moses, "Now go, I am sending you," (Exodus 3:10) God had already implied that He would accompany Moses. Why then did Moses demur, saying, "Who am I?" forcing God to reply, "Because I will be with you"? What did God mean by emphasizing that the Jews would worship Him "on this mountain"? Was it not sufficient to say, "All of you will then worship God"?

We learn in the Talmud (*Menachoth* 110a): "Resh Lakish said, 'What is the significance of the verse (Leviticus 7:37) "This is the Torah for the burnt offering, for the meal offering, for the sin offering, and for the guilt offering"? It teaches that when someone busies himself with the study of Torah it is as though he were offering a burnt offering, a meal offering, a sin offering and a guilt offering.' Rava asked, 'Why then does the verse say, "For the burnt offering, for the meal offering, etc.?" It could have said more succinctly, "a burnt offering, a meal offering." Rather,' Rava explained, 'it teaches that whosoever busies himself with the study of Torah will not need either burnt offering, meal offering, sin offering, or guilt offering.'" Rashi (ibid.) explains Rava as saying: "The study of Torah atones for one's sins."

If Rashi is correct, we need to understand what Rava's explanation adds to that of Resh Lakish, when both teach the same idea: that Torah study atones for one's sins.

A simple analysis could suggest that the difference is only in how Resh Lakish and Rava read the words of the biblical verse. Resh Lakish emphasizes the words "this is the Torah," while Rava emphasizes the words "Torah for the."

Besides the simplest explanation, there may be a deeper teaching, which requires examining how Torah study atones for one's sins. Perhaps according to Resh Lakish, until a person learns Torah, he remains connected to his sin, as does any sinner requiring atonement. Rava adds that atonement is not necessary at all, because the Torah erased the sin before it could connect with the person, who consequently passed no time with the sin. It is well known that the longer a person waits before making amends, even if he does not continue to sin, the sin of which he has not repented grows more deeply rooted within him. That is, the longer guilt remains with the person, the more work is required to remove it.

The Talmud (*Yebamoth* 48b) notes: "Why are proselytes these days oppressed and afflicted?" and answers: "Because they were tardy before coming to nestle beneath the wings of the *Shechinah*." The idea is the same. Proselytes endure suffering because they spent time mired in sin. An example of this phenomenon can be seen when an article of clothing is stained. If it is cleaned immediately, only minimal effort is required to remove the stain. If the stain is left unattended, however, it becomes ingrained, and then in order to remove the stain, the article of clothing must be thoroughly washed and scrubbed and bleached. These are the sufferings endured by proselytes, because they procrastinated.

In order for man not to allow his sins, small or great, to become ingrained, he needs to fear sin. Even when not faced with the opportunity or desire to sin, a person still needs to have a visceral fear of sinning. He should never feel safe from sin just because he has not transgressed in thought, word, or deed; for it is not only what has been explicitly forbidden and proscribed by the Torah and by our sages, of blessed memory, that is sinful, and it is not just over these that we have to repent.

How a person perceives sin depends upon how much he truly wants to cleave to God. If this is his only desire, then anything contrary to the will of God, whether in thought, word, or deed, is perceived as a sin for which he repents. It is not enough for him to know intellectually that whatever disconnects him from God is wrong; he must go beyond that and become afraid lest he do, or find that he has already done, something to distance himself from God.

There are those who know only how bitter is the punishment for every sin, may the Merciful One protect us, and then there are those who have attained a higher level, for whom the sin against God is in itself a bad thing—and not only outright sin, but anything that is against the will of God. Nevertheless, even at this level the person still may not look for sin inside himself; he may not nourish in his heart a terror of sinning. Consequently, he adamantly insists that he is a good person, and that he does only what is right. At a still-higher level than this is the person who is always afraid of sinning, whose heart is always broken, constantly asking himself, "Who knows if I am not right now rebelling against God?" Someone whose heart is softened by his constant fear of sinning will always find blemishes within himself.

The difference between them is as follows: At the lowest level, though a person may be aware of the evil inherent in every sin, it is only intellectual awareness and not a viscerally felt fear of the sin. At that level, a person's heart does not shudder at the thought of committing a sin. At the higher level, however, the fear has entered deeply inside him. His body, mind, and heart are softened, and they convulse in terror at the thought of committing a sin. Such a person always finds faults within himself, and is afraid lest his faults lead him into sin. He worries about them, and immediately upon identifying the faults in himself repents of them. He does not hesitate even for a moment, and so his character defects are not allowed to take root. Since he has put the fear of sin and thoughts of repentance before the sin itself, the repentance is actually in place before a sin has even been committed. So, if there are any shortcomings in such a person, God forbid, repentance comes swiftly.

The truth is that the fear a person feels at the thought of being punished for a sin, or at the thought of sin itself, is drawn from the *sephirah* of *Gevurah*, Fear—the fear manifest in the Supernal Worlds, the fear that angels show. This exalted fear is drawn downward into this world and clothed in sackcloth. It manifests as one person's fear of committing a sin and being punished, or fear at becoming distanced from God in the case of another more evolved person, each experienced at his own level. This is not the case, however, with a person whose constant fear precedes any actual sin. Such a person's fear is pure and exalted. It is that of the Supernal Worlds. Such a person is elevated and sanctified by the fear itself, until neither body nor soul are able to stand any kind of blemish, and so his repentance is instantaneous.

Now, while every head sickens and every heart grieves, some say that this is not the time to talk of piety, repentance, or fear—whether of this sort or that—that it is enough just to observe the simple, practical commandments. They are mistaken, for two reasons. First, because even now we must worship with all the means at our disposal, with every type of worship. The second reason—which argues quite to the contrary—is this: Any person practicing spiritual reflection, suffering the fears we have described, worrying whether he may be sinning this way or that, and always looking inside himself for any kind of blemish, eventually experiences the most profound joy. After periods of introspection such as these, he begins to feel elevated and, because his fear is pure, tastes the sweetest, most rapturous essence of fear, described in the Sabbath hymn "God I desire" (by R. Aaron the Great of Karlin). It is a supernal fear, which elevates the man.

With this, perhaps we can understand a teaching found in the holy Zohar (vol II, *Acharey* 69b): "Before the creation of the world, the Torah said to God, 'Man, whom You are about to create, is going to sin, and if You do unto him as he deserves, he will not survive.' God answered the Torah, 'Is it for nothing that I am called (Exodus 34:6) God of mercy, Gracious, Long of patience . . . ?'" It is difficult to understand why the Torah would ask this question in the first instance, when it must surely have been aware that written in the Torah are the words "Repent unto God your Lord." (Deut. 4:30)

From what we have said above, it may be understood as follows: It is not just repentance that had to precede the creation of the world, but also the fear of sinning. The Torah itself brought this fear into existence, by voicing its fear that man would sin in the future. So, by holding onto the Torah a Jew can reach this level, where the fear of sinning, God forbid, is rooted in his heart, preceding any sin. This is how every person, each at his own level, upon realizing that he has just sinned, can prevent the defect he has just acquired, God forbid, from working its way deep into his soul, by repairing it and repenting immediately.

This is implied by the Talmud in the passage quoted above. Rava said, "Whosoever busies himself with the study of Torah needs neither burnt offering, nor meal offering, nor sin offering, nor guilt offering." For such a person, no time is spent in sin, because the fear and thoughts of repentance are already rooted within him before the sin happens. Why? Because he has busied himself with the Torah, and it was with the Torah that the fear of sin originated, introducing thoughts of repentance before the creation of the world. Through learning Torah, a person becomes connected to the fear of sin that is in the Torah. Thus, "whosoever busies himself with the study of Torah does not need a burnt offering. . . ."

Our teacher Moses said this to the Jewish people after the revelation at Sinai: "For in order to test you, has God come, that His fear may be on your face, so that you not sin." (Exodus 20:16) Rashi (ibid.) explains: "The Hebrew word *nasoth*, "test" can also be translated "raise."

The verse according to Rashi would, at first glance, appear to contain two distinct ideas. First, the issue of elevating the Jewish people, about which Moses says, "in order to *nasoth* (raise) you." Second, the fear of sin, about which Moses says, " in order . . . that His fear be upon your face." The fear, which is merely the medium preventing sin, explains the end of the sentence: "so that you not sin."

But with what we have said above, we can interpret Rashi's explanation in a new way. The two issues are actually one and the same. Moses is telling the Jewish people what to expect from the proper fear of God: that they will achieve a constant fear of sinning—the purest, most elemental fear, which elevates a person to the highest realms of awareness, to the experience of profoundest joy. "For in order to *nasoth* (raise) you, has God come, that His fear may be on your face." It is the sweetest, most pleasant, essential fear, as we said above. And naturally, since they will have been so elevated in their worship, the Jewish people will be able to stand proud vis-à-vis the nations of the world, without fearing them.

This is what Moses was hinting at when he said, "Who am I that I should go to Pharaoh? And how can I possibly get the Jews out of Egypt?" Moses was the most humble person ever to walk the earth. He was constantly asking himself, "Who am I? And how can I possibly . . . ?" So God said to him, "It is not true that you are not fit, and it is not true that you have faults and blemishes, God forbid. Your self-doubting is itself a form of worship, the type of worship that illuminates the world, coming as it does through a chain of causality from the name of God that is the future." It comes from the name of God, *EHYE*—"I will be." When a person feels that there is nothing worth looking at in his heart, but says, "I am nothing right now, but from now on I will try to be something," his worship takes on the aspect of God's Name, *EHYE*–I will be. It draws out a reciprocal promise of *EHYE*—I will be.

God said to Moses, "Because I will be with you. . . . And this is the proof that I have sent you . . . you will then worship God on this mountain." God emphasizes "on this mountain" because it is written (Exodus 3:1): "And he [Moses] came to the mountain of God at Horeb." The Talmud (*Shabbath* 89a) asks: "Why was Mount Horeb later called Sinai?" and answers: "Because the Hebrew word *Sinai* is a cognate of *sina*, 'hatred.' Sinai was the mountain around which hatred for the gentiles came into the world." Since the whole purpose of the worship that God promised Moses the Jewish people would do on "this mountain" is to raise (*nasoth*) and exalt the worshipper, God emphasized "this mountain" because once we are elevated by worship, every accuser is struck dumb and all enemies are engulfed with shame, and we, all the Jewish people, will be rescued with salvation and favors.

# *VaEra*–January 17, 1942

"Elohim *(God) spoke to Moses, saying, 'I am* YHVH *(God). I appeared to Abraham, Isaac, and Jacob as* El Shaddai *(God Omnipotent), and I revealed not My name* YHVH *to them*. . . . *Therefore, tell the Jewish people, "I am* YHVH. *I will take you away from your forced labor in Egypt and free you from their slavery*.'" (Exodus 6:2–6)

The following is taught in the Talmud (*Arachin* 10b): Rava b. Shila, in the name of R. Mat'nah, on the authority of Samuel, said: "There was a *magrefa* [a shovel-shaped musical instrument] in the holy Temple that had ten holes, each of which produced ten different kinds of music. A *Tanna* taught: It was one cubit long, one cubit broad, and from it projected a handle with ten holes. Each hole produced one hundred kinds of sounds, amounting for the whole to one thousand tunes."

Rashi (ibid.) explains that the *magrefa* was a sort of trowel or spade, used in a daily Temple ritual of *Terumath Hadeshen* (Tithing the Ashes), in which the ashes on the sacrificial altar were gathered, heaped, and removed. We need to understand: Why does an implement used for moving ashes need to sing—and not just to sing, but to sing a thousand songs, which is something that other instruments cannot do? In fact, from other references to the *magrefa* in the Mishnah (*Tamid* 3:8), we learn that this instrument was so loud, its sound could be heard as far away as Jericho.

The Tosaphists, in their commentary to the Talmud (*Arachin* 10b), argue with Rashi, contending that the *magrefa* is a tympanum and not a shovel. But let us try to understand the meaning according to Rashi, who says the *magrefa* is a shovel. What is the significance of a shovel that can produce the sound of a thousand voices? Why did it produce this sound when it was shoveling ashes, and what can we learn from this teaching?

The Mishnah (*Tamid* 2:2) teaches: "On the Pilgrimage Festivals, the daily rite of removing the ashes from the altar was not performed, because they beautified the altar." The ashes were allowed to pile up, in order to decorate and beautify the altar so that all might see that many sacrifices had been offered. Let us try to understand what this teaches us, for, surely, everything that was done in the Temple was done for a reason. We need to understand why the ashes of burnt offerings, and not some other display, were used as evidence of the great number of sacrifices that were offered up on the Festivals.

The explanation is this: All sacrifices brought upon the altar were analogous to the "in place of his son" explicitly noted regarding the Patriarch Abraham, who sacrificed a ram "in place of his son" Isaac (Genesis 22:12–18). Anyone seeking atonement for sins, or those bringing burnt offerings as gifts, were required to offer up their souls as a sacrifice to God. The Torah provided the sacrificial rite as a way of offering an animal in place of one's own soul. The ritual heaping of the ashes of the animal sacrifices showed that only after the sacrificial rites had been performed, when the accumulated ashes were actually seen, could there be any real appreciation of the magnitude of the sacrifice.

This is also the case when Jews depart at God's will, because it arose thus in the Divine Thought that they would be brought as sacrifices to Him, blessed be He. For it is only after they have departed that we can appreciate their greatness, in quantity and quality.

In the past, when they were with us, even though we treasured and protected them like the pupil of our eye, the spirit in our body and soul, and as much as we rejoiced and delighted in them, we did not really know how to appreciate them. We could not know how good things were when they were here with us. Now that they are missing, may the Merciful One protect us, we can see plainly how very much we miss them. The heart yearns for them and the pain will not be comforted, except with the words of God to Moses, "So did it arise in the thought before Me." (Talmud, *Menachoth* 29b) Moses asked of God, "You have shown me his [R. Akiba's] Torah, now please show me his reward." "Turn around," commanded God. Moses turned around and saw them weighing R. Akiba's flesh in the slaughterhouse. "Is this the Torah and its reward?" he asked. "Silence!" spoke God. "So did it arise in the thought before Me."

The ritual shovel, the *magrefa*, which was specifically made for moving the ashes of the sacrifices on the altar in the Temple, resounded with loud music.

The purpose of all the music and singing in the Temple was to raise a clamor on high, in heaven. The music was for God to hear, as it is written (Numbers 10:9–10): "When you go to war . . . you shall sound a staccato on the trumpets. You will then be remembered before God your Lord, and will be delivered from your enemies. On your days of rejoicing, on your festivals, and on your new moon celebrations, you shall sound a note with the trumpets over your burnt offerings and your peace offerings. This shall be a remembrance before your God." So, it is not just we on earth who are more moved by the ashes remaining after the sacrifices have risen up on high. In heaven too, there is a similar heightening of appreciation. What people were unable to achieve during their lifetime, they can achieve now on high, by arousing an awakening in heaven of the profoundest mercy and salvation for the Jewish people, immediately and without delay.

This explains what we learn in the Talmud (*Berachoth* 3a); R. Jose said: "I was once traveling on the road, when I entered into one of the ruins of Jerusalem in order to pray. Elijah the prophet, of blessed memory, appeared. . . . He said to me, 'My son, why did you enter this ruin?' I replied, 'To pray.' . . . He said to me, 'My son, what sound did you hear in this ruin?' I replied; 'I heard a Divine Voice, cooing like a dove, saying, "Woe to Me, that I razed My house, burned My temple and exiled My children among the Gentiles!"' He said to me, 'By your life and by your head! It is not only now that God exclaims thus; He does so thrice each day!'" If, as Elijah the prophet told R. Jose, God laments the destruction of Jerusalem every day, why did R. Jose not hear God crying every time he prayed? Why did he hear God only upon entering one of the ruins of Jerusalem to pray?

It is understandable because Rabbi Jose was praying amidst the ruins and ashes of Jerusalem, and when someone is looking at the ashes, it intensifies the Divine pain and increases God's compassion to the point where R. Jose could hear what he was unable hear before—the weeping of God.

What can this teach us, that we may use in our worship? There is a teaching in the book *Sha'ar HaKedusha*, by R. Chaim Vital, of blessed memory: "The evil inclination in man is patterned on the four elements from which human beings and the entire universe are fashioned. From the element of Fire comes anger. From the element of Air comes pride. . . . From the element of Earth comes sloth and indifference."

In his holy book *Imrei Elimelech* (p. 40) my late father, of blessed memory, explains how one may exploit the passion inherent in the evil inclination derived from the element Fire, by harnessing it to good purpose and using it to worship God. "The same passion a person might use to do wrong can be used for doing good, because a person in his progress toward spiritual renewal can utilize passion. However, the principle does not work with the characteristics of sloth and indifference resulting from the evil inclination derived from the element Earth. There we are dealing with Amalek, who functions by chilling the passions of the Jewish people. Indifference and cynicism are devoid of passion, so they cannot be inverted and sanctified."

The evil inclination is, as it were, fourfold, and tries to use the four elements to achieve its ends. The aspect of the evil inclination that is Amalek, the serpent in the Garden of Eden who was forever cursed to eat earth, governs the element Earth. We need to understand what this means. Could not sloth or apathy be inverted and used as excuses to avoid doing something sinful, thereby utilizing the element Earth in the fight against the evil inclination? Why cannot the element Earth also be used in the service of God?

The reason is this: Indifference, passivity, apathy, and insensibility damage faith, and so are of no use to anyone except the evil inclination. So long as Amalek does not use the element of Earth to damage a person's faith, it is possible to use passivity and laziness for good, sanctifying them, as is the case with the evil inclinations derived from the other Elements. But once Amalek uses Earth to chill a person's faith, God forbid, then the element Earth cannot be enlisted in the war against sin, because it engenders only indifference regarding worship and the fulfillment of sacred duties. Once a person's faith is damaged and his passion dies, he can no longer use indifference or passivity creatively, nor can he make use of his passion, turning it into a passionate awakening.

One might ask how laziness and the Earth element damage faith, and how does the evil inclination ruled by Amalek use someone's Earth element to ruin his faith? The answer is as follows: We have previously described how a Jew's faith originates in the spirit of sanctity residing in every Jew, making him capable of faith far beyond his comprehension or intellectual abilities. However, once the Jew is trapped in depression and apathy, his heart, mind, and all those parts of his body influenced by the evil inclination are dragged down, growing incapable of shaking off their depression. When thus prevented from cleaving to holiness, his faith is damaged, God forbid. That explains why calamities and crises that beset a person, God forbid, breaking him or forcing him to succumb, can also damage his faith. At first, even though a person does not have heretical thoughts, God forbid, he also does not have exalted, spiritual, faith-filled thoughts either, because he is so numbed, dumb, and stolid, choked in heart and brain. Then, little by little, impious and irreverent thoughts may begin to creep in, God forbid.

This is why even in the Temple, where the Jewish people offered sacrifices upon the holy altar, wanting nothing but to elevate everything to God in a fire of holiness, the ashes—the element of Earth—remained on the altar. The Earth element could not be elevated to holiness, and so the ashes had to be consecrated in the daily ritual of *Terumath Hadeshen*, Tithing the Ashes. How can this tithing be done? Only with the music of the *magrefa*, representing *simcha* (joy) and salvation of Israel—for with *simcha* and an expression of salvation anything can be elevated, and darkness can be transformed into light.

That was why *Terumath Hadeshen* was not done during the great pilgrimage Festivals. At those times, nothing upon the altar needed elevating, because the Festivals themselves are a time of *simcha*, brilliance, liberation, and tremendous sanctity. They are a taste of the World to Come, when everything will be elevated to holiness.

There is perhaps a still deeper level of understanding that even we with our meager comprehension can add. It is well known that the four Elements are drawn from the four-letter name of God, *YHVH* (*Yud*, *Heh*, *Vav*, *Heh*), and that the Earth element is drawn from the fourth and final letter, the second *Heh*, representing the *sephirah* of *Malkhut*. When the final *Heh* is, God forbid, sundered from the Name of God, *YHVH*, and falls, there occurs something akin to the words of the famous kabbalistic poem *Kel Mistater* (a hymn from the Sabbath afternoon liturgy, after Proverbs 16:8): "Who disunites the One, will see no light." This is a state similar to that of the moon, who brought about the loss of her own luminosity (see Talmud, *Hullin* 60b).

When the *sephirah* of *Malkhut* is aroused to connect with her beloved, she begins by singing, (Isaiah 35:1–2) as is well known, "Arousing the Lily of Sharon to song . . . abundance will blossom, and rejoice with joy and singing." (See Midrash, *Tanchuma*, Deut. 2:2) Only then does it become obvious that the detachment had to precede the arousal. The longing for union grows out of the feelings of disconnection, and so the song issues directly from the pain of separation. This is why the "Song of Songs" is all about separation and then closeness, e.g., "My beloved is slipped away and gone," (Cant. 5:6) which brings the state of "My heart dissolved when he spoke," (ibid.) as is well known. The song is actually born of longing and pain brought about by separation and distance. This same process can also be experienced in the link between father and son, for, as we see, the more they are parted the more their love burgeons and intensifies.

This is the significance of the music that came from the *magrefa* with which the ritual of *Terumath Hadeshen* was performed. The ashes themselves, because they were so disconnected from their spiritual source, were filled with longing and, hence, even more song. This is why the ashes were left on the altar on Festival days: because they beautified the altar, bringing about even greater unification within and between heaven and earth.

Let us return to what we were saying above: Why was it only when he was praying in the ruins that R. Jose heard the voice of God saying "Woe to Me . . ."?

The answer is that there in the ruins, out of the pain of the Jewish people, Divine compassion for Jews was raised to a new level.

In the reading from Exodus with which we began this chapter, "*Elohim* spoke to Moses, saying 'I am *YHVH*. I appeared to Abraham, Isaac, and Jacob as *El Shaddai*, and I revealed not My name *YHVH* to them," we can see that it was only after God revealed Himself in the aspect of *Elohim* (Strict Judge) that *YHVH* (All Merciful God) was revealed. Rashi (ibid.) explains God as saying: "I appeared to the Patriarchs, but I did not keep my promises to them. So I am going to act upon those promises now. And now that I have mentioned them, there is an awakening of great sorrow for those who are gone, but not forgotten." The reawakening of the awareness of loss arouses salvation, as it is written: "And I am bringing the Jewish people out of the Land of Egypt . . ."

# *Bo*–January 24, 1942

*"God said to Moses and Aaron in the land of Egypt. 'This month shall be the head month to you. It shall be the first month of the year. Speak to the entire community of Israel, saying . . .'"* (Exodus 12:1)

Rashi (ibid.), quoting the *Mechilta* (*Bo*:1:2), explains: "The unnecessary reference to the land of Egypt in the first verse is there to emphasize that this revelation occurred outside the city. Moses and Aaron left the presence of Pharaoh and the city to distance themselves from loathed idols and other offensive objects. If even a simple prayer like that which Moses offered up in aid of Pharaoh during the plague of hail could not be uttered within the city precincts for that same reason (see Exodus 9:29), how much more so a weighty commandment such as this?"

Let us try to understand an apparent contradiction: When Moses said to Pharaoh, "So says God. . . ." (Exodus 11:4) Rashi (ibid.) explains that the prophecy was actually received by Moses where he stood, while he was in the palace standing before Pharaoh. Perhaps the solution is as follows: Prayers and Torah Commandments were not uttered by or given to Moses in Pharaoh's palace because the palace was an unclean place, and unfit for the revelation of prophecy. But revelation concerning the punishment of the wicked or the redemption of the Jewish people is permissible anywhere, and should never be delayed. It is always the right time and place for this type of revelation.

Nevertheless, we still need to understand why it is written, "God said to Moses and Aaron in the land of Egypt." Why does the fact that this revelation took place not in Pharaoh's palace but outside the town need to be emphasized at all?

We learn in the Talmud (*Baba Kamma* 54b); R. Hanina b. Agil asked R. Hiyya b. Abba: "Why does the first set of Ten Commandments (Exodus 20) contain no mention of the word *tov* (Good), whereas the second set of Ten Commandments (Deut. 5) contains the word 'good'? (See Rashi [Deut. 5:16]: This is a reference to the fifth commandment, to honor one's parents, where it is said: "You will then live long and have it good on the land that God your Lord is giving you.") R. Hiyya b. Abba replied: "Before you ask me *why* the word 'good' is mentioned, ask me *whether*, in fact, the word 'good' is mentioned. I'm not quite sure whether the word 'good' is there or not. Go, therefore, to R. Tanhum b. Hanilai who was close to R. Yehoshua b. Levi. He is an expert in *aggadah* (homiletics). He will tell you if the word 'good' appears, and why."

It is difficult to accept that any one of the sages quoted in the Babylonian Talmud was unsure not only of why, but even whether the word "good" appears in the Ten Commandments. Is it possible, God forbid, that the sage did not actually know a verse in the Torah, and especially the Ten Commandments? Even assuming this to be so, why did he not refer R. Hanina to an expert in scripture before sending him to an expert in homiletics? If he himself did not know the verse, then possibly the expert in *aggadah* also would not know it.

Perhaps the explanation is as follows: There is a well-known teaching in the Zohar (vol. I, 103a) about the verse (Prov. 31:14) "Her husband is well known in the gates. . . ." The Zohar explains this verse with a play on the Hebrew word *b'she'arim*, "in the gates": "*she'ar*, normally translated as 'gate,' can also mean 'estimation,' 'calculation,' and 'valuation.' The 'husband' in the verse is the Holy Blessed One, Husband of the human soul, Who is known by each person inasmuch as that person in his heart esteems and values Him."

From this we can learn that a Jew's fear and love of God are each a sort of revelation. They are what God personally reveals of Himself to that individual. Even if the person's fear of God is no more than fear of being punished, and his love of God is really just in order to receive a reward, it is still a revelation of God, because God is manifest in this person's fear of punishment and desire for reward. How much greater is the revelation, however, when someone truly loves and fears God, trying to be a true worshipper and servant of God alone.

No one today sees visions of God in the way that revelation was bestowed upon prophets of antiquity. What we have is our fear of God, our love, and our faith in Him. These are an individual's revelation, through which his soul perceives God. This is similar to what is said in the Book of Daniel 10:7: "And I, Daniel, alone, saw the vision. The men who were with me saw not the vision, but a tremendous trembling and fear and awe fell upon them."

The extent to which a person journeys spiritually, preparing himself and making ready to receive God's revelation, is a measure of his faith, love, and fear of God. Any grasp of the Torah he may have acquired, whether of the revealed or the hidden Torah, is his personal revelation of God, because God is found within the Torah. A person learning a page in the Talmud (*Baba Metzia* 2a) concerning two people who have simultaneously found a lost object and are both tightly holding the same *tallit*, saying, "It's all mine." " No! It's all mine." has grasped something of God's light, found only on that page in the Talmud. Although he may think he is studying simple case law concerning mundane people and everyday things—two people, the *tallit*, and the dispute over ownership, etc.—he is actually experiencing a revelation of God.

So every Jew learning the Torah must strive to reach for the hidden, the secret, within it. Whether he is learning the text on a simple scholarly level or studying the arcane meaning, he must always try to reach for the mystery, which is the light of God in that Torah.

In the holy book *Ma'or VaShamesh* we learn that when we refer to the "mysteries of the Torah" we are not talking about Kabbalah. Whatever is written, published, and can be learned out of a book cannot be the "mysteries of the Torah." If anyone and everyone can discuss it and teach it to their friends, there is no point in calling it a "mystery." The real "mystery" is in each individual's revelation of God through his own study of Torah. That is truly a mystery, because no one can teach a friend or a pupil this secret. It remains for everyone to acquire his own understanding of God, at the level he reaches and with the effort he invests.

Besides taking personal inventory every few months, or at the very least every few years, to assess his relationship to God, every person must stop and take stock immediately after learning Torah, even if the learning was only for an hour. Also after prayer and after worship, a person needs to look inside himself and ask whether he is completely changed or not. He may find that he has not been elevated entirely, and cannot say he has fulfilled the verse (Psalms 24:3) "Who climbs God's mountain, standing in His holy place?" However, even if he cannot say that he remains elevated, standing "on the mountain," he should at least discover that after an hour of study or prayer he is not the same person as he would have been after an hour of idleness.

From this we can understand why Rashi, citing a Midrash (Exodus Rabbah 25:2), makes the following comment on Exodus 17:7: "When the Jews asked, 'Is God among us or not?' they started a chain of events that brought Amalek down upon them. This is why the following verse begins, 'Amalek arrived and attacked Israel there in Rephidim.' (Exodus 17:8)" The Midrash (*Tanchuma, B'Shalach* 25), however, suggests a different cause for the attack by Amalek. The verse says that the Jewish people arrived in "*rephidim*." The root of the Hebrew word *rephidim* is *rapha*, "weak." That is, "Because their hands were weakened from neglecting the Torah, Amalek came and attacked them."

From what we have said above, it is clear there is really no distinction between the two Midrashim. "Their hands were weak from neglecting Torah," because although they studied Torah, they never got a "handle" on it; it never reached "their hands." We learn in the Mishnah (*Uktzin* 1:1): "Something may act as a handle if it is properly attached, as for example a stalk attached to a fruit can be used to grasp and move the fruit. Holding the handle is then technically the same as holding the fruit." When the Jewish people were not attached to Torah properly, then, as the Midrash *Tanchuma* says, their hands (handles) were weak. They had not discovered the mysteries of the Torah. In fact, they had reached a low point where, as the Midrash Rabbah quoted by Rashi says, they even questioned whether God was inside them or not. This reconciles the two Midrashim.

To return to what we were saying above; all types of worship and understanding of the Torah are revelations of God. This, as we said, is the meaning of the passage in the Zohar, "Her husband is well known in the gates . . ." The Husband is known and revealed to the soul only to the degree with which the soul is familiar with Him.

With this we can understand why, when R. Hanina b. Agil asked R. Hiyya b. Abba why the Torah says, "Honor your father and mother, so that you may live long and have it good on the land that God your Lord is giving you," R. Hiyya could not answer. R. Hiyya said he did not know whether the word "good" appears or not. What he was really saying is that his knowledge of God did not take into consideration what God might do for him in return. R. Hiyya's worship of God was not about obtaining a reward, so he could not say why or even whether the second set of Ten Commandments promises a good life while the first Ten Commandments do not. His knowledge of Torah and his fulfillment of the commandments had nothing to do with his rational understanding; it was all a revelation, as was explained above. God reveals Himself to each person according to the extent of that person's worship, and since R. Hiyya did not worship in order to obtain a reward, he could not explain the verse. But why did he then refer R. Hanina to R. Tanhum, who was an expert in homiletics?

We learn in the Talmud (*Shabbath* 30a); The question was asked before R. Tanhum of Neway: Is it permissible to extinguish a burning lamp for a sick man on the Sabbath? R. Tanhum first responded to the question with a lengthy homiletic exegesis, and then finally answered, "A lamp is a lamp, while the soul of man is called a lamp of God (Prov. 20:27). It is better that a person's lamp be extinguished, before the lamp of God be snuffed out."

Rashi (ibid.) comments: "This is not to say that we learn all the laws pertaining to saving human life on the Sabbath from R. Tanhum's sermon. The law that saving human life overrides Sabbath prohibitions is established elsewhere. We derive the concept from the injunction (Leviticus 18:5) 'Observe the Torah commandments and live by them,' which means to live by them, and not to die by them (*Yoma* 85b). If this is the case, why did R. Tanhum give this lengthy homiletic sermon in answer to the original question? Because many of those who came to hear R. Tanhum speak that day were peasants and other simple, unlearned people. The crowd included women and children, as well as scholars. R. Tanhum, as a master of the *agadda*, was trying to draw and speak to people's hearts."

This tells us that the Torah revealed to the preacher is not only at the level of his own understanding, but also at the levels of those who are listening to him. So, R. Hiyya referred R. Hanina to R. Tanhum, assuming that R. Tanhum would be able to answer the question—not that he was implying that R. Tanhum himself was someone whose worship of God was in order to obtain a reward, and would therefore be able to answer the question, but rather that his unique skills as a preacher gave him insights not otherwise granted to other such holy men. Precisely because R. Tanhum was a master of the *agadda*, a speaker to people at all levels of understanding, it was given to him to understand the verse "You will then live long and have it good . . ." He understood it even at the level of those who worship and fulfill the commandments of God only in the hope of obtaining reward. Many in R. Tanhum's audience worshipped God at that level.

Furthermore, a master of the *agaddah* not only has his own insights into Torah but also experiences revelations of Torah that are beyond and above his level of understanding. The reason for this could be as follows. We learn this in the *Tanya* (Epistle 23), from the Rav, R. Shneur Zalman of Liadi: "This is what I heard from my teachers: 'If an angel should find itself among any gathering of ten Jews, even when they are not speaking of Torah, such an unfettered dread and terror would befall the angel at the *Shechinah* (Divine Presence) resting upon the Jews, that it would disappear into oblivion."

When ten Jews are dispersed, each in his own home, each is an individual, and the *Shechinah* (Divine Presence) resting upon them is not as great as when they are all together. When they come together to hear the words of the Living God from a master of the *agaddah*, from a single person, there occurs a confluence of all the people who have come to listen within the one person who is about to teach Torah to them. Within the master preacher himself there occurs a revelation of God, clothed in the words of Torah. It is not only those things that people need to hear that are revealed to the speaker; as was said above, the preacher may be given an understanding of why the second set of Commandments contain the promise of a reward, in the word "good"—a concept at a much lower level than his own understanding of Torah. The teacher may also be given insights into new, higher levels of the Torah just because people have come to listen to him teach, even if they themselves are not ready for those levels.

This is the point: There are levels of understanding that belong solely to the teacher, the results of his own Torah and worship and the personal revelation of God within him, at a much higher level than those who are listening to him can appreciate. His audience is not connected to these elements of their teacher's personal understanding. However, regarding the revelation that comes to the teacher only because he is teaching these very people, even though the listeners are not yet at a level to comprehend what has been revealed to the teacher, they are nevertheless still connected to it. It may still go through a layered process whereby it becomes manifest to them.

The teacher's own revelation and the revelation that comes to him because he is teaching are analogous to the Written Torah and the Oral Torah. The Written Torah comes from a greatly exalted place, higher than the Oral Torah and Kabbalah. Nonetheless, the Written Torah has been drawn down into our world, the universe of *Assiya* (Action). The Oral Torah and the Kabbalah, which were initially lower than the Written Torah and derived from it, are now in the exalted worlds, the universes of *Atzilut* (Archetypes), *Briyah* (Creation), and *Yetzirah* (Formation), as is well known.

This is the meaning of the verse (Malachi 2:7) "The lips of the *cohen* will guard knowledge, and the Torah will be sought from his mouth, because he is an angel of God." It hints at the following. People seek Torah at the *cohen*'s mouth even though he is an angel of God and his Torah level is much higher than theirs. But because the *cohen* actually teaches words of Torah to the public with his mouth, the students are right there in his mouth, so to speak, and even though his Torah is very exalted, it is drawn down and made available to them in this way.

There is a well-known teaching in the Talmud (*Yebamoth* 97a): "When anyone repeats the Torah of a dead scholar, the lips of the dead, though lying in a grave, mutter along with the speaker." That is, particularly the lips and particularly in the grave, because in the upper worlds, in the Academy of Heaven, everyone learns Torah all the time anyway. For someone to speak Torah in his grave, someone living must be repeating the dead person's Torah. The dead man had a connection with his students during his lifetime, and so the students were in his mouth and his Torah was in their hearts. His students retain this powerful connection with him even after his death, and thus his lips move "in the grave." Furthermore, anyone who repeats the Torah of a dead teacher becomes his student even after the teacher's death, and the lips of the dead teacher begin to speak in the grave as this new student begins to draw Torah from the mouth of the teacher, as we said above, "And the lips of the *cohen* will guard knowledge, and the Torah will be sought from his mouth . . ." It is only when the teacher has students and they fill his mouth with Torah that he transcends his own personal understanding. It follows, therefore, that even after a teacher has died he still remains connected to his students in this world. Similarly when a student dies, he remains connected to the teacher's continued learning of Torah in this world. The student is still connected to the teacher because he was in the mouth and in the heart of the teacher. The revelation of Torah that came to the teacher only came to him because he had this particular student.

Let us now return to the quote with which we began this chapter, "God said to Moses and Aaron in the land of Egypt." Even though Moses and Aaron were outside the city, God still spoke to them in Egypt. The emphasis on Egypt is because Egypt was where the Jews, Moses' students, were. The Torah he was being given and the Commandment to purchase and prepare a kid on the tenth of the first month in preparation for the Egyptian Passover Festival was solely for the benefit of the Jewish people at that time and in that place. This was a once-only Festival. Subsequent Passover celebrations were quite different. Moses was favored with this revelation only because of his students, the Jews who were still in Egypt—because, as we said, it is the students who bring about the revelation in their teacher, each according to his own level.

# *B'Shalach*—January 31, 1942

*"Moses and the Israelites then sang this song to God. And they spoke, to say, 'I will sing to God for His great victory.'"* (Exodus 15:1)

Rashi (ibid.) says of the phrase "I will sing" that when the miracle happened, it occurred to them to sing at some point in the future. We learn in the holy book *Kedushath Levi* (ibid.), concerning Rashi's comment, that "I will sing" refers to a future time. He says, "When the Jewish people were still in Egypt, they had such faith that God would save them, they already thought of the song they would sing upon gaining their freedom." Hence "I will sing," in the future.

One might add that from a reading of the text it would appear that not only did they think about the singing they would do in their freedom, but while they were still in Egypt they actually thanked and praised God, as it is written (Exodus 12:27): "The people bowed and prostrated themselves."

With this introduction, it is possible to understand why in an earlier verse (Exodus 6:9), when Moses first told the Jewish people that he had been sent to redeem them, "They did not listen to Moses, because of their shortness of breath and the hard work." What was it that they needed to hear? Furthermore, Moses said to God (Exodus 6:12), "If even the Israelites will not listen to me, how can I expect Pharaoh to listen to me?" The Torah then goes on to say, "God spoke to Moses and Aaron, and commanded them regarding the Israelites." What did He command? Rashi (ibid.) explains: "God commanded them to lead the Jewish people with gentleness, and to have patience with them." Does this suggest that up until that point Moses did not lead them gently and patiently, God forbid? How does this answer the question asked by Moses, "If even the Israelites will not listen to me, how can I expect Pharaoh to listen to me?"

The Talmud (*Berachoth* 7b) on the verse (Psalms 3:1) "A song of David, when he fled from Absalom his son" asks: "'A song of David?' It ought to have been 'a lamentation of David.'" The Talmud answers: "When the Holy Blessed One said to David (II Samuel 12:11), 'Behold, I will raise up evil against you out of your own house,' David began to worry. He thought, 'It may be a slave or a bastard who will have no pity on me.' When he saw that it was Absalom, his son, he said, 'Any normal son has a care for his father,' and so he rejoiced. Hence, 'A song of David.'" Similarly, regarding "A Song of Asaf. O God, Gentiles are come into Your inheritance. They have polluted Your holy sanctuary and turned Jerusalem into rubble," (Psalms 79) the Talmud (*Kiddushin* 31b, see *Tosaphot*) asserts: "It ought to be a 'lamentation of Asaf!'"

We need to understand the original question posed by the Talmud. The law states clearly (Mishnah, *Berachoth* 9:5): "A man must bless God for the evil that happens to him as for the good that happens." If it must be accepted with joy, why does the Talmud ask: "'A song of David?' It ought to have been 'A lamentation of David?'" Furthermore, why according to the Talmud quoted above was it called "a song," in gratitude for the grain of good found even in the pain, when the psalm itself speaks only of suffering?

It is possible to accept suffering and endure it with love, and to have faith that everything is from God, but to actually sing while enduring it is difficult. In order for a person to sing, his essential self—his soul and his heart—must burst into song. One of the conditions of prophecy was the necessity for the prophet to be in a state of *simcha*—blissful joy—at all times, even while in pain, as we learn in the book *Sha'ar HaKedusha*, by R. Chaim Vital, of blessed memory. Yet, we learn that when the prophet Elisha wanted prophecy to rest upon him and his normal blissful state was not sufficient, he needed more joy, and so he said (II Kings 3:5), "'Bring me a minstrel.' And it came to pass, when the minstrel played, that the hand of the Lord came upon him." We see clearly that something good has to occur, there must be salvation, for the heart to rejoice. Then, when a level of *simcha* has been reached, a person can sing to God about his pain as well. This is the meaning of the Talmud's question, "A song of David?" The question is: How was King David able to sing? The Talmud answers that in the suffering he saw a miracle from heaven, because things could have been so much worse, God forbid. King David rejoiced over this miracle until he could also sing about his pain.

This is an important rule for us. In all suffering, when there is nothing with which to encourage ourselves, we must strengthen ourselves and rejoice in the reflection that it could have been, God forbid, so much worse. This is like David, who rejoiced because the evil could have come from one of his servants, instead of from his son. But when, God forbid, the suffering is so great that one is completely crushed and the mind has crumbled, when there is insufficient personality left intact for it to able to be strengthened, then it is difficult to rejoice in reflections like those of King David. This is the reason why the Israelites "did not listen to Moses."

We learn in the Talmud (*Sotah* 30b) of an argument among *tannaim*: "How did the Israelites sing the 'Song of the Sea'? R. Nechemia declared that all the Jewish people achieved a state of prophecy: They were all given the 'Song of the Sea' together and they sang together with Moses. R. Akiba and R. Eliezer son of R. Jose said that only Moses achieved prophecy, and so Moses sang the song while the Jewish people repeated it after him." Both of these explanations are the words of the living God. At the sea, the *Shechinah* (Divine Presence) rested so much upon the people that, as we learn in the *Mechilta* (ibid.), even the lowliest maidservant saw visions that were not revealed to Ezekiel the prophet. Everyone achieved a state of prophecy, and they could sing even without first hearing the words from our teacher Moses. So, when our teacher Moses started to sing, they were able to sing the words along with him. This was not the case, however, when they were still in Egypt. There, though the people wanted to sing and praise God, they had not achieved the high level of prophecy, so they had to listen to Moses and respond after him.

When Pharaoh hardened his spirit, and increased the workload of the Jewish people, saying (Exodus 5:7), "Do not give the people straw for bricks as before. Let them go and gather their own straw," their spirit fell so much that they were unable even to listen to Moses and repeat the song after him. This is the meaning of "'They did not listen to Moses, because of their shortness of breath and the hard work." Therefore, when our teacher Moses said, "The Israelites will not listen to me," God instructed him to lead them with gentleness and patience. The meaning of this is that it was the duty of the shepherds of the Jewish people to bring about a change in Heaven's policy regarding the Jews, forcing it to administer the world with gentleness and patience, instead of inflicting pain, God forbid. This would allow the people to listen and to sing.

The verse says, "God spoke to Moses and Aaron, and commanded them regarding the Israelites." In general, the way that the Jewish people bring about God's salvation is through prayer, but when, God forbid, danger is imminent and there is no time to pray, then salvation is brought about by decree, as the Talmud (*Sotah* 12a) says: "The *tzaddik* (pious person) decrees, and the Holy Blessed One fulfills." Similarly, when God tells the Jewish people to awaken heaven's mercy, sometimes He requests it of them, as described in the Talmud (*Berachoth* 7a): "God said to R. Ishmael b. Elisha, 'Ishmael, My son, bless Me.' What was Ishmael's blessing of God? 'May it be Your will that Your mercy suppress Your anger and Your mercy prevail over Your other attributes, so that You treat Your children mercifully. And may You, on their behalf, stop short of the letter of the law.'" However, in times of great suffering, it is written, "God commanded them regarding the Jewish people." He commanded that, by decree, a change must be wrought in the Divine administration of the world, decreeing that the Jewish people be led mercifully. This would bring an end to their slavery, and enable them, even while they were still in Egypt, to sing and praise God and to prepare themselves for the singing and praising they would do upon their redemption. This is the meaning of (Exodus 14:31) "The Israelites saw the great power that God had unleashed in Egypt." Already, when still in Egypt, they could see God's salvation, and so they were able, in their minds, "to sing in the future."

In "Moses and the Israelites then sang this song to God. And they spoke, to say . . ." "to say" implies that they succeeded in establishing this for future generations—to say: that out of their heart and soul it be said. In Yiddish it would be translated as *Es zol sich zugen shirah*—The song should say itself.

# *Yithro*—February 7, 1942

*"Remember the Sabbath day to sanctify it. Work during the six weekdays and do all your tasks. But keep the seventh day a Sabbath for God your Lord; do not work on that day, neither you, your son, your daughter, your slave, your maidservant, your animal, nor the stranger in your gates. Because God created heaven and earth, the seas and all that they contain, in six days, and He rested on the seventh day. God therefore blessed the Sabbath day and sanctified it."* (Exodus 20:8–11)

Why is it that the Torah first says we should sanctify the Sabbath, and then ends by saying it is God who sanctifies the day?

We learn the following in the Talmud (*Shabbath* 10b) on the verse (Exodus 31:13) "Speak to the Children of Israel, saying, 'Only observe My Sabbaths, because they are a sign between Me and you for all generations, so that you know that I, God, am sanctifying you.'" "The Holy Blessed One said to Moses, 'I have a precious gift in My treasure house. It is called "Sabbath," and it is my desire to give it to the Jewish people. Go and inform them.' From this, R. Simeon b. Gamliel deduced: If one gives a loaf to a child, he must inform the child's mother. But did not R. Hama b. R. Hanina teach: If one makes a gift to his neighbor, he need not inform him, as deduced from Scripture (Exodus 34:29): 'And Moses did not know that the skin of his face shone by reason of His speaking with him?' There is no real difficulty. R. Hana refers to a gift that will be revealed anyway, while R. Simeon refers to one that is not likely to be revealed. But surely, the Sabbath is a matter that stood to be revealed. Why then did God have to inform them? Yes, the Sabbath would be revealed, but its rewards were not obvious. And so, God told Moses, 'Go and inform them . . .'"

We need to understand why the Talmud says, "If one gives a loaf to a child, he must inform the child's mother." Why does it not say, "He must inform the child's parents"? Perhaps because it is usually the mother who bakes the loaf and gives it to the child, and so it is she who benefits from the giving of the loaf. But that is not entirely true, since it is usually the father who earns the money to buy the ingredients for the loaf, and so he benefits even more from the gift of the loaf to the child. Why then do we inform the mother, who may only have toiled to bake the loaf?

The intention of the teaching could be as follows. It is not only when you give your own bread to a child that you must inform both parents, because both benefit from the gift—the father by not having to pay for bread, and the mother by not having to bake it and feed it to the child. But even if you feed the child with the bread his mother provided, and it is only of benefit to the mother in that she is spared the small task of having to feed the child herself, it is still necessary to inform her. The proof of this teaching is the Sabbath itself. It is well known that while still in Egypt, Moses begged Pharaoh to give the Jewish people a day on which to rest and that Pharaoh granted the request. This is why in the Sabbath morning liturgy we say, "Let Moses rejoice in the gift of his portion" (since it was because of Moses that the Jewish people observed the Sabbath while still in Egypt). If this is so, then even though the Sabbath exists because it is the day on which God rested, nevertheless when God gave it to the Jewish people, it was as if He was giving them something that they already possessed. As a result of the efforts of our teacher Moses, they already observed the Sabbath while still in Egypt, and yet God told Moses to "go and inform them." From this we learn that even if one feeds a child with a loaf that already belongs to him, one must still inform his mother of the gift.

It is noteworthy that in the Talmud quoted above, God says, "I have a precious gift in My treasure house," while the Torah itself is called "a hidden treasure." In the Talmud (*Shabbath* 88b) we learn: "When Moses ascended on high, the ministering angels said to the Holy Blessed One, 'Sovereign of the Universe, what business has one born of woman amongst us?' God answered, 'He has come to receive the Torah.' They said to Him, 'That hidden treasure, which was hoarded nine hundred and seventy-four generations before the world was created, You desire to give to flesh and blood?'" The angels did not say, "hoarded in Your treasure house." They simply said "hoarded." Obviously, "the treasure house" of the Holy Blessed One is far beyond our comprehension.

However, what may be within reach of our limited understanding is as follows. Perhaps, when speaking of something in a treasure house, the thing itself is perceivable, and cannot be seen only because it is hidden inside the treasure house.

This is comparable to a house whose walls conceal its contents. When, on the other hand, we talk of a "hidden treasure," we do not mean that it is concealed in a treasure house. We mean that the thing itself is invisible, and not simply concealed from view. It is hidden because it is so much beyond our ability to perceive it, and even though nothing hides it from view, we are still unable to see it.

This was the chief argument of the angels, when they called the Torah "the hidden treasure" and not the precious object "in a treasure house." "Look," they said, "The Torah is right here in front of us and yet we are unable to perceive it, because it is so lofty and its Light so tremendous. How can You be contemplating giving it to flesh and blood?" The Talmud goes on to say that in response, the Holy Blessed One said to Moses, "Give them a rebuttal." Moses replied, "Sovereign of the Universe, I am afraid that they will consume me with their fiery breath." God said to him, "Hold on to My Throne of Glory, and give them a rebuttal." This in itself was their answer: that the Jew, who exists in the temporal world below—this human, who was so contemptible in their eyes that they must refer to him as "born of woman"—was yet grasping the very Throne of Glory, far above them. The angels exist in *Yetzirah*, the universe of Formation, while the Throne of Glory is in *Briyah*, the universe of Creation.

The fact is that, like the Torah, the Jew exists right in front of everyone and yet cannot be perceived, because he is as exalted as the Throne of Glory and his Light is so tremendous. The very angels see him without comprehending him at all. Even the person himself does not perceive his own essence. Moses was afraid of being consumed by the angels; he obviously had no idea that he was so much greater than they were. Although there is no real basis for comparison, nonetheless, when Gentiles look at a Jew and see someone contemptible, it is because they cannot perceive the actual Jew. It is precisely because Jews are a "hidden treasure" and not hidden in a treasure house, because they are simply beyond perception and due to their greatness impossible to grasp, that they are the only proper receivers of the Torah, which is itself a "hidden treasure."

Of the Sabbath, God said to Moses, "I have a precious gift in My treasure house. It is called 'Sabbath,' and it is my desire to give it to the Jewish people. Go and inform them." The Talmud concludes that God was telling Moses to inform the Jewish people about the rewards of the Sabbath. What was the purpose of the information? We are all, thank God, Jews, and so each one of us must have been informed by God. Each, at his own particular level, must know what God meant when he said, "Go and inform them of its rewards," as the Talmud concluded. The purpose is to be aware, to know that "I, God, am sanctifying you."

In the *Tanya* (Epistle 23), R. Shneur Zalman of Liadi explains the difference between Divine Inspiration and Divine Reward. "Divine Inspiration means that a tremendous light comes to rest upon the Jew—a light much greater than the person himself can grasp, and far greater than that which could actually enter into him. A Divine Reward, however, is Divine Light that has been restricted and limited to the amount the person is capable of absorbing."

According to what we have said above, it is appropriate that the Jewish people receive the Torah, which, because of its great light, is a hidden treasure. This is because the Jewish people are also hidden, and cannot be grasped, because of their great light and exalted status. While the Torah can rest upon them, at the level of Divine Inspiration, the Jew can actually grasp the light of the Sabbath, because, as we said above, it is "a precious gift in My treasure house"—something that can be perceived and grasped when not concealed behind walls. Through the Sabbath, God constricted that part of the Torah that He desired to channel and give to the Jewish people. In this way it could penetrate right into their being, into their essence, under the guise of "I have a precious gift in my treasure house, called the Sabbath." God did not give away the entire Torah in heaven, but only that portion that could be received by the Jewish people. He drew it down and constricted it from the level of a "hidden treasure" to the level of "a precious gift in a treasure house," as He did with the Sabbath. The Torah was thus reduced from Divine Inspiration to the level of a Divine Reward, whereby it could enter into the Jewish people.

As the Talmud says (*Shabbath* 86b), "Everyone agrees that the Torah was given on the Sabbath." If it had not been given on the Sabbath, the Torah would have remained at the level of Divine Inspiration. Because the Torah was given on the Sabbath, however, the Jewish people connected with it at the level of a Divine Reward, about which God said, "Go and inform them." Torah is an inferior variety of Divine Wisdom, as we know from the Midrash (Genesis Rabbah 17:5): "R. Hanina b. Yitzchak said that there are three inferior, premature, unripe varieties. Sleep is a variety of death, dreams are a variety of prophecy, and the Sabbath is a variety of the World to Come. R. Abin added another two. The globe of the sun is a variety of Divine Light, and Torah is a variety of Divine Wisdom." Divine Wisdom is inspirational, and so God gave the Jewish people the lesser variety, at the level of "Go and inform them."

Why the Torah was given specifically on the Sabbath, we cannot know. But with our limited perspective, perhaps it is possible to suggest as follows. The Sabbath is both the *sephirah* of *Binah* (Understanding) and the *sephirah* of *Malkhut* (Sovereignty). The *sephirah* of *Malkhut* is also known as *K'nesseth Yisrael* (Congregation of Israel). When the Torah is given on the Sabbath, therefore, the Light is reduced and constricted within bounds, according to the capacity of each individual Jew to receive it.

Another reason could be that during the Six Days of Creation, God worked in the world, and what then was missing? Rest. With the Sabbath came rest, as Rashi explains (Genesis 2:2). What is "rest" in human terms? It is the restoration of a person's soul, a process that happens inside him. A similar change from external to internal processes occurs in the spiritual world. During the six days of the week, the holiness that is drawn down is external to the person, in the form of Divine Inspiration, but on the Sabbath, the holiness is internal. Because the Sabbath was the day on which the Torah was given, the Torah can be drawn inward even during the six days of the week, depending only upon how much we connect the Sabbath with the weekdays. In the lyrics of the Sabbath hymn "God I Desire" by R. Aaron the Great of Karlin, we sing, "Save me from behind, from parting with the Sabbath, not to lock out of Sabbath, the six days."

Each person apprehends the Torah at the levels of *p'shat* (meaning), *remez* (allegory), *d'rush* (homily), and *sod* (mystery), according to his particular mindset. Regarding these four layers of Torah understanding, the Holy Blessed One had no need to tell Moses, "Go and inform them." The whole Torah was given for Moses to tell to the Jewish people—and not only to tell it, but also to lay it out like a table set before them, as Rashi explains on the verse (Exodus 21:1) "These are the laws that you must set before them": "Like a table properly set and laid." "Go and inform them," therefore, means that it was Moses' duty to help them perceive and experience what was otherwise impossible to grasp: the Light of the Hidden Treasure and the Divine Inspiration that surrounded them.

Every Jew experiences an exalted state from time to time, whether during prayer, on Sabbath, during the Festivals, or at other particularly uplifting times. He may not know why he experiences this exaltation at that time. Indeed, it is forbidden to reflect upon causes and reasons while it is happening, because introspection and intellectualizing actually undermine the exaltation. Nevertheless, it is felt. It is a connection between the levels of Divine Inspiration and the Divine Reward of "Go and inform them," which informs their innermost and essential selves.

This does not only apply in times of exaltation. We need to bear in mind that although, generally speaking, arrogance is a most destructive character defect— the Talmud (*Sotah* 5a) describes God saying, "I and he cannot live in one world"— nonetheless, a person must never see himself as hollow or contemptible. For when someone considers himself hollow and contemptible, he behaves in a hollow and contemptible way. A person needs to feel that he is a Jew, a chasid, and a God worshipper, for that feeling is a spark, a flash of the Light of Divine Inspiration penetrating him. Even though he is lowly in his own estimation, always seeing his own faults, nevertheless he feels within himself that he is a Jew and a chasid, at the level of (II Chronicles 17:6) "And his heart grew haughty in the ways of God." Not only does this not cause him to act arrogantly; on the contrary, it humbles him in his own eyes, so that he is always looking at his own faults and character defects. It is obvious that anyone feeling hollow and contemptible, God forbid, thinks that only the most grievous sins are forbidden him. When he finds himself innocent of such grievous sins, he is already arrogant and proud. This is not the case with someone who feels himself to be a chasid and God worshipper, for whom even a trace of a trace of evil is intolerable. Not only that, but such a person knows just how easy it is to fall into the very deepest pit, God forbid, and his heart is always broken inside him.

Thus, the terrible sufferings, may the Merciful One protect us, aside from the fact that they are evil in themselves, are also destructive in that they cause people's spirits to fall, preventing them from feeling their own greatness and nobility. We must strengthen ourselves, even in this suffering. We must each be like a captured prince, who, even though tortured, is nonetheless a tortured prince. God will have mercy, and rescue us immediately and forthwith.

"Go and inform them . . . so that you know that I, God, am sanctifying you." With this knowing, a person is aware that he is a chasid. This knowing is part of God's knowing, and with it, the person knows. It is a well-known teaching of Maimonides, of blessed memory, and taught by the kabbalists, that God's omniscience is with His self-knowledge. We have previously discussed how God knows of a person's piety and worship through His self-knowledge. A person's piety and worship are actually God's, because God is the one who gives the desire and the strength, the mind and the heart, to worship. When God gives part of His knowledge to someone, and with it knows the person's worship, then the person sees that the worship was not his, and that everything is God's. Then he understands that he of himself does nothing, and regards only his faults as his own—because they are his own; he made them—and so his heart falls and his spirit breaks.

It is well known that in Egypt it was the *sephirah* of *Da'at* (Knowing) that was in exile. The letters of the Hebrew name Pharaoh—*peh*, *resh*, *ayin*, *heh*—can be inverted to read *ha'oref* which, translated, means the back of the neck, opposite the face, the occiput, which prevents *da'at* (knowing) from expanding. In this our current exile, it is the *Da'at* of the lower *sephirot*—the *Midoth* (Characteristics) as opposed to the *Mochin* (Mentalities)—that are in exile. The task is to bring *Da'at* out of exile. That is why it is written (Exodus 2:25), "And God saw the Children of Israel, and God knew." The people were brought out of Egypt ". . . so that you know that I, God, am sanctifying you." Of the coming of the Messiah, it is said (Isaiah 11:9), ". . . and the world will be filled with knowledge of God."

Although they suppress *Da'at* (Knowing), God forbid, nonetheless all our sufferings now, as in Egypt, have a purpose. Their purpose is to crush and remove "common knowledge," with which man thinks that he knows, and upon which he relies, while in the words of the verse (Ecclesiastes 1:18), "He adds knowledge, he adds pain." Their purpose is to beat it and eradicate it, so that afterwards God's knowing can be revealed inside each person, and in the entire world.

"Remember the Sabbath to sanctify it. . . . God therefore blessed the Sabbath day and sanctified it." Why does the Torah say first that we should sanctify the Sabbath, and end by saying that it is God who sanctifies the day? If we remember the Sabbath and sanctify it, then we will know that it is really God who sanctifies it. It is not our doing, but ". . . so that you know that I, God, am sanctifying you." We will know that God sanctifies it, and we will feel God's holiness within us.

# *Mishpatim (Parshat Sh'kalim)*— February 14, 1942

*"And these are the Judgments that you must set before them."* (Exodus 21:1)

We learn in the Talmud (*Berachoth* 3a); R. Jose said: "I was once traveling on the road, when I entered into one of the ruins of Jerusalem in order to pray. Elijah the Prophet, of blessed memory, appeared and waited for me at the door until I had finished my prayer. Whereupon, he said to me. 'Peace be with you, master!' And I replied, 'Peace be with you master and teacher!' He said to me, 'My son, why did you enter this ruin?' I replied, 'To pray.' . . . He said to me, 'My son, what sound did you hear in this ruin?' I replied, 'I heard a Divine Voice, cooing like a dove, saying, "Woe to Me, that I razed My house, burned My temple, and exiled My children among the Gentiles!"' He said to me, 'By your life and by your head! It is not only now that God exclaims thus, He does so thrice each day! And even more than that, whenever Jews go into synagogues and studyhouses and respond, "May His great name be blessed!" the Holy Blessed One nods His head and says; "Happy is the king who is thus praised in his house! Woe to the father who banishes his children, and woe to the children who are banished from their father's table!"'"

We have previously discussed why R. Jose heard the Divine Voice only when he was praying amidst the ruins, even though the Holy Blessed One speaks thus three times every day. For behold! A Jew, tortured in his suffering, may think he is the only one in pain, as though his individual, personal pain, and the pain of all other Jews, has no affect Above, God forbid. But, as the verse (Isaiah 63:9) says, "In all their pain is His pain," and as we learn in the Talmud (*Hagigah* 15b) in the name of R. Meir, "When a person suffers, to what expression does the *Shechinah* (Divine) give utterance? 'O woe! My head, O woe! My arms.'" In sacred literature we learn that God, as it were, suffers the pain of a Jew much more than that person himself feels it.

Possibly because God is infinite—and hence unknowable in the world—His pain at the suffering of Jewish people is also infinite. Perhaps it is not just impossible for any human to feel such immense pain, it is impossible even to apprehend the level of God's pain, to know that He bears it. Just to hear God's voice saying, "Woe to Me, that I razed My house, burned My temple, and exiled My children among the Gentiles!" is impossible, because it is beyond the boundaries of human comprehension. It was only when R. Jose entered into the devastation of one of the ruins of Jerusalem, letting go somewhat of his self-centeredness, that the boundaries restricting his perception were also destroyed and he was able to hear the voice of God. Even then, he heard only a little of the voice, for, as he said, "I heard a Divine Voice, cooing like a dove," while we know from the verse (Jeremiah 25:30) "God roars, howling over his city," that God roars, as it were, like a lion, over the destruction of the Temple.

And so, the world continues to exist steadfast, it is not obliterated by God's pain and His voice at the suffering of his people and the destruction of His house, because God's pain never enters into the world. This could explain the teaching in the Midrash (Lament. Rabbah, Intro. 24.): "At the hour of the destruction of the Temple, God wept, saying, 'Oh! Woe unto Me, what have I done? I brought my *Shechinah* (Divine Presence) down to dwell below, for Israel's sake, and now I am retreating to My original position, to be the laughingstock of Gentiles, reviled among creatures.' At that moment the angel Metatron appeared, and falling upon his face he begged, 'Master of the Universe, allow me cry, and then You need not cry.' God replied, 'If you do not leave Me to cry now, I will go somewhere you have no permission to enter, and I will cry there, as it is written (Jeremiah 13:17): "For if you listen not, My soul will weep in *mistarim* (concealment)."'"

In the Midrash (*Tanna D'bai Eliyahu* Rabbah 17) we learn: "Why does God weep in private? Because it is unseemly for a king to cry in front of his subjects." If the only reason the angel Metatron asked leave to cry in God's stead was because it is unseemly for God to cry publicly, the angel could simply have left God's presence, leaving God to cry privately. But with what we have said above, it may be explained thus. What the angel meant is that it is a shame for his subjects that their king should have to cry at all. But since His pain is, as it were, infinite—pain greater than the world can discern—and consequently cannot enter the world, so the world does not even tremble at it, the angel made his proposal, saying, "Allow me to cry, and then You need not cry." Although angels are messengers of God, through whom God performs

His acts, this is why this angel wanted to be allowed to do God's weeping, as it were, to introduce it into the world, so that God, as it were, would not have to cry: because, no sooner would the world listen to the sound of God's crying, as it were then it would hear and explode! If but a single flash of God's pain, as it were, would enter the world, all His enemies would be scorched. At the Red Sea, the Holy Blessed One said to the ministering angels (Talmud, *Megillah* 10b), "My handiwork drowns in the sea, and you want to sing?" And now, when the Jewish people are drowning in blood, the world continues to exist? "Allow me to cry," said the angel, "and then You need not, because Your crying would no longer be necessary."

At the time of the destruction of the Temple God wanted to atone for the sins of the Jewish people, but it was not yet a time of salvation. So, He said to the angel, "I will go somewhere you have no permission to enter, and I will cry there." Now, the pain is so great, the world cannot contain it; it is so far beyond the world. God's pain and suffering have increased so greatly, they are beyond even the angel's ability to perceive it, even he cannot see God's pain. We learn in the Talmud (*Hagigah* 5b): "The Holy Blessed One has a place for weeping. It is called *Mistarim*. . . . Is there such a thing as weeping before God; has not R. Papa said, 'There is no grief in the presence of the Holy One, blessed be He'? There is no contradiction; *Mistarim* refers to inner chambers, while R. Papa is referring to outer chambers." The Maharsha (ibid.), in his commentary, teaches that the "inner chambers" refer to the *sephirah of Binah* (Understanding). It is understandable according to what was said earlier, because the *sephirah of Binah* is described in the book of the Zohar (Intro., 1a) as "open to inquiry but closed to comprehension." Because it is beyond the capacity of the mind to comprehend, God's pain is, as it were, hidden from the angel and from the rest of the world.

This, though, is the difference. We spoke last week about the Torah, which, before it was given on Sinai, was referred to as a "hidden treasure," not as a precious object in a treasure house. We explained that it was incomprehensible, hidden by its own greatness. At the time of the destruction of the Temple, even though God's pain was, as it were, hidden even from the angels and from the whole world, it was not incomprehensible due to its immensity. Note the word "chambers"—how the text uses the phrase "inner chambers," because everything exists here in this world, in the Torah. Since, as we explained last week, the Torah was given on the Sabbath because everything had to be compressed and constricted for the sake of the Jewish people, it means that through the Torah absolutely anything can be revealed in the world. This includes even what has been concealed within "chambers," hidden by the vessels containing it.

We learn in the Mishnah (*Ta'anith* 2:1): "What is the order of service for fast days? The ark, which houses the Torah scroll, is taken out into the open space of the city." In the holy Zohar (vol. III, 71a) we learn that in times of trouble, may the Merciful One protect us, the Torah scroll was even taken out of its ark. Besides the reason given in the Talmud, to publicize the fast, it may be hinting at what we have said above. Through the Torah we are capable of revealing even the most sublime and concealed Light, even that which is usually hidden from the world because it is so exalted. It can even reveal God's pain and His weeping, as it were, over the pain of the Jewish people. Then, as it is written (Psalms 94:4), "All who have wrought evil will crumble," and our salvation will be revealed swiftly, immediately, and forthwith.

It is possible that this is the meaning of the verse (Psalms 22:2) "My God, my God, why have You forsaken me, so far from me, my salvation, the words of my pleading?" Of course, we believe that You will save us, that You have not forsaken us completely, God forbid. But, in feeling "forsaken," we refer to our salvation that is so far away and the suffering that just goes on and on. The psalm continues, "You are holy; You dwell in the supplications of the Congregation of Israel."

We learn in the teachings of the holy Rav, R. Shneur Zalman of Liadi, of blessed memory, that *kadosh* (Holy), is an expression of separateness and distinction, as in (Deut. 22:9) "Do not plant different species in your vineyard . . . lest the yield of both the crops be *tukdash* (condemned)." Meanwhile, as Rashi explains on the verse (Genesis 38:21) "There was no *kedesha* (prostitute) here," *kedesha* means separated and distinguished for a single purpose.

This, then, is the meaning of God's *Kedusha* (Holiness): that He is separate and distinct from all worlds. Thus, the verse reads, "Why have You forsaken me . . . You who are holy [i.e., separate and distinct]?" But the truth is, "You dwell in the supplications of the Congregation of Israel." You are to be found in Torah and in the prayers of Jews, which are called "the supplications of the Congregation of Israel." But how can You bear the humiliation of the Torah and the pain of the Jewish people, who are being tortured only because they observe the Torah?

Therefore, it is incumbent upon us, the Jewish people, to grasp the Torah, wherein is the Holy Blessed One. By entering into the Torah, by learning it and observing its commandments, we are actually entering into God's presence. Then His weeping and His voice, as it were, which laments our suffering, will be revealed, and all evil, like smoke, will just disappear. It is true that in times of suffering it is very difficult to learn, and there are Jews who find it difficult to observe certain commandments. But the Jewish people have been skilled at suffering for ages, and have never slackened their observance of Torah and its commandments. Speaking generally, the Torah was not given to us on condition that when things go well for us, we will observe it, and when things are bad for us, God forbid, we will abandon it, God forbid. God is always our God, and we will always learn His Torah and observe His commandments.

Let us return to our previous discussion. Through the Torah that we learn and observe, God's voice, roaring over the destruction of the Temple and the Jewish people, will be revealed and salvation will come hurriedly and swiftly. For He, God, and His voice, which are in *mistarim*—concealment, at the level of "My soul shall cry in *mistarim*"—will be revealed through the Torah, because although the Torah was once a "hidden treasure," nonetheless it was revealed to the Jewish people. All the holiness of heaven can, likewise, be revealed through the Torah. Furthermore, Torah not only brings about a revelation of God and of His weeping, it also sweetens all the pain and judgments. At the simplest level, the sweetening of judgments is the reward for learning Torah, as is promised (Leviticus 26:3): "If you follow My laws and are careful to keep My commandments, I will provide you with rain at the right time. . . ."

Aside from that, as we learn in sacred literature, sin does not just draw *din* (judgment) down in retribution; sin and *din* are intrinsically connected. Similarly, the good brought about by observing Torah and *mitzvot* (commandments) is not just a reward; goodness is intrinsically and essentially a fact of Torah and *mitzvot*. For example, in the book *Sha'are Orah* (intro.), we learn that anyone who knows how to concentrate upon the meaning of his prayers has the keys to open all the gates of heaven in his hands. Since the flow and revelation happen through the letters and the names of God, when a person knows how to combine them, he is able to repair the conduit and restore the flow of abundance. Similarly, with Torah and *mitzvot*, good does not come only by way of a reward, but happens intrinsically. So it is with this. Aside from the rewards it brings with it, the Torah unifies all the voices into one voice, which is the voice of the Torah.

We learn in the Midrash that God's voice at the giving of the Torah went from one end of the world to the other. We also learn that the Jewish people heard God's voice coming from all directions—east, west, north, and south. Besides the literal explanation, this hints to us that we should not think the physical world too distant from and antithetical to the Torah, for this is not so. We can hear the Torah coming from everywhere in the world because the world was also created at the word of God. His word is the very essence of the world. It seems otherwise only because people utilize the world evilly, destroying thereby the world that was created with ten Divine statements. But he who uses the world to do good finds himself being assisted by the world in his Torah and in his worship.

In the Talmud (*Baba Kamma* 72b) we learn; R. Nachman said to Rava: "The reason why I did not tell you this in the morning was because I had not yet eaten beef." Through eating meat, his knowledge of Torah increased. The simple reason for this is, as everyone understands, the living soul dwells inside the body, while the human mind, which is the seat of the soul, reposes in the brain. When a person's brain is starved, it is difficult for him to acquire Torah, but when he eats as much as he needs, his mind is strengthened and gains the power to comprehend, and it becomes easier to increase his knowledge of Torah. Thus it seems that bread and meat can enable a person to hear the Torah. But at the time of the revelation of the Torah, the voice of Torah was heard from the whole world. Even now, a person can still hear the voice of Torah coming from everywhere in the whole world—not just from those parts of the world that merge with him and become a part of his body, as through eating and drinking, but also from the world that is external to himself.

The world was created at the word of God, and the Torah is the word of God. Truly, He, God, is One, and His word is One. The whole Torah was included in the Ten Commandments, and the Ten Commandments were uttered in one word, as is written in the Midrash (*Yalkut Shimoni* 250). Likewise, God's word at the creation of the world and God's word at the giving of the Torah are the same, one word. With *hishtalshelut*—the process of becoming physical in this world—the word of God separates into two elements, two manifestations of speech. For the world, God's word becomes the *mitzvot* (commandments) to be observed by mankind and commands to the created world to come into existence. At God's decree the sun shines by day and the moon at night, and so forth. For the Jewish people, God's word becomes the Torah and *mitzvot* that sustain them and the world.

When examined at a higher level, the Ten Commandments are one word and the ten statements of creation are one. On the first day, everything was already created, as Rashi explains (Genesis 1:1). When examined at a still higher level, the word of the ten statements and the word of the Ten Commandments are also one word, because He and His word are One. Just as He is One, so all His words are also One.

A person who is elevated and united with the single voice of God in the Torah can hear the voice of the Torah from everywhere in the world—from the twittering of the birds, from the lowing of cattle, and from the voices and cacophony of people. Out of all of these, he hears the voice of God in the Torah. At the revelation of the Torah, it is written (Deut. 5:18), ". . . They heard a great Voice that did not cease. . . ." Rashi (ibid.) says that the Voice giving the Torah never ceased and can always be heard. Because it goes on forever and can be heard from everything, thus all evil is elevated to good. All the evil speech and evil doctrines spoken by the enemies of Israel are transformed into the voice of the Torah, because they also exist in the world. Their vitality is drawn from the voice of God in the Torah, which has branched out into evil words. It is simply that the words of admonishment to be found in the Torah have become physical and manifest to the point where the enemies of Israel—these ones or those ones—can talk of physically beating and inflicting pain on a Jew, God forbid. When everything is unified with the Torah, they also are elevated to become the voice of Torah, and all evil is sweetened.

To return to the verse with which we opened this chapter, "And these are the judgments that you must set before them," Rashi (ibid.) explains that wherever the phrase "And these" is used in a sentence, it adds something to the previous subject, in that it forms a continuation of it. Here, the phrase "And these" adds these laws to the previous ones. Just as the previous ones, the Ten Commandments, were given at Sinai, so these too are from Sinai. With Torah, we can fix those words that are judgments, as is written (II Kings 25:6): "And they spoke judgments to him."

The judgments must be set before the people according to their needs, and not, God forbid, in opposition to them. For these judgments also are from Sinai, and they are also the voice of God. It is just that they have branched out into *din* (judgment), into words, and even into the evil deeds of the enemies of Israel. In the Midrash (*Tanchuma*, Exodus, *Ki Thissa* 3) we learn: "Moses said to God, 'But once I am dead, I will not be remembered.' God replied, 'I promise you: Just as you are standing here now, elevating them and teaching them the chapter of the *shekel*s, so every year as they read the chapter of *shekel*s before Me, it will be though you were standing right here elevating them.'" The Midrash explains that this is why the verse in the Torah does not say "count/raise their heads" but rather "You will count/raise their heads." (Exodus 30:12) When, God forbid, there is fear lest there be a plague due to the census, their heads can be lifted through reading the Torah, because everything may become Torah, and everything can be sweetened into good.

# Parshat Zachor—
# February 28, 1942

*"Remember what Amalek did to you on the road, on your way out of Egypt. They met you on the road, cutting off those stragglers at the rear, when you were tired and exhausted, and they did not fear God. Therefore, when God gives you peace from all the enemies surrounding you in the land that God your Lord gives you, to occupy as a heritage, you must obliterate the memory of Amalek from under the skies. You must not forget."* (Deut. 25:17)

Of course God needs to do now, what He must to fulfill His promise to "obliterate the memory of Amalek from beneath the skies." (Exodus 17:14) But the Torah applies everywhere and all the time, so how can we also, right now, fulfill our obligation to "obliterate the memory of Amalek"?

Examining the narrative of Israel's war with Amalek (Exodus 17:8), let us try to understand how Moses could have lowered his hands even for a moment, when this would mean, God forbid, victory for Amalek? What can it teach us? Similarly, what can we learn from the following talmudic interpretation (*Rosh Hashanah* 29b) of the biblical narrative "When the Jewish people look up toward heaven, and they enslave their hearts to their Father in heaven, they are victorious?" Surely, even when their eyes are not directed heavenward, people may still have their hearts bent upon their heavenly Father? Furthermore, the *Halachah* (Law) states that when praying, a person's eyes ought to be lowered (*Shulhan Aruch*, *Orach Chaim* 95:2).

Let us examine in some detail the verses we recite as part of the weekday morning liturgy. After donning *T'fillin* (phylacteries), we say, "Imbue me of Your wisdom, Exalted God, and inform me with Your understanding. With Your *chesed* (Loving-Kindness) do greatly with me, and with Your *gevurah* (Judgments) cut down my enemies. . . ." This is taken from a verse in Psalms (143:12), but the actual text of the psalm says, "With Your *chesed* cut down my enemies." Why did the authors of the liturgy choose to ignore the text, substituting the word "judgment" for the word "loving-kindness"? There may be a source elsewhere in Scripture containing the expression "With Your judgment cut down my enemies," but we do not recall such a verse and I have searched for it without success.

Perhaps the word *chesed* is used in the psalm because when God destroys the wicked enemies of the Jewish people, Jews sometimes suffer "collateral damage." As the Talmud says (*Bava Kama* 60a), "Once permission has been given and the destroyer is unleashed, it does not distinguish between the pious and the wicked." This is why Moses warned the Jews in Egypt about a plague intended to smite the Egyptian firstborn. Fearing the "collateral damage" mentioned above, he said (Exodus 12:22), "Let no one leave the door of his house until morning."

The Jewish people have often had to endure calamities whose sole purpose was the destruction of wicked Gentiles. At such times, Jews are imperiled through no fault of their own. We ourselves witnessed this, observing Jews suffering through the war preceding this one. Only afterwards were we able to see that all had been from heaven, in order to rid the world of the enemies of the Jewish people: the Russian czar and his wicked regime. Before the advent of that war, no one could have foreseen such consequences. Nevertheless, Jews who were caught up in the events suffered. This is why King David begs of God, "When You punish the wicked enemies of Israel, please do not use the attribute of *gevurah* (Judgment), lest, God forbid, Jews should also be caught up in the destruction. For even a single Jewish person is precious in Your eyes, O God." Then David prays, "With Your *Chesed* (Loving-Kindness) cut down my enemies," so that no Jew should have to suffer, God forbid.

The *Shevirath HaKelim* (Shattering of the Vessels), from which all judgment and punishment stems, was wrought through the attribute of *chesed*. We learn this from the teachings of R. Isaac Luria (*Etz Chayim*, Gate 11:6, infra iv.). There he explains why there was no shattering in the three supernal *sephirot*. The "Shattering of the Vessels" occurred only in the seven lower *sephirot*, because the supernal *sephirot* are all *Chesed*. The lower *sephirot* are within the realm of *gevurah*, so when they were inundated with a surfeit of Light from Above, itself a type of *Chesed*, they were incapable of containing it, and so they shattered.

According to our sages, of blessed memory, in the Talmud (*Sanhedrin* 95b), it was *Chesed* that wrought the downfall of Senacherib's army in the days of King Hezekiah. When Senacherib's soldiers came to make war against Israel, "they heard the song of the angels, and died." Their deaths were at the level of "With your *Chesed* destroy my enemies." The divine and infinite Light that is the song of angels, when revealed to the armies of Senacherib, was sufficient to kill them all without harming a single Jewish person. The people of Israel slept in their beds, while their enemies were destroyed.

This could possibly provide the explanation for the entire verse in Psalm 143:12. "And in Your loving-kindness cut down my enemies, and destroy all those who afflict my soul, for I am Your servant." King David means: "Please destroy my enemies, but only with the attribute of *Chesed* and not with the attribute of *gevurah*. Destroy all those who hate my soul." And why do they hate my soul? Precisely "because I am Your servant," and because I am Your servant, they do not just hate my physical body, they hate my soul even more. So when You destroy them with *gevurah*, they win anyway. First, they win with the death of those holy Jews who are caught up in the destruction, God forbid. And second, even those whom the Guardian of Israel protects from being killed will still be profoundly affected. In a situation such as this, everyone is bound to suffer heavily and everyone endures tremendous pain and bitter anguish, whether the agony is his own or that of all the Jewish people. When a person starts to think about it, his heart is ripped to shreds and his life is embittered and soured. Jews walk around broken in pieces, bent to the ground, and filled with the deepest despair and depression.

All of these emotions are diametrically opposed to the proper conditions for learning Torah, for prayer, or for the worship of God. God's worship requires strength and *simcha* (joy). This is especially true when the troubles carry on for a long time. For then, even someone who at first was able to brace himself and encourage others, also loses strength, becoming weary of comforting himself and others. Even if he tries to brace himself to console and bolster others, he cannot find the words. He has used and repeated them so often that anything he has had to say is by now old and stale. It no longer has any effect, on either the speaker or his audience.

Incidentally, it seems that this is also part of the test. Although a person needs to hope at every moment to be saved by God, he must not depend entirely upon his hope that the outcome will be immediate salvation. For if he puts all his trust in this hope and, God forbid, time passes and rescue still does not come, he suffers what is described in the verse (Proverbs 13:12) "Expectation long deferred makes the heart sick." This is especially so when people place all their faith in a prediction they were given or in some natural event, saying, "Ah! Now the salvation must happen." When rescue does not materialize, the person's spirit falls even further and he becomes even more broken. Therefore, concomitant with belief in immediate redemption, we must also repeat the words of Eli the High Priest: "He is *Elohim*—God—and will do what's best in His eyes." (I Samuel 3:18)

The entire world belongs to God. Even we belong not to ourselves but to God. We came to this world at the will of God, our existence is at God's discretion, and we will go to the higher world at His blessed desire. The definition of "good" is what He, blessed God, desires. We have no right to flail, God forbid, at His will. We need to pray and beg Him to treat us with *chasadim tovim* (good loving-kindness), the sort of goodness we can appreciate as *Chesed*, revealed kindness. But if, God forbid, He, blessed be He, does want to torture us, this also we must accept with love, hoping that He will not abandon us, but rescue us and draw us close to Him.

Consequently, if a person sustains himself only with his belief in imminent salvation, then his experience of agony and suffering remain unmitigated, and it is difficult for him to bear when, God forbid, salvation is delayed. This is not the case if together with the belief in salvation he also bows his head, saying, "He is God, and will do what's best in His eyes." This actually softens and absorbs the bitterest feelings, and lessens the sting of pain at what is happening. A person is then able to bear more, and his faith has more power to boost his spirits, even when, God forbid, salvation does not come as soon as he had hoped.

With this it is possible to understand the hint given in the story of Jacob the Patriarch: "All his sons and daughters tried to console him, but he refused to be comforted. 'I will go down to the grave mourning for my son,' he said. His father wept for him." (Genesis 37:35)

One might ask: Why is it written "all" his sons and daughters, and not just "his sons and daughters"? What was the purpose of specifying all his sons and all his daughters? What difference would it have made if it had simply said, "And his sons and daughters tried to console him?" Rashi (ibid.) quotes a number of interpretations. The first, giving the plain meaning of the text, explains that Jacob was predicting he would mourn for his son for the remainder of his life. But that itself begs the question: Why was Jacob predicting he would never be comforted? Didn't he accept that everything came from God? There is another question. Why does Rashi, interpreting the phrase "His father wept for him," explain it to mean that Isaac cried for Jacob? What was wrong with the more obvious interpretation that Jacob, refusing to be comforted, cried for Joseph?

With what we have said above, it might be explained thus: not that Jacob refused to be comforted, but that Jacob, believing Joseph was dead, said that he was prepared to be comforted only by the knowledge that it was all the will of God, and thus had to be. He was refusing to accept only the words of comfort offered by his children. "What use are your speeches?" he said. "Even if you succeed for the moment to beguile me into repose, long before I die the passage of time and Joseph's continued absence will have caused me to mourn for him again. By then, you will have repeated these words of comfort so often, they will be of no avail." This, then, is the meaning of "All his sons and daughters tried to console him." Even though all his children tried consoling him, and though they tried in various ways to comfort him, still Jacob said, "I will go down to the grave mourning for my son." It is better to take comfort only in this, that "He is Lord, and will do what's best in His eyes." All their words and all their consolation could never be enough to console him continuously throughout the remainder of his life. The verse is not telling us that Jacob refused to be comforted at all, but that he was simply refusing to be beguiled. Rashi's explanation that the phrase "His father wept for him," refers to Isaac's crying for Jacob means that in fact, Jacob himself was able to take comfort in the knowledge that what had happened was God's will, and had ceased weeping.

Let us return to our earlier thought, that King David prayed, "And in Your *Chesed* cut down my enemies." He asked for loving-kindness so that no Jew would be caught up in God's judgments upon the Gentiles. The verse continues, "and destroy all those who afflict my soul, for I am Your servant." King David was saying, "They hate my soul, afflicting it because I am Your servant. If, God forbid, the judgment against them also harms me, then my enemies will have succeeded. Even when a person is not damaged directly by the judgment, if he nevertheless has to endure great suffering, and is broken and depressed, he will not be able to worship You with strength, in which case his enemies will have already won."

To understand why after putting on *t'fillin* we say, "With Your *Chesed* do greatly with me; with Your *gevurah* cut down my enemies," we will need to study the liturgical meditation recited prior to donning *t'fillin*. In it we remind ourselves that God commanded us to put *t'fillin* upon the arm to recall God's "outstretched arm," so prominent in the Exodus from Egypt. The "outstretched arm" was a unique symbol of both "plague and healing," (Isaiah 19:22) for in Egypt, although the plagues punished Egyptians, they were healing for Israelites, as is well known. The execution of Judgment did not harm the Jewish people at all because the *Din* (Judgment) was for the benefit of Israel. And so *Din* [symbolized by the left hand] was wrapped inside *Chesed* [symbolized by the right hand] (Zohar, vol. II, 56b).

We can also understand why, if the *t'fillin* of the arm are in memory of the "outstretched arm," we put them not on the right hand, representing *Chesed*, but on the left hand, representing *gevurah*. Even though the verse (Exodus 15:6) of the song at the splitting of the Red Sea says, "Your right hand, O God, is awesome in power; Your right Hand, O God, crushes the foe," it resolves itself when we bear in mind that during the period of the Exodus from Egypt the left hand was wrapped inside the right.

By way of homily, a suggestion as to why the verse (Exodus 14:31) says, "Israel saw the great hand that God unleashed against Egypt." Perhaps it was called the "great hand" because it was not just a single hand; it actually consisted of the two hands, one wrapped inside the other.

We have learned the following in sacred literature. The Light of God is beyond *Din* (Judgment), and only enters the realms of *Din* when the Light undergoes a downwards *hishtalshelut* (process). Correspondingly, when Light is elevated and Jews ascend to higher worlds through an upwards *hishtalshelut*, *Din* becomes *Rachamim* (Mercy) for Israel. In the writings of his honor, his holiness, my father, the Rabbi of sacred, blessed memory, we learn the following: "Since the original thought of Creation contained the idea that *Din* would be beneficial for the Jewish people, wherever the 'original thought' is revealed we find that *Din* manifests as *Rachamim* toward Jewish people."

Let us try to understand a little more fully the concept of "original thought," wherein *Din* is actually *Chesed* for Israel, and learn how with our limited intelligence this understanding can be applied to our present, sorry state. To do this we need to understand Rashi's comment (Genesis 1:1), "In the beginning, the original thought was to create the world with the attribute of *Din*. Seeing, however, that it could not last, God preceded it with *Rachamim* and made it partners with *Din*."

Rashi's comment raises a host of questions. How do the principles of *Briyah* (Creation) and *Din* (Judgment) operate simultaneously? How could it have arisen in God's thought to Create with the attribute of Judgment, when it is taught in the Zohar in Elijah's opening speech (*Tikunim*, Intro. II) that *Din* is "short," intrinsically restrictive, i.e., it conceals Light and withholds revelation. How do they work together when the very essence of *Briyah* is revelatory?

Perhaps it can be explained using a human analogy. If a person does a small favor for someone, the attribute of *gevurah* (Judgment) need not be utilized; but if he wants to do something great—for example, to give a large sum of money—he may well have to overcome his own tendency to withhold. He may need to use the attribute of *gevurah* to awaken and reveal his *Chesed* before he can bring himself to do any great act of giving. What he actually does with the attribute of *gevurah* is use it against himself. It may be difficult for him to give away so a large sum of money, so he has to use the power of the attribute of *gevurah* to overwhelm his own resistance.

This, however, is the difference: When a person uses *gevurah* on himself, it can be used to reveal kindness. In fact, certain acts of great kindness cannot happen without using *gevurah* in this way. This is not the case when *gevurah* is being used against someone else, for then it is always punitive, involving *hester* (Concealment).

This is why, for God to create the worlds of *Tzimtzum* (Constriction) He had to use the attribute of *gevurah* against Himself, as it were, because God, blessed be He, is utterly above, beyond, and without boundaries or restriction. What is more, as is well known, the original *Tzimtzum* preceding Creation—that which produced the original brilliance—was, as it were, a constriction in the Light of the Infinite Self. That is why Rashi says: "In the beginning, the original thought was to create the world with the attribute of *Din*." For, as is well known, "God and His knowing are One," and so any reference to original thought is a reference to God's Self. It was in the very Self of God, then, that the original constriction occurred, at the beginning of Creation. For this to happen, God had, as it were, to overwhelm and restrict His Light. The *gevurah* God used, as it were, was upon Himself and not against anything else. It was only when the *Din*, constriction, and withholding began to permeate creation that God saw the world could not stand it, and so He introduced the attribute of *Rachamim*. Nevertheless, the attribute of *gevurah* that arose in the original thought was no less than the original revelation of *Chesed*.

The roots of the Jewish people are also in the "original thought," where even *Din* is *Chesed*. This is why when the "original thought" was revealed during the Exodus from Egypt there was "plague and healing" together—plague for Egyptians and healing for Israel. *Din* was at the level of "the great hand," as we said above. So, after putting on *t'fillin*, which is also in memory of "the great hand" that was revealed in Egypt, we say, "and with Your *gevurah* cut down my enemies." We are not afraid of any Jew being harmed, God forbid. On the contrary, there will be only goodness and kindness.

We can learn from this that if, God forbid, we see *Din* (Judgment), then the appropriate response is for us to use *gevurah* (Judgment) upon ourselves: because the origin of *gevurah* was the overcoming of the Self, and it was from this that *Chesed* was revealed. In the present situation it is obvious that *gevurah* has spread beyond the Self and is directed at others, and so we must try to apply this principle. When a Jew succeeds in overcoming himself, he elevates the *gevurah* to its original source, which is, as it were, the *gevurah* of God over Himself, and this reveals tremendous *Chesed* in this world as well, and it will address all of our physical needs.

In the past, when facing the challenge to conquer ourselves, we had to overcome our desires and evil inclination, as it says in the Mishnah (*Avoth* 4:1): "Who is a strong? He who conquers his desires." Now, however, we have another, additional challenge: to conquer our despair and bolster our broken spirit, to take strength in God. Doing so is very, very difficult, because the agony is unbearable, God will have mercy. But while so many Jews are being burned alive for God's name, when they are murdered and slaughtered only because they are Jews, then we must at least be able to withstand this test. With the very same selflessness that they display, we too must conquer ourselves and find strength in God.

This is hinted at in the verses with which we opened this chapter, "Remember what Amalek did to you on the road, on your way out of Egypt. They met you on the road, cutting off those stragglers at the rear. . . ." The Hebrew word *karcha*, "met you," also translates as "chilled you," meaning, "they were trying to degrade you." The Hebrew words *hanecheshalim acharecha*, "those stragglers at the rear" can also be translated as "those who had fallen into despair," or as one might say in Yiddish, *Di vas fallen unter sich*, because it was their inner spirit that had collapsed. It was these stragglers whom Amalek was able to attack and damage. Moses taught us that even in the midst of war, even when Amalek is dominant—when, according to all the evidence of our eyes, there is no hope of salvation—we must continue to look heavenwards, persisting in our belief in the supernatural ability of God to save us. Moses lowered his hands and allowed Amalek momentary victory in order to teach the Jewish people that even when Moses' hands are lowered and Amalek is winning, they must still turn their faces heavenwards and hope. Not just this, but even when salvation is not forthcoming we must enslave our hearts to our Father in heaven, accepting everything with love. Then, our acceptance arouses the transformation of *Din* into *Rachamim*, as we said above, fulfilling the promise to "obliterate the memory of Amalek from beneath the skies." (ibid.)

"The name of God is not whole, and the throne of God is not whole, until the seed of Amalek is exterminated." (Rashi Exodus 17:16, quoting Midrash *Tanchuma, Ki Taytzay* 11) Why stress the "seed" of Amalek? While it is true that the progenitor of the nation was named "Amalek," and so all his descendants are "the seed of Amalek," nevertheless as the nation itself is also called "Amalek" ("Amalek lives in the Negev," Numbers 13:29; see I Samuel 15:8, "Agag, King of Amalek"), why not simply say, "until Amalek is exterminated"? The implication is that we have to obliterate the seeds Amalek has planted, because otherwise, after Amalek himself is destroyed, the seeds that he planted will remain.

Who knows how long the Sabbath that today so many Jews, constrained by Amalek's torments, are forced to desecrate, God have mercy, will remain so desecrated? After this war is over, people will not be as afraid of doing work on the Sabbath as they once were. The precaution against eating forbidden foods will for many of them never again be as strictly observed as it was before Amalek forced the consumption of nonkosher foods upon them. Those young people who are forced to abandon the Torah now, who are enduring so much pain and suffering they do not even know if they are alive: Will they put their whole heads and bodies back into the study of Torah, after the destruction of Amalek?

Thus, "God's name is not whole, and the throne of God is not whole, until the seed of Amalek is exterminated." This refers to the seeds Amalek has sown in and among us. "Therefore," says God, "I will totally [obliteratingly] obliterate the memory of Amalek." (Exodus 17:14) The repetition of the Hebrew word for "obliterate" in the text emphasizes the speed with which this will be done, as Joseph explained to Pharaoh: "His dream was repeated twice to emphasize the swiftness of the impending fate." (Genesis 41:32)

Similarly, when God calls "Moses Moses" from the burning bush (Exodus 3:4), the repetition of Moses' name without a dividing comma is to emphasize the urgency. The Midrash (Exodus Rabbah 2:12) explains with a parable: "A man who is foundering beneath an unbearable weight calls to whomever is nearest, 'Hey! You you come quick, help me shed this load!'" When something is said twice, it means that it is to be done quickly, and so when God says, "I will totally [obliteratingly] obliterate the memory of Amalek," He meant "Quickly, so that he does not have the chance to leave too many seeds behind."

# *Purim*—March 3, 1942

*"Jacob's lily rejoiced and cheered,*
*seeing together*
    *Mordechai in royal blue revered.*
*You were forever their salvation,*
*and their hope*
*in every generation."* (A song from the Purim liturgy.)

    The principle joy of the Jews was at being rescued from annihilation, not at seeing Mordechai dressed in royal blue and regal attire. Why does the song speak first of the joy of seeing Mordechai dressed in royal blue before saying, "You were forever their salvation, and their hope in every generation"?

    Psalm 102 begins: "A prayer for the afflicted when he is wrapped, pouring his plaint before God . . ." The meaning is this. When a person suffers light pains, God forbid, he may be able to hide his pain within himself. Because it is not so great, he can therefore wrap himself around it, encompassing it within him. However, when the pain increases, reaching a point where he can no longer surround and contain it within himself, he may no longer be able to keep it hidden, and so is forced to reveal it in words, in crying, or with screams.

    Should the pains continue increasing, God forbid, the sufferer may reach the point where the pains surround *him*, and he becomes wrapped up in *them*, as in: "He encompasses me with bitterness and frustration." (Lament. 3:5) This is the meaning of Psalm 102, "A prayer for the afflicted . . ." When the afflicted one's whole being is wrapped in distress and pain, he is compelled to pour out his plaint before God. His whole self is poured out in prayer, as it says in Psalm 22:15: "God, my God, why have You forsaken me? . . . I am spilt like water. . . ."

The exact opposite occurs in the event of a reprieve from pain. When God rescues someone from a desperate plight, the person may contain his salvation. However, when the salvation is much greater than the person needs, then redemption encompasses the person, and he is enveloped by it. Thus in our liturgy (*Yotzer* for *Parshat HaChodesh*) we refer to the month of Nissan as the month "encompassed by salvation."

The reason is perhaps as follows: It is said of the *aurot* (lights) and the *sephirot* (emanations) that each comprises an *Aur P'nimi* (Inner Light) and an *Aur Makif* (Encircling Light). The Inner Light is the lesser of the two, and can be contained within the *keli* (vessel). The Encircling Light is much greater, and because the vessel cannot contain this light within it, the light escapes the vessel, encircling and wrapping itself around it.

All salvation flows to us from God through the *sephirot*, as is well known. So when God sends salvation to a person through the medium of a particular *sephirah*, the effect upon the person depends upon whether it was the Inner or the Encircling Light that was sent. If the salvation is at the level of the Inner Light of the *sephirah*—even if this Inner Light is much greater than the Encircling Light of the person receiving it—because it is Inner Light, the person receiving it can encompass it within himself. The salvation is just sufficient to meet the person's needs. Not so, however, when the salvation is from the Encircling Light of the *sephirah*. Then it is an all-enveloping salvation, wherein the person may be given much more than is necessary just to meet his needs.

Perhaps this explains the miracle of Chanukah, which happened in the Land of Israel at a time when the Temple still stood and was a salvation in line with our needs, but not greater than them. We were given victory over the enemies who beset us, but we did not go on to invade and conquer them in their lands. On Purim, however, we received a different kind of salvation. Even though we were in a foreign land and, as the Talmud says (*Megillah* 14a), "We are still in servitude to Ahasuerus," nevertheless we were given much more than simple reprieve from death or the meeting of our immediate needs. "Everything was turned upside down, that the Jews dominated their enemies," (Esther 9:1) and we killed tens of thousands of them.

We learn in the holy book *Pardes Rimonim* that it is impossible to blemish or damage the *Aur Makif* (Encircling Light). Therefore a person may use the toilet while wearing a *tallit katan* and *tzitzit*. The *k'lipoth* (husks) prevalent in a lavatory cannot attach themselves to these garments, because the *tallit katan* and *tzitzit* is a form of *Aur Makif* that surrounds and envelops.

The miracle of Chanukah came to us in the Land of Israel while the Temple still stood. We deserved salvation, and so it could come to us from the Inner Light, giving us no more than we required at that time. This was not so on Purim, when the Jews were in exile and, as it says in the Talmud, ". . . still in servitude to Ahasuerus." There, in Persian exile, we were not as deserving of salvation. As we know from the Midrash (Talmud, *Megillah* 12a), at that time there were well-founded accusations against the Jewish people, and there was, God forbid, a sentence of death already signed and sealed, hanging over them. In order to be saved at all, we needed to be completely surrounded and encompassed. This is why salvation had to come from the Encircling Light, which cannot be blemished or damaged by accusation or *k'lipoth*. And so, when salvation did come to us, it was much greater than was required to meet our immediate needs.

This is the meaning of "Jacob's lily rejoiced and cheered, seeing together Mordechai in royal blue revered." When the Jews saw that in the physical world Mordechai was dressed in the clothing of salvation, they understood that the redemption was coming to them from the Encircling Light. They rejoiced, because they understood that "You will be forever their salvation, and their hope in every generation." That is, it was an eternal salvation, and their hope would continue for all generations. Whether or not the generation was entirely worthy of redemption, the Purim story contained the promise of salvation for the entire Jewish people in every generation. Because the salvation on Purim was from the Encircling Light, which cannot be blemished or damaged by any accusation, it continues and can be drawn upon forever.

# *Parshat Parah*—March 7, 1941

*"God spoke to Moses and Aaron, saying, 'The following is the Torah's decree, commanded by God: Speak to the Children of Israel and have them bring you a completely red heifer, having no blemish, and which has never borne a yoke . . .'"* (Numbers 19:1–2)

Rashi (ibid.) explains: "The Torah tells us that this is a decree, because Satan and the Gentile world taunt the Jews, asking, 'What is this commandment, and what reason does it have?' That is why the term 'decree' is used to describe it. 'It is my decree, and you are forbidden to conceptualize it.'"

It may in fact be that these two issues—the purification ritual using the ashes of the red heifer, and the prohibition against pondering the meaning of the statute—are not separate issues; rather, the prohibition against questioning is actually part of the purification ritual.

R. Akiba says in the Mishnah (*Yoma* 8:9): "Just as the *mikveh* (pool of water) purges defilement, so does the Holy Blessed One purify Israel."

A *mikveh* can purify someone only if he immerses his whole body in it. If one limb remains outside the *mikveh*, the person will not be purged of his defilement. This is why we must abandon our selfhood and throw ourselves completely into God's dominion. Anyone imagining they have autonomous existence and independent consciousness is already, God forbid, without God.

We must completely abandon ourselves, affirming that we are null; that our consciousness is null; and that the Holy Blessed One, alone, exists. His sanctity and His will, alone, are all and everything. What God commands in the Torah, and how He governs the world, is "Good," and we have no right to conceptualize beyond that.

With this we can explain what Rashi means when he says, "Satan and the Gentile world taunt the Jews, saying, 'What is this commandment, and what reason does it have?'" For while it is possible that Satan tries to influence people's thoughts, where do we find the Gentile world taunting us over this particular commandment? They oppress and taunt us over the whole Torah in general, not specifically about the commandment of the red heifer.

It can be understood as follows: When receiving the Torah at Sinai, we said to God (Exodus 24:7), without pondering or questioning, "We will do and we will listen." Not so, the nations of the world; when they were offered the Torah they asked, "What is written in it?" One commandment did not appeal to this nation, while another did not appeal to some other nation (see *Sifrei Devarim*, *Piska* 343).

So, Satan taunts us "with" the nations of the world, saying, "You Jews did not ask 'What is this commandment, and what is the reason behind it? Does it suit us or not?' while the Gentile world did ask. Now see for yourselves who dominates whom, who oppresses whom." This is why it is written: "This is the decree of the Torah . . ."—because we are forbidden even to ponder upon this puzzle. We must persist in our belief that whatever God does is exactly what must be done. This is how the red heifer purifies and atones; because we enter into the *mikveh* with our whole being, abandoning ourselves to the Holy Blessed One.

In the Midrash (Numbers Rabbah 19:4) we learn: "When Moses our teacher ascended to heaven, he heard the voice of God expounding the Law of the Red Heifer, in the name of R. Eliezer: 'Eliezer says: The calf must be one year old, and the heifer two years old.' Moses asked God, 'May it be Your will, Lord of the Universe, that this Eliezer be of my descendants.' God granted Moses' request and confirmed it in the Torah: 'The name of the one was Eliezer . . .'(Exodus 18:4)."

Why did Moses, upon hearing God repeat this particular law in the name of R. Eliezer, beg God that R. Eliezer be his descendant? We know that God taught Moses the entire Oral Torah, mentioning the names of all the rabbis as He quoted their teachings, as is taught in the Talmud (*Hagigah* 15b): "The Holy Blessed One credits the Torah issuing from the mouths of all rabbis." Why then did Moses ask specifically that R. Eliezer, and not some other Rabbi, be his descendant?

Rashi (Numbers 27:16) quotes a Midrash (Numbers Rabbah 21:15): "Moses wanted to ask of God that his children inherit his greatness, but God told him that it could only go to Joshua." We need to understand why Moses wanted this favor of God. It certainly was not motivated by personal pride, God forbid. Similarly, we learn that King David, upon hearing from the prophet that his children would inherit his throne and sovereignty for all eternity, immediately began singing praises and giving thanks to God (II Samuel:7:18). What was the cause of King David's happiness?

With our limited understanding, it might be explained as follows: Perhaps Moses reckoned that if his children were to lead Israel on the right path of Torah and worship, in his footsteps, this might be of benefit to his soul in the other world. It would then be as if he himself were still leading the Jewish people, even after his death. The Talmud (*Shabbath* 88a) says: "When the Jewish People said, 'We will do and we will listen,' one hundred and twenty thousand angels came down with crowns for them. After worshipping the golden calf, the crowns were removed and given to Moses. Moses took them until some future time, when he will return them."

Let us understand: Does this mean, God forbid, that Moses will be less great in the future because he will no longer have possession of those crowns? The truth is that when Moses took the crowns, he did not snatch them for himself, God forbid. He took them only for safekeeping, so that they should not be returned to heaven, because if they had been returned to their source, then the Jews would not have been able to enjoy them at all. In his role as the leader of the Jewish people, Moses could pass some of the light provided by the crowns on to the Jews. When Moses studied Torah with the Jews, he removed the veil from his face (Exodus 34:34) so that the Jews could enjoy the beams of light that had come to him when he absorbed the light of all the crowns, as Rashi, on the Talmud (*Shabbath* 88a), explains. Even now we can still enjoy these beams of light, through the extension of Moses that reaches into every generation. This is what prepares us for the coming Redemption, when Moses will return the crowns to each of us.

Moses heard the voice of God teaching the Oral Torah, repeating a teaching in the name of R. Eliezer: "A one-year-old calf and a two-year-old heifer," as we said above. The Law of the Red Heifer is Torah at the level of "We will do and we will listen." We do not conceptualize or even ponder the meaning of this Torah. We do not question God's laws. We do not ask, "What is this commandment?" as did the Gentile world. Since Moses had been informed that his own children would not be leading the Jewish people into the future, he knew that the light of the myriads of crowns earned by the Jewish people for saying "We will do and we will listen" would not be restored to them through his children. Therefore he begged that at least R. Eliezer be one of his descendants, because it is in the name of R. Eliezer that we open the Oral Torah concerning the red heifer—which is Torah at the level of "We will do and we will listen." Through R. Eliezer, Moses is able to shed the light from the crowns upon all of Israel, bolstering our faith and giving us the strength to cast ourselves entirely upon God, to believe without even pondering, God forbid, that everything God decrees and does is perfectly good.

We learn from this that the underlying meaning of the Law of the Red Heifer is a return to the level of "We will do and we will listen."—not to question, God forbid; just to believe that since everything is from God, it is good. Faith such as this both purges and atones, and the faith itself advocates on behalf of the Jewish people, as though to say, "Look, the Gentile world, at the giving of the Torah, asked, 'What is written there?' But Jews, God forbid, never ever think of such a question."

Before we could merit receiving the Torah we had to say, "We will do and we will listen." Before the reading next Sabbath (Parshat HaChodesh) of the Chapter of the New Moon, containing the very first commandment the Jews received from God (Exodus 12:1) we need this week's reading of the Chapter of the Red Heifer, at the level of "We will do and we will listen." With this we draw upon ourselves the redemption from Egypt, and as in the days of our Exodus from Egypt, God will show us miracles and salvation (Michah 7:15) and all good things, immediately and forthwith. Amen.

# *Parshat HaChodesh*—
# March 14, 1942

*"This month shall be the head month to you. It shall be the first month of the year. Speak to the entire community of Israel, saying, 'On the tenth of this month, every man must take a lamb for each extended family, a lamb for each household. . . .'"* (Exodus 12:1–4)

Why were these two Commandments—the institution of the lunar calendar and the preparation of the Paschal lamb—commanded at the same time? According to R. Simeon b. Gamliel in the Talmud (*Pesachim* 6b), the juxtaposition of the two commandments was meant to teach us that there is an obligation to discuss the laws of Passover two weeks before the festival. However, as the *halachah* (law) is not decided in favor of R. Simeon's reading, why were the two commandments given together?

At the simplest level it might be argued as follows: It is well known that although God told Abraham that his descendants would be slaves in Egypt for four hundred years (Genesis 15:13), the Jewish people did not actually spend four hundred years in Egypt. Numerous reasons for this discrepancy have already been suggested, but apart from the explanations given by our holy sages, of blessed memory, another reason may be that before God said to Moses, "This month shall be the head month to you . . ." the Jewish people used a solar calendar. Before leaving Egypt, God told them, "This month shall be the head month to you . . ." meaning that henceforth, Jews must use the lunar calendar. Following this commandment, all calculations based on the old calendar were voided, and all calculations of year numbers were inapplicable. Once God decided that the reason for the Jews' sojourn in Egypt, originally scheduled to last four hundred years, had been fulfilled, there was no reason to delay the Exodus. This is the reason for the connection between the first commandment, "This month shall be the head month for you . . ." and the commandment relating to preparations for the Paschal lamb. God told the Jewish people, "Start counting lunar months and you will be able to leave Egypt immediately. Therefore, speak to the entire community of Israel, saying, "On the tenth of this month . . .'"

There is another possible explanation. The verse tells us that at the crossing of the Red Sea, "The Israelites saw the great power that God had unleashed against Egypt, and the people were in awe of God. They had faith in God and in His servant Moses." (Exodus 14:31) The question regarding this verse posed by the holy Zohar (vol. II, 53b) is well known. If the Israelites actually saw the hand of God, of what relevance was their faith?

In our situation, we may understand this to be hinting at the following: We have already said, quoting sacred literature, that a Jew's faith in God is not simply something to fill the gaps created by his lack of certainty. Faith is the soul's way of knowing and seeing. The soul of a Jew senses something of the illumination cast by the holiness and greatness of God, hence the knowledge and belief his faith affords is more reliable than anything provided by his rational mind. This ability of our soul to perceive is akin to prophecy, the only difference being that for the prophets the revelation was experienced as a visual image, a sensory event, while our soul-sight is an inner, faith-based knowing, a non-sensory certainty. The Jewish people have inherited this soul-sight from their ancestors, as we learn in the Talmud (*Pesachim* 66a): "Leave it to the Jews! If they are not actually prophets themselves, they are the children of prophets." We learn in the Midrash (Exodus Rabbah 3:15) that God told Moses, "They are believers, children of believers." It means that the faith of Jews is an inherited trait, passed down from their ancestors, because they are all the children of believers.

It seems that there are two types of faith in man. When he is feeling strong, and especially when he is joyful, faith is a sensation of certainty. But if a person is depressed, and especially if he is utterly broken, God forbid, it is possible for him to have faith that he does not experience at all. This is because faith is in some way a manifestation of prophecy, and a basic prerequisite of prophecy is profound *simcha* (Joy). Just because a person does not feel his faith, however, does not mean that he does not believe, God forbid. He is a believer even though at that particular moment he may be unable to access his faith.

If we look at a person's body, we see that those functions absolutely crucial to sustain life are not dependent upon the person's conscious will. He is not informed of the function of his digestive tract, nor does he know about the operation of his heart or his lungs. The only awareness he can have of the workings of his digestion or of his heart or lungs is an objective, detached sort of knowledge. He cannot be conscious of them in the way that he is aware of his self. He knows he has lungs, because he observes himself breathing, inhaling and exhaling, in the same way as he may be aware of another person's lungs, through hearing that person breathe. His heart impinges upon his consciousness only when its rate is accelerated. This tells us that consciousness of his organs and limbs is correlative to a person's ability to act upon them. He is conscious of his arms and his legs because they do not operate without his input. This is not true of the heart and the lungs, etc. Their function is absolutely essential to a person's survival, and so they cannot depend upon a person's consciousness but must continue to function whether the person wills them to or not; hence the person is unconscious of their operation.

Because the body clothes the soul, the same can be said of the soul. All the spiritual functions absolutely necessary to the continued survival of the soul in a person's body—like the innate love every Jew has for God and for his fellows, and like faith, as we have said above—are independent of a person's consciousness and out of his control. According to the Rav, R. Shneur Zalman of Liadi, of blessed memory, this is because these functions are innate, inherited traits, and are absolutely vital to the continued functioning of the soul. A person may perhaps become aware of his faith only when he consciously chooses to exercise it. When he practices loving he becomes aware of his innate love, and when he practices faith he becomes aware of his faith. It may be true that without the inherited faith and love that we already possess by virtue of our ancestry, we might not be able to practice or increase our love or faith. Nevertheless, because we make the conscious decision to practice love or faith, the added portion, the amount by which it increases, is our own. It becomes love that we are consciously aware of and it enables us to experience the sensation of certainty in our own faith.

Clear proof of this is in the Talmud (*Pesachim* 66a) quoted above: "Hillel was consulted regarding the laws of a Passover that falls on the Sabbath: 'What if a man forgot and did not bring a knife [to the Temple for his sacrifice] on the eve of the Sabbath?' 'I have heard this law,' Hillel answered, 'but have forgotten it. But leave it to the Jews! If they are not prophets themselves, they are the children of prophets!' On the morrow, [they saw] he whose Paschal offering was a lamb stuck the knife in its wool; he whose Paschal offering was a goat stuck it between its horns."

How is it that Hillel, himself a child of prophets, did not know the answer? With what we have said above it all becomes clear. The innate prophecy within us, inherited from our ancestors, governs those functions that are absolutely vital to the continued well being of the soul. However, this prophecy cannot be accessed at will unless it is voluntarily exercised. In the Talmud quoted above, it was only on the following day, when everyone was required to be in the Temple with a knife for the Paschal sacrifice, that the innate prophetic powers of the Jews were called into play. Had they been asked in advance to describe the proper procedure, they too, just like Hillel the sage, would have been unable to answer.

Incidentally, this explains the Talmud (*Baba Kamma* 9b): "A *mitzvah* (Commandment) requires that we expend extra effort in order to beautify it, because it is written, 'This is my God and I will glorify Him.' (Exodus 15:2) How much extra must we be prepared to spend? The beautification of a *mitzvah* demands as much as a third in excess of the norm."

Let us try to understand. How did our holy sages learn from the verse "This is my God and I will beautify Him," that the extra amount one must be prepared to spend for the beautification of a *mitzvah* is exactly one-third?

There are three partners in the creation of every person: God, and both parents. If this is so, then the sanctity a person has—his love, faith, and the desire to observe the *mitzvot*—can be divided equally among the three partners. As we have already mentioned, our vital functions are inherited from our ancestors. How are we related to our ancestors, but through our parents! Our fathers and mothers received their innate gifts from their parents, and this goes all the way back to the prophets and to the holy patriarchs and matriarchs of our people. This means that each person has within himself, inherited through his father and mother, an unconscious force endowing him with faith and the desire to love and worship.*

There is another part to these visionary gifts: the part that a person receives from the third partner in his creation, God. It is either bestowed as a gift when God arouses in him the desire to worship, or it can be attributed to the person himself when he arouses that part of himself that desires to cleave to God. As we have said above, we are unaware of those parts of ourselves that are absolutely vital to us. Therefore, in the two thirds inherited from our father and mother, which are vital to the functioning of our soul, we cannot really "beautify the commandment," as we have no access to it. We cannot do more than that which the commandment requires. Only that part that we ourselves have awoken, or that God has aroused in us from above, are we able to enhance and beautify. It is this part of himself that a

---

*Author's note: This is not to say that every man is constrained by his nature and lacks free will. At most the innate and inherited traits incline him towards love, faith, and worship. Man still retains the choice of ignoring his innate tendency, God forbid. This is similar to what Maimonides in his work *The Eight Chapters*, writes concerning man's nature and instincts.

person can know and through which he can become impassioned, in order to beautify and glorify his actions even more than is just necessary in fulfilling the requirements of a commandment.

This is hinted at in the verse "This is my God and I will beautify Him," meaning "I will beautify that part of me that is of God, by observing the commandments." Then the verse continues, ". . . the God of my father, and I will exalt Him," for in addition to the instinctive faith that I inherit from my parents, whose energy is manifest in the *mitzvah* I am about to perform, I also have something from God, to which I can add my own energy, above and beyond the two thirds given me by my parents. Thus, the Talmud tells us that only one third must be enhanced, because the two thirds inherited from our parents are beyond our control. Since it is only in the final third that free will exists, the commandment to enhance and beautify applies only to this final third.

Returning to the original issue, we Jewish people are always filled with love and fear of God, and our faith is steadfast. These traits are instinctive, as they are inherited from our ancestors. As an extreme example of this, we learn in the Talmud (*Berachoth* 63a): "A thief during his burglary calls upon the Merciful One." The urge to pray is so automatic that even when a person is about to break one of the Ten Commandments, his instinct forces him to call upon God, praying not be caught in the act of his transgression. It is just that without exercising or adding to it, a person remains unaware of his natural faith, love, or devotion. Only when he does something to increase his faith, love, or devotion do they become obvious to him, and he is able to feel them.

As well as the preparations we need to make within ourselves, through our own exertion in the areas of love, fear, faith, and other prerequisites for divine inspiration, we also need vigor and joy in order to merit added inspiration. In times of desperate affliction, God forbid, when we lack vigor and joy, we are in a state of spiritual lethargy and feebleness. It is not, God forbid, that we have no faith, and to insinuate as much would be grossly reprehensible. All Jews believe in God, but at times they feel neither their faith nor the certainty it reveals.

Our teacher Moses said to God, "But they will not believe me. . . . They will say, 'God did not appear to you.'" (Exodus 4:1) Do not think for a moment that Moses the faithful shepherd was speaking ill of the Jews. He was defending them. He was saying, "The Jews in Egypt are in so much pain that their faith is only feebly experienced." From this we can understand God's reply. God said, "And if they do not believe these two signs [the staff turning into a serpent, and the leprosy of Moses' hand], and still do not take you seriously, then you must take some water from the Nile and spill it on the ground. The water that you take from the Nile will turn into blood upon the ground." (Exodus 4:9)

It could be asked: If the first two signs were insufficient to convince them, what was so powerful about the third sign, the turning of water into blood, that would force the Jews to believe? That is, if disbelief was still possible after the first two signs, perhaps the third sign would fail as well.

We learn in the Midrash (Genesis Rabbah 48:9): "When Abraham the patriarch saw three angels who appeared to him as humans, he said to himself, 'If I see them paying respect to one another, I will know that they are respectable people.'"

This is an important rule, applicable to the world in general. If a person is devoid of humane, decent feelings, he will invariably assume that others are equally deficient, and that they therefore deserve no respect. A person who is himself decent and self-respecting, on the other hand, will always treat others with respect. The same is true of pious people. They tend to have the most faith in other pious people, because they recognize in others what they see in themselves. A wicked person has no faith in the righteous because he sees no virtue in himself and suspects everyone else of being equally corrupt.

Thus Moses was saying to God, "Of course the Jews have faith. They inherited it from their ancestors. But right now they are in so much pain they cannot feel their faith; it is buried too deep inside them. And because they cannot access their faith, even though their belief in God is a glowing ember of prophecy, inherited through the chain of ancestor prophets (as was said above), they have no faith in their own prophetic abilities. So, they will not believe that I have had this prophetic vision either." Moses said, "They will not listen to me. They will say, 'God has not appeared to you.'" This is why God gave Moses the signs. They were not just miracles with which Moses could convince the Jews that he had seen God; they were also intended to lift the spirits of the Jews, by showing them that God would save them. And so God said, "If they also do not believe these two signs, then you must take some water from the Nile and spill it on the ground. The water that you will take from the Nile will turn into blood on the ground." This last sign was greater than the first two because even though it was just a small splash of water on the ground that turned into blood, it foreshadowed the plague of blood that was to be visited upon the Egyptians. The Jews would soon see Moses begin to smite the Egyptians, and their spirits would start to lift, and some of their depression would fade away. They would be able to lay hold of a little joy, and their faith would increase. They would then also believe in the prophecy of Moses.

This is what is meant by the verse quoted above, "And the Jews saw the great power that God had unleashed in Egypt, and the people were in awe of God. They believed in God and in Moses His servant." (Exodus (14:31) At the time of their salvation, when they were feeling joy, the Jews felt all their own natural faith

A person whose intention is to fulfill the desire of God fears the sins of other Jews, and also fears the suffering of Jews, God forbid, because the Jewish people are (Deut. 9:26) "Your people and Your portion." They are the children of God, as it is written (Exodus 4:22): "So says God: 'Israel is My son, My firstborn.'" Such a person is in pain when, God forbid, the Jewish people suffer pain.

In the writings of my holy father, of blessed memory, we also learn, regarding self-sacrifice, that while a person who loves the king will give his life for the king, someone who loves the king even more powerfully will also give his life for the son of the king. Similarly, a person who really loves God powerfully is willing to give his life for Jews, and certainly suffers when he sees Jews in pain. This is true not just when they are in spiritual distress, but when they are in physical pain as well—when another Jew is in poor health, God forbid, or has nothing to eat or drink, nowhere to live, and nothing to wear, etc.

God said to Moses (Exodus 23:20–21), "I will send an angel before you to safeguard you on the way, and bring you to the place that I have prepared. Be careful in his presence and heed his voice. Do not rebel against him, since My name is in him. He will not bear your sins." Rashi (ibid.) explains: "'The angel will not bear your sins,' because angels belong to a class of beings who never sin, and are therefore unaccustomed to sin." In view of what was just said, we can propose another reason for the angel's lack of forbearance. It might be due to a misapprehension on the angel's part. Angels may be of the opinion that abandoning the body and ascending to a more spiritual world is a great boon. Therefore, "he will not bear your sins," because of his belief that it is preferable to die and be elevated beyond the physical. But He, God, reigns everywhere; His sanctity can also be found in all things physical. The truth is actually quite contrary to the angel's perception. Angels are unable to conceive of the fact that the Torah always combines with physical things and permeates them. This is why we learn in the Talmud (*Shabbath* 88b): "The angels said to God about the Torah: 'That hidden treasure, which was hoarded nine hundred and seventy-four generations before the world was created, You desire to give to flesh and blood?'"

It may be that this is hinted at in the verse (Numbers 20:15) "Our fathers migrated to Egypt, and we dwelt there a long time. The Egyptians mistreated both our fathers and us." Rashi (ibid.) explains: "From this verse it may deduced that the Patriarchs suffer in their graves when punishment meets the Jewish people." Why does Rashi specify that they suffer "in their graves," when the souls of holy persons dwell Above? Only their holy bodies are buried in graves, together with the spirit of their bones, those parts of the personality below the level of the mind, as is discussed in the works of R. Isaac Luria, of blessed memory. From what was said earlier it can be explained thus. If Rashi had said only that the Patriarchs feel pain when we are in pain, we might have understood it to mean that the souls of the holy ones suffer when souls of the Jewish people are in pain. But then I might not have inferred that the Patriarchs feel pain over the physical pain experienced by people, or over physical needs that are not met, for even when they were alive the holy ones had transcended their physical needs, and they rose even higher after their deaths, ascending beyond the scope of any physicality. Therefore, Rashi wrote that the Patriarchs suffer in their graves. The only things remaining in the grave are their holy bodies, which endure pain over the physical pain of Jews. Even though the holy ones are in heaven, they know that all the greatness they achieved in this world was achieved through their physical, holy bodies. We have a tradition that when we who are alive in the world study the teachings of those who are dead, their lips move in their graves. In the Garden of Eden and in the Academy of Heaven, their souls continue learning the Torah, but for their lips to continue mumbling Torah in the grave, it is necessary for Jews to inhabit corporeal bodies in this world. Therefore, their bodies in the grave also suffer over the physical pain of the Jewish people.

God said of the angel, "He will not bear your sins," because, "My name is in him." But God "carries sins and passes over transgressions," (Micah 7:18) so how can the reason why the angel "will not bear your sins" be "My name is in him"? The verse may be hinting, to us in our situation, at the following. It is well known that in the matter of the *sephirot* (Divine Apparel) there are two different categories: circles and lines. With circles, the larger encircles the smaller, extending outward as far as God, who encircles everything. The world we inhabit, the universe of *Assiya* (Action), is at the center of all circles. In the category of the straight line, however, the shortest line includes the longer, up to the level of the line stretching from infinity, which is at the very center. The line representing the universe of *Assiya* is the outermost garment, as is mentioned numerous times in the book *Etz Chayim*. It is also well known that the fundamental origin of *kelim* (vessels), receptacles of the Divine Light, is the void created by the absence of the Infinite Light that encircles everything, as is taught in the book *Etz Chayim* (1st gate, 2nd section; see notes supra. II).

We learn that the root of all things physical is in the circle that surrounds everything, where the greater always encircles the lesser, and He, God, surrounds everything, for, as the Midrash teaches (Genesis Rabbah 68:9), "He is the Place of the world." Everything exists within Him. The soul, however, is in the category of the straight line, in which the lesser clothes the greater, and the line stretching from Infinity is the innermost. This is what the verse is hinting at with "He will not bear your sins, for My name is in him." Unlike a human being, the angel does not have a body at a much lower level than his soul. The whole angel is a soul, which is in the category of the straight line that houses the Divine, as was said, "My name is in him."

The body of the angel surrounds the Infinite Light because the soul, and not the body, is the principle thing. Therefore, "He will not bear your sins," because, for the angel, the divesting of the body and the ascension of the soul are the only important factors.

Our teacher Moses prayed (Exodus 32:13–14), "Remember Your servants Abraham, Isaac, and Jacob . . . Remember the holy ones suffer in their graves," over the physical suffering of the Jewish people, as we said above. Thus Moses, by mentioning the Patriarchs, prayed that God grant the Jewish people life and physically rescue them. This is the meaning of "My prosperity is not Your charge. But for the holy ones who are in the earth and the heroes in whom all my longing dwells."—that is, not just for the sake of their souls in heaven but also for the bodies in the earth, because they suffer in the grave at the physical pain of the Jewish people. "Save us," we pray, "in these physical matters too," so that we may serve God from abundance. Amen, may it so be Your will.

# *Chukath*—June 27, 1942

*"It was there that Miriam died and was buried. There was no water for the people, so they assembled against Moses and Aaron."* (Numbers 20:1–3)

There was no water because the wellspring from which the Jews drew water throughout their forty years of journeying in the wilderness flowed only in Miriam's merit (see Rashi [ibid.] quoting Leviticus Rabbah 27:6).

Let us attempt to understand why it was in the merit of Miriam that the water flowed—not that we are presuming to understand what it was that she did in order to so exclusively merit the wellspring. We cannot comprehend Miriam's piety or that of the other people of her stature living at that time. We are merely trying to infer something from the story that is applicable to us.

With respect to the verse "It was there that Miriam died," Rashi (ibid.) explains: "Miriam also died with a kiss. The text however, does not tell us 'she died at the mouth of God,' as it does in describing the deaths of her siblings Moses and Aaron, because this was not the respectful way from on high." What is Rashi suggesting? At the simplest level, what could be disrespectful about saying that Miriam died at the mouth of God? Surely it is obvious that the kiss was not, God forbid, a physical kiss.

There is a well-known teaching, found in the writings of his honor, his holiness, my father, my teacher, of sacred, blessed memory. "A Jew needs to bear in mind that even when he believes he is having a spiritual awakening as a result of his own actions, it is still always God, infusing him with belief and desire from above, Who engenders his awakening from below." In other sacred writings this idea is requence of four universes. The first universe, that of *Atzilut* (Archetypes) precedes the universe of *Briyah* (Creation), because it was in the universe of Archetypes that the concept of Creation came into being as an archetype. In the universe of *Atzilut*, as the Zohar (vol. III, *Rayah Mehemnyah* 225a) says, "God and His life are one," implying that God is unknowable in that universe, and it is only through Creation that He is revealed. Thus the universes and the *sephirot*, which are a sort of revelation of God, operate mainly through birth, creativity, and renewal.

Throughout the biblical narrative of the creation of the world, the Torah refers to God as *Elohim* (Lord), and only afterwards, in the recapitulation on the sixth day, is it written (Genesis 2:4): "On the day that *YHVH-Elohim* created heaven and earth." This is the first mention of God by the four-lettered name *YHVH*.

Rashi (ibid.) explains: "In the beginning, there arose in the original thought to create the world with the attribute of *Din* (Judgment, *Elohim*). Seeing, however, that under those conditions the world could not endure, God (*YHVH*) preceded it with *Rachamim* (Mercy) and made it partners with *Din*."

We learn from this that "Creation" and "Existence" are two distinct concepts. The original thought was to create, even though Creation would not endure. As we learned above, the primary revelation of God is the revelation of His Light through Creation. This revelation can best be served through continuous creation, whereby this gives birth to that and that to the next, and so on. Subsequently, God added the attribute of Mercy so that individual man might also have permanence.

With this, we can answer the well-known question: How do we explain the idea that there was an Original thought that required subsequent emendation? Such inconsistency can only occur to a human who may at first see something one way, but later change his mind when viewing it from a different perspective. This, God forbid, cannot be said of God. With what we have said above, however, the paradox disappears. God created the world in this way in order to allow for the existence of freedom of choice.

If, in God's original intention, Creation and Existence were one and the same—with no other thought—then humans would have been neither permitted nor able to sin. Sin brings death into the world, which interrupts existence. (The only existence that remains once sin is introduced is the survival of the species as a whole through continuous procreation.) If Creation and Existence were identical and could not be sundered from one another, there would be no allowance for sin, because the end of Existence would also be the end of creation. This would either preclude the existence of humanity or otherwise negate the revelation of God, which was the whole purpose of Creation/Existence.

Therefore, in the Original Thought, it arose to create the world with the attribute of *Din* (Judgment). This was Creation distinct from Existence. In this design, the permanent existence of any individual person was precluded from the outset, and permanence was intended only in the sense of continuous creation. It was only afterwards that God added the attribute of *Rachamim* (Mercy), through which an individual might also attain some permanence, in that he might not die immediately after sinning. This allowed for freedom of choice, whereby a person can sin and interrupt his own existence, while still allowing for the existence of the species through the process of birth and continuous Creation as it arose in the Original Thought.

But Jews, "You are children of God, your Lord (of *YHVH*, your *Elohim*)." (Deut. 14:1) You are children of *YHVH-Elohim* because the strict *Din* of *Elohim*, which allows only for the existence of the species, is mitigated by *YHVH,* of infinite Mercy, allowing for the existence of the individual, as we have said above. "In the beginning, the Original Thought was to create the world with the attribute of *Din* (*Elohim*). Seeing, however, that it could not long exist, God associated Judgment with the attribute of *Rachamim* (*YHVH*)." Through this partnership, the individual was also given permanence.

Now, at this time, the permanence that we have and with which we relate to God is only the permanence of the human species. This is at the level of *Din* (*Elohim*) and is achieved only through our procreation. In the future, however, we will relate to God at the level of *Rachamim* (*YHVH*), and then there will also be permanence in the existence of the individual.

Our permanence now as a species is achieved only through our children—not solely through physically giving birth to children and parenting them, but also through the teaching of Torah to Jewish children, as the Talmud states clearly (*Sanhedrin* 19b): "Anyone who teaches Torah to the child of a friend is credited by the Torah as having given birth to that child." This is analogous to the birth we find regarding the *sephirot*, through which their holiness and light is revealed.

This is the greatness of children who learn Torah. In the Zohar (*Tikunim*) we learn that children learning Torah are the Face of God. In light of what has been said above, children learning Torah are the Face of God not only because of the Torah they are studying, but also because they are being taught Torah. A teacher of children is a type of creator, since he is considered to have given birth to them. The creativity of a teacher is similar to that which reveals the Light in the creation and birth of the *sephirot*.

As was said above, Creation is Revelation, since it is through Creation that God reveals Himself. Thus, not only are children a physical renewal because they are children, they are also revelations of the Torah, because through them fresh Torah is born, since teaching Torah is also a type of birth, as was said above. Because children are Creation, and Creation is the medium for the revelation of God, "Children learning Torah are the Face of God," through whom the *Shechinah* (Presence of God) is revealed, as was said above. Also, the only permanence that Jewish people can have in this world is through their children. This is why the original anti-Semite,

Pharaoh, conspired against Jewish children, proclaiming, "Every boy who is born must be cast into the Nile. . . ." (Exodus 1:22)

Again and again, in observing the pitiless behavior of the Jew-haters, there is always something unique in their savagery toward Jewish children—whether, God forbid, they want to kill them, or whether they are trying to force them to convert, as we know from all the decrees in the previous hundreds of years.

Oh, how it breaks our hearts to witness this now, too. For with all the unrelenting pitiless cruelty and murderous ferocity, too awesome to describe, being poured out upon the House of Israel, the savagery without compassion shown our small sons and daughters outweighs everything. Oh Woe! What has happened to us?

It is not just that they plot, God forbid, to exterminate all Jewish children, but when the children are killed, it also affects their parents and their grandparents who are already in the Garden of Eden. The only permanence that their parents and grandparents had in this world was through the existence of these children, as explained above, and when God forbid, they exterminate the children, the existence of the parents and grandparents, may the Merciful One protect us, is also negated. This is why we pray, in the High Holidays and fast days liturgy, "Our Father, our King, have mercy upon us, upon our children and our infants," because our children and our infants are not merely our offspring, they are our very selves.

Every Jew has faith that there exists nothing else but God. As is explained in sacred literature, when the Torah says, "There is none but Him" (Deut. 4:35), it does not simply mean that there is no god but God, it means that nothing exists but God. The universe and everything in it is the Light of God. Therefore, we must grasp everything in the world, not as something individual unto itself, but as a revelation of God's Light. Even our Jewish children must not be seen as just another category of persons, just our children; Jewish children, in addition to being the permanence and existence of the Jewish people, are Creation and Renewal, the revelation of God.

Likewise, the Torah that we teach to schoolchildren, or that one person teaches his friend, even if he merely gives him a word of caution or guidance, should not be seen as events unto themselves but as tremendous revelations of God. Each instance is a renewal and a birth, for each learning event is a creation and renewal. Before studying and learning, the person may not have been a Torah student or a principled person, and now, through learning, he has undergone a renewal and birth. As we said above, any person who teaches Torah to another is considered by the Torah to have given birth to him, and every birth and renewal is a revelation of God, because there is nothing else, and nothing else but God exists in the world.

It follows then, that everything a Jew does or says is actually an expression of his inner soul, which is always acting for and talking to God, because the soul knows that there is nothing but God. His soul knows that everything is Godly and every action or word is directed toward God. We ourselves may be unconscious of this because the physical body, besides blocking our awareness of the sanctity of our soul and its yearning for God, also blocks our awareness that whatever we are doing is actually for God. Though a person may think that he is acting or speaking on his own behalf, as for example when a Jew asks his friend for a favor, in reality his soul knows that his friend cannot grant the favor, that favors come from God. His soul knows that the one of whom the favor is being asked has merely been designated as the agent of God in the granting of this favor. So, while a person may think that he is begging a favor from another, his inner soul is begging God all the time for help, because God is omnipotent, He is the Merciful Father and He will show mercy and save us.

When we hear the shrieks of the tortured, old and young, screaming *Ratevet, Ratevet* ("Save us, save us"), we know that they are not crying out to us. Their souls are screaming, as all our souls scream out to God, "Merciful Father, *Rateveh Rateveh* (Help, help)," for as long as we have a breath of life within us.

The truth is, it is a marvel how the world exists after so much screaming. When the Ten Rabbis martyred by the Romans were suffering, the ministering angels cried out, "Is this Torah, and this its reward?" A voice from heaven responded, "If I hear one more cry I will turn the whole world back to water." Yet now, immaculate children, purest angels, together with the greatest, holy Jews, are murdered and butchered just because they are Jews, who are greater than any angels, filling the whole vast emptiness of the universe with their screaming, and the world does not turn back into water? It remains standing, steadfast, as though God is untouched by events, God forbid?

We learn in the Talmud (*Berachoth* 32b); R. Elazar said: "Since the day the Temple was destroyed, a wall of iron has separated the Jewish people from their Father in Heaven." Why is an iron wall necessary? Because prayers of the Jewish people can break down stone walls, and so an iron wall was erected. But against screams like these, how can even an iron wall remain standing? It is impossible to comprehend. For we are certainly not alone in our prayers. Our fathers and our mothers, all the prophets and prophetesses, all the righteous men and women are not at rest, they are not silent while we suffer. They are surely turning the whole Garden of Eden and all the holy palaces upside down, on account of our suffering. It is certain they take no consolation in saying, "Despite everything, one way or another the Jewish people will survive," because in order to save one individual Jew who is in danger, one is even obliged to desecrate the Sabbath. The souls of the righteous, when they were in this world, did not just pray for the whole congregation of Israel in general, they prayed for each private individual Jew. Certainly now they are all still praying and storming this same way on behalf of every Jew.

". . . My welfare is not Your charge. For the holy who are in the earth, for the heroes in whom all my longing dwells" (Psalms 16:2–3)

We may conclude from all that has been said so far that there is nothing else but God, and that everything is a revelation of God's Light. All birth and all creativity, and even what one person teaches another—nothing is isolated unto itself, because everything is a revelation of God. Even a simple choice, when a Jew chooses to do something good, this also comes from God because nothing else exists but Him. So what can a person do, in order that God endow him with desire and knowledge to choose "good"? Why does God give one person a greater abundance of desire and knowledge than he gives to another? At the very least a person needs to long for God, to want God to endow him with yearning and the knowledge that he needs in order to worship. He should also prepare himself to be capable of receiving the Light of holiness, yearning, and knowledge from Above.

While Miriam was alive, as we said above, she performed even those deeds that she was not obliged to perform. It was obvious that the force driving her to such exalted heights of piety was an exceptional yearning that gushed out from within her. With it she was able to inspire the whole Jewish people with a longing to yearn for God, and to prepare themselves properly to receive the supernal Light that our teacher Moses was to bring down for them. As we have quoted previously from sacred literature, our teacher Moses was equerry to the King. His function was to bring down the Light from Above. But once Miriam died, the Jewish people were no longer able to access this great yearning, and so they were no longer properly prepared to receive the Light that Moses brought down from Above.

Moses needed to lower himself to the level of the Jewish people, in order to raise them and arouse this yearning in them. How did Moses lower himself to their level? By sinning. He did what for him was counted a sin. They complained of the lack of water, whereupon Moses hit the rock twice, even though God had specifically said to him, "Speak to the rock." (Numbers 20:8)

We know from sacred literature that to fulfill any obligation on behalf of others, a person must first be included in the obligation himself (Mishnah, *Rosh Hashanah* 3:8). Thus, in order to help others, pious people sometimes have to sin, each according to his own level. One assumes that Moses immediately and straight away repented for his sin of disobedience in hitting the rock, so that we, the Children of Israel, could also participate in his longing for total forgiveness. The whole Jewish people were elevated thereby, and as a result, a copious flow of water was forthcoming, and there was abundance and great salvation.

# *Mattoth—July 11, 1942*

*"Moses spoke to the tribal heads of the Israelites, saying, 'This is the word that God commanded.'"* (Numbers 30:2)

The question is well known: Why does the chapter not open with a verse explaining that God spoke to Moses, as it does in most other places? Rashi (ibid.) explains that while other prophets announced their prophecy with the words "So says God," Moses' prophecy was superior in that he announced it with "This is the word." If this is so, then why, at the time of the exodus from Egypt, when there was such tremendous revelation, did Moses say (Exodus 11:4), "So says God," while here, at this juncture, he said, "This is the word"?

We learn in the Talmud (*Berachoth* 10a); R. Samuel b. Nahmani said in the name of R. Yochanan: "Every chapter of Psalms that was particularly cherished by David, he commenced with 'Happy' and concluded with 'Happy.' He began with 'Happy' as it is written, 'Happy is the man,' and concluded with 'Happy' as it is written, '. . . happy are all they that take refuge in Him.'" The Tosaphists (ibid.) ask: "Why does R. Samuel say 'Every chapter' when only one chapter in the entire Psalms begins and ends with 'Happy?' The very first Psalm begins, 'Happy is the man,' and the second Psalm ends, 'happy are all who take refuge in Him.'" [Psalms 1 and 2 are one long chapter.] The Tosaphists answer: "Perhaps the Talmud does not mean specifically "happy," but, more generally, whenever the closing lines resemble the opening lines, e.g., those Psalms beginning with 'A song of David' and ending with 'I sing,' or those beginning and ending with 'Hallelujah,' etc."

Let us attempt to learn something appropriate to our situation from this teaching. We need to understand why David ended every chapter that he cherished with the same expression as that with which he opened.

Perhaps it is thus. In the introduction to the holy Zohar (1a), we learn that the *sephirah* of *Binah* (Understanding) is sometimes called the world of *Miy*—Who, since it is open to inquiry but cannot ever be known, as it is so far beyond the boundaries of comprehensibility. The *sephirah* of *Malkhut* (Sovereignty) is sometimes called the world of *Mah*—What, because a person questions and inquires, trying to peer and penetrate from one level to the next, to the ultimate level where, upon his reaching it, we ask, "What do you know? What did you see?" For it is all is as mysterious as before he began searching. The *tikun* (Restoration) of the *sephirah* of *Malkhut* to its original perfection happens only when the unknowable quality of *Mah* is clearly revealed.

We learn in Talmud (*Hullin* 60b) on the verse (Genesis 1:16) "God made two great luminaries, the greater light and the lesser light" that the moon said to the Holy Blessed One, "Sovereign of the Universe! Is it possible for two kings to wear one crown?" God responded to the moon, "Go then and make yourself smaller." When the Moon—*Malkhuth* (Sovereignty) proposed equality with the five higher *sephirot* of *Ze'er* (Small Faces), she caused a blemish. She wanted to be known, and the response to the moon was "Go then and make yourself smaller," because fixing the blemish required the moon to negate her desires. She had to become unknowable, to be at the level of *Mah* (What). So it is with a person who, after all his worship and Torah study, realizes that he has not worshipped and has not grasped anything. As the holy Zohar said: "What do you know? What did you see? All is as mysterious as before." The person becomes a manifest revelation of *Koach Mah*, The Power of What. [The Hebrew word for wisdom is *chokhma*, and the four Hebrew letters that make up the word *chokhma*—*cheth*, *chaf*, *mem*, and *heh*—can be rearranged to read *Koach Mah,* which translates as The Power of What.] By realizing that he knows nothing, the person becomes a revelation of the *sephirah* of *Chokhma* (Wisdom), which is *Koach Mah*, The Power of What. This is a revelation of the supernal *Chokhma* within his lower *Chokhma*, as is well known. *Malkhut*, the World of *Mah* that we all inhabit, is also known as the lower *Chokhma*. Hence the well-known kabbalistic aphorism "Father establishes Daughter," *Chokhma* (Wisdom) = *Malkhut* (Sovereignty).

King David was the paradigm of *Malkhut*, and, as the Talmud tells us, whenever he cherished a particular psalm, he began and ended it with the same phrase. What it means is this: As we said earlier, the *tikun* (restoration) of the *sephirah* of *Malkhut* happens only when the unknowable quality of *Mah* is clearly revealed, and so whenever David set about perfecting the world, the beginning and the end of his psalms had to be the same. Above, at the beginning, are the two supernal *sephiroth, Chokhma* and *Binah*, Wisdom and Understanding, *Koach Mah* (The Power of What) and *Miy* (Who). Below, at the end, is the lower *sephirah* of *Malkhut* (Sovereignty), which is only perfected when *Mah* (What) is revealed. This is why David closed with the same phrase he used in the opening.

Another possibility could be this. We learn in the Talmud (*Pesachim* 117a): "Why do chapters sometimes begin, 'To David, a Psalm,' and sometimes, 'A Psalm of David'? 'To David, a Psalm' indicates that the Divine Presence rested upon him before he composed the psalm, while 'A Psalm of David' indicates that he began composing that particular psalm, and only later did the Divine Presence come to rest upon him." Obviously, when he composed a psalm before the Divine Presence come to rest upon him, the beginning of the psalm could not have been the same as the end, because it began without Divine Inspiration. When, however, the Divine Presence rested upon him from the outset, then the beginning was the same as the end. This is what was so cherished by David, for then the whole chapter was composed with Divine Inspiration. It rested upon him right from the beginning, and therefore he made the beginning and the end the same, for both beginning and end were equally infused with the spirit of prophecy. This was not the case with those psalms that opened without the Divine Presence—when the Divine Presence came to rest upon him only later. Then, the beginning and end were not the same quality and David did not give them endings that mirrored the beginnings.

If, as the Talmud states, whenever it is written "To David, a Psalm," the Divine Presence rested upon him before he began, then the beginning and the end of these chapters should always be the same—but this is not the case. An explanation may be as follows. Only when the Divine Presence came to rest upon him as a consequence of his own devotions, after he had "awakened it from below," did David make the psalm's opening and closing the same, for when this happened, he himself was the same at the beginning and the end. But when the Divine Presence rested upon him as a gift, without his prior devotions, as "an arousal from Above," then he himself was not in the same state at the end as he was in the beginning. To begin with, he was unprepared for Divine Inspiration, while by the end, he would have aroused himself to that level. Therefore, in those psalms he did not make the end the same as the beginning. In fact, a close reading of the text in the Talmud quoted above reveals a hint at this idea. The Talmud reads: "Every chapter that was particularly cherished by David." When the chapter was accomplished by David, and brought about by his devotion as an "awakening from below," he made the end the same as the beginning.

With this we can understand why the Talmud says that every chapter of Psalms particularly cherished by David commences with "Happy," etc. As the

Tosaphists say, this does not refer just to "Happy," but to whenever he opened and closed with similar phrases, as in "I sing" and "Hallelujah" and so forth. Why does the Talmud specify "Happy"? Informed by what was just said—that it depended on whether David brought the Divine Presence to rest upon him through an "awakening from below"—the answer may be as follows. David could only achieve an awakening from below when he was happy, not when he was in pain and grief, and so the Talmud says, "He commenced with 'Happy,'" because this—his happiness—enabled him to begin and end his psalm with the same expression.

It is impossible for someone to draw the Divine Presence down upon himself in times of pain and grief, may the Merciful One protect us. In the holy book *Etz HaChayim* by R. Chaim Vital, of blessed memory, we learn that one of the conditions of prophecy is that even in times of pain and suffering the prophet must be in a state of *simcha* (joy). Nonetheless, the prophet Elisha said (II Kings 3:15), "Bring me a minstrel," in order to bring himself to a state of *simcha*. This would seem to indicate that even though he was always in a state of joy, nevertheless his pain blemished the joy, destroyed the conditions for prophecy, and prevented the resting of the Divine Presence, especially as it was to be brought about with "an awakening from below."

This could also be one of the reasons why our sages, of blessed memory, say that the prophet Jeremiah wrote the Book of Lamentations before the actual destruction of the Temple, for the Book of Lamentations was dictated by Jeremiah and written by Baruch b. Neraiah (Jeremiah 36:4). We can understand this with what was said above. Lamentations was uttered with the spirit of prophecy, as the verse (Jeremiah 36:1) says: "Thus came the word of God to Jeremiah, saying, 'Take a scroll and write in it all the words that I have spoken to you.'" After the destruction of the Temple, Jeremiah's pain was so great that he would have been unable to utter Lamentations with any Divine Inspiration, because without at least some scrap of joy it is impossible to cry and lament with any spirit of prophecy. This is why he had to write the Book of Lamentations before the actual destruction of the Temple.

It is impossible to achieve prophecy in a state of depression. The Talmud (*Shabbath* 30b) says: "The Divine Presence rests upon a person only through *simcha*, and similarly in matters of *Halachah* (Law)." This also affects one's ability to take some homiletical teaching from the painful experience, for even this is impossible if a person is grief-stricken and spirit-crushed. There are even times when it is impossible for a person to force himself to say anything or to interpret events because of the immensity of the breakdown and decline, may the Merciful One protect us.

With what can he strengthen himself, at least a little, so long as salvation has not appeared? And with what can the spirit be elevated, even the tiniest bit, while crushed and broken like this? Firstly, with prayer and with faith that God,

Merciful Father, would never utterly reject His children. It cannot be possible, God forbid, that He would abandon us in such mortal danger as we are now facing for His blessed Name's sake. Surely, He will have mercy immediately, and rescue us in the blink of an eye—but with what shall we gather strength over those, the holy ones, who have already, God protect us, been murdered—relatives and loved ones, and other, unrelated Jews, many of whom touch us like our very own soul? And how will we encourage ourselves, at least somewhat, in face of the terrifying reports, old and new, that we hear, shattering our bones and dissolving our hearts? With the thought that we are not alone in our suffering; God, blessed be He, bears it with us, as it were, as it is written (Psalms 91:15): "I am with him, in distress." And not with just this thought, but with another, additional reflection: There is suffering we endure individually for our sins, or pangs of love that soften and purify us. In all of this, God merely suffers with us. But then there is suffering in which we merely suffer with Him, so to speak—suffering for the sanctification of God's name. In the liturgy for fast days and High Holy days, we say, "Our Father, our King, act for the sake of those who were murdered for Your Holy Name." They are murdered, as it were, for Him, and for the sanctification of His blessed name. In the Hosanna liturgy of the Sukkoth Festival we say, "Hosanna, save the one who bears Your burden, Hosanna," because Jews are carrying His burden. The chief suffering is really for God's sake, and because of Him we are ennobled and exalted by this sort of pain. With this, we may encourage ourselves, at least a little.

The liturgy reads: "Hosanna, save those who learn Your fear, Hosanna. Hosanna, save those who are slapped upon the cheek, Hosanna. Hosanna, save those who are given to beatings, Hosanna. Hosanna, save those who bear Your burden, Hosanna." By "those who learn Your fear" we mean those who learn the whole Torah, of which it is written (Exodus 20:16): ". . . and so that God's fear be upon your faces." How is it possible to learn when we are being "slapped upon the face" and "given over to beatings"? Because Israel knows that she "bears Your burden," and from this she is able to take some little encouragement.

How can we tell whether our suffering is due only to our sins, or whether it is in order to sanctify God's name? By observing whether our enemies simply torture us, or whether we only are being tortured as a consequence of their hatred for the Torah. Regarding the decree of Haman, the Talmud (*Megillah* 12a) asks: "What did the Jews in that generation do, to deserve extermination? It happened because they partook of the feast of that wicked one [King Ahasuerus]." Yet, regarding the decrees against the Jews by the Hellenes in the story of the miracle of Chanukah, the question "What did they do to deserve it?" is not asked by the Talmud, even though many thousands of Jews were murdered, almost the whole Land of Israel was conquered, and the Hellenes penetrated the holy Temple. This was because Haman's decree was only against Jews, and so people were sure it must be due to their sin that it had come about. The Talmud, therefore, asks, "Which particular sin warranted this decree?" This was not the case with the Hellenes. We say (Chanukah liturgy), "In the days of Matithyahu the High Priest . . . when the evil Hellenic kingdom rose up against Your people Israel to make them forget Your Torah and compel them to stray from the statutes of Your will." There is no need to ask what sin brought it about, because it was suffering for the sanctification of God's name, even though they may simultaneously have been cleansed of any sins they may have had.

"Return O God, until when?" (Psalms 90:13) Jews are giving their lives for the sanctification of God's name. "Please, O God!" He will have mercy on His people and on His children who are killed and tortured for His blessed sake.

"When the Ark went forth, Moses said, 'Arise, O God, and Your enemies will scatter and Your foes flee before You!'" (Numbers 10:35) The enemies of the Jewish people are the enemies of God, as Rashi (ibid.) explains. This is what our teacher Moses meant when speaking of the Ark and the stone tablets it contained. As we have said above, the proof that the pain being endured is for the sanctification of God's name, and that the enemies of the Jews are the enemies of God, is when they conspire against the Torah. And so Moses says, "Arise, O God, and Your enemies will scatter and Your foes flee before You!" Arise, O God!

We learn the following in the Midrash (Exodus Rabbah 23:1) concerning the verse (Exodus 15:1) "Then (*Oz*) Moses and the Israelites sang this song." "The verse (Psalms 93:2) says, 'Your throne has been fixed since *oz*—then; You, God, are eternal.' What it means is this: Your throne was not consolidated nor was it known in the world, until the Jewish people sang the 'Song of the Sea,' beginning with the word *oz*. A parable: What is the difference between a King and an Emperor? The first is depicted standing, while the other is always depicted seated." When God sits, lowering Himself, so to speak, in this world, there is a greater revelation than when He stands. Thus, "Your throne has been fixed since *oz*," because when the Jewish people were rescued and they sang the song, there was a revelation of God. Hence "Your throne has been fixed since *oz*." But when, God forbid, the Jewish people are in pain, then we say, as it were, "Arise, O God," for it is a desecration of God's name when He is not depicted sitting. Therefore, "Your enemies will scatter and Your foes flee before You!"

Let us return to what was said above. Every chapter that was "cherished by David," was cherished because it began with "an awakening from below," when he drew down upon himself the Divine Presence. So, when the Torah wants to hint to us that our teacher Moses was greater than other prophets, in that his prophecy began, "This is the word," it does not first say, "God spoke to Moses," even though

God actually did speak to Moses. The inference is that it was not with an "awakening from above" that God spoke, but solely with an "awakening from below." Moses brought the prophecy about with his own effort, and this is what makes the greatness of his prophecy—"This is the word"—so complete. This was not the case in Egypt, when Moses said, "So says God." Rashi (Exodus 11:4) explains: "While Moses was still standing before Pharaoh, this prophecy was spoken to him." In those circumstances, it must have been an "arousal from above." That is why, in that instance, the Torah does not mention the extra quality of his prophecy, "This is the word." It is mentioned only here, in our opening quote, where there was the "arousal from below"—from Moses himself.

# Shabbath Chazon—July 18, 1942

*"A vision, shown Isaiah son of Amoz, concerning Judah and Jerusalem, in the days of Uzziah, Ahaz and Hezekiah, kings of Judah."* (Isaiah 1:1)

Let us try to understand why this Sabbath is named for the *Haftorah*, the weekly reading from the Prophets. There are other Sabbaths of which the same is true: Shabbath Nachamu and Shabbath Shuva are also named after the *Haftorah* read on that day. One assumes there is a good reason why each of them is distinguished from the other Sabbaths of the year, which are not named after their *Haftorah* readings. If the reason for this Sabbath being called Chazon is because it occurs within the three straitened weeks separating 17 Tammuz and 9 Av, and because the *Haftorah* speaks of the destruction of the Temple, then the same ought to apply to the previous two Sabbaths. The *Haftorah*s of the two previous weeks, which also occur within the three straitened weeks, are taken from the prophecies of Jeremiah, who lived many years after Isaiah, and was there in Jerusalem at the time of the destruction. Yet those two Sabbaths are not named for their *Haftorah*s.

However, we learn in the Midrash (Cant. Rabbah 3:2): "There are ten expressions of prophecy, but which is the harshest of all? R. Eliezer said, 'A vision is the harshest,' as it is written (Isaiah 21:1), 'A cruel vision was told me.'" Of prophecy in general, we know nothing. But a simple explanation, reflecting our situation, may be as follows. We have previously spoken about how apparent it has become that hearing and speaking of pain and suffering is a very far cry from actually experiencing it. Hearing and speaking of it is vastly distant from having to witness it, let alone undergoing it, God forbid. When in Scripture and in the writings of our blessed sages we studied descriptions of the agony endured at the destruction of the Temple, we thought we had some notion of pain. At times we even cried while learning their teachings. But now, it is plain that hearing about sufferings is vastly different from seeing them, let alone enduring them, God forbid. They cannot be compared even minimally. Therefore, of the various levels of suffering revealed to the prophets—whether through a verbal prophecy, the Divine Voice heard from heaven, or other types of prophecy— the harshest level of all was when prophets were shown a "vision." The harshest of all prophecies was when they had to watch a realistic simulation of the pain and suffering. This is the meaning of "A cruel vision was told me."

This was what Ulla and other sages of the Talmud meant when they spoke of the birth pangs of the Messiah (*Sanhedrin* 98b); Ulla said: "Let the Messiah come; I will not see it." Even though they knew of the suffering that will accompany the birth pangs of the Messiah, they did not want to actually witness the Jewish people enduring such agony. According to what we have said above, their intention was not simply to spare themselves the discomfort of having to witness such pain. They were responding to other sages who had so much to say about the agony that precedes the birth of the Messiah. They were expanding upon the words of those other sages, saying, "As much as we know, and as much as we imagine we are describing the suffering in words, we are still far, far short of the truth. Knowing of pain and speaking of suffering are nothing like having to watch it. So, even though I know about them, I still do not want to see them. Let the Messiah come; I will not see it.

This is the meaning of God's words to Moses (Exodus 3:7), "I have truly seen the suffering of My people in Egypt . . . because I know his pain." At the simplest level, it might be asked: Why does God say, "I know," after already having said, "I have seen"? A father may know that his son will benefit greatly from surgery, and yet be unable to stand and watch the operation being performed upon him. As we said above, knowing about pain cannot be compared to actually watching it. And so, even though the surgery is for the son's good the father is unable to watch, for while it is happening, the father's knowledge is void; he cannot bear in mind the benefits of the operation because he is aware only of his son's pain. Like all the other exiles and sufferings, the exile in Egypt was for the benefit of the Jewish people. This is what God meant when He said, "I have truly seen the suffering of My people," meaning, "Because I have seen and watched, I know only their pain. I cannot bear in mind the benefits that will come of it. I know only the pain they feel. . . ." Therefore, God continued, "Now go. I am sending you to Pharaoh. Bring My people, the Israelites, out of Egypt."

Shabbath Chazon, the "vision" of Isaiah, is the harshest prophecy of all, because it is cruel to have to witness pain. Therefore, we read this *Haftorah* in the week in which Tisha B'Av—the 9th of Av—occurs, and the Sabbath is called by the name of the *Haftorah*, Shabbath Chazon, Sabbath of "Vision." In heaven, they are already seeing the pain of the Jewish people, as God says, "I know his pain"—and only his pain, not the benefit that will come of it. With this we can bring about the salvation, at the level of "Open Your eyes, and see." (Daniel 9:18) The *Haftorah* begins with a "vision," which is harsher than all other levels of prophecy, but it ends with salvation (Isaiah 1:27): "Zion will be redeemed with justice, and her captives with charity."

# General Index

Aaron   30, 32, 66, 98, 188–189, 268, 274, 277, 305, 322
Abraham   13, 30, 52, 77–78, 100, 132, 140, 150, 153, 157, 162, 164, 167, 225, 231–232, 233, 246–250, 263, 267, 309, 314, 321
Absalom   276
Acrostic   18, 104, 169, 183, 199, 229, 233
Action   60, 97, 191, 222, 247, 258
Adam and Eve   99, 167, 197, 222–224, 231, 233
Adulterers   234
Afterlife   161, 307, 318, 320
Aharon of Karlin, Rabbi   260, 283
Aharon Yechiel, Rabbi   255
Ahasuerus   41, 103, 105, 240, 303–304, 334
*Akeidah See* Binding of Isaac

Akiba, Rabbi   11, 67, 96, 139, 172, 174–175, 206, 263, 305, 377
  martyrdom of   11, 96, 174, 202, 205–206, 224, 248, 252, 263
Altar   41–42, 52, 54, 136, 163, 204, 232–235, 262–263
Altruism   122, 225
Amalek   38, 55–57, 265, 270, 293, 299–301
Analysis of purpose   116, 189
Ancestors   105–106, 160, 178–179, 214, 250, 310–314, 328
Angel   17, 19, 43, 52–74, 84, 99, 108, 109, 140, 151–153, 207–208, 245, 251, 259, 272–273, 280–281, 287–288, 314, 319, 320–321
  accusing   74, 78
  calling   52–53, 108

Angel (*continued*)
  empowering the  53, 307
  fixing the  9
  holy  20
  *Metatron*  287–288
  Michael  136, 163, 232–233
  ministering  33, 52, 53, 108, 136, 152, 222–223, 232–233, 280, 288, 328
  name  19, 319
  nullified  49, 272
  Sammael  19
  song of the  294
Anger  264
Anguish/Agony  21, 54, 57, 62, 93, 158, 295, 299
Animal sacrifice *See* Sacrifice
Animal soul  222
Anniversary *See* Yahrzeit
Anti-Semite
  the original  326–327
Anxiety  5, 54, 62, 192
Apathy  265
Apple  168, 256
Arab  227
Aramaic  52, 63, 212
Archetypes  153, 197, 222
Aristocrat  103
*Arizal*  90, 180, 197, 224, 234, 294, 319
Ark  48, 103, 107, 109, 153, 288–289, 335
Arms/Legs  194, 297, 311
Arrogance  264, 283–284
Asaf  138, 276
Ascension  232, 251
Ashes  262–266, 305
*Atbash*  61
Athaliah  194

Atonement  54, 58, 136–137, 152, 196, 205, 235, 257, 263, 288, 306, 308
Autonomous existence  305, 327
Av, Ninth of, (*Tish'a B'Av*)  337, 339
Awakening from below/above  332–336

Ba'al Shem Tov  234
Babylon  315
Babylonians  141
Backside  189, 255
Baking  280
Balaam  111
Balak  111
Banquet  237
Bar mitzvah  61
Barrel  41, 93, 98, 99, 105, 240
Baruch b. Neraiah  333
Baruch of Medzbusz, Rabbi  21
Beatings *See* Torture
Beauty  57, 193, 224, 243, 312
Beginning  90, 177
Beitar  251
Belief *See* Jewish faith
Beloved  211
Benjamin  26, 204
Bezalel b. Uri b. Chur  48, 223
Binding of Isaac  14, 52–54, 132, 136, 139, 140, 157, 235, 263
Birth
  and death  198, 324–326, 329
  pangs  196–198, 338
Bitterness/frustration  187, 189, 295, 296, 302
Blessing  15, 19, 24, 84–89, 98, 123, 194, 201, 210, 211, 243, 279, 285
  of the child  29

of God    28, 53, 69, 70, 89, 108,
    118, 135, 244, 264, 276,
    277, 278, 286
of Jacob    15, 154, 156, 241,
    243, 244
of Joseph    28, 323
Moses'    210
priestly    98, 101, 107
over the Torah    31
Blood    41, 52, 113, 141, 162, 163,
    222, 232, 233, 288, 313–314
B'nei Brak    67, 172
Book of Lamentations    333
Brain    290–291
Bricks    122, 277
Bride and groom    146, 239
Broken
    heart    36, 50, 53, 58, 64, 100,
        108, 124, 206, 209, 259,
        277, 284, 315, 326
    spirit    115, 133, 155, 160–161,
        209, 212–213, 250, 277, 284,
        295, 299, 300, 315, 333
Brother    151, 157, 245, 254
Burning bush    52, 54, 155, 157,
    300, 315
Burnt offering    87, 108, 136, 142,
    247, 263–264
Businessman    149, 206

Caleb    110, 165
Calendar, solar/lunar    309–310, 317
Calling    52, 53, 54, 64
Calumny    44, 129
Canaan    21, 30, 59, 82, 110, 159,
    161–165
Captives    118, 120, 150, 227
Catastrophe/calamity    27, 124,
    140, 200, 205

Cattle    291
Causality    24
Cause and effect    24, 197
Chambers, inner/outer    288, 315,
    316
Chanukah    249, 303–304, 334
Chaos    191, 192
Charity    53, 133, 158, 234, 339
Chasid    283–284
Children
    blessing the    28, 101, 323
    cruelty towards    327
    death of    201, 214
    giving birth to    197–198
    God's    229, 324
    of Israel    76, 174
    learning Torah from    183
    learning Torah like    185
    and parents    129, 178, 180,
        243, 279, 296
    patriarchs'    77, 93, 140, 157, 162
    of prophets    310
    teaching Torah to    69, 114–115,
        160, 170, 179, 272, 326
    we and our    125, 207
Chulda the prophetess    193
Circles and Lines    320
Clothes, Clothing    115, 122, 258,
    302, 304, 311
Clouds of Glory    35, 36, 246–247
Circumcision    64, 162, 163, 166, 212
Comma    54, 157, 301
Commandments
    and statutes    65, 221
    to acquire merits    64, 163, 166
    becoming the    90
    before the    62
    to be joyous    58, 123, 160
    to be steadfast    75

Commandments (*continued*)
  bring down divine light  61, 170
  to bring the red heifer  305, 307
  delight the heart  183, 229
  divinity of Torah  57
  to don *t'fillin*  297
  exemption from  60
  first  66, 274, 317
  to honor the dead body  74
  irrational  88, 306
  juxtaposition of  59, 162, 309
  to light the menorah  188
  longing to fulfill  209
  to love God  96, 174, 252
  not intended to provide enjoyment  26
  not to be a glory-seeker  132
  to obliterate Amalek  293, 300
  observance of  49, 67, 80, 93, 97, 100, 191, 210, 240, 243
  posthumous observance of  51
  practical  153, 222, 259, 291
  purpose of  82
  questioning the  175
  to redeem captives  246
  sanctify us  89
  from Sinai  92
  suffering is also a  160
  Ten  102, 131, 220, 269, 271
  transformative power of  99
  in the world of action  50, 247, 255, 289–290, 312, 323
Commerce  36, 93, 97, 115
Compassion  193–194, 229, 252, 327
Complaint  77, 78, 100, 164, 210
Complimentarity  205
Comprehension  176, 288, 331

Concealment (*Hester*)  74, 108, 185, 210, 232, 247, 250, 298, 315
Conceptualizing (*Hirhur*)  305, 307
Congregation of Israel  88, 107, 155, 156, 172–175, 194, 231, 233, 282, 289, 328
Consciousness  176, 213, 305, 310–311, 316, 328
Consolation  200–201, 296, 328
Constancy  157
Constriction (*Tzimtzum*)  298
Contention  73
Corruption  57, 65, 78, 99, 314
Cosmic reciprocity
  damage  29
  reciprocity  12, 53, 103, 133, 165, 166, 229, 230, 247
Counting  87, 90, 91, 155, 157
Courage  23, 210, 213, 237
Covenant  13, 30, 40, 41, 92, 204, 209
Creation  24–25, 59, 61, 79, 103–105, 108, 112, 144, 147, 177, 180, 182, 191, 197–198, 222–223, 228, 231, 260, 282, 290–291, 297–299, 324
  continuous  325–327
  purpose of  4, 5, 8, 34, 77, 97, 147, 149, 222
Creativity  223, 325, 326, 329
Credit  62, 105, 191, 231, 233
Crown  194, 307, 308
Cruelty  214, 327
Crying *See* Weeping
Culture  56–57, 253
Curse  82, 121, 122, 210, 211, 265
Czar of Russia  294

Daniel  269
Death  19, 115, 123, 138, 140, 155, 181–183, 193, 195–196, 198, 200, 206, 234, 263, 282, 295, 325
  Abraham's  13
  decomposition  198
  desire for  11, 96, 234–235, 319
  by disease  242
  in the future  19
  for God's Name  299
  by hanging  73, 154
  Martyr's  11, 96, 174, 202, 205, 234, 235, 248
  Miriam's  194–195, 322, 329
  Moses'  49, 322
  praying/studying for the dead  50
  Sarah's  13
  sentence of  304
  by shooting  242
  by starvation  242
  Ulla's  198, 338
Debate  110
Decadence  57, 65, 314
Decency  57, 314
Defilement  305
Deliberation  256
Delight  21, 183
Depression  265, 295, 314, 333
Desert  164, 194–195
Deserving  31, 60, 62, 64, 78, 166, 190, 304
Desire  108, 140, 165, 168, 204–206, 247, 255, 299, 329
Despair  197–198, 213, 295, 299

Destruction  26, 36, 50, 160, 186, 206, 208, 242, 250, 251, 276, 287–288
Diaspora  89
Digestion  311
*Din* (Judgment)  144–145, 180–181, 243, 247, 290, 292, 297–298, 299, 300, 325
  abundance  237, 290
  attributes  90, 144, 278
  compassion  194, 264, 267
  essence  90, 164
  face, *See* God's Face
  inspiration  281–282, 313, 331–332
  light  57, 60, 61, 144–146, 169–171, 181, 183, 198–199, 206, 210, 224, 229, 233, 247, 253, 282, 294, 295, 320
  Name, *See* God's Name
  promise  80
  spark  253, 283
  unification  49, 90, 169, 206
  will  48
Dreams  282
  Jacob's  17
  Joseph's  22
  Pharaoh's  301
Doorposts  53, 130, 234
Doubts  83, 115–116, 132, 160, 166, 242, 250–252, 296
Dove  264, 286
Drawing lots  234
Drinking  148–149
  drinking houses  147
Duress  41, 94, 98–99, 105
Dust and ashes  234

# General Index

Earth   191–192, 264–265, 318
Eating and drinking   93, 97, 112, 115, 149, 234, 243, 291
Education   115
Egypt   27–30, 33, 54–56, 67–70, 76, 78, 79, 81, 93, 104, 156, 160, 161, 163, 165, 170–172, 179, 186–187, 220, 228, 250, 257, 261–262, 267–268, 274–278, 280, 284, 293–294, 297, 299, 308–309, 310, 313, 31–, 319, 330, 336, 338
Egyptians   24–25, 33, 77–78, 100, 123, 170, 186, 190, 195, 209, 214, 297, 314, 317
Eighth Day festival   145–146, 237–238
Elazar b. Ararch, Rabbi   84
Elazar b. Azaria, Rabbi   67, 172
Elazar b. R. Simeon b. Yochai, Rabbi   159, 315
Eli the High Priest   295
Eliezer b. Hyrcanus, Rabbi   67, 84, 114–115, 172, 306–307
Eliezer b. R. Jose Hagllili, Rabbi   277
Elijah the prophet   36, 44, 50, 194, 199, 229
Elimelech of Grodzysk, Rabbi   162, 318
Elimelech of Lyzhensk, Rabbi   84
Elimelech, Rabbi   138, 231
Elisha b. Abuya   148
Elisha the prophet   80, 181, 276, 333
Ellul   211, 219
Emorites   82
Endurance   151, 199
Enjoyment   26, 147

Ephraim   323
Esau   19, 154–158, 180, 219, 241, 244245, 248
Essential self   276, 283
Esteem   269
Esther   22, 103
Eternity   169, 241–243
Ethics   57
Evil   56, 109, 115, 121, 132–133, 151, 161, 201, 276, 284, 289, 291
Evil Inclination   8, 57, 60, 148, 193, 212, 264–265, 299
Exile   9, 16, 23, 27, 31, 57, 77, 78, 108, 150, 160–161, 232, 236, 250, 264, 284, 286, 304, 315, 338
Existence   325–326
Ex nihilo   105
Exodus   34, 40, 62, 67, 79, 81, 104, 160, 172, 179, 262, 267, 297, 299, 308, 310, 330
Extermination   334
Eyes   239, 293, 300
Ezekiel the prophet   38, 277
Ezra   167–169

Face   182, 189, 208, 255, 261, 279, 307, 334
Faith *See* Jewish faith
Family   59, 62, 156, 166, 175, 309
Fasting   3, 46
  as praise of God   5
  as sacrifice   52, 233
  on Yom Kippur   58
  and daughter   331
  and son   266–276, 286, 338
Fat   154, 162, 166, 175

Fear
  arousing our   4, 313, 334
  as revelation   269
  of erring/sin   4, 85, 258–261, 318
  exalted   85, 258–261
  of God   3, 18, 34, 54, 63, 108, 201, 255, 260–261, 269, 293, 310
  of heaven   63–64, 84–85, 190–191
  of pain/punishment   4, 84–85, 98–99, 116, 133–134, 157, 190–192, 240, 245, 258–259, 269, 281
Fearing (*Gevurah*)   90, 139, 155, 194, 259, 294–295, 297, 299
Feminine flow (*Mayin Nukvin*)   169, 232
Festival/Pilgrimage   46, 89, 91, 138, 143, 219, 221, 235–238, 263, 264, 266, 274, 309, 334
Field   23, 92
Fiftieth gate   160
Fire   35, 45, 54, 98, 102, 186, 240, 264
First day   291
Fish   143, 46
Fixing (*Tikun*)   220, 331
Flesh and blood   182, 206, 214, 222, 252, 263, 280–281, 319
Flogging   185
Food   112, 115, 141, 160, 225, 234
Fool   70, 132
Forbidden
  foods   300
  sex   65, 151
Forgiveness   3, 4, 43, 54, 173, 329

Formation (*Yetzirah*)   222, 281
Four
  elements   264–265
  sons   69, 172, 175
  species   46
Free will/Choice   34, 247, 312–313, 325
Friends   234, 270
Fruit   173, 198, 271
Future   207, 209, 238, 275, 278

Garden of Eden   50–51, 68, 265, 320, 327–328
Gates   234, 269, 290
Gehenna   68, 148, 251
Gematria   20, 45, 183, 229
Genesis   40, 56, 59, 62, 323
Gentiles *See* World, nations of the.
Gentleness   30, 275, 277
Germ   173–174
Germination   198
Giddal, Rabbi   167–168
Gifts   109, 136, 279, 280–281, 311, 312, 332
Ginnai River   226, 228
God
  abandoning oneself to   97, 136, 255, 305–307
  of Abraham   18, 140, 250
  acknowledging   6, 76, 90, 181, 232
  Almighty   24, 57
  alone exists   305, 327
  approaching   256, 316
  assisting   135, 157–158, 168, 249
  awareness of 6, 34, 90
  awe of   4, 76, 68, 85
  begging   328

God (*continued*)
  blessing  28, 53, 69–70, 89, 181, 243, 276–278, 286
  Body/Self/Soul of  18, 89, 104, 153, 183, 287, 299
  bonding with  18, 60–64, 65, 89–93, 104, 124, 152, 160, 174, 191, 247, 250, 255
  bringing into this world  152, 153, 168, 232–233, 247
  calumny against  44
  changing  152, 153, 277
  children are the revelation of  327
  closeness to  4, 60, 64–65, 75, 89, 90, 93, 104, 118, 124, 152, 165, 168, 191, 247, 250–251, 258, 296, 316
  clothed in Torah  272
  champion of the Jews  165, 166, 249, 253
  cleaving unto  255–258, 312
  creating and destroying worlds  224
  doing away with  211, 249
  desecrating the Name of  335
  dying for  334
  fear of  3, 18, 34, 54, 63, 64, 68, 84, 85, 102, 108, 201, 255, 269, 293, 310
  the forgiving  3, 72, 74, 163
  and His Court of Law  35, 130
  and His knowing are One  299
  husband of the human soul  269
  imminence of  5, 73, 75, 90, 104, 110, 118–119, 168
  of Isaac  140, 250
  of Israel  167–168
  of Jacob  140, 221, 250
  knowledge of  34, 90, 108, 111, 119
  laughing stock of gentiles  287
  love of  18, 85, 90, 99, 174, 235, 248, 252, 255, 269, 315, 316, 318
  man's resemblance to  74, 152
  Merciful  180–181, 200, 328, 334
  mind of  247, 251
  needing Pharaoh  170
  Omnipotent  328
  Omnipresent  38, 69, 72, 320
  Omniscient  284
  our  168–169, 250, 316–317
    Father  160, 163, 293, 300, 328, 334
    hope  302
    King  180, 334
    Redeemer  180–181
  of our fathers  70, 78, 100, 250
  proximity to  5, 64, 75, 160, 165, 168
  questioning  251–252
  rebelling against  259, 296
  receiving from man  54, 90, 168, 277, 278
  revelation of  5, 6, 24, 49, 50, 72, 77, 90, 104, 108, 118, 119, 144, 145, 168, 183, 187, 198, 210, 211, 220, 229, 232, 233, 247, 270, 327, 328
  roaring like a lion  287, 290
  sanctifying  334
  seeing  49, 72
  trusting  185
  war against  253
  Who gives Himself  211

Who says, "Enough" 24, 224, 235
Who teaches Torah 89, 102, 103, 118–119, 136–137, 184–185, 291, 306, 316, 326
yoke of 5, 6, 93
your 118–119, 120, 200, 316
and Israel are One 74, 89, 104, 146, 152–153, 168–169, 232, 233
and Torah are One 89, 104, 152, 291
God's
abode 315
abundance 15, 181
affection 52
anger 28, 68, 111–113, 140, 226, 278
arm 74, 154, 155, 171, 287
attributes 24, 28, 139, 144, 152–153, 155, 278
bearing iniquity 44, 73
begrudging 21
blessing 19, 98, 123, 241–242, 279, 285
bread 136
burden 54, 157–158, 334
calling to man 53, 54, 64, 96, 119, 154, 157, 158, 255, 277–278, 300
coercion of the Jews 41, 94, 98–99, 105
compassion 194, 264, 267
congregation 73, 89
cooing like a dove 264, 286–287
constriction of Himself 299
coronation 221, 223

curse 74
decree 304, 335
desire to be known 18, 50, 92, 104, 108, 118–119, 247
dwelling in the human heart 50, 160
ears 124
enemies 288, 335
eternity/infinity 242, 287
eyes 239, 240, 295–296
face 98, 108, 210–211, 232, 255, 315, 326
favoritism 44, 98
giving 15, 18, 99, 104, 168, 241
birth 198
glory 52, 72, 74, 77, 131–132, 155, 163, 168–169, 186, 189, 220–233
goodness 72, 83, 99, 112–113, 132, 305
head 154–155
hands 72–75, 79, 81, 85, 112, 171, 200, 201–202, 210, 297, 299, 310
healing of the sick 24, 241–242
heart 74
hiddenness 49, 106, 108, 118, 177, 210–211, 220, 232, 287, 290
hidden treasure 280, 319
holiness 84, 86, 108, 198, 202, 250, 289, 306, 310
howling 287
instrument 122
joy 34
Judgments (*Gevurah*) 24, 28, 31, 35–36, 93, 104, 122, 136, 137, 142, 144, 210, 219, 221, 294, 297

God's (*continued*)
  knowing   164, 251, 284, 299, 338
  lament   264, 286–289, 316
  light   189, 233, 250, 270, 281–282, 295–299, 310, 320, 324–329
  love of Jewish People   50, 104, 106, 180, 113, 163, 202, 240, 250, 252, 266
  loving-kindness (*Chesed*)   139, 194, 204, 209, 210, 225, 247–248, 255, 294, 297, 323
  luck   50
  mercy (*Rachamim*)   24, 28, 108, 131, 144–146, 152, 155, 161, 201, 206, 209, 215, 235, 238, 249, 253, 260, 278, 334
  misleading the Jewish People   44
  mistreatment of the Jews   31, 122, 136, 145, 164, 277
  mockery of Egypt   33, 170
  mouth   194, 196, 199, 322, 323
  Name of *See* God's Names
  needs   249
  observance of the Torah   10, 16, 102, 136, 227, 293
  Oneness   236, 248, 291, 299, 317
  pain   54, 154, 158, 163, 211, 264, 286, 287, 289, 315, 316, 333, 334
  palms   202
  patience   73, 163, 164, 165
  pleasure   34, 90, 131, 132, 151, 220, 237
  presence   289

  promise/oath   17, 77, 80, 81, 100, 157, 162, 204, 209, 267
  punishment of the Jews   77, 83, 93, 113, 129–130, 136
  purpose   116
  regrets   10, 36, 50, 154, 264, 286
  rejoicing in destruction   33
  repentance   10, 120, 134, 203
  righteous acts   111, 132, 133
  shadow   48
  self knowledge   284
  sovereignty   5, 8, 24, 129, 130, 131, 135, 168, 178, 194, 220–222, 232–233, 306
  spoken word   18, 77, 80, 102, 103, 112, 131, 192, 219–220, 290–291
  suffering   287, 289, 333–334
  thoughts   24, 108, 144, 149, 247–248, 263, 298, 325, 326
  throne   49, 55, 132, 220, 281, 300, 335
  treasure   64
  treasure house   280, 288
  triumph   33, 104, 249
  truth   210, 211, 219, 220, 241, 243
  understanding   251, 294
  voice   103, 104, 154, 157, 158, 264, 266, 286, 287, 290, 306
  ways   161
  weeping/crying   264, 266, 286, 287, 289, 315, 316
  will   48, 132, 156, 166, 227, 245, 247, 296, 306

wisdom 282, 294
withholding 194, 298
written word 18, 74, 102, 104, 192
yearning 34, 54, 63, 93–97, 154, 237
God's Names 11, 18, 72, 74, 85, 98, 101, 108, 113, 165, 168, 181–183, 199, 229, 231, 249, 250, 290, 299, 300
*Adon* 167
*Adonoy* 167
*Adonai* 20, 118, 142, 144, 221–225, 231, 232, 233
*Adonai-Tz'vaoth* 167
All Merciful 180, 181, 200, 201, 267
Almighty 24, 57, 164
*Creator* 210
*Ehyeh* 56, 261
*El* 24, 164, 180, 181, 187, 255
*El Shaddai* 24, 30, 164, 262, 267
*Elohim* 30, 31, 32, 86, 200, 201, 220, 243, 262, 267, 295, 325, 326
*HaMakom* 38
ineffable 167, 168
I Will Be Whom I Will Be 56, 261
Judge 200, 201, 267
Lord of Hosts 52, 54, 167, 207, 208
Most High 111
Omnipotent 114, 262, 267
Omnipresent 38, 320
*Shaddai* 24, 85, 164
*Yah* 221–224

*YHVH* 20, 21, 24, 30, 31, 32, 56, 61, 86, 144, 155, 164, 165, 167, 200, 201, 220–225, 262, 266, 267, 325, 326
*YHVH-Elohim* 25, 325–326
Gold 77, 78, 100, 256
Golden calf 43, 152, 195, 307
Good
 deeds/Righteousness 159, 249, 250, 290, 296, 306, 329
 tidings 213
Grace 31, 98, 260
Grain 154, 157
Grapes 168
Graves 195, 242, 273, 296, 319, 320, 321
Greatness 63, 284, 306
Grief 200, 201, 209, 259, 296, 316, 333
Grievous sins 284

*Haftorah* 226, 337, 338
*Hagaddah* 68–70, 80, 93, 170–175, 179, 180, 181, 188
Hair 193
*Halachah* 36, 60, 145, 180, 293, 309, 333
*Hallel* 76, 181, 229
Hallelujah 330, 333
Hama b. Hanina, Rabbi 279
Haman 240, 334, 335
Handle 271
Hands 63, 72–74, 160, 180, 219, 271, 290, 293
Hanina, Rabbi 60, 268, 271
Hannah 167
Hannaniah, Mishael, and Azariah 196

Harvesting  23, 92
Hasmoneans  249, 253
Healing  24, 200, 241–243, 248, 297
Heart  160, 191, 206, 230, 233, 239, 252, 255, 256, 269, 272, 276, 293, 300, 311, 315, 316
Heathen  38, 87, 88, 89, 138, 140
Heaven  36, 53–58, 79, 80, 103, 121, 135, 154, 164, 165, 171, 177, 182–185, 191–193, 219, 220, 222, 232, 234, 264, 273, 277, 290, 293, 300, 306, 318, 320, 321
  and earth  104, 106, 147, 149, 154, 169, 170, 222, 266, 280, 325
Heavenly echo  36, 50, 152, 229, 328
Heaven-sent  63
Heaven's sake, for  190–193, 225, 232, 299
Hebrew letters  18, 19, 46, 56, 61, 85, 135, 144, 167, 183, 185, 284, 290
  alef  46, 185, 228
  ayin  284
  beth  46, 185
  chaf  144, 331
  cheth  169, 194, 331
  daleth  56, 85, 183, 185
  gimmel  183, 185
  heh  45, 56, 61, 167, 169, 221, 222, 224, 266, 284, 331
  kaf  18, 56
  lamed  56, 169, 228
  mem  19, 61, 144, 194, 331
  nun  107, 109, 144, 169
  peh  144, 284
  resh  56, 85, 194, 228, 284
  shin  85, 228
  tzaddi  61, 85, 144
  vav  167, 169, 222, 224, 266
  yud  56, 61, 85, 165, 167, 169, 221, 222, 228, 266
Hebron  165
Heel  20, 209
Hellenes  249, 253, 334, 335
Heretic/Heresy  70, 253, 265
Hidden light  61
High Court  89
High Holidays  219
Hillel  145, 311, 312
History  180, 195, 224, 251, 338
Hitting the rock  323, 329
Hiyya, Rabbi  178, 268, 271
Holy/holiness/sanctity  23, 27, 46, 60, 62, 84, 86, 90
  accessing/feeling  69, 86, 90, 99, 148, 168, 169, 174, 183, 186, 198, 204–206, 229, 234, 245, 246, 247, 250, 265, 279, 281, 283, 285, 316
  the—field  23
  holy, holy, holy  52, 53, 108
  holy of holies  204, 276
  intrinsic  46, 62, 84, 100, 112, 31
  practical details of  50
  sparks  160, 161
Honoring one's parents  220, 269, 271
Hope  295
Horeb  261
Hosea the prophet  230
House  53, 82, 156, 264, 281, 286, 294

Household   59, 156, 162, 166, 309
House of study/prayer   207, 229, 264, 286
Human knowledge   284
Human mind   176, 288, 290
Humility   68, 69, 109, 261, 283
Hunger   122, 242

Icon   182, 183, 187
Idolatry/Idols   63, 66, 70, 78, 132, 156, 196, 234, 268
Illness   24, 67, 84, 200, 241, 242, 243, 247, 259, 271
Indifference   264, 265
Individual
  eternity   324
  revelation   270, 271
  suffering   286
Individuality   61, 65, 155, 172, 173, 174, 197, 198, 228, 229, 282, 316
Inheritance   250, 306, 307, 310, 311, 316
Inspiration   281, 282, 283
Instinct   324
Intellectualization   57, 65
Intelligence   56, 116, 176
Intention *See* Sacred meditation
Inundation   169, 232, 252, 294
Isaac   15, 23, 30, 132, 139, 140, 164, 180, 231, 233, 235, 241, 243, 244, 247, 250, 263, 267, 296, 297, 321
Isaac, Rabbi   59
Isaac Luria, Rabbi *See Arizal*
Isaiah b. Amoz the prophet   48, 54, 337, 338
Ishmael b. Elisha, Rabbi   28, 87, 88, 234, 277, 278

Israel   20, 30, 31, 32, 38, 45, 59, 63, 64, 74, 76–78, 88, 92, 96, 100, 105, 107, 109, 111, 121, 122, 123, 155, 162, 164, 174, 182, 184, 185, 191, 212, 213, 224, 225, 229, 237, 239, 249, 250

Jacob   15, 19, 23, 26–30, 64, 78, 105, 111, 156, 158, 159, 160, 161, 164, 180, 202, 219, 231, 233, 242–244, 248, 250, 267, 296, 321
  blessing   24, 28
  dream   17
  suffering   25, 245, 248, 296
Jeremiah the prophet   194, 333, 337
Jerusalem   36, 50, 108, 135, 138, 141, 152, 169, 200, 201, 229, 230, 236, 251, 264, 276, 286, 337
Jewish
  calendar   89, 309, 310, 317
  culture   56
  faith   59, 78, 83, 110, 115, 123, 160, 161, 170, 182, 185–187, 207, 210, 230, 249–253, 265, 269, 300, 310, 313, 316, 327
  intrinsic/innate   250, 265, 311, 313
  irrational   160, 250, 300, 306, 316
People
  accusers of the   8, 45, 70, 78, 104, 131, 261, 304
  advocacy of   235, 277, 308
  always in God's sight   202

Jewish
  People (*continued*)
    appreciating   263264
    the ardor of—for God   38,
      85, 89, 90, 92, 96, 108,
      131, 169, 170
    assisting God   135, 157, 158,
      222, 247
    banishment of the   8, 130, 131
    bearing God's burden   334
    body and soul of the   253
    broken   22, 54, 58, 77, 86,
      108, 131, 155, 163, 170,
      207, 213, 230, 250, 265,
      277, 295, 299, 313
    children of God   44, 147,
      160, 163, 264, 278, 286,
      319, 324, 326, 333
    chilling of the   56, 57, 265,
      300
    coerced into compliance   41,
      94, 98, 99, 105, 240
    collective needs of the   229,
      277, 304
    consciousness of the   8, 54,
      56, 85, 89, 90, 99, 118
    create worlds   222, 224
    cries of   5, 77, 124, 125,
      130–131, 158, 214, 225,
      232, 328
    crushed   22, 54, 83, 100,
      108, 131, 163, 207, 213,
      230, 250, 265, 277, 299,
      313
    in danger   105, 157, 163,
      186, 220, 224, 227, 242,
      245, 249
    destruction of the   242, 290,
      295, 299, 327
    divinity of the   74, 84, 89,
      109, 112, 152, 155, 202,
      281
    dying for the   140, 174, 234–
      235, 319
    dying to sanctify God   335
    empowering the angels   53,
      163
    enemies of the   19, 55, 56,
      108, 109, 113, 118, 120,
      123, 130, 131, 141, 163,
      179, 202, 205, 220, 224,
      234, 235, 242, 249, 253,
      261, 164, 289, 291, 294,
      295, 297, 303, 315, 326,
      327, 335
    in exile   9, 28, 129, 130,
      131, 220, 232, 236
    forced to be small
      minded   22, 56, 207,
      300, 313
    giving to one another   53,
      174, 193, 234, 327
    God's abode   50, 51, 64,
      160, 168, 189, 202, 205,
      250, 316
    God's firstborn son,   8, 130,
      131, 160, 319
    God's glory,   8, 135, 163,
      17, 168, 206, 222, 242,
      312, 324
    God's love for   50, 54, 64,
      131, 155, 158, 169
    God's portion   212, 213,
      253, 276, 319
    heart of the   28, 58, 85, 124,
      160, 168, 206, 242, 311
    holiness of the   205, 206,
      263, 279, 281

honor of the  163–166
ignorance of the  8, 250, 272,
    253, 277, 294, 315, 317,
    319, 327, 328, 334
individual needs of  35, 50,
    100, 116, 117, 119, 156,
    164, 166, 174, 192, 193,
    225, 229, 234, 239, 292,
    299, 303, 304
indomitable  113, 152, 255,
    237, 284, 324, 328
joy of the  58, 230, 242
love for  139, 163, 174, 235,
    319
make new Torah  222, 274
in modern times  8, 56, 83,
    115, 116, 284, 294, 327
murder of  140, 142, 155,
    157, 163, 202, 206, 232–
    235, 2, 422, 512, 632,
    993, 260
in need of forgiveness  43, 78,
    152
in need of mercy  43, 131,
    152, 193, 277, 317, 319
power of the  89, 109, 152,
    205, 222
prayer for  139, 163, 165,
    193, 277
praying for one another  53,
    139, 165, 193
ready to die for God  165,
    252, 253, 317, 335
reason for Creation, the  8,
    121, 122, 147, 149, 220,
    288
remorse of the  8, 77, 85
reveal God's light  222, 229,
    232, 233, 281, 288, 289

sacrifice of the  41, 52, 140,
    163, 232, 234, 263
sin of the  72, 74, 77, 131,
    151, 152, 202, 288
six hundred thousand  229,
    233
spiritual heights of the  85,
    104, 109, 112, 152, 174,
    175, 205, 206
spiritually diminished  22, 56,
    83, 85, 86, 108, 160,
    170, 207, 237, 265, 300,
    313
suffering of the  8, 11, 29,
    34, 36, 52, 53, 54, 77,
    85, 93, 108, 109, 112,
    113, 122, 130, 131, 145,
    155, 157, 158, 163, 164,
    170, 186, 192, 193, 197,
    198, 210, 212, 213, 220,
    224, 225, 230, 232, 233,
    234, 236, 250, 251, 267,
    277, 286, 287, 294, 299,
    313, 319, 132, 327, 328,
    335, 338
and the Torah are One  89,
    104, 174, 191, 253, 274,
    174, 191, 205, 206, 240,
    258
triumph of the  20, 55, 113,
    221, 249, 293, 324
under threat from God  40,
    77, 94, 98, 99, 105, 240
soul  4, 89, 90, 163, 174, 175,
    224, 232, 240
worship  140, 152
Job  115, 201
Jose, Rabbi  36, 50, 141, 229, 230,
    264, 266, 286

Joseph  22, 26, 28, 35, 161, 202, 205, 255, 256, 300, 323
Joseph, Rabbi  60, 227, 228
Josephus Flavius  253
Joshua b. Nun  55, 165, 183, 223, 306
Joy/Rejoicing/Simcha  3, 4, 36, 58, 100, 102, 109, 181, 210, 235, 242, 259, 261, 266, 276, 295, 302, 307, 310, 314, 315, 333
Judah  254, 255, 256, 337
Judah, Rabbi  60
Judah the Prince, Rabbi  159
Judah b. Illai, Rabbi  208
Judgment/*Gevurah* See also *Din* (Judgment)  25, 31, 35, 36, 73, 74, 85, 86, 90, 121, 131, 139, 145, 160, 180, 181, 185, 191, 201, 210, 211, 221, 243, 248, 286, 292, 294, 299
Justice  210, 211, 250, 252, 339

Kabbalah  119, 270, 273, 284, 331
*Kavanah* (Sacred Meditation)  49, 90, 124, 125, 140, 205, 206, 248
*Kavanot*  49, 90
King
  of beasts  113
  David  102, 194, 196, 230, 241, 276, 277, 294, 295, 297, 307, 307, 330–335
  Hezekiah  21, 243, 294
  of Israel  48, 80
  Josiah  193
  Nimrod  153
  Saul  103
Kiss  26, 88, 150, 193, 107, 322, 323

*K'lipoth* (Husks)  224, 303
Knees  114–116
*K'neseth Israel*  155, 156
Knife  311, 312
Knowledge (*Da'at*)  176, 223, 273, 284
Kosher  87, 160, 300

Lamb/kid  59, 62, 63, 93, 162, 166, 170, 274, 309, 317
Lament  209, 276, 333
Land of Israel  26, 38, 55–57, 62, 74, 79–81, 88, 92, 164
Leadership  30, 100, 114–116, 122, 207, 275, 277, 278, 307
Learning Torah *See* Torah
Leprosy  160, 313
Letters of the alphabet *See also* Hebrew letters  46, 183
Lid  105, 106
Life  200, 201, 212, 225, 233, 235, 242, 321, 323
Light  57, 60, 62, 183, 205, 206, 223, 266, 270, 289, 303, 307
  inner/encircling  303–304
Lion  111, 113, 148, 287
Listening  103, 212, 213, 250, 275, 276, 277
Liturgy
  before blowing shofar  3, 129, 131, 133, 219, 225
  Chanukah  249, 253, 335
  before donning *T'fillin*  297
  daily  100, 118, 250, 255
  fast days  232, 288, 289, 334
  Festival Mussaf  76, 107
  Friday night  21
  grace after meals  324

Hallel 181, 229
High Holy Days 73, 131–33, 225, 227, 327, 334
Hoshanna Rabbah 236
morning 31, 53, 69, 293, 294
Parshat Hachodesh 62, 303
Passover Haggadah 93, 172, 175, 179, 180, 214
Purim 302
before reciting psalms 76
Rosh Hashanah 9, 221
Sabbath 21, 91, 168, 180, 260, 266, 280, 282, 283
Sukkoth 334
Lips 54, 88, 137, 191, 212, 213, 226, 234, 273, 320
Lord 20, 150
Love 87, 88, 99, 152, 160, 162, 169, 174, 175, 240, 248, 266, 296, 311, 313, 318
Loving 90, 139, 252, 311
Loving-kindness (*Chesed*) 31, 90, 100, 102, 108, 112, 118, 123, 132, 139, 145, 151, 152, 155, 187, 194, 239, 247, 248, 255, 294, 296

Maggid of Mezeritch 73, 118, 255
Maidservant 38, 277, 323
Maimonides 284, 312
Manasseh 48, 73
Manna 36, 122
Marriage 159, 174
Martyrdom 11, 138, 140, 224, 232–235, 248, 252
  pleasure in 11, 96, 205, 248, 252
Master 16, 190, 192, 286

Mattityahu b. Yochanan, High Priest 249, 335
Meditation 49, 205, 297
Medium 182, 183
Meir, Rabbi 148, 154, 155, 286
Menachem Mendel of Rymanov, Rabbi 14
Men of the Great Assembly 118, 255
Menorah 188, 249
Mercy (*Rachamim*) 31, 86, 102, 108, 123, 131, 144, 146, 155, 158, 193, 229, 298
Merit 64, 70, 92, 133, 160–163, 166, 180, 181, 186, 317, 322
Messiah 196–199, 246, 284, 338
Messianic era 179
Midrash 251
*Mikveh* (Pool) 160, 305
Milk
  and honey 62
  and meat 65
*Miluy* 46, 56, 85
Miraculous/miracles 102, 106, 122, 163, 170, 197, 235, 236, 240, 276, 303, 304, 308, 334
Miriam 194, 322, 329
*Mishna* 50, 84
*Mitzvah* 61
*M'NaTZ'PaCh* 144
Moab 111
Mockery 33, 54, 131
Money 101, 173, 200, 298
Month 59, 62, 66, 160, 161, 162, 166, 194, 211, 219, 221, 224, 268, 303, 309, 310, 317
Moon 221, 266, 291, 331
Mordechai 22, 124, 302, 304

Moses
  admonishing the Jewish
    People   179
  arguing with God   160, 163,
    212, 250, 257, 277, 313
  asking to be shown God's
    glory   72, 74
  being commanded by God   30–
    33, 92, 98, 103, 144, 170,
    186, 279, 305, 317, 338
  blessing Israel   48
  at the burning bush   155, 157
  calling upon God   107, 114,
    335
  challenging God   31, 122, 145,
    164, 248, 252, 261, 263
  concerned about posterity   50
  death of   322
  editor of the Torah   14, 45, 196
  fear of God   64
  fighting Amalek   293, 300
  God and—studying Torah
    alone   104
  God calling to   52, 54, 119,
    301
  God revealing Himself to   30,
    167, 267
  Israel's faith in   76, 182, 310
  Israel, the cause of—
    greatness   274
  Joshua and   165, 223
  love of God   44
  permeates all Jews   51, 199,
    234, 307
  pleading on behalf of Israel   43,
    151, 152, 165, 213, 314,
    319, 321
  reading the Book to Israel   40
  receiving Jethro   38
  receiving the Torah   53, 109,
    135, 184, 306
  Sabbath—gift   280
  sin of   323, 329
  singing   78, 275, 278
  standing before Pharaoh   99,
    164, 268
  taking Joseph's bones   35
  teaching the Jewish People   63,
    66, 102, 260, 283
  "telling" the Jewish People   188
Moses Cordovero, Rabbi   184
Mothers   157, 195, 279
Mountain   105, 109, 163, 184,
  240, 246, 247, 257, 261, 270
Mourning   123, 200, 296, 297
Mouth   54, 70, 88, 136, 194, 208,
  213, 234, 256, 273, 274
Murder   57, 65, 140, 155, 206,
  234, 242, 251, 299, 333
Music/musician   181, 262, 266,
  276, 333
Musical instrument   262, 266
Muteness   22, 181
Mystery/mysteries of the
  Torah   119, 152, 183, 270–
  271, 281, 331

Nachman, Rabbi   290
Nachshon b. Aminadav   185
Names of God *See* God, Hebrew
  words
Naming   222–224, 231, 318
Naomi   194
Natural law   24, 65, 110, 122,
  144, 235, 323
Nazirite   192, 193

Neck 26, 235
Nehemiah, Rabbi 277
New moon 59, 62, 89, 264, 308
Nightfall 36
Nile River 313, 314, 327
*Nissan* 62, 170, 303
Noah 31, 150, 153
Nobility 284,
Nostrils 185.186
*Notariqon See* Acrostic
Nothingness 40, 305
Novelty 184, 185
Numbness 214, 265

Oath 192, 193, 204, 209
Offering *See also* Sacrifice
  bullocks/oxen 237
  burnt 87, 108, 136, 142, 247, 257, 263, 264
  departed souls 136, 140, 163, 195, 202, 232, 233
  guilt 257, 263
  meal 257
  paschal lamb 50, 62–64, 80, 93, 162, 163, 166, 170, 309–312, 317
  peace 264
  trespass/sin 193, 257, 263
Oil 150
*Omer* 87, 90, 91
Oneness *See* Unification
Oral Torah 87, 88, 94, 270, 273, 306, 315
Originality 61
Original Thought 149, 298, 299, 325, 326
Other side 115
Ownership 173, 270

Pain 7, 11, 12, 54, 77, 108, 109, 131, 136, 137, 154, 155, 158–164, 185, 192, 200, 204–207, 214, 225, 229, 232
  ennobling 334
  psychic versus physical 320
Papa, Rabbi 288, 315
Paradise *See* Garden of Eden
Parents/Grandparents 28, 280, 312, 326, 327
Passion 36, 264, 265
Passover 67, 76, 79, 80, 87, 90, 91, 167, 170, 172, 175, 179, 181, 182, 226, 274, 309, 311
Patriarchs/Matriarchs 19, 41, 59, 77, 140, 152, 165, 234, 312, 319, 320, 321
Peace 98, 159, 161, 181, 293
Perception 176, 281
Permanence 323, 327
Perversion 65, 151, 251
Pharaoh 30, 33, 35, 99, 122, 163, 164, 165, 170, 186, 212, 213, 254, 257, 261, 268, 275, 276, 277, 280, 284, 301, 315, 327, 335, 338
Philosophy 56, 57
Phylacteries *See T'fillin*
Piety 259, 294, 315, 322
Pillar
  of cloud 35, 36
  of fire 35, 36
Pinchas b. Yair, Rabbi 226–228, 245, 246–247
Pious women/men 194, 294, 314, 322, 329
Plagues 34, 82, 268, 292, 294, 297, 313, 314

Power
- of names   223
- of question (Koach Mah/Miy)   170, 177, 178, 331
- of uncleanness   56, 160, 161

Prayer   6, 15, 23, 31, 36, 50, 54, 70, 72, 73, 77, 93, 97, 114, 119, 120, 124, 129, 130, 136, 158, 161, 165, 181, 186, 195, 208, 209, 219, 220, 225, 229, 245, 247, 248, 255, 256, 264, 268, 277, 283, 286, 289, 290, 306, 313
- automatic   313
- before and after   16, 99, 114, 256, 270, 295
- with a broken heart   36, 119, 120, 130, 193, 209, 256, 264
- conditions for   295
- emotional   6, 93, 130, 193, 230, 251, 264
- facing God during   255, 256
- grudging   31
- without heart   256
- with joy   36, 160
- joyless   31, 230
- loud   6, 124, 130, 137, 230
- with love   36, 96, 193
- for pain   159
- passionate   6, 36, 93, 100, 119, 130, 193, 230, 251
- requires Torah   118, 219, 247
- revelation through   119, 124, 247, 248, 256
- torrential   230, 251

Priest/High Priest/Cohen   87, 101, 118, 141, 168, 188, 201, 234, 249, 255, 273

Pride   264, 283, 284

Prophecy   23, 38, 49, 181, 268, 269, 276, 277, 282, 310, 312, 315, 316, 330, 332, 333, 336, 338

Prophets/seers/children of   80, 102, 143–145, 181, 269, 276, 277, 306, 310, 311, 316, 328, 330, 333

Proselytize/proselyte   38, 258

Psalms   36, 76, 138, 183, 209, 276, 294, 318, 330, 331, 332

Punishment   34, 54, 77, 85, 107, 108, 122, 129, 130, 137, 144, 145, 191, 192, 197, 200, 201, 210, 268, 294, 318

Purification   152, 305, 306

Purim   58, 302, 304

Questioning   175–178, 250, 251, 270, 271, 306–, 308

Rabba b. b. Channa   139

Rabbinical ordinance   88, 89, 90

*Rachamim* (Mercy)   144–146, 180, 181, 194, 299–300, 325–326

Rachel   254

Rain   290

Ram   263

Rationalizing   110, 114–116, 250

Rav   167, 168, 178, 184

Rava   257, 258, 290

Rebbe   116, 178, 184

Receiving   53, 54, 60

Reconciliation   210

Redemption/Salvation   12, 16, 19, 24, 25, 31, 34, 55, 56, 57, 58, 62, 64, 77, 78, 80, 93, 99,

## General Index

100, 104, 108, 110, 116, 122, 123, 142, 146, 158, 159, 160, 161, 162, 164, 165, 166, 171, 179, 180, 181, 193, 195, 198, 199, 208, 209, 213, 215, 220, 225, 233, 235, 238, 239, 241–244, 248, 249, 253, 256, 261, 264, 266–268, 276, 278, 284, 288, 289, 290, 295, 300, 302, 302, 307, 308, 314, 317, 321, 327, 329, 333, 339, 277, 288, 297, 310

Redeeming captives  226–228, 245, 246
Red Heifer  195, 305–308
Red Sea  22, 33, 38, 56, 81, 185, 186, 227, 228
Remembering  51, 55, 64, 219, 238, 264, 293
Remorse  6, 129, 130
Renewal  223, 224, 325, 327
Rennet  87
Repentance
  creative  223
  God's  10, 120, 134, 203
  beneath God's honor  73
  habitual  8
  individual  10, 58, 85, 120, 130, 131, 133, 134, 140, 141, 158, 172, 203, 221–226, 229, 230, 258, 329
  principles of  11, 133, 137
  before the sin  259, 260
  year-round  6, 258
Reprieve  31, 54–57, 235, 303
Resolve  151, 153, 186
Resurrection of the dead  143, 155, 201, 209, 324
Retribution  197

Revelation  49, 50, 72, 73, 77, 80, 102, 119, 144, 145, 164, 165, 168, 170–178, 184–187, 197, 198, 220, 229, 232, 234, 247, 256, 260, 268–271, 289, 291, 297, 306, 315, 317, 324, 325, 326, 327
Reward  60, 94, 115, 190, 191, 210, 248, 263, 269, 271, 272, 281, 282, 290, 323, 328
Righteous/pious people  21, 73, 105, 136, 148, 150, 155, 159, 161, 165, 186, 196, 198, 232, 277, 294, 323, 328
Robbery  57, 59, 65, 74, 131, 173
Rock/Rocky mountain  72, 73, 323
Romans  202, 205, 224, 234, 252, 315, 328
Rosh Hashanah  3, 9, 46, 129, 219, 223, 225, 238
Ruins/rubble  36, 50, 54, 138, 229, 230, 264, 267, 276, 286

Sabbath  21, 45, 46, 87, 90–93, 160, 206–209, 279–, 285, 288
  connecting with  283
  delighting in the  21
  desecration of the  45, 47, 148, 160, 206, 227, 228, 234, 235, 271, 300, 328
  God's precious gift  279–282
  honoring the  21, 208, 279
  light of the  281, 282
  liturgy of  21, 91, 168, 180, 260, 266, 280, 282, 283
  before Passover  63, 64, 167, 168, 170, 171, 311
  of repentance  230

Sabbath (*continued*)
   rewards of the   280, 281
   sanctifying the   21, 208, 279, 285
   and the world to come   282
Sacred meditation *See* Kavanah
Sacrifice   52, 53, 135, 136, 139, 140, 141, 143, 162, 163, 164, 194, 195, 202, 232, 233, 262, 263
Saints   138, 139, 190, 224, 225, 229, 232, 235, 277, 323, 328
Salvation *See* Redemption
*Sammael See* Angel
Samuel b. Nahmani, Rabbi   330
Scholar/scholarship   114, 148, 159, 184, 206, 224, 272, 273
Self
   abnegation/abandonment   90, 99, 174, 175, 197, 198, 225, 232, 235, 250, 252, 299, 305, 306, 317, 331
   awareness   311
   centeredness   4, 99, 191, 192, 193, 197, 252, 287
   confidence   30
   denial   5, 174, 192, 225, 299
   examination   5, 234, 251, 261, 270, 316
   justification/satisfaction   5, 234, 316
   respect   314
   sacrifice   27, 43, 52, 136, 140, 232, 233, 235, 250, 252, 263, 299, 317
*Sephirot*   152, 155, 169, 176, 178, 197, 222, 232, 262, 284, 294, 303, 320
Serenity   21, 159, 161

Serpent/snake   121, 160, 161, 265, 313
*Shavuoth*   102, 104
*Shechinah*   50, 154, 155, 189, 258, 272, 277, 326
Sheep   114–117
Shekel   50, 51, 292
Shepherd   114–117, 161, 193, 277, 313
*Sh'ma*   27, 96, 161, 172, 205, 206, 248, 252, 316
*Sh'mini Atzeret*   146, 237, 238
*Shofar*   6, 46, 136, 219, 220, 221, 224
Sickness *See* Illness
Signs   160, 279, 314
Silence   21
Silver   77, 78, 100, 256
*Simchat Torah* 238
Simeon, Rabbi   73
Simeon b. Gamliel, Rabbi   234, 235, 279, 309
Simeon b. Lakish/Resh Lakish, Rabbi   191, 257, 258
Simeon b. Yochai, Rabbi   73, 159, 205, 234, 315
Simeon the Just   193
Simple Son   175, 178, 179
Sin   44, 54, 72, 85, 93, 95, 99, 133, 141, 151, 157, 158, 164, 173, 192, 193, 195, 196, 197, 200, 201, 210, 225, 235, 237, 251, 253, 257–260, 263, 290, 313, 318, 319, 323, 325, 329
Sinai   40, 45, 52, 92, 98, 99, 102, 104, 105, 109, 135, 152, 184, 220, 234, 260, 261, 288, 292, 306, 317

# General Index

Servant/slave/slavery  36, 77, 93, 150, 170, 190, 192, 214, 220, 225, 262, 276, 278, 293, 295, 297, 303, 304, 309
Slaying of the firstborn  104, 294
Song  33, 76, 77, 78, 79, 80, 143, 146, 181, 182, 186, 241–244, 266, 275, 276, 277, 278, 295, 297, 302, 307, 330, 333, 335
Song of Songs  147, 266
Soul/souls  50, 51, 70, 75, 103, 136, 139, 156, 174, 182, 223, 232, 233, 241, 251–253, 263, 269, 276, 283, 295, 297, 310, 311, 316, 318, 320, 327
Sovereignty (*Malkhut*)  169, 194, 199, 232, 266, 282, 290, 307, 331
Speech  79, 97, 103, 112, 144, 212, 213, 258, 302
Spies  110, 165, 223
Spirit  70, 74, 277
Spiritual
 awakening  322–323
 journey  269
Statutes  64, 65, 88, 160, 221, 249
Stiff neckedness  150–153
Stragglers  55, 56, 57, 293, 299, 300
Straw  122, 148, 277
Struggle  19, 20, 74
Stubbornness  151–153, 161
Students  175–178, 184, 205, 208, 234, 247, 252, 270, 273, 274
Submission  62, 160, 161, 178, 206, 221, 232, 243, 248
Suffering
 after  19, 85, 86, 133, 155, 161, 181, 192, 196, 243

as atonement  52, 136, 137, 192, 193, 196, 197, 205, 334, 335
as seasoning  14
avoiding  197, 206
before  196, 206, 232
beneficial  160, 170, 185, 192, 193, 206, 232, 250, 284, 316, 338
causes of  161, 224
covenantal  14, 100
damaging  14, 85, 86, 133, 134, 145, 149, 159, 160, 161, 193, 206–209, 213, 225, 250–252, 265, 277, 282, 297, 300, 316, 333
fulfills a commandment  160, 185
hearing and witnessing  337–338
is Torah  185, 232
joy in  181, 276
posthumous  319, 328
to sanctify God's Name  334–335
times of  90, 97, 130, 145, 146, 149, 154, 159, 160, 163, 179, 181, 192, 197, 206, 209, 210, 214, 224, 229, 232, 237, 240, 251, 252, 277, 284, 289, 295, 300, 313, 328, 333
unbearable  14, 100, 122, 123, 129, 130, 133, 145, 155–160, 196, 197, 206, 213, 225, 232, 277, 284, 295, 296, 299, 301, 302, 328
worshipping while  16, 74, 90, 100, 134, 145, 149, 153, 181, 187, 206, 237, 252, 276, 300

Sukkoth   35, 46, 138, 143, 235, 237, 238
Sun   49, 282, 291, 331
Supernal light   61, 62
Supernal source   174
Supernatural   122, 123, 300
Sweetening judgments   85, 99, 145, 160, 185, 186, 193, 208, 209, 290, 292
Symbol   46, 107, 160
Synagogue   29, 36, 50, 83, 180, 219, 229, 264, 286

Tabernacle   48, 103, 152
Talmud, Babylonian   251, 269, 270
Tanchum b. Hanilai, Rabbi   269, 271, 272
Tannaim   262, 277
Tarfon, Rabbi   73, 172
Targum   52, 63, 212, 223
Teaching/teacher   38, 53, 176–178, 184, 205–208, 271, 272, 273, 274, 286, 326
Tears   77, 315
Temple   26, 79–81, 135, 139–145, 152, 168, 169, 180, 186, 201, 204, 234–236, 249, 262, 263, 264, 265, 286, 287, 288, 290, 303, 304, 311, 312, 333–338
Ten
   Commandments   102, 131, 133, 220, 268–271, 291, 292, 313, 315
   expressions of Creation   290–291
   expressions of Prophecy   337
   Jews   272
   Jewish martyrs   202, 224, 234, 252, 328
Territory   26
Terror   196, 209, 252, 258, 272, 333
Test/trial   140, 206, 209, 246, 250, 260, 295, 299
Tetragrammaton *See also* YHVH, God's Names
*T'fillin*   49, 89, 93, 94, 153, 175, 293, 294, 297, 299
Theft   57, 313
Thirteen
   attributes of mercy   152
   principles of faith   210
Thought   56, 57, 97, 140, 144, 149, 177, 180, 184, 222, 248, 255, 258
Throne of Glory   49, 55, 132, 220, 281, 300, 335
Tithes/tithing   245, 262, 266
Tongue   70, 121, 212, 234
Torah
   abandoning   300
   accepting the   163, 166, 191, 192, 240
   and God are One   89, 104, 183, 270, 271, 291, 316
   and Israel are One   89, 104, 174, 184, 191, 227, 274, 288
   applies everywhere, always   293, 319
   before and after studying   270, 327, 331
   begging for more   88, 153, 176–178, 208, 273, 315
   being one with the   66
   blessings over the   31, 184
   the Body/Soul/Self of God   18, 89, 104, 183, 270, 271, 281, 291, 316
   books of the   40, 59, 62

children are revelations of   326
children learning—are God's
    face   326, 327
chronology of the   40, 59, 60
damaged   29, 147, 250, 251
editing of   14, 103, 107
end to the   83, 250
fence around the   88, 89, 90, 94
fixed times for study of   148,
    149, 238
four levels of (Pardes)   328
God's hidden treasure   280–
    282, 288, 290, 319
is joy   102, 104, 153
is life   201, 219
learning   26, 104, 114, 269,
    273, 289, 291, 295, 315
letters of   229, 233
the medium of creation   103,
    153, 183, 222, 260, 288,
    291, 316
narrative of the   40, 59, 60, 61,
    103, 107, 325
neglecting the   253, 271
novelty in   184, 185, 222, 315,
    316, 326
oral   87, 88, 94, 270, 273, 306,
    315
reaching for   316, 333
the reason for creation   147,
    149, 191, 260
revealed and hidden   269, 270,
    271, 281, 288
revelation/receiving the   37, 89,
    99, 102, 103, 106, 109,
    163, 176, 184, 185, 208,
    239, 240, 247, 270, 271,
    272, 280, 306, 315–317,
    326

requires prayer   118, 247
for the sake of Israel   99, 274,
    227, 274
scroll   148, 229, 288, 333
seventy faces of the   62, 151
soul of the   174, 176, 183, 233,
    270
sounds of   180, 219, 220, 248
speaking—while suffering   248,
    315, 316, 333
study of   26, 53, 56, 57, 66, 93,
    96, 97, 100, 133, 136, 148,
    153, 172, 184, 190, 191,
    192, 206, 247, 248, 257,
    258, 270, 272, 300, 315,
    320
study of—atones for sins   258
studying—together with
    God   316
suffering is   185, 186
teaching the   68, 69, 83, 89,
    102, 118, 136, 184, 205,
    272, 273
teaching the—to children   326
written   88, 102, 183, 233, 251,
    273, 338
Torment   4, 34, 54, 57, 77, 108,
    122, 124, 129, 130, 192,
    251
Torture   30, 57, 122, 132, 196,
    206, 213, 248–253, 289, 291,
    327, 334
Tosaphists   41, 98, 136, 197, 240,
    262, 330
Total immersion   305
Touch   105
Trades   115
Tradesman   149
Tragedy   85, 201

Tribe
    of Benjamin   185, 204
    of Judah   204, 223
    of Levi   145, 180
Tribes   202, 330
Truth   90, 131, 132, 133, 149,
    210, 211
T'shuvah *See* Repentance
Tzaddik *See* Righteous people, Saints

Ulla   196, 197, 198, 338
Understanding (*Binah*)   169, 176–
    178, 223, 232, 251, 272, 282,
    288, 331
Unification of everything   290–291
Unifying God's Name   49, 173,
    205, 232, 233, 236, 248, 291
Unworthiness   74, 78, 92, 132,
    158, 162

Vessels   46, 48, 77, 100, 106, 224,
    303, 320
Vineyard   92, 289
Visions   38, 72, 246, 269, 277,
    310, 337–338
Voice   124, 129–131, 143, 180,
    190, 214, 219, 229–230
Void and Chaos   191, 192, 320

Walls   144, 281, 282, 328
War   17, 56, 118, 120, 230, 253,
    263, 293, 284, 300
Water   322, 329
    Water drawing ceremonies   235
Weekday   45, 279, 282, 283
Weeks   87, 161
Weeping   26, 70, 77, 84, 159,
    190, 195, 201, 234, 264, 296,
    302, 315

Wellsprings   322, 323, 329
Wicked
    people   33, 56, 65, 69, 73, 108,
        249, 294, 314
    son   172–179
Wilderness   37, 186, 322
Wine   80, 87, 88, 150, 154, 192
Wisdom (*Chokhma*)   176–179, 183,
    222, 223, 232
Wise
    man   183
    son   176–179
Withholding   139, 146, 194, 298
Women   194, 272
Wood   148, 186
World/Universe
    of Action   49, 50, 51, 79, 80,
        81, 189, 222, 247, 248,
        273, 320
    of Archetypes   197, 222, 273,
        325
    belongs to God   296
    birthday of the   5
    to come   20, 21, 68, 76, 114,
        140, 144, 145, 159, 161,
        169, 180, 181, 189, 190,
        197, 200, 201, 221, 266,
        282
    of Creation   222, 273, 281, 324,
        325
    evolving   24, 189
    expanding   24
    of fixing   224
    of Formation   22, 273
    hidden   108, 189, 197
    nations of the   17, 56, 59–61,
        64, 169, 220, 237, 261, 264,
        276, 281, 286, 287, 294,
        297, 305, 306, 307, 308

revealed   108, 189, 197, 199
of Speech   79, 189, 247, 248
this   94, 136, 145, 152, 153,
    159, 161, 164, 165, 169,
    170, 181, 184, 186, 187,
    190, 197, 201, 221, 222,
    247, 273, 274, 287, 290,
    324, 328
of thought   11, 56, 189
true meaning of   149
upper/spiritual   136, 155, 161,
    165, 169, 170, 180, 181,
    184, 186–189, 197, 222,
    259, 273, 282, 286, 296,
    298, 324
Work   45, 46, 282
  on the Sabbath   45, 47, 148,
    271, 279, 300
World War I   294
Worship *See also* Prayer   5, 6, 15,
    23, 27, 36, 37, 49, 50, 93,
    100, 108, 125, 136, 140, 153,
    155, 160, 165, 168–170, 172,
    180, 190–192, 232, 233, 236,
    243, 250, 259, 261, 270, 271,
    316
  before and after   270, 295
  creative   229, 233, 234, 259,
    264
  decision to   212, 243, 312, 316
  exalts the worshipper   261
  individual/private   316
  innovative   234, 235, 261
  is revelation of God   270, 271
  longing to   209, 312, 316
  lowest forms of   192, 318

public   125, 257, 317
requires joy   315
through fasting   5
unconditional   190, 191
while in pain   109, 136, 259,
    316
with fear   108, 318
with love   36, 96, 125, 136,
    190, 191, 312, 318
Wrath   108
Writing   46, 144

*Yahrzeit*   138, 140, 162, 165, 190,
    231, 318
Yiddish   278, 300
Yearning   200, 204, 208
Yechezkel HaCohen, Rabbi   241
Yehoshua, Rabbi   67, 84, 87, 88,
    172
Yehoshua b. Levi, Rabbi   269
Yerachmiel Moshe, Rabbi   21
Yeshiva   29, 83, 206, 207, 209,
    219
Yochanan, Rabbi   73, 139, 330
Yochanan b. Zakai, Rabbi   67, 84
Yoke of Heaven   26, 27, 93, 96,
    161, 169, 178, 206, 221, 222,
    248, 305
Yom Kippur   3, 46, 58, 63, 141,
    225, 238

*Ze'er Anpin* (Small Faces)   232,
    331
Zion   108
Zohar   315
Zusia of Anipoli, Rabbi   84

# Index of Hebrew, Yiddish and Aramaic Words

*aba* 232
*acharecha* 300
*achara* 115
*ad* 169
*adam* 223
*adama* 223
*Adonai* 20
*aggadah* 269, 272
*akeidah* 136, 246, 247, 250
*alef* 46
*ally* 95
*almut* 22
*alumati* 23
*alumim* 23
*alumoteichem* 23
*amidah* 138, 246
*ana* 104
*anashim* 229
*ani* 18, 104
*anochi* 18, 104, 220
*anpin* 232
*anshei* 139
*asher* 55

*assiya* 222, 273
*at* 175, 179
*ata* 175
*atereth* 194
*atzilut* 197, 222
*aur* 303
*aurot* 303
*avodah* 66
*ay-ly* 95

*ba'alah* 194
*bereshith* 238
*beth* 46, 139
*bezal-el* 48
*binah* 169, 176, 177, 178, 232, 282, 28, 331, 332
*briyah* 222, 273, 281, 298
*b'she'arim* 269
*b'simcha* 315

*chacham* 148
*charish* 21
*chasadiim* 296

*chasid* 139
*chasidim* 138, 140
*chasidut* 315
*chayil* 194
*cheder* 83, 160
*chesed* 118, 132, 139, 140, 145, 151, 152, 155, 169, 210, 239, 247, 248, 255, 295, 296, 297
*chevlay* 197
*chiktha* 169
*chodesh* 224
*chokhmah* 176, 177, 178, 179, 232, 331, 332
*clal* 173, 174, 175
*cohen* 104, 107, 118, 207, 255, 273

*Da'at* 284
*derech* 56
*devarim* 45
*di* 300
*din* 144, 145, 146, 180, 181, 211, 247, 292, 297, 325
*dinim* 210
*d'rush* 283

*Ehyeh* 56, 261
*ekev* 209
*El* 24, 164, 180, 181, 255
*eleh* 45
*Eli* 187
*Elohim* 30, 200, 201, 325
*El-Shaddai* 24, 25
*epikoros* 70
*es* 278
*esheth* 194

*fallen* 300

*gadol* 63, 64
*gamur* 197, 198
*gedulah* 90
*gevurah* 90, 139, 155, 194, 259, 294, 295, 297, 299
*gidin* 188, 189

*hachamor* 246
*hacharaish* 22
*hadeshen* 262, 266
*hadevarim* 45
*haftorah* 137, 337, 338
*hagaddah* 68, 69, 70, 80, 93, 170, 171, 172, 173, 175, 179, 180, 181, 188
*hagadol* 63, 170
*hakelim* 294
*halachah* 36, 60, 145, 293, 309
*hallel* 76, 181
*HaMakom* 38
*hanecheshalim* 300
*haolam* 169
*haoref* 284
*harim* 105
*hasechel* 177
*hashkafa* 123
*hashoevah* 139
*hassidut* 207
*hester* 74, 108, 185, 210, 232, 239, 247, 250, 298, 315
*higayon* 114, 115, 116
*higayonot* 116
*higid* 188
*hikdim* 25
*hishtalshelut* 182, 183, 197, 291, 297, 324
*hod* 90
*horim* 105

## Index of Hebrew, Yiddish and Aramaic Words

*hoshua* 223
*hu* 199

*im* 22, 246
*ima* 232

*kaddish* 50
*kadmut* 177
*kadosh* 289
*karcha* 55, 300
*katan* 303
*katavit* 104
*kavanah* 124, 125
*kavanot* 49, 90
*k'chu* 226
*kedusha* 289
*keli* 303
*kiddush* 230
*k'lipoth* 224
*k'neseth* 155, 194, 282
*koach* 176, 331, 332
*kosher* 87
*kriah* 52

*lachash* 121
*l'Adonai* 169
*l'alafim* 169
*l'hagid* 189
*l'havi* 179
*l'israel* 229, 233
*l'torah* 229, 233

*maaseh* 139
*magrefa* 262, 263, 266
*mah* 176, 177, 199, 331, 332
*makif* 303
*malachim* 245
*malkhut* 90, 155, 169, 104, 199, 222, 232, 266, 282, 331, 332

*matzo* 80
*mavet* 19
*mayin* 169, 232
*meAlmim* 23
*medaber* 103
*midoth* 90, 284
*mikveh* 83, 305, 306
*miluy* 46, 56, 85
*min* 169
*minyan* 83
*mishna* 50
*mistarim* 287, 288, 290, 315
*mitdaber* 103
*mitzvah* 61, 312, 313
*mitzvot* 290, 291
*miy* 177, 178, 331, 332
*mochin* 284
*moshe* 199
*moshiach* 197
*mussaf* 107

*na* 77
*nachal* 169
*nafshai* 104
*nafsheinu* 169
*nasoth* 260, 261
*nazir* 192, 193
*nazirim* 192, 193
*ne'eman* 109
*netzach* 90
*nevelah* 87
*nikud* 125
*nishmat* 180
*nissan* 62
*nistar* 108, 118, 239
*nitzav* 73
*nitzavim* 73
*nitzavta* 73
*nitzim* 73

*nochach* 108, 118
*notariqon* 104, 169, 229, 233
*nukvin* 169, 232

*olam* 169
*omer* 87
*otiot* 229, 233
*oz* 335

*panim* 108, 185, 210, 250
*pharo* 284
*pikudei* 183
*pnimi* 303
*p'shat* 185

*rabbah* 63
*rachamim* 144, 145, 146, 180, 181, 194
*rachmaniyoth* 194
*rapha* 270
*rateveh* 328
*ratzon* 204
*rechem* 194
*rega* 112, 113
*remez* 283
*rephidim* 270
*reshith* 147
*riboah* 229, 233

*sael* 20
*sammael* 19
*sar* 20
*sela* 241, 242, 243
*sephirah* 155, 176, 178, 194, 199, 222, 232, 259, 266, 282, 284, 288, 303, 331, 332

*sephirot* 152, 155, 178, 197, 222, 232, 284, 294, 303, 320, 324, 325, 326, 331, 332
*Shabbat* 63, 170
*Shaddai* 24, 85, 164
*she'ar* 269
*shechinah* 50, 154, 155, 189, 204, 258, 272, 287, 326
*she'haya* 199
*shevirath* 294
*shirah* 278
*shishim* 229, 233
*shivyo* 120
*sh'ma* 27, 53, 67, 96, 161, 172, 205, 206, 248, 252, 316
*shuva* 226, 230
*sich* 278, 300
*siddur* 139
*simcha* 266, 276, 295, 310, 315
*simchath* 139
*sina* 261
*sitra* 115
*sod* 283

*tacharishi* 22
*tacharishun* 22
*tachat* 57
*tallit* 270, 303
*talmid* 148
*tameh* 82
*tannaim* 84, 262, 277
*t'chila* 233, 234, 235
*terumath* 262, 266
*t'fillin* 49, 89, 93, 94, 153, 175, 293, 294, 297, 299

*tifferet* 90, 155, 194
*tikdash* 289
*tishm'un* 209
*t'lamdeynu* 136
*tov* 269
*tovim* 296
*tzaddik* 105, 197, 198, 277
*tzaddikim* 174, 232
*tzimtzum* 298
*tzinor* 204
*tzitzit* 303
*tzomah* 63
*Tz'vaoth* 167

*unter* 300
*ushpizin* 139, 235

*vas* 300
*vayechtar* 73
*vaye'etar* 73
*v'shavitha* 120

*Yah* 221, 223, 224
*yahavit* 104
*yesh* 229, 233
*yesod* 90
*yetzer* 85
*yetzirah* 222
*YHVH* 20, 21, 24, 30, 31, 32, 56, 61, 86, 155, 164, 165, 167, 325, 326
*YHVH-Elohim* 25, 325, 326
*yisrael* 228, 233

*zarah* 66
*ze'er* 232
*zol* 278
*zugen* 278

# Source Index

Genesis
- 1:1   147, 223, 239
- 1:16   331
- 1:27   112
- 2:4   25, 325
- 2:19   223
- 3:16   197
- 4:7   95
- 6:8   31
- 6:9   150
- 15:6   249
- 15:8   231, 233
- 15:12–13   232, 309
- 21:23   324
- 22:1   140
- 22:2   247
- 22:4   246
- 22:5   246
- 22:11   54, 157
- 22:12   140
- 22:12–18   263
- 22:13   136
- 22:14   52
- 23:1   13
- 25:7   13
- 27:22   180, 219
- 27:27   23
- 27:28   15, 154, 241
- 27:33   241
- 28:13   17, 18
- 28:15   17
- 32:4   245
- 32:11–14   157
- 32:12   245
- 32:27   19
- 37:1   21, 159
- 37:7   22
- 37:11   209
- 37:35   296
- 38:21   289
- 41:32   301
- 43:14   24
- 44:18–33   254
- 45:14   26

Genesis (*continued*)
  45:15   26
  46:26   156
  47:28   28
  48:15   28, 323

Exodus
  1:22   327
  2:23   225
  2:25   284
  3:1    261
  3:4    52, 54, 157, 301
  3:7    164, 338
  3:10   257
  3:11   163, 257
  3:13   249
  3:15   144
  4:1    160, 313
  4:9    313
  4:10   212
  4:22   8, 319
  4:31   249
  5:1    164
  5:5    145
  5:7    277
  5:21   164
  5:22–23   122, 164
  6:1    31, 123, 164
  6:2    167
  6:2–6   262
  6:2–13   30
  6:6    123, 164
  6:9    212, 249, 275
  6:12   212, 275
  8:22   317
  10:1   33, 170
  10:26  99
  11:2   77, 100
  11:4   268, 330, 336
  12:1   59, 66, 268, 308
  12:1–3   162, 170
  12:1–4   309
  12:12   104
  12:15   80
  12:16   46
  12:21   63
  12:22   294
  12:27   275
  13:8   69, 172
  13:17–20   35
  13:21   35
  14:1–4   33
  14:14   22
  14:15   163, 186, 317
  14:27   228
  14:30–15:1   76
  14:31–15:21   182
  14:31   278, 297, 310, 314
  15:1   243, 275, 335
  15:2   100, 312
  15:6   297
  15:17–18   79
  17:8   269, 293
  17:14   293, 300
  18:1   38
  18:4   306
  19:2   105
  19:3   52
  19:6   99
  19:9   188
  19:17   40
  19:22   297
  20:1   131, 167, 220
  20:2   220
  20:8–11   279
  20:12   131, 220
  20:15   102
  20:16   260, 334

## Source Index

20:17   102
20:18   317
21:1   35, 116, 286
21:26–27   136
22:22   9
23:20-21   17, 43, 44, 74, 319
24:6–8   41
24:7   40, 94, 152, 306
25:8   50
30:2   223
30:12   50, 292
31:13   279
31:14   46
31:18   184
32:7   213
32:13–14   321
32:14   10
32:32   315
33:2–4   151, 152
33:7   169
33:15   43
33:18–23   72
33:19   152
33:20   48
33:31   43
34:6–8   152
34:6   72, 260
34:7   44
34:9   151
34:29   279
34:34   307
35:1   45
39:43   48

Leviticus
  1:1   52, 119
  2:13   14
  7:37   257
  14:34   82

14:35   83
14:38–40   82
18:5   272
19:18   174
20:7   84
20:17   151
22:31   89
23:2   89
23:4   89
23:15–16   87
25:1–5   92
26:3   290
26:9–13   95
27:32   202

Numbers
  6:2   193
  6:18   193
  6:22–27   98
  7:89   103
  8:3   188
  10:9–10   264
  10:35   335
  13:16   165, 223
  13:28   110
  13:29   300
  13:30   110
  14:17   135
  19:1–219:35–36   107
  20:1   194
  20:1–3   322
  20:8   329
  20:11   323
  20:15   190, 195, 319
  23:8   111, 112
  23:21   111
  23:24   111
  27:15   114
  29:35   237

## Numbers (*continued*)
29:36–39   143
30:2   330
33:2   196

## Deuteronomy
4:7   64, 168
4:27   41
4:30   260
4:35   327
4:37   106
5:18   291
5:22–24   179
6:5   12, 38, 96, 174, 205, 248, 252, 315
6:7   148
6:8   94
7:12   204, 209
9:9   184
9:26   319
9:29   213
10:10   184
10:12   63, 85
11:26–28   210
14:1   324, 326
16:3   179
18:13   212
21:10   118
21:20–21   74
22:9   289
25:17   39, 55, 293
26:6–7   214
26:14   123
26:15   121
28:69   14
29:27   83
29:28   124
30:11–14   255
32:3   135
33:12   204
34:11   239
34:12   239

## I Chronicles
16:27   315
16:36   167

## II Chronicles
17:6   283
33:13   73
34:22   193

## I Kings
18:37   44

## II Kings
3:5   276
13:15–19   80, 181, 333
14:14   85
25:6   292

## I Samuel
3:18   295
15:8   300

## II Samuel
7:18   307
12:11   276

## Ezekiel
16:6   64, 162, 163
16:7   162
18:6   105

## Hosea
14:2   10, 137, 226

## Isaiah
1:1   337
1:27   339
6:1   49

## Source Index

6:3   52, 53, 108
6:5–7   54
11:9   284
12:3   235
19:22   297
21:1   337
25:8   19
26:4   221
28:13   16
30:20   233
33:6   64
38:9   241
38:19   241
40:1–2   200, 201
40:26   177
42:8   223, 231
47:8   196, 242
48:13   79
49:3   8
49:16   74, 202
52:8   143
55:6   5
58:13–14   22
63:9   286
66:1   55
66:9   198

Jeremiah
2:3   147
2:13   201
2:27   8
13:17   287, 315
25:30   287
36:1   333
36:4   333

Malachi
2:7   207, 273
3:6   152
3:7   120, 134

Micha
4:6   44
6:5   111
7:15   308
7:18   320

Job
4:4   115
42:10   201

Zachariah
9:9   246

Nehemiah
8:6   167

Daniel
9:18   339
10:7   269
10:21   163

Psalms
3:1   276
3:2   241
5:5   202
7:12   111
8:5   109
12:12   207, 208
16:2   138, 231, 318, 329
19:9   183, 229
22:2   289
22:15   303
24:3   270
25:14   119
30:6   112
33:20   169
34:14   133
44:5   159

Psalms (continued)
    44:9   160
    52:3   255
    62:13  323
    76:9   191
    79:1–2  138, 276
    81:4   221, 224
    82:1   73
    90:13  10, 335
    91:15  54, 154, 158, 211, 315, 334
    93:1   73
    93:2   335
    94:2   136
    94:4   289
    102:1  302
    110:4  118, 255
    111:6  59, 61
    113:4  169
    115:1  229.
    115:17–18  181
    118:5  3, 225, 230
    118:18  196
    119:76–78  102
    119:89  79
    119:108  136
    119:122  133, 219
    119:160  131, 219
    121:1  104
    130:1  124
    130:3  221
    130:4  3, 4
    130:5  225
    135:5  169
    138:3  230
    139:13  152
    143:12  294, 295
    147:19  64, 65

Esther
    4:1    124
    4:14   22
    7:5    103
    9:1    303
    9:27   41, 240

Canticles
    1:2    87, 89
    1:3    88
    2:16   92
    4:9    239
    5:6    103, 266
    6:3    92, 95
    7:11   92, 95
    8:6    74, 202

Ecclesiastes
    1:9    199
    1:18   284
    3:14   4

Lamentations
    1:8    201
    3:5    302
    3:56   3, 129, 219
    5:21   120, 134, 203

Proverbs
    3:16   201
    8:22   147
    10:27  201
    13:12  295
    16:8   266
    20:27  271
    25:11  256
    26:4   70
    27:19  96, 119

28:9    118, 219, 247
29:4    130
31:14   269

*Midrash*
Mechiltah
   Bo 1:2    268
   Bo 5:1    162
   Bo 11:2   63
   Bo 13:3   135
   B'Shalach 3:1    277
   B'Shalach 14:16  317
   Yithro 20:1    102

*Torath Cohanim*
   Kedoshim    65

Sifrah
   VaYikra 1:2    119
   Kedoshim 2:12    174

Sifrei
   Devarim, Piska 343    306

Tannaim
   Deuteronomy 26:6–7    214

Rabbah (edit. Wilna)
Genesis Rabbah
   3:7    224
   5:5    228
   5:8    24
   12:1   116
   17:5   282
   29:1   31
   51:2   35
   17:4   167, 222
   17:5   231, 233

48:9    314
54:2    324
55–56   247
65:20   219
68:9    320
68:14   17
75:4    245
84:1    159
93:3    256

Exodus Rabbah
   2:5    155
   2:12   54, 157, 301
   3:15   310
   23:1   335
   25:2   269
   30:9   10, 69
   41:1   123
   41:5   184

Leviticus Rabbah
   4:6    156
   20:2   246
   22:1   234
   27:4   323
   27:6   322
   29:6   224

Numbers Rabbah
   19:4   306
   21:15  306

Deuteronomy Rabbah
   2:36   53

Ruth Rabbah
   7:14   194

# Source Index

Canticles Rabbah
  2:4   182
  3:2   337
  4:2   186
  4:6   186
  6:6   201

Ecclesiastes Rabbah
  9:3   3

Lamentations Rabbah
  intro 2   180
  intro 24   287

Tanchuma (edit. Buber)
Genesis
  Noah 2   94
  Vayishlach 2   54

Exodus
  Vaera 1   164
  B'Shalach 25   270
  Ki Thisa 3   49, 292

Leviticus
  Tazria 6   198
  Tazria 11   253

Numbers
  Pinchos 16   143, 237
  Massay 2   199

Deuteronomy
  Deuteronomy 2   266
  Ki Taytzay 9   55
  Ki Taytzay 11   300

Yalkut Shimoni
  Vol I cap. 250   291
  Vol.II cap. 355   64

Psalms 887:138   131
Proverbs 950   148
Lamentations 10

Tana D'bei Eliyahu
Rabbah
  cap. 17   287
  cap. 25   105

*Mishna*
Berachoth
  9:5   276

Shabbath
  15:1   148

Rosh Hashana
  3:8   329

Yoma
  8:5   235
  8:7   227
  8:9   11, 96, 305

Sukkah
  5:1–4   139

Taanit
  2:1   288

Avoth
  1:3   115, 190
  2:8   84
  3:16   62
  5:6   228
  5:7   176
  6:5   176
  6:11   132

# Source Index

Avoth d'Rebbe Natan
    38:3    234

Sanhedrin
    6:7    154
    10:1    210

Tamid
    2:2    263
    3:8    262

Uktzin
    1:1    271

*Talmud*
Baylonian Talmud (edit. Wilna)

Berachoth
    3a    36, 229, 264, 286
    5a    13, 136
    6a    115
    7a    28, 111, 277
    7b    167, 225, 231, 276
    9a    77, 100
    10a    330
    13b    178
    17a    232
    20a    44
    28b    67, 84, 114
    31b    44, 167
    32a    148, 213
    32b    328
    33b    63
    55b    177
    61b    12, 96, 174, 205, 248, 252
    63a    313

Shabbath
    3b    178
    10b    279

    13a    197
    13b    214
    22b    189
    25b    208
    30a    271
    30b    333
    55a    48
    70a    45
    86b    282
    87a    188
    88a    40, 94, 98, 99, 105, 152, 191, 240, 307
    88b    109, 239, 280, 319
    89a    135, 261
    89b    139
    104a    109, 183
    105a    18
    113a    21
    115a    107
    118b    46
    133b    243

Pesachim
    6b    309
    50a    18, 144
    66a    310, 311
    112a    205
    117a    332

Rosh Hashanah
    17b    72
    18a    5
    28a    26
    29b    293

Yoma
    9a    201
    38a    221
    66b    141

Yoma (continued)
    69b    167
    75a    36
    85b    58, 272
    86b    173
    87a    68

Moed Katan
    17a    297

Hagigah
    5b     288, 315
    12b    135, 163, 224
    15b    154, 286, 306

Ta'anith
    4a     74, 202
    7a     184

Megillah
    2b     144
    10b    33, 288
    12a    304, 334
    14a    303
    14b    193
    16a    103
    21a    184
    25a    85

Baba Kamma
    9b     312
    27b    173
    54b    268
    60a    294
    72b    290
    87a    60
    91b    193

Baba Metzia
    2a     270
    84b    159
    85a    178

Avodah Zarah
    3a     60
    19a    190
    29b    87
    35a    88

Sanhedrin
    38a    155
    38b    70
    47a    138
    59b    121
    65b    191
    81a    105
    91b    143
    95b    294
    98b    196, 338
    101a   147
    103a   73
    104a   150
    108a   31
    110b   139

Makkoth
    10a    68, 184
    22b    148

Kiddushin
    2b     16
    31a    220
    31b    276
    68a    246
    82b    115

Gittin
    60b    102

Kethuboth
    33b    196
    Nedarim 32a    232
    64b    73

## Source Index

Arachin
  10b  262

Nazir
  4b  193
  10a  192

Sotah
  5a  283
  12a  277
  30b  277
  38a  18
  43a  318

Yebamoth
  48b  258
  49b  48
  97a  273

Hullin
  7a  62, 226
  7b  245
  35b  155
  49a  98
  60b  266, 331

Zevachim
  53b  204

Menachoth
  29b  221, 248, 252, 263
  53a  231
  65b  87
  110a  232, 257

*Jerusalem Talmud (edit. Wilna)*
Rosh Hashanah
  7b  10, 69

Peah
  5a  121

*Zohar (edit Constantinople)*
Vol.I
  intro 1a  288, 331
  intro. 1b  177
  intro. 4b  222
  103a  269
  227b  28, 323

Vol.II
  9b  169
  20a  9
  42a  139
  53b  310
  56b  297
  69b  260
  Raya Mehemnia 120b  199
  Raya Mehemnia 225a  325

Vol.III
  71a  289
  84b  220
  94a  46
  168b  186
  220b  176

Tikunei Zohar
  intro. 1  194, 199
  Tikun 6  225
  Tikun 6:22b  50
  Tikun 19  53
  Tikun 21  118

*Rashi*
Genesis
  1:1  25, 59, 144, 147, 180, 291, 298

*Rashi*
Genesis (*continued*)
  2:2   283
  2:4   325
  1:27   112
  6:9   150
  7:13   153
  21:23   324
  23:1   13
  25:7   13
  27:27   23
  27:28   15, 156
  28:13   17
  32:4   245
  32:13   157
  37:1   21
  37:35   296
  38:21   289
  45:14   26
  46:30   27
  47:28   28

Exodus
  3:2   315
  3:11   163
  6:1   164
  6:2   267
  6:13   30, 275
  11:4   268
  12:1   268
  12:6   162
  14:2   186
  14:15   186, 317
  15:1   275
  15:17   79
  17:15   55
  17:16   300
  17:17   270
  18:1   38
  20:15   102
  20:16   260
  21:1   116, 283, 292
  24:7   40
  33:18   72
  39:43   48

Leviticus
  1:1   52, 119
  7:37   257
  14:14   82
  25:1   92

Numbers
  6:27   98
  8:3   188
  10:35   107, 335
  13:16   165, 223
  19:2   131, 195, 305
  19:5   77
  20:1   194, 195, 322
  20:15   195, 319
  27:16   306
  30:2   330
  33:2   199

Deuteronomy
  5:16   269
  5:18   291
  5:24   179
  6:5   38
  10:10   184
  18:13   212
  29:35   237
  32:3   135

Isaiah
  49:16   202
  52:8   144

# Source Index

Psalms
   119:160   131

Shabbath
   30a   271
   87a   188
   88a   106, 307

Baba Kama
   27b   173

Arachin
   10b   262

*Tosaphoth on Talmud*
Berachoth
   10a   330

Shabbath
   88a   98, 240

Hagigah
   12b   163

Kiddushin
   31b   276

Menachoth
   110a cit. Michael   136, 232

Baba Kama
   91b   193

Arachin
   10b   262

*Maharsha on Talmud*
Hagigah
   5b   288

Sanhedrin
   104a   150

Hullin
   7a   227

*Shulchan Aruch*
Orach Chaim
   cap. 95:2   293
   cap. 402   63

*Maimonedes on Mishnah*
   Eight Chapters 6   65

*Shaarei Orah*
   intro.   290
   cap. 1   183, 229

*Likutei Shas (Arizal)*
Berachoth
   61a   224

*Etz HaChaim*
   Gate 1:2   320
   Gate 3:2   229
   11:6   294

*Tanya*
   cap. 47   168
   cap. 25   253
   epistle 23   272, 281

*Kedushath Levi*
   B'Shalach   275

*Divrei Elimelech*
   89   21
   145   212

*Divrei Elimelech* (continued)
   154   77, 100
   175   43
   275   82
   440   318

*Imrei Elimelech*
   40   264
   114   163, 165
   148   56

   183   63
   330   7, 129

*Ohr Hachaim*
   Exodus 25:8   50

*Tosfos Yom Tov*
   Avoth 5:6   228

*Arvei Nachal*
Numbers
   Massei   11

## ABOUT THE TRANSLATOR

**Rabbi J. Hershy Worch** was born in Manchester, England, in 1955, and ordained in 1992 by Rabbi Shlomo Carlebach, who also introduced him to the work of Rabbi Kalonymus Kalmish Shapira, author of this book. Rabbi Worch has served as rabbi of Congregation Ohave Sholom of Pawtucket, Rhode Island, and as Hillel Director in Melbourne, Australia, and at the University of Illinois, Champaign-Urbana. Rabbi Worch is an artist, musician, dramatist, and poet. His writings on a variety of subjects, ranging from Maimonides to Generation X, have appeared in books, newspapers, and journals worldwide. Rabbi Worch welcomes comments, suggestions, and feedback about his work. His email address is: j.h.worch@worldnet.att.net

## ABOUT THE EDITOR

**Deborah Miller** is a writer and journalist living in Melbourne, Australia. Her novel *The Company of Words* (Papyrus Publishing) was published in 1998.

*Recommended Resources*

**I Will Be Sanctified: Religious Responses to the Holocaust**
translated by Edward Levin                                    1-5682-1943-1

**Conscious Community: A Guide to Inner Work**
by Kalonymus Kalman Shapira
translated and introduced by Andrea Cohen-Kiener    1-5682-1897-4

**The Holy Fire: The Teachings of Rabbi Kalonymus Kalman Shapira, the Rebbe of the Warsaw Ghetto**
by Nehemia Polen                                              0-8766-8842-3

**To Heal the Soul: The Spiritual Journal of a Chasidic Rebbe**
by Kalonymus Kalman Shapira
translated and edited by Yehoshua Starrett           1-5682-1306-9

**A Student's Obligation: Advice of the Rebbe of the Warsaw Ghetto**
by Kalonymus Kalman Shapira
translated by Micha Odenheimer                        1-5682-1517-7

Available at your local bookstore
online at www.aronson.com
or by calling toll-free 1-800-782-0015